ASSESSING MULTICULTURALISM IN GLOBAL COMPARATIVE PERSPECTIVE

In *Assessing Multiculturalism in Global Comparative Perspective*, a group of leading scholars come together in a multidisciplinary collection to assess multiculturalism through an international comparative perspective.

Multiculturalism today faces challenges like never before, through the concurrent rise of populism and white supremacist groups, and contemporary social movements mobilizing around alternative ideas of decolonization, anti-racism and national self-determination Taking these challenges head on, and with the backdrop that the term multiculturalism originated in Canada before going global, this collection of chapters presents a global comparative view of multiculturalism, through both empirical and normative perspectives, with the overarching aim of comprehending multiculturalism's promise, limitations, contemporary challenges, trajectory and possible futures. Collectively, the chapters provide the basis for a critical assessment of multiculturalism's first 50 years, as well as vital insight into whether multiculturalism is best equipped to meet the distinct challenges characterizing this juncture of the 21st century.

With coverage including the Americas, Europe, Oceania, Africa and Asia, and thematic coverage of citizenship, religion, security, gender, Black Lives Matter and the post-pandemic order, *Assessing Multiculturalism in Global Comparative Perspective* presents a comprehensively global collection that is indispensable reading for scholars and students of diversity in the 21st century.

Yasmeen Abu-Laban is Professor of Political Science and Canada Research Chair in the Politics of Citizenship and Human Rights at the University of Alberta. She is also a Fellow at the Canadian Institute for Advanced Research. Her published research addresses themes relating to ethnic and gender politics; nationalism, globalization and processes of racialization; immigration policies and politics; surveillance and border control; and multiculturalism and anti-racism. Her most recent book, with Ethel Tungohan and Christina Gabriel is *Containing Diversity: Canada and the Politics of Immigration in the 21st Century* (2023). She has served as President of the Canadian Political Science Association, and as Vice-President of the International Political Science Association.

Alain-G Gagnon is the Founding Director of the Interdisciplinary Research Center on Diversity and Democracy (CRIDAQ), and Professor in the Department of Political Science at the Université du Québec à Montréal (UQAM) where he holds the Canada Research Chair in Quebec and Canadian Studies. He is the author of *The Legitimacy Clash: Challenges to Democracy in Multinational States* (2023). He is president of the Royal Society of Canada. In 2020, he received the Mildred A Schwartz Lifetime Achievement Award from the American Political Science Association.

Arjun Tremblay is Associate Professor in the Department of Politics and International Studies at the University of Regina, Saskatchewan. He specializes in the field of comparative politics. He obtained his PhD in Political Science from the University of Toronto, Ontario, in 2017 and was a Postdoctoral Fellow (2017–2018) at the Canada Research Chair in Québec and Canadian Studies (CREQC) at the Université du Québec à Montréal. His publications include *Diversity in Decline? The Rise of the Political Right and the Fate of Multiculturalism* (2019) and as co-editor, *Federalism and National Diversity in the 21st Century* (2020).

ASSESSING MULTICULTURALISM IN GLOBAL COMPARATIVE PERSPECTIVE

A New Politics of Diversity for the 21st Century?

Edited by Yasmeen Abu-Laban, Alain-G Gagnon and Arjun Tremblay

LONDON AND NEW YORK

Designed cover image: Getty Images

First published 2023
by Routledge
605 Third Avenue, New York, NY 10158

and by Routledge
4 Park Square, Milton Park, Abingdon, Oxon, OX14 4RN

Routledge is an imprint of the Taylor & Francis Group, an informa business

© 2023 selection and editorial matter, Yasmeen Abu-Laban, Alain-G Gagnon & Arjun Tremblay; individual chapters, the contributors

The right of Yasmeen Abu-Laban, Alain-G Gagnon & Arjun Tremblay to be identified as the authors of the editorial material, and of the authors for their individual chapters, has been asserted in accordance with sections 77 and 78 of the Copyright, Designs and Patents Act 1988.

All rights reserved. No part of this book may be reprinted or reproduced or utilised in any form or by any electronic, mechanical, or other means, now known or hereafter invented, including photocopying and recording, or in any information storage or retrieval system, without permission in writing from the publishers.

Trademark notice: Product or corporate names may be trademarks or registered trademarks, and are used only for identification and explanation without intent to infringe.

ISBN: 978-1-032-05420-9 (hbk)
ISBN: 978-1-032-05419-3 (pbk)
ISBN: 978-1-003-19748-5 (ebk)

DOI: 10.4324/9781003197485

Typeset in Bembo
by Deanta Global Publishing Services, Chennai, India

CONTENTS

List of Figures viii
Editor Biographies ix
Acknowledgments xv

Introduction 1

Reflecting on Multiculturalism at Its Semicentennial:
Over the Hill or Just Getting Started? 3
Yasmeen Abu-Laban, Alain-G Gagnon and Arjun Tremblay

PART 1
Multiculturalism and Citizenship 19

1 Multiculturalism as Citizenization: Past and Future 21
   Will Kymlicka

2 Multiculturalism and Inclusive Democracy: Canadian
   Multiculturalism and Immigrant Citizenship 41
   Irene Bloemraad

3 Multicultural Citizenship in Singapore 60
   Terri-Anne Teo

Part 2
Multiculturalism, History and Intersectionality   81

4 Multiculturalism and Decolonization   83
   Avigail Eisenberg

5 Multiculturalism in the Post-Colony: Shadows of
   Agamben in South Africa   99
   Amanda Gouws

6 Language and Multiculturalism in the United States   119
   Dan Freeman-Maloy and Raymond Tatalovich

7 Framing Diversities: European Approaches to Minorities
   within Minorities   134
   Dolores Morondo Taramundi

Part 3
Multiculturalism, Religion and Secularism   151

8 Interculturalism and the Fair Management of Diversity
   in Multinational Democracies: The Contribution of
   Quebec–Canada Dynamics   153
   Félix Mathieu

9 Multiculturalism: The Place of Religion and State–
   Religion Connections   170
   Tariq Modood

10 Hinduizing Nation: Shifting Grounds of Secularism,
   Diversity and Citizenship   186
   Mohita Bhatia

Part 4
Multiculturalism's Meaning and Value   203

11 Oh Canada, Your Home's on Native Land: Narratives of
   the Missing in a Multicultural Home   205
   Kiera L Ladner, Hope Ace, Marcus Closen and Dane Monkman

12 Black Lives Matter, Social Justice, and the Limits of
    Multiculturalism   223
    Debra Thompson

13 Hungary and the Paradoxes of Illiberal Anti-Multiculturalism 237
    Zsolt Körtvélyesi

Part 5
Multiculturalism, Pandemic, Populism and the
Political Right   261

14 Rethinking Membership under a Pandemic Crisis   263
    Anna Triandafyllidou

15 Imperiled Multiculturalism? COVID-19, Racism and
    Nation-Building in Australia   276
    Tim Soutphommasane

16 Immigration, Multiculturalism and Tolerance: Canada's
    Two Images   292
    Paul May

    Conclusion: Towards a New Diversity Politics for the 21st
    Century? Building on Multiculturalism through Solidarity   308
    Yasmeen Abu-Laban, Alain-G Gagnon and Arjun Tremblay

Index   *323*

FIGURES

1.1 Immigrants   28
1.2 Aboriginal Peoples Source: Harell et al. 2021a.   29
1.3 French-Speaking Québécois Source: Harell et al. 2021a.   29
2.1 Relative Prevalence of the Word "Multiculturalism" in
     English-Language Books, 1950–2019   44

EDITOR BIOGRAPHIES

Yasmeen Abu-Laban is Professor of Political Science and Canada Research Chair in the Politics of Citizenship and Human Rights at the University of Alberta. She is also a Fellow at the Canadian Institute for Advanced Research. Her published research addresses themes relating to ethnic and gender politics; nationalism, globalization and processes of racialization; immigration policies and politics; surveillance and border control; and multiculturalism and anti-racism. Her most recent book, with Ethel Tungohan and Christina Gabriel, is *Containing Diversity: Canada and the Politics of Immigration in the 21st Century* (2023). She has served as President of the Canadian Political Science Association, and Vice-President of the International Political Science Association.

Alain-G Gagnon is the Founding Director of the Interdisciplinary Research Center on Diversity and Democracy (CRIDAQ), and Professor in the Department of Political Science at the Université du Québec à Montréal (UQAM) where he holds the Canada Research Chair in Quebec and Canadian Studies. He is the author of *The Legitimacy Clash: Challenges to Democracy in Multinational States* (2023). He is president of the Royal Society of Canada. In 2020, he received the Mildred A Schwartz Lifetime Achievement Award from the American Political Science Association. He received many other awards and distinctions, among which in 2019 the Order of Canada and in 2022 the National Order of Québec.

Arjun Tremblay is Associate Professor in the Department of Politics and International Studies at the University of Regina, Saskatchewan. He specializes in the field of comparative politics. He obtained his PhD in Political Science from the University of Toronto, Ontario, in 2017 and was a postdoctoral fellow

(2017–2018) at the Canada Research Chair in Québec and Canadian Studies (CREQC) at the Université du Québec à Montréal. His publications include *Diversity in Decline? The Rise of the Political Right and the Fate of Multiculturalism* (2019) and as co-editor *Federalism and National Diversity in the 21st Century* (2020).

Contributor Biographies

Hope Ace is Anishinaabek from M'Chigeeng First Nation and has settler roots. She is a PhD student in Indigenous Studies at the University of Manitoba with a research focus on necro politics, treaty, gender and Indigenous sovereignty.

Mohita Bhatia is Assistant Professor in Sociology at Saint Mary's University, Nova Scotia. Previously she has been a Fulbright postdoctoral scholar at the Centre for South Asia, Stanford University, USA. She holds a PhD in Sociology from the University of Cambridge, UK, where she was the recipient of a four-year Gates–Cambridge scholarship. Her research spans areas of ethnic conflicts, borderlands, everyday nationalism, refugee issues, citizenship processes, religion and secularization. Ethnography has been at the core of her various research works including her recent book *Rethinking Conflict at the Margins* (2020).

Irene Bloemraad is the Class of 1951 Professor of Sociology, University of California, Berkeley, USA. She also serves in multiple leadership roles, as the Thomas Garden Barnes Chair of Canadian Studies at Berkeley, the founding Director of the Berkeley Interdisciplinary Migration Initiative, and as co-director of the Boundaries, Membership and Belonging program of the Canadian Institute for Advanced Research. Her publications include *Becoming a Citizen: Incorporating Immigrants and Refugees in the United States and Canada* (2006) and as a co-editor *Civic Hopes and Political Realities: Immigrants, Community Organizations, and Political Engagement* (2008), *Rallying for Immigrant Rights* (2011) and *The Oxford Handbook of Citizenship* (2017).

Marcus Closen is a PhD student in political science at the University of Toronto, Ontario. His primary research interests are gender and diversity in legislative representation and constitutional politics.

Avigail Eisenberg is Professor in the Department of Political Science at the University of Victoria, British Columbia. Her research focuses on issues at the intersection of political theory and Canadian politics. Her publications have been translated into French, Polish, Spanish, Japanese and Mandarin. Her publications include *Reasons of Identity: A Normative Guide to the Political and Legal Assessment of Identity Claims* (2009) and as a co-editor of *Minorities within Minorities* (2005) and *Recognition versus Self-determination: Dilemmas of Emancipatory Politics* (2014).

Editor Biographies **xi**

Amanda Gouws is Distinguished Professor of Political Science at Stellenbosch University, South Africa. She holds an NRF Chair in Gender Politics. Her specialization is South African Politics and Gender Politics. Her research focuses on women and citizenship, the National Gender Machinery and women's representation and she has published widely in these areas. Her publications include as editor *(Un)Thinking Citizenship: Feminist Debates in Contemporary South Africa* (2005) and as a co-editor *Gender and Multiculturalism: North-South Perspectives* (2015), *Nasty Women Talk Back* (2018) and *COVID Diaries: Women's Experience of the Pandemic* (2021). She was a Commissioner for the South African Commission for Gender Equality, 2012–2014.

Zsolt Körtvélyesi is Research Fellow at the Centre for Social Sciences (Hungarian Academy of Sciences) and Associate Professor in the Faculty of Social Sciences at Eötvös Loránd University, Hungary. He holds a law degree (University of Szeged, Hungary, 2006) with specialization in French Law (University of Paris Nanterre, France, 2005) and European Studies (University of Szeged, 2005), a Nationalism Studies MA (Central European University, Austria, 2009), an LLM (Harvard Law School, USA, 2014, on Fulbright Scholarship) and an SJD (Central European University, 2016). He has research experience in questions of comparative constitutional law, citizenship, nationalism, minorities, human rights and the rule of law in the US and in the EU.

Will Kymlicka is the Canada Research Chair in Political Philosophy at Queen's University, Ontario. He has published 8 books and over 200 articles, which have been translated into 32 languages, and has received several awards. His books include *Contemporary Political Philosophy* (1990; second edition 2002), *Multicultural Citizenship* (1995), which was awarded the Macpherson Prize by the Canadian Political Science Association, and the Bunche Award by the American Political Science Association, and *Multicultural Odysseys: Navigating the New International Politics of Diversity* (2007), which was awarded the North American Society for Social Philosophy's 2007 Book Award. In 2019 he won the highest honor, the Gold Medal, from the Social Sciences and Humanities Research Council of Canada for his work in diversity and democracy.

Kiera L Ladner is Professor in the Department of Political Studies and holds a Canada Research Chair in Miyo we'citowin, Indigenous Governance and Digital Sovereignties at the University of Manitoba. Her publications include *This Is an Honour Song: Twenty Years Since the Blockades* (2010) co-edited with Leanne Simpson, and *Surviving Canada: Indigenous Peoples Celebrate 150 Years of Betrayal* (2017) co-authored with Myra J Tait.

Dan Freeman-Maloy is Fonds de recherche du Québec—Société et culture (FRQSC) Postdoctoral Fellow in the Department of Political Science at the

Université du Québec à Montréal (UQÀM). Within the department, he is affiliated with the Chaire de recherche du Canada en études Québécoises et Canadiennes (CREQC). He completed his PhD at the University of Exeter, UK, where he served as assistant director of the European Centre for Palestine Studies (ECPS), with the support of a doctoral fellowship from the Social Sciences and Humanities Research Council of Canada (SSHRC).

Félix Mathieu is Assistant Professor in the Department of Political Science at the University of Winnipeg, Manitoba. His work focuses on the theory and practice of federalism, nationalism, and the management of diversity in a comparative perspective. He published in 2022 *Taking Pluralism Seriously: Complex Societies Under Scrutiny*.

Paul May is Assistant Professor in the Department of Political Science, Université du Québec à Montréal (UQAM). His research focuses on the impact of immigration on Western societies. Before joining UQAM, he completed a postdoctoral program at Queen's University, Ontario, and another one at Harvard University, USA, where he taught from 2016 to 2019. His publications include *Philosophies du multiculturalisme* (2016), "French Cultural Wars: Public Discourses on Multiculturalism in France (1995–2013)" (2015, *Journal of Ethnic and Migration Studies*) and "Exercising Agency in a Hostile Environment: How Do Refused Asylum Seekers Find Work?" (2020, *Ethnicities*).

Tariq Modood is Professor of Sociology, Politics and Public Policy and founding Director of the Centre for the Study of Ethnicity and Citizenship at the University of Bristol, UK, and Fellow of the British Academy. His latest publications include *Essays on Secularism and Multiculturalism* (2019), *Multiculturalism: A Civic Idea* (2nd ed.; 2013); co-editor, with Thomas Sealy, of "Special Issues on Racism and Anti-Racism in Asia and the Middle East" (in *Political Quarterly*) and on the Global Comparative Governance of Religious Diversity (in *Religion, State and Society*, both 2022). His website is tariqmodood.com.

Dane Monkman (Giizhebaabi Migizii) is an individual of Cree, Anishinaabe and settler ancestry. He is a MA student at the University of Manitoba in the department of Political Studies studying Indigenous Governance and Treaties.

Dolores Morondo Taramundi is Head of Research at the Human Rights Institute of the University of Deusto, Spain, and a member of the European Network of legal experts in gender equality and non-discrimination. Her teaching focuses on human rights, legal theory, critical approaches and legal methodology. Her publications include "Escaping the Ivory Tower: Legal Research on Human Rights from a Critical Perspective" (2019, *The Age of Human Rights Journal*), "Minorities-within-Minorities Frameworks, Intersectionality and

Human Rights: Overlapping Concerns or Ships Passing in the Night?" (2018, in *Ethno-Cultural Diversity and Human Rights*), and "Is Multiculturalism Bad for Women, Still? Persisting Dilemmas in Cultural and Religious Accommodation in Europe" (2014, in *Found in Multiculturalism: Acceptance or Challenge?*).

Tim Soutphommasane is Chief Diversity Officer at the University of Oxford, where he is also Professor of Practice in Political Theory and Human Rights in the Department of Politics and International Relations. He is also Professor of Practice (Sociology and Political Theory) at the University of Sydney, Australia. From 2013 to 2018 he was Australia's Race Discrimination Commissioner. His research focuses on patriotism, multiculturalism, national identity and race. His publications include *On Hate* (2019), *I'm Not Racist But …* (2015), *Don't Go Back to Where You Came From* (2012), *The Virtuous Citizen* (2012) and *Reclaiming Patriotism* (2009).

Raymond Tatalovich is Professor Emeritus in the Department of Political Science at Loyola University, Chicago, USA, and a specialist in American and Canadian politics. His co-edited books include *Moral Controversies in American Politics* (2005) and he also co-authored four more including *The Modern Presidency and Economic Policy* and a presidency text, *To Govern a Nation: Presidential Power and Politics* (1998), as well as being the sole author of two scholarly works: *Nativism Reborn? The Official English Language Movement and the American States* and *The Politics of Abortion in the United States and Canada* (1997). His recent co-authored books include *Cultures at War: Moral Controversies in Western Democracies* (2003) and *The Rise and Fall of Moral Conflicts in the United States and Canada* (2018).

Terri-Anne Teo is Lecturer in the Politics of Race and Ethnicity at Newcastle University, UK. She holds a PhD in Politics from the University of Bristol, UK. She writes about race, citizenship, multiculturalism and migration. Her recent publications include "Minstrelsy beyond the 'West': Deflections, Continuities and the Un/Knowing of Race in Singapore" (2022, *Journal of Intercultural Studies*), "Multiculturalism beyond Citizenship: The Inclusion of Non-Citizens" (2021, *Ethnicities*) and "Silent Citizenship: Choices, Tactics and Claims-Making among Sexual Citizens" (2021, *Citizenship Studies*). She is the author of *Civic Multiculturalism in Singapore: Revisiting Citizenship* (2019) and co-editor of *Postcolonial Governmentalities: Rationalities, Violences and Contestations* (2020).

Debra Thompson is Canada Research Chair in Racial Inequality in Democratic Societies and Associate Professor in the Department of Political Science at McGill University, Quebec. Her work has appeared in journals such as the *Canadian Journal of Political Science*, *Ethnic and Racial Studies*, *Social and Legal*

Studies, and the *Cambridge Review of International Affairs*. Her publications include *The Schematic State: Race, Transnationalism, and the Politics of the Census* (2016) which received three awards from the American Political Science Association: the Race and Ethnic Politics section best book award in race and comparative Politics, the Seymour M Lipset award for the best book in Canadian politics, as well as honorable mention from the International Politics and History section.

Anna Triandafyllidou holds the Canada Excellence Research Chair in Migration and Integration at Toronto Metropolitan University (formerly Ryerson), Ontario. She was previously based at the European University Institute (EUI) in Florence, Italy, where she held a Robert Schuman Chair on Cultural Pluralism in the EUI's Global Governance Program. She is Editor of the *Journal of Immigrant and Refugee Studies* and Chair of the IMISCOE editorial committee publishing a highly cited book series on international migration with Springer. Her recent books include *Rethinking Migration and Return in Southeastern Europe* (with E Gemi, 2021) and an edited volume on Migration and Pandemics (2022). Her recent journal publications have appeared in *Journal of Ethnic and Migration Studies* (2022), *Environment and Planning A: Economy and Society* (2022), *Ethnicities* (2022), *International Migration* (2021) and *Nations and Nationalism* (2020).

ACKNOWLEDGMENTS

The initial inspiration for this volume stemmed from the longevity of multiculturalism in Canada—which in 2021 reached its 50th year as an official national policy. In early discussions, prior to COVID-19 being declared a pandemic, we had envisioned bringing scholars from around the country and world to Canada. In Canada, we would all reflect on the possibilities, limitations and challenges of multiculturalism globally on this momentous occasion.

With the COVID-19 pandemic our initial plans for travel and face-to-face discussions never came to pass. That we were nonetheless able to discuss, exchange, write and complete this volume despite this extraordinary world health emergency stems from the dedication and support of many individuals and organizations.

From Routledge we are especially grateful for the expert guidance and enthusiastic support of Natalja Mortensen (based in the USA). At different phases of this project, we were also happy to receive the encouragement and adept assistance of Charlie Baker (based in the UK).

We benefitted from supports and resources given by our respective universities and departments at the University of Alberta, Université du Québec à Montréal and University of Regina. We also acknowledge the support of the Canada Research Chairs Program as well as the Canadian Institute for Advanced Research.

We were especially pleased that we were able to count on the Zoom webinar platform to bring scholars together across borders and continents in a lively exchange. This took place on October 8, 2021, exactly 50 years from when Prime Minister Pierre Elliott Trudeau announced a policy of multiculturalism within a framework of English and French bilingualism. From University of

Regina Information Services, we thank Stephen Martin for his dedicated and professional support.

We are also very appreciative of Salina Abji for her expert, timely and dedicated editorial support.

We sincerely thank the anonymous reviewers for their careful and constructive suggestions and comments, as well as their time.

We also are grateful for the competent and contributory research assistance we received, and thank Alanna DeCorby, Nariya Khasanova, Jaya Mallu, Rylan O'Connor and Gustavo Gabriel Santafé.

Last, but not least, we are so thankful to our many contributors from across Canada and around the world. Their willingness to share their expertise online and in writing made for lively conversation, reflection and exchange. Their efforts in meeting deadlines despite the many challenges of the pandemic made this collection possible.

Yasmeen Abu-Laban Alain-G Gagnon and Arjun Tremblay

Introduction

Reflecting on Multiculturalism at Its Semicentennial

Over the Hill or Just Getting Started?

Yasmeen Abu-Laban, Alain-G Gagnon and Arjun Tremblay

Introduction

Multiculturalism today faces challenges like never before. The rise of populism and the growth of white supremacist groups in many countries undercuts the pluralistic inclusion that multiculturalism promises. Across states, a common response to the COVID-19 pandemic was to shut borders to immigration, in effect shutting off a key source for population diversity. Not the least, many of today's social movements concerned with challenging exclusion have mobilized around ideas like decolonization, anti-racism and national self-determination. In other words, many vibrant contemporary movements—such as Black Lives Matter, Idle No More, the Dakota Access Pipeline Protests, Rhodes Must Fall and the Catalan independence demonstrations—have not explicitly embraced "multiculturalism" as the primary framework or discourse for inclusion. Taking these trends and challenges head on, this volume gives sustained attention to multiculturalism's promise, trajectory and possible futures. With country coverage from the Americas, Europe, Oceania, Africa and Asia, as well as thematic coverage of citizenship, religion, security, gender, Black Lives Matter and the post-pandemic order, this collection provides a global comparative perspective on multiculturalism's near and longer-term prospects in the 21st century.

The comparative discussion offered in this volume is set against the backdrop of the 50th anniversary of the first ever official multiculturalism policy. On October 8, 1971, Canadian Prime Minister Pierre Elliott Trudeau made a statement to the House of Commons that served as the point of genesis for official multiculturalism in Canada. Owing to the fact that Canada was the first Western country to adopt an official policy of multiculturalism, the 50th anniversary of this experiment was salient for us as editors based in different parts of

DOI: 10.4324/9781003197485-2

the country. Indeed, as we discuss further below, despite its longevity, multiculturalism has long been viewed with suspicion by successive governments in the province of Québec, where a majority of French speakers reside. But we also felt this anniversary demanded not only national but global comparative reflections on multiculturalism's current state and its potential trajectories over the next 50 years. This is because we understand multiculturalism to not only be an official Canadian policy, but also a concept, ideology, ideal, topic of debate and even sometimes a policy that has had uptake in other countries including Australia, the United States, many European nation- states and even in non-Western contexts.

There are other important reasons to examine multiculturalism at this juncture. In the last decade, global migratory movements, including those of refugees, have been on the rise which has resulted in the further diversification of societies across the world along cultural, religious and linguistic lines. And as noted above, the last decade has seen a remarkable number of social movements mobilize in liberal democracies around issues of diversity, recognition and anti-discrimination and, at that, often in contexts with seemingly robust minority rights frameworks. One might therefore have expected to hear demands for more multiculturalism or for the design and implementation of multicultural institutions; perhaps surprisingly, the words multiculturalism and multicultural are rarely heard. Instead, current social movements are mobilizing around other ideas, such as decolonization, anti-racism, abolition/defund the police and Indigenization, among others. These choices may suggest more than that multiculturalism is not as compelling as other ideas as a rallying point. These choices might even suggest that multiculturalism is no longer seen as best suited either for tackling the inequities and exclusions identified by these movements or, more generally, as the politics of diversity needed to fulfill the promise of democracy in the 21st century.

There are still other signs that multiculturalism's days may now be numbered. For one, after several decades of implementation of multiculturalism policies, there remains significant debate about multiculturalism and whether it actually aids or hinders citizenship and immigrant integration. It is also increasingly unclear—although it was once taken for granted—whether multiculturalism is capable of reconciling multiple diversities, such as those pertaining to language, nation, gender and Indigeneity. Additionally, after 9/11, more attention came to be placed by analysts on religion as well as how to understand different forms of secularism and the governance of religious diversity. Multiculturalism's relationship with religion and religious accommodation remains nebulous at the very time when tensions between secularizing polities and religious minorities have intensified. And, the overall fate of multiculturalism as an ideal for facilitating the inclusion of majorities, minorities and newcomers alike has been brought into serious question by exclusionary populist discourses, parties and movements. The reality of border closures as the preferred state response to the

COVID-19 pandemic, and the scapegoating and fearmongering unleashed by the pandemic, may be seen to have furthered these discourses.

Rather than ignore the significant challenges we have outlined that face multiculturalism as it extends past its 50th anniversary, this volume brings these issues front and center into analytic, theoretical, comparative and empirical consideration. In doing so, we ask, Does multiculturalism help or hinder citizenship? Is multiculturalism capable of reconciling multiple diversities, such as those pertaining to language, nation, gender and Indigeneity? Is there a future for multiculturalism in secular and secularizing polities? Does multiculturalism still have heuristic, mobilizational or policy value for state and social actors? Can multiculturalism survive populism and the pandemic?

In addressing these questions, this volume illuminates multiculturalism's prospects, limitations and ultimately, its promise in the decades beyond its semicentennial. Taken together, the volume's chapters provide a critical assessment of multiculturalism's first 50 years, as well as vital insight into whether multiculturalism or another type of diversity politics is best equipped to meet the distinct challenges characterizing this juncture of the 21st century. To situate the discussions in chapters written by world-leading experts covering themes relating to multiculturalism and its successes and challenges, below we proceed in four parts. First, we consider the origins of multiculturalism. Second, we discuss the expansion of multiculturalism (albeit in different ways and forms) beyond the national federal level in Canada, as well as beyond Canada. Third, we highlight recent critiques of multiculturalism launched by state and civil society actors. Finally, we overview the key sections and chapters of this volume.

Multiculturalism's Origins and the Centrality of the Canadian Experience

Since Canada forms an important backdrop to the discussion of multiculturalism in this book, we begin with a brief overview of the etymology of the word "multiculturalism" itself. The term multiculturalism is widely seen to have originated in Canada in the discussions emerging from the *Royal Commission on Bilingualism and Biculturalism* (also called the B and B Commission) (Abu-Laban, 2018). The B and B Commission was formed by Prime Minister Lester B Pearson in 1963, in response to the resurgence of nationalism in Québec and demands for greater autonomy by the majority Francophone population in that province. The tenor of this period was symbolically captured in the popular slogan of Québec's Liberal Premier Jean Lesage, who stressed the idea of "Maîtres Chez Nous" ("masters in our own home"). The slogan was linked to a period in which greater provincial powers were sought by the Québec government in education, healthcare, pensions, hydroelectricity, as well as the quest for constitutional recognition and a veto on constitutional changes (Abu-Laban, 2018).

As the B and B Commission gained traction, challenges to the idea of "biculturalism" were voiced, especially outside Québec. This was particularly evident in western Canadian provinces like Alberta, where multiple groups contested reference to two cultures (English and French) in defining the country. Amongst those critical of the bicultural framing were Ukrainian-Canadians, who had arrived in western Canada in greater numbers between the late 19th century and World War One, and who were then reaching into the second and third generations (see e.g., Lupul, 2005). However, contestations also included growing numbers of immigrants arriving from outside of Europe, as Canada's immigration policy shifted in the 1960s to being officially non-discriminatory as concerns race/ethnicity, and the policy's overt preferences for immigrants from Europe were removed. The driving concern of groups challenging the terms of the B and B Commission was to ensure symbolic recognition from the state for their contributions in shaping the country, something that was seen to have been made invisible in the language of biculturalism (Breton, 1984). In this way, multiculturalism's roots arguably had their basis, at least in part, in civil society demands.

However, state actors also advanced multiculturalism, sometimes for complex reasons that extended beyond the symbolic recognition of groups that were neither French nor British in origin. Reflecting the tenor of debates of the day, for example, Alberta Premier Harry Strom pushed the idea of multiculturalism at the June 1971 Victoria constitutional conference. He did this not only to recognize the claims that were emerging from individuals and groups in Alberta, but also to reject the centrality of Canadian dualism (Abu-Laban and Nieguth, 2000: 480) and to advance the idea, in distinction to Québec's demands, of Alberta as an equal partner in Confederation in any constitutional changes (Alcantara, Levine and Waltz, 2014).

Months later, on October 8, 1971, responding to the reports of the B and B Commission whose Book IV was tellingly entitled *The Cultural Contribution of Other Ethnic Groups* (Canada, Royal Commission, 1970), Prime Minister Pierre Elliott Trudeau announced a policy of multiculturalism *within* a framework of English and French bilingualism. In Trudeau's words, "although there are two official languages there is no official culture" (Canada, House of Commons, 1971: 8545). To be clear: Pierre Trudeau's rationale for advancing a policy of multiculturalism was to promote "national unity" (Canada, House of Commons, 1971: 8545). But, in point of fact, it was never an entirely unifying formulation. Many Québec-based scholars, as well as successive Québec governments, have rejected the federal multiculturalism policy. Indeed, Québec adopted the terminology of "interculturalism" in interfacing with diverse communities (Abu-Laban and Stasiulis, 1992: 357–368; see also Félix Mathieu's chapter in this volume). Indigenous peoples (First Nations, Métis and Inuit) have also shown little interest in the policy, instead advancing their claims through different mechanisms, including treaties (see also the chapter by Kiera L Ladner, Hope Ace, Marcus Closen and Dane Monkman in this volume).

Nonetheless, the term and policy have shown longevity in Canada, and Canada is also relevant for being widely seen both by citizens and the broader world as "the place" where multiculturalism somehow exists (Hinz, 1996). In fact, in 1982, with the adoption of the *Canadian Charter of Rights and Freedoms* (a bill of rights entrenched in the constitution) multiculturalism was given recognition in Section 27 which holds that "this Charter shall be interpreted in a manner consistent with the preservation and enhancement of the multicultural heritage of Canadians" (Canada, Department of Justice, 2019). In 1988, the federal government passed *The Canadian Multiculturalism Act* which gave multiculturalism a firm basis in law. The policy not only continues at the federal level but has both provincial and municipal variants.

In the late 1980s and throughout the 1990s, Canadian scholars like Will Kymlicka, Charles Taylor and Michael Ignatieff as well as many others outside of Canada began to address multiculturalism as an ideal. Indeed, multiculturalism was so ubiquitous that the late conservative political theorist Kenneth Minogue, who was a UK-based critic of multiculturalism, once quipped that Canada should apologize and make reparations to the world for introducing the word (Stockland, 1996). It is to multiculturalism's expansion both within Canada and as a global phenomenon that we now turn.

Multiculturalism's Expansion within Canada and across the Globe

In the 1970s, 1980s and early 1990s, eight of Canada's ten provinces implemented a politics of difference in the form of acts and statutes largely modeled after Canada's federal level policy of official multiculturalism (see Garcea, 2006). More recently, Newfoundland and Labrador published its "Policy on Multiculturalism" in 2008 (see Tremblay and Bittner, 2011). In Québec, scholars and some political actors have advocated the implementation of "interculturalism" as a policy framework. In contrast to multiculturalism, interculturalism is a policy for managing diversity meant specifically for a minority nation based on two main principles; on the one hand, interculturalism embraces immigration and cultural pluralism as essential for Québec's survival and its democratic flourishing while, on the other hand, interculturalism also requires an unbreakable commitment to ensuring the continuity of the French language and Francophone culture. Although Québec interculturalists agree on these two main principles, they differ in their understanding of how much the latter can trump the former if the two principles come into conflict. Likewise, Québec interculturalists differ over what constitutes acceptable and accommodatable forms of cultural pluralism (see Mathieu's chapter in this volume). More recently, questions are being raised as to whether interculturalism, a policy that was never formally adopted but that influenced Québec politics for close to four decades, has now ceded way to a policy stress on state secularism (see Gagnon and Tremblay, forthcoming).

As multiculturalism became generally entrenched at the sub-state level in Canada, it also caught on globally during the late stages of the 20th century. Countries such as Australia, the Netherlands and Sweden adopted what are widely considered to be countrywide multiculturalism policies, albeit in distinct ways and for different reasons. In Australia, official multiculturalism emerged in the wake of the end of racial restrictions in immigration policy and the ensuing increase in immigration from Southeast Asia. Its first iteration resulted in the creation of the Australian Institute of Multicultural Affairs in 1979, which was tasked *inter alia* with promoting awareness and appreciation of cultural diversity (Australian Institute of Multicultural Affairs Act 1979, Part II; Section 5). In the Netherlands, official multiculturalism became government policy in the early 1980s and was embodied in two policy documents: the *Minderhedenbeleid* (i.e., the Ethnic Minorities Policy) and the *Minderhedenotta* (Memorandum on Minorities). The implementation of official multiculturalism in the Netherlands came in the wake of a series of terrorist attacks committed by Moluccan immigrants, who had come to the Netherlands following the collapse of the Dutch East Indies and who had suffered severe economic deprivation and social exclusion after their arrival (see Chin, 2017: 108–110). In Sweden, official multiculturalism—in the form of the 1975 Immigrant and Minority Policy—was implemented not only in response to a linguistic, cultural, and religious diversification of constituency brought about by labor migration but also, as Karin Borevi argues, because "it fitted in well with the national self-image developed in the post-war period of Sweden as a pioneer in human rights issues" (Borevi, 2013: 145).

Apace with these developments, multiculturalism policies were also implemented in countries that never adopted official multiculturalism as countrywide policies. Strikingly, multiculturalism policies were implemented in France and the United States, countries where the word "multiculturalism" has often negative connotations, and in the United Kingdom, a country that rejected a proposal from the Commission on the Future of Multi-Ethnic Britain that it "should formally declare itself a multicultural state" (Banton, 2000: 721).

Evidence of this kind of global engagement with multiculturalism has been documented by researchers at Queen's University, Canada, in a project led by Keith Banting and Will Kymlicka called the "Multiculturalism Policy Index" or MPI, for short. The MPI traces the adoption of 23 multiculturalism policies—eight for immigrants, nine for Indigenous peoples and six for national minorities—for 21 OECD countries from 1960 to 2020. The MPI gives a score of 1 for a fully adopted multiculturalism policy, a score of 0.5 for a partially adopted multiculturalism policy and a score of 0 for a multiculturalism policy that has not yet been adopted or for a policy that was once fully implemented

TABLE 0.1 Multiculturalism Policies (2020)

Country	Immigrant Multiculturalism Policy Score (out of 8)
Australia★	8
Austria	1.5
Belgium★	5.5
Canada★	7
Denmark	1
Finland★	7
France	1.5
Germany	3
Greece	2.5
Ireland	4.5
Italy	1.5
Japan	0
Netherlands	1
New Zealand	6.5
Norway	4.5
Portugal	3.5
Spain	3
Sweden ★	7
Switzerland	1
United Kingdom	6
United States	3.5

Source: Multiculturalism Policy Index, http://www.queensu.ca/mcp/ (accessed May 29, 2022).
★ countries with a score of 1 for "affirmed multiculturalism and has an implementing body."

but has since been abandoned. Table 0.1 provides an overview of country-level commitments to immigrant-centered multiculturalism policies in 2020. As indicated, countries (Australia, Belgium, Canada, Finland, Sweden) that in 2020 had still fully "affirmed multiculturalism" and also had "an implementing body" tended to have high overall multiculturalism policy scores. But the vast majority of countries that had *not* done so have nevertheless adopted one or more forms of immigrant-centered multiculturalism policies.

Multiculturalism's implementation across these democracies coincided with and is perhaps in part attributable to a "rebirth of minority rights" (Kymlicka, 2007: 31) in international law. Will Kymlicka describes this "rebirth" in *Multicultural Odysseys: Navigating the New International Politics of Diversity* (2007), arguing that it is due to a shift in the public perception of the relationship between minority rights and universal human rights. Whereas it was once largely believed that the protection of minority rights would impede the global enshrinement of universal human rights, "it is increasingly asserted that virtually all of the goals and values of the international community—whether it is human rights, peace and security, democracy or economic development—depend on the recognition of minority and indigenous rights" (ibid., 45).

Within this new context, during the 1980s and 1990s, international organizations articulated new formal commitments to minority rights emphasizing the recognition, protection and preservation of diversity. These commitments included (ibid.: 32–37): the International Labour Organization's Convention 169 (Indigenous and Tribal Peoples Convention, 1989); the United Nations 1992 Declaration on the Rights of Persons Belonging to National or Ethnic, Religious and Linguistic Minorities; the Council of Europe's European Charter for Regional or Minority Languages (1992) and Framework Convention for the Protection of National Minorities (1995).

In East Asia, the Middle East, as well as Central and Eastern Europe, multiculturalism's expansion has faced significant hurdles during the late 20th century and at the turn of the millennium. These hurdles have been brought to light by Kymlicka and collaborators in a series of groundbreaking comparative studies of immigrant, Indigenous and national minority multiculturalism policies. In "Liberal Multiculturalism: Western Models, Global Trends, and Asian Debates" (2005: 41–50), Kymlicka argues that the recognition and empowerment of national minorities has clashed with longstanding communitarian values emphasizing mono-nationalism, while the entrenchment of Indigenous land rights and self-government rights butts up against a "belief that they impede economic development" (50). In *Multiculturalism and Minority Rights in the Arab World* (2014: 9–15), Kymlicka and Eva Pfostl argue that opposition to multiculturalism in the Middle East is rooted in three factors: 1. the collective memory of the Millet system, a system that recognized diversity but that also subordinated non-Muslim minorities (i.e., "The Millet Legacy"); 2. the practice of colonial powers deploying minority rights as means to demobilize movements for national liberation (i.e., "The Colonial Legacy"); and 3. the development of "unamist" (15) Arab nationalisms following the collapse of colonial empires (i.e., "Postcolonial Nation-Building"). And, in "Multiculturalism and Minority Rights: West and East" (2002), Kymlicka points to two main impediments to multiculturalism's development in Eastern and Central Europe, specifically as it relates to the devolution of political authority to national minorities: the fear that devolution will empower illiberal minority elites, on the one hand, and the widely-held belief that minority nationalism has a shelf life and is bound to peter out.

It is only in Latin America where multiculturalism—in the form of the recognition and accommodation for Indigenous peoples—appeared to have been substantively adopted, as Donna Lee Van Cott demonstrates in "Multiculturalism versus Neoliberalism in Latin America" (2006). However, even here, there is also evidence of an inverse relationship between the depth of recognition and accommodation and the size of the Indigenous populations (278–279). In brief, and contrary to trends in North America and Western Europe, the more extensive multicultural policy frameworks were implemented in countries with the smallest minority populations.

State and Societal Questioning of Multiculturalism's Effectiveness in the 21st Century

After many favorable years for multicultural politics, things seem to have changed in the 21st century. Prior to this, multiculturalism offered an expression of social inclusion and participation in public life, and as such, took root in Canada, Australia, the United Kingdom and in many other countries. For one, the Netherlands was once part of the vanguard of states to adopt official multiculturalism. However, the country has since veered towards civic integration as a model of immigrant integration. Following the events of September 11, 2001, we have also witnessed a rise and mainstreaming of anti-Muslim racism (also called Islamophobia). At the beginning of the second decade of the 21st century, leaders in France (Nicolas Sarkozy), Germany (Angela Merkel) and the United Kingdom (David Cameron) expressed strong opposition toward multiculturalism and decried its apparent tendency to create two "parallel" societies, one of which comprises the majority community while the other isolates minority communities. Additionally, the last two decades have seen the rise of a right-wing populist discourse across the world that is distinctly mono-cultural, anti-immigrant and that harkens back to assimilationist ways of engendering social cohesion. At the same time, in many circles, multiculturalism has become a convenient scapegoat for austerity-inclined political actors. These actors have set their sights on ostensibly costly social policies and a bloated state apparatus, positioning austerity measures as a solution to problems caused, at least in part, from multicultural policy efforts.

There are still other sources of criticism of multiculturalism that come from civil society. For example, the intense forms of surveillance and racialized violence stemming from the post 9/11 "war on terror" has led some members of targeted minority groups to express their discomfort with multiculturalism for seemingly limiting their social space, for boxing them into specific cultures, and for depriving them of agency (Abu-Laban and Nath, 2007). Additionally, there is also a complex relationship between national and immigrant minorities within the context of multiculturalism. On the one hand, we have seen national minorities such as the Basque people deploy multiculturalism in the process of immigrant integration in opposition to the development of a restrictive immigration system by the Spanish government (Jeram, 2013). On the other hand, national minorities in South Tyrol (Wisthaler, 2016) and in Belgium (Jacobs, 2000) have sometimes seen immigrants and immigration as threats to their own political aspirations.

Multiculturalism has also been subject to still other criticisms in Canada from some scholars and civil society voices for its inability to deal with racism, causing division, not dealing adequately with socio-economic inequalities and severing language from culture by not promoting multilingualism (Abu-Laban and Stasiulis, 1992; Haque, 2012; see also chapters in this volume by Debra Thompson, by Avigail Eisenberg and by Kiera Ladner, Hope Ace, Marcus

Closen and Dane Monkman). Criticisms of multiculturalism have only amplified since the term went global. Indeed, on the heels of Canada's adoption of a multicultural policy, Australia also implemented federal level multiculturalism (see Soutphommasane in this volume), and in the 2010s some politicians decried multiculturalism as a failure in Europe (see Morondo Taramundi in this volume).

In brief, as we can see in the foregoing discussion, any scholarly engagement with multiculturalism must take place and must necessarily contend with a range of often contextually specific understandings of multiculturalism and its impact. Clearly multiculturalism has developed globally beyond the Canadian context. Yet it also seems that after more than 50 years of its deployment in policy and public discourse, multiculturalism has yet to be fully embraced in the hearts and minds of the citizens of liberal democracies. To what extent, then, does multiculturalism have a future? Should multiculturalism *have* a future? The chapters in this volume, concerned with a wide range of regions and countries, shed light on these questions.

To be sure, the temporal backdrop to the focus on multiculturalism in this volume stems from a particular marker, namely the semicentennial celebration in 2021 of the policy of official multiculturalism within a bilingual framework. However, given all the debates and variance within and beyond Canada, we find it highly important to pay attention to how multiculturalism is being used in specific contexts, and what we might learn in the years to come about the promise and limits of multiculturalism as a "21st century" diversity. This includes whether multiculturalism is being invoked positively or negatively, and it also entails whether multiculturalism is being used to reference demographic diversity (or specific groups), an actual policy or the philosophical ideal of cultural pluralism.

The following chapters foreground an analysis on the viability of multiculturalism in the 21st century, an issue that is often an afterthought in discussions on multiculturalism. The volume's comparative ambit allows for a comprehensive account of multiculturalism's global trajectory which includes Australia, North America, Western Europe, Asia, South Asia, South-East Asia and Eastern Europe. Furthermore, by discussing multiculturalism as a policy and discourse but also as a demographic phenomenon relating to increased population diversity and set of ideals, the volume will, we hope, provide a better understanding of multiculturalism's problems, promise and possibilities as we move into the second quarter of the 21st century.

Overview of the Book

Contributors to this volume include some of the world's leading scholars on multiculturalism, citizenship, immigration, religion and diversity as well as language, Indigenous politics, race and (settler) colonialism. The volume's chapters are divided into five parts which cover a range of countries pertaining to key thematics that beset debates over multiculturalism. *Part 1: Multiculturalism and Citizenship* comprises three chapters, each of which engage the longstanding connection between minority recognition and accommodation, on the one hand, and the notions, expectations and modalities of belonging in modern liberal democracies, on the other. In "*Multiculturalism as Citizenization: Past and Future*," Will Kymlicka discusses key tenets of liberal multiculturalism and addresses their challenges. Based on global comparative findings, Kymlicka shows that some groups suffer from "membership penalties" despite decades of multiculturalism. Nevertheless, he argues that the solution seems to lie in more, rather than less, multiculturalism. In "*Multiculturalism and Inclusive Democracy: Canadian Multiculturalism and Immigrant Citizenship*," Irene Bloemraad addresses criticisms that multiculturalism, as a normative ideal, contributes to a divided citizenry lacking a common identity and that, as a public policy, multiculturalism impedes immigrant integration and leads to siloed communities. Her chapter shows that, while multiculturalism is not a panacea, it does indeed have some very important "citizenizing" effects, at least in Canada. In "*Multicultural Citizenship in Singapore*," Terri-Anne Teo examines the racialized framework of multiculturalism in Singapore and its close relationship with immigration policies. Importantly, Teo presents a case where "multicultural citizenship" cannot be cleanly separated from "multicultural non-citizenship." Within this context, Teo further demonstrates that, despite the adoption of group-differentiated policies in Singapore, there remain systemic inequalities affecting minority groups in both the citizen and non-citizen populations.

There are four chapters in *Part 2: Multiculturalism, History and Intersectionality* which together grapple with issues of colonialism, postcolonialism and decolonization, along with intersectionality (or what is sometimes framed in multicultural debates as "minorities within minorities"). In "*Multiculturalism and Decolonization*," Avigail Eisenberg considers whether multiculturalism has been a help or hindrance to decolonization. Eisenberg argues that, in Canada, multiculturalism presents important obstacles to decolonization including its reliance on liberal ideas about citizenship, integration and state authority. In "*Multiculturalism in the Post-Colony: Shadows of Agamben in South Africa*," Amanda Gouws examines the difficulties in applying the concept of multiculturalism to post-apartheid South Africa. In doing so, Gouws seeks to understand if it is possible to reconcile interpretations of a settler colonial past with the liberal individual interpretation of multiculturalism, all the while paying attention to the intersectionalities of race, class, gender, sexuality and nationality in race engagements. In "*Language and Multiculturalism in the United States*," Dan Freeman-Maloy and Raymond Tatalovich explore the legislative achievements of "official English" movements in the United States and their place within a wider critique of the perceived fragmentation of US civic life. The authors show how the debate over multiculturalism has come to uneasily group together questions of language, race and nationality in the land that has embraced the motto, *E pluribus unum* (out of many, one). In "*Framing Diversities: European Approaches to 'Minorities within Minorities'*," Dolores Morondo Taramundi examines the competing and complementing understandings of "minorities within minorities" at the supranational level in Europe. Morondo Taramundi shows that, while there is a substantive discussion on these minorities, the term and concept of "multiculturalism" is conspicuously absent in new and emerging legal and policy frameworks.

Part 3: Multiculturalism, Religion and Secularism comprises three chapters addressing the relationship between multiculturalism and secularism, as well as trends and debates in the governance of religious diversity. In "*Interculturalism and the Fair Management of Diversity in Multinational Democracies: The Contribution of Quebec–Canada Dynamics*," Félix Mathieu situates his discussion of multicultural and intercultural models of pluralism against the backdrop of the ongoing debate over state secularism in Québec. He argues that the former is best suited for minority nations but that neither interculturalism nor multiculturalism are immune to (re)producing discriminatory practices. Consequently, the chapter concludes by identifying an analytical and practical framework that can help to identify both legitimate and illegitimate intercultural policies. In "*Multiculturalism: The Place of Religion and State–Religion Connections*," Tariq Modood expands on the key features of what has been called the Bristol School of Multiculturalism: a bottom-up politics that seeks an egalitarian public recognition for the minority identities important to their bearers, without exceptionalizing or obviating religion, as some liberal multicultural schools of thought do. In discussing the Bristol School approach, this chapter offers an account of political secularism that is compatible with multiculturalism and conducive to being "multiculturalized." In "*Hinduizing Nation: Shifting Grounds of Secularism, Diversity and Citizenship*," Mohita Bhatia discusses India's constitutional multicultural commitments to minorities. Bhatia traces how the Indian government has turned its back on these commitments following the ascendancy of the Narendra Modi-led Bharatiya Janata Party (BJP) in 2014.

The three chapters in *Part 4: Multiculturalism's Meaning and Value* examine the potentialities of multiculturalism when faced with historic legacies of slavery and colonialism, persisting anti-Indigenous and anti-Black racism and a contemporary context of democratic backsliding. In "*Oh Canada, Your Home's on Native Land: Narratives of the Missing in a Multicultural Home*," Kiera L Ladner, Hope Ace, Marcus Closen and Dane Monkman ask whether or not the discourse and policy of multiculturalism in Canada can live up to what it promises. They argue that, in actuality, Canadian multiculturalism reconciles diversity and inclusivity with a history of racism and exclusion and therefore does little to address the dispossession and subjugation of Indigenous nations and the continued denial of legal and constitutional pluralism and treaty recognition. In "*Black Lives Matter, Social Justice, and the Limits of Multiculturalism*,"

Debra Thompson makes two key arguments. First, that Black Lives Matter, one of the most significant social movements of the 21st century, has exposed the conceptual limits of the multicultural model. Second, that the Movement for Black Lives not only goes beyond liberal multiculturalism, but it also proposes a more radical approach emphasizing the political, economic and moral imperatives of social justice and democratic repair. In *"Hungary and the Paradoxes of Illiberal Anti-Multiculturalism,"* Zsolt Körtvélyesi analyzes how "illiberal" multiculturalism has caught on in Hungary post-2010 under the Orbán regime. The chapter also sheds light on the superficial nature of Hungary's past commitment on minority rights and on how multiculturalism policies have been deployed to serve electoral rather than integrationist objectives.

This volume's final three chapters are included in *Part 5: Multiculturalism, Pandemic, Populism and the Political Right*. These chapters grapple directly with xenophobic populist trends and racism, as well as the fallout from the COVID-19 pandemic and the resurgence of an anti-immigrant political right. In *"Rethinking Membership under a Pandemic Crisis,"* Anna Triandafyllidou reflects on the effects of the global pandemic and on the challenges and opportunities that it has presented to denizen populations—like refugee claimants and temporary workers. The chapter concludes by offering preliminary insight on whether or not this global shock may actually lead to a revival of multiculturalism from a civic responsibility perspective. In *"Imperiled Multiculturalism? COVID-19, Racism and Nation-Building in Australia,"* Tim Soutphommasane explores the historical development of multiculturalism in Australia from a comparative perspective. He argues that Australian multiculturalism has been seriously wounded by the COVID-19 pandemic and assesses Australia's capacity to bounce back from a lapse in nation-building imagination. In *"Immigration, Multiculturalism and Tolerance: Canada's Two Images,"* Paul May examines multiculturalism as it relates both to the flattering self-image that Canada projects outwardly to its global counterparts and to Canada's real image as a state with a very restrictive immigration regime. Within this context, May argues that a key area of Canada's actual influence in terms of multiculturalism lies in providing a blueprint for a European political right concerned with limiting the diversification of their respective states.

The volume's concluding chapter, *"Towards a New Diversity Politics for the 21st Century? Building on Multiculturalism through Solidarity"* reviews the major findings and conclusions stemming from contributor chapters. Our review shows how "diversity politics" is also related to diverse polities, necessitating attention be paid to geographic and temporal context. The chapter considers the relevance of these insights in relation to the terminological complexity besetting multiculturalism stemming from its contextual specificity, multiculturalism's mixed record of effectiveness, as well as multiculturalism's near and longer-term futures. We consider the case for the continued value of a revamped and modernized multiculturalism that is attuned to the complexity of the politics of diversity in the 21st century. The complexities include the exacerbation of racism in the age of populism and during the global pandemic as well as emerging discussions on citizenship and belonging that are now set against the backdrop of 50 years of multiculturalism. Within this context, we point to the critical importance of civil society in the 21st century and to the need for an emboldened politics of diversity and a solidaristic multiculturalism.

References

Abu-Laban, Yasmeen and Daiva Stasiulis. 1992. "Ethnic Pluralism under Siege: Popular and Partisan Opposition to Multiculturalism." *Canadian Public Policy XVIII* (4): 365–386.

Abu-Laban, Yasmeen and Nisha Nath. 2007. "From Deportation to Apology: The Case of Maher Arar and the Canadian State." *Canadian Ethnic Studies 39* (3): 71–97.

Abu–Laban, Yasmeen and Tim Nieguth. 2000. "Reconsidering the Constitution, Minorities and Politics in Canada." *Canadian Journal of Political Science 33* (3): 465–497.

Abu-Laban, Yasmeen. 2018. "Recognition, Re-distribution and Solidarity: The Case of Multicultural Canada." In *Diversity and Contestations Over Nationalism in Europe and Canada*, John-Erik Fossum and Birte Siim (eds.) London: Palgrave Studies in European Sociology, 237–261.

Alcantara, Christopher, Renan Levine and James C. Walz. 2014. "Canadian First Ministers' Conferences and Heresthetic Strategies: Explaining Alberta's Position on Multiculturalism at the 1971 Victoria Conference." *Journal of Canadian Studies 48* (2): 100–121.

Australia. *Australian Institute of Multicultural Affairs Act 1979*, Part II; Section 5.

Banton, Michael. 2000. "A UK Perspective" In *Report on the Future of Multi-Ethnic Britain: UK, North American and Continental Perspectives*, Michael Banton, Will Kymlicka, Charlie Westin (eds), *26* (4): 720–723.

Borevi, K. 2013. "The Political Dynamics of Multiculturalism in Sweden." In *Challenging Multiculturalism: European Models of Diversity*, Raymond Taras (ed.) Edinburgh: Edinburgh University Press, 138–160.

Breton, Raymond. 1984. "The Production and Allocation of Symbolic Resources: An Analysis of the Linguistic and Ethnocultural Fields in Canada." *Canadian Review of Sociology and Anthropology 21* (2): 123–144.

Canada, Department of Justice. 2019. "Section 27—Multicultural Heritage." 17 June. https://www.justice.gc.ca/eng/csj-sjc/rfc-dlc/ccrf-ccdl/check/art27.html (Accessed 22 August 2021).

Canada, House of Commons. 1971. *Debates*, 12 October: 8545–8548.

Canada, Royal Commission on Bilingualism and Biculturalism. 1970. *The Cultural Contribution of the Other Ethnic Groups*. Ottawa: Information Canada. Edmonton and Toronto: Canadian Institute of Ukrainian Studies Press.

Chin, Rita. 2017. *The Crisis of Multiculturalism in Europe: A History*. Princeton, NJ: Princeton University Press.

Framework Convention for the Protection of National Minorities. 1995. Council of Europe Press.

Gagnon, Alain-G. and Arjun Tremblay. 2023. "Interculturalism and the Plea for an Informal Constitution: Responding to the Challenge of Polyethnicity in Québec."

In *A Written Constitution for Québec?*, Richard Albert, Léonid Sirota and Patrick F. Baud (eds.) Montreal and Kingston: McGill-Queen's University Press, 137–161

Garcea, Joseph. 2006. "Provincial Multiculturalism Policies in Canada, 1974–2004: A Content Analysis." *Canadian Ethnic Studies 38* (3): 1–20.

Haque, Eve. 2012. *Multiculturalism within a Bilingual Framework: Language, Race and Belonging in Canada*. Toronto: University of Toronto Press.

Hinz, Evelyn. 1996. "What Is Multiculturalism? A Cognitive Introduction." *Mosaic 29*: 3.

International Labour Organization. 1989. *Indigenous and Tribal Peoples Convention (no. 169)*. Geneva: United Nations.

Jacobs, Dirk. 2000. Multinational and Polyethnic Politics Entwined: Minority Representation in the Region of Brussels-Capital." *Journal of Ethnic and Migration Studies 26* (2): 289–304.

Jeram, Sanjay. 2013. "Immigrants and the Basque Nation: Diversity as a New Marker of Identity." *Ethnic and Racial Studies 36* (11): 1770–1788.

Kymlicka, Will. 2002. "Multiculturalism and Minority Rights: West and East." *JEMIE - Journal on Ethnopolitics and Minority Issues in Europe 4*: 1–24.

Kymlicka, Will. 2005. "Liberal Multiculturalism: Western Models, Global Trends, and Asian Debates". In *Multiculturalism in Asia*, Will Kymlicka and Baogang He (eds.) Oxford: Oxford University Press, 22–55.

Kymlicka, Will. 2007. *Multicultural Odyssey: Navigating the New International Politics of Diversity*. Oxford: Oxford University Press.

Kymlicka, Will and Eva Pföstl. 2014. *Multiculturalism and Minority Rights in the Arab World*. Oxford: Oxford University Press.

Lupul, Manoly. 2005. *The Politics of Multiculturalism: A Canadian-Ukrainian Memoir*. Multiculturalism Policy Index. http://www.queensu.ca/mcp/ (accessed: 22 August 2021).

Office of the High Commission. 1992. *Declaration on the Rights of Persons Belonging to National or Ethnic, Religious and Linguistic Minorities*. Geneva: United Nations Human Rights.

Stockland, Peter. 1996. "Not All Cultures Equally Developed." *Calgary Herald*, 8 November.

Tremblay, Reeta and Amanda Bittner. 2011. "Newfoundland and Labrador: Creating Change in the 21st Century." In *Integration and Inclusion of Newcomers and Minorities Across Canada*, John Biles, Meyer Burstein, Jim Frideres, Erin Tolley, and Rob Vineberg (eds.) Montreal and Kingston: McGill-Queen's University Press, 325–354.

Van Cott, Donna Lee. 2006. "Multiculturalism versus Neoliberalism in Latin America." In *Multiculturalism and the Welfare State: Recognition and Redistribution in Contemporary Democracies*, Keith Banting and Will Kymlicka (eds.) Oxford: Oxford University Press, 272–296.

Wisthaler, Verena. 2016. "South Tyrol: The Importance of Boundaries for Immigrant Integration." *Journal of Ethnic and Migration Studies 42* (8): 1271–1289.

PART 1
Multiculturalism and Citizenship

1
MULTICULTURALISM AS CITIZENIZATION

Past and Future

Will Kymlicka

Since multiculturalism first emerged as a political claim and political commitment in Canada 50 years ago, critics and defenders have debated how multiculturalism affects our ideas and practices of citizenship. For many observers, this is indeed the crucial factor in assessing multiculturalism: does it enrich or diminish our status as citizens and our practices of democratic citizenship? This focus on citizenship is not surprising, given that citizenship is often seen as the defining achievement of the modern age. Whereas premodern polities treated people as mere subjects of the state, modern societies turn subjects into citizens, turning "the citizen" into the central protagonist of modern history and politics (Dahrendorf, 1974). Following James Tully, we can refer to this as "citizenization" (Tully, 2001)—the broad historical process of converting historic relations of political domination and hierarchy into relations amongst peers who collectively determine the terms of their shared social world.

Until recently, most people viewed citizenization as an unalloyed good. Contemporary political philosophy, at least its Western liberal-democratic strand, is fundamentally "citizenist" (Bloom, 2017). The field of political philosophy has often understood its historical calling as a matter of turning subjects into citizens, to theorize and justify these processes of citizen-making or citizenization. And this goal was shared by the progressive left. As Baines and Sharma put it, citizenship has been the "preferred social justice strategy for many on the Left" (2002: 75). Throughout the 20th century, struggles for social justice have paradigmatically been "citizenship struggles." Writing near the end of the 20th century, Fraser and Gordon could say:

> "Citizen" and "Citizenship" are powerful words. They speak of respect, of rights, or dignity ... We find no pejorative uses. It is a weighty, monumental, humanist word.
>
> *(Fraser and Gordon 1994: 90)*

For those who view citizenship in this way, as the core of social justice and moral progress, multiculturalism is worth defending if and insofar as it is compatible with and contributes to citizenization.

Not everyone today, however, endorses the exaltation of citizenship. As far back as 1998, Linda Bosniak proposed "giving up on citizenship as an aspirational project altogether" (Bosniak, 1998), and today pejorative references to citizenship abound. Dimitry Kochenov, for example, labels the defense of citizenship as racist, sexist and indeed "totalitarian" (Kochenov, 2019). There are multiple strands to this critique of citizenship, but a central concern is that it is ultimately a tool of state power. States have a vested interest in promoting citizenship, and in sorting humanity into (loyal) "citizens" and (excludable) "aliens" or "foreigners." It is only when we are "seeing like a state" (Scott, 1998) that we would want to bind people to particular states, and to view a truly human life as one that is led within "national containers." On this view, far from being a "weighty humanist word," state-based citizenship is in fact a betrayal of humanism, an imprisoning of human identities and aspirations within the limits and boundaries set for us by the nation state (Favell, 2019). For those who see citizenship as an obstacle to social justice and moral progress, multiculturalism will be worth defending if and insofar as it contributes to the desanctification of citizenship and the liberation of humanity from citizenship categories.

My aim in this chapter is not to resolve this dispute about the merits of citizenship, which runs deep in contemporary political thought.[1] But I hope to show how this underlying debate has shaped assessments of multiculturalism, both its past performance and its future prospects.

As we will see, both sides of this debate have criticized multiculturalism. Many of those in the pro-citizenship camp have argued that multiculturalism weakens citizenship. Rather than helping us relate to each other as political peers who co-author a shared world, multiculturalism instead divides us into hostile tribes who are unable or unwilling to cooperate or commit to shared political projects. This indeed was central objection to multiculturalism for the first few decades of its existence, and it remains a concern for many on the right (Ryan, 2010).

In my view, defenders of multiculturalism have offered compelling responses to this critique, providing both empirical evidence and theoretical reasons why multiculturalism, at its best, can be a project of citizenization. We now have 50 years of experience with multiculturalism, and I think we can now safely put to rest some of the speculative fears about how multiculturalism would erode citizenship. I discuss this in the following section.

However, the very success of this defense of multiculturalism-as-citizenization has now laid multiculturalism open to the opposite critique. For a growing number of commentators, multiculturalism is flawed precisely because it *is* a form of citizenization. Multiculturalism ties recognition of diversity and plurality, not to people's humanity, but to their membership in and loyalty to the state. Multiculturalism makes room for diversity, but only insofar as people are able and willing to subsume expressions of diversity to the boundaries and limits of state-based citizenship. For some critics, this linking of multiculturalism to state citizenship may once have been necessary and legitimate, but is now historically obsolete, and so we need to cut the umbilical cord between multiculturalism and citizenship.[2]

Confronted with this new critique, defenders of multiculturalism have two possible responses. One is to sever the link between multiculturalism and citizenship and argue that multiculturalism can and should take a more unbounded and cosmopolitan form. The second is to defend the link between multiculturalism and citizenship, and to argue that multiculturalism-as-citizenization remains essential to moral progress and social justice. I will discuss this choice in the second half of the chapter, and its implications for the future of multiculturalism.

Multiculturalism as (Incomplete) Citizenization

The link between multiculturalism and citizenship can be understood at two levels. First, we can ask whether multiculturalism is tied as a matter of formal policy to the possession of citizenship: that is, is multiculturalism something that we can claim *as citizens*? I will call this the direct or formal linking of multiculturalism and citizenship. Second, we can ask whether multiculturalism promotes the moral ideals or purposes of democratic citizenship—that is, does it promote *citizenization*? For example, does it challenge inherited political hierarchies and promote a sense of civic equality and participatory parity?

In the Canadian case, the existence of a direct formal link between multiculturalism and citizenship is particularly clear, due to its distinctive history. The multiculturalism policy was originally demanded in the 1960s by long-settled and well-integrated European ethnic groups—Ukrainians, Italians and Poles—whose members had been in Canada for decades, if not generations, and who were therefore already citizens. And their claim for multiculturalism was in large part a demand for recognition of their historic contributions to the nation: helping to "settle" Western Canada;[3] serving in the Canadian Army during World War II; playing important roles in the economic and civic life of the country through churches, family businesses, labor unions and civic associations. So, the policy implicitly assumed that its beneficiaries were already

Canadian citizens and was formulated as an attribute of Canadian citizenship. It was a new way of understanding one's Canadian-ness, not an alternative to being (or becoming) a Canadian. The policy said that one appropriate and honorable way of being a Canadian and participating in Canadian democracy is to be a proud member of one's ethnic group—to be a proud Ukrainian-Canadian, say, or Italian-Canadian (Kymlicka, 2015).

Canadian multiculturalism therefore had a different origin than in Germany, for example, where (a form of) multiculturalism was adopted as a policy for "foreigners" or "aliens" who were not able to become citizens (Schönwälder, 2010). Multiculturalism in Germany was a consolation prize to make non-citizenship bearable, and to facilitate migrants' return to their countries of origin. This is sometimes called "returnist multiculturalism," premised on the idea that migrants are foreigners who should return to their real home. In Canada, by contrast, multiculturalism was a policy claimed by citizens, as a way of valorizing the role of all ethnic identities and ethnic groups in the exercise of Canadian citizenship.

The initial focus of multiculturalism on long-settled citizens changed in the 1970s as a result of changing immigration. Canada increased its overall immigrant intake, and removed explicit racial preferences in admissions, leading to the emergence of several new non-European immigrant communities. These groups, which were not part of the original 1960s debate on multiculturalism, faced a number of integration challenges that were not faced by the long-settled European ethnic groups. As a result, multiculturalism evolved to intervene earlier in the integration process, to help people in the first stages of their settlement and integration.

But even as multiculturalism programs adapted to serve the needs of newcomers who may not yet be citizens, it remained primarily conceptualized as a policy about what it means to be a Canadian citizen. Multiculturalism has never been seen in Canada as an alternative to citizenship, or as a transitional phase that immigrants pass through on the road to becoming "real" Canadians who no longer need multiculturalism. Multiculturalism is a right in Canada, but it is a right that one possesses *as a Canadian*. The policy articulates a model of *multicultural citizenship*—by showing that one way of being a proud and active Canadian citizen is by being a proud and active Greek-Canadian or Vietnamese-Canadian. One striking consequence of this citizenship-centric understanding of multiculturalism is that temporary migrants to Canada, such as the temporary farm workers who regularly come to work in Canada on a seasonal basis, are not eligible for most multicultural programs. Whereas "returnist multiculturalism" in Germany was designed for migrants who were expected to return to their country of origin, citizenist multiculturalism in Canada is not even available to migrants who are expected to return.

So as a matter of formal policy, multiculturalism in Canada is clearly linked to the possession of citizenship.[4] What is less clear is whether multiculturalism is "citizening" in the more substantive sense. Does multiculturalism help replace relations of domination and subjection with relations of equality and cooperation? And how would we test this claim? What are the metrics of citizenization, and how would we determine whether multiculturalism promotes or inhibits it?

This is contested territory, which I have tried to explore in more depth in other publications (e.g., Kymlicka, 2012). So let me just quickly sketch how I see the issue. We can start by asking: what is the problem that multiculturalism is supposed to fix? What was the gap or deficit in citizenization that multiculturalism was intended to overcome?

According to Nancy Fraser's influential formulation, we can think of society as containing two intersecting domains of injustice: an unfair distribution of material resources, determined by one's location in the labor market, and an unfair distribution of cultural recognition, determined by one's location in relation to cultural schemas of worthiness (Fraser, 1995). Multiculturalism arose to challenge the latter injustice. Members of ethnic minority groups often feel that their identities and interests are seen by the larger society as less valid or less worthy. The two dimensions of injustice are closely linked, since we know that perceptions of worthiness shape people's attitudes towards material issues, such as support for access to welfare benefits, or support for access to political power. On all of these issues, around the world, majorities tend to think of minorities as deficient in relation to cultural schemas of worthiness, and therefore less "deserving" in terms of access to benefits, rights and power.[5] Being seen as less worthy is both an inherent injustice, and also contributes to reproducing injustice in material resources.

Why are minorities seen as less worthy and less deserving? There are many possible reasons, but we might categorize them under two broad headings. First, minorities are often subject to dehumanizing forms of stigma or prejudice—they are seen as *deficient in humanity*.[6] Second, even if their humanity is recognized, minorities are often seen as not really "one of us:" they are seen as *insufficiently Canadian*. Needless to say, these two attitudes often go together. Those who are seen as deficient in humanity are unlikely to be accepted into the circle of the nation. But the two are not reducible to each other, and the absence of dehumanizing prejudice does not guarantee recognition of inclusion in the "we." For example, many majority Canadians accept that immigrants are hard-working, law-abiding and loving parents, but still worry that they are merely "Canadians of convenience," who have no sense of loyalty or commitment to Canada.[7] They may be good humans, viewed from an abstract or universal perspective, but they are not seen as committed to "us"—they do not live up to the expectations of an "ethics of membership."[8] And as we will see, this matters for perceptions of their deservingness of state support or political power.

A central task of citizenization, therefore, is to challenge these hierarchies of worthiness. And, for many of its proponents, multiculturalism was seen as citizening in precisely this way: it was intended to challenge perceptions that ethnic minorities were deficient either in their humanity or their Canadian-ness.

Has multiculturalism in fact advanced these citizening goals? I think there is evidence for such citizening effects, albeit incomplete and fragile. In previous work, I have tried to pull together a range of different studies that provide correlational, longitudinal and experimental data suggesting that adopting multiculturalism policies leads both to lower levels of dehumanizing prejudice and to more inclusive conceptions of "we-ness" (Kymlicka, 2012). And as a consequence, multiculturalism is associated with higher levels of public support for the right of minorities to access welfare benefits, to have cultural accommodations and to share political power.[9]

However, these citizening effects of multiculturalism are deeply uneven, fragile and incomplete. For example, while Canadians often express positive attitudes towards immigration and multiculturalism in general, this co-exists with deep prejudices and anxieties about particular minorities, including Blacks and Muslims.[10] And even the more general positive attitudes often seem skin-deep, valued more in rhetoric than in lived practice, and easily overridden by perceived fears, particularly about security.[11]

Given these mixed results, I think a fair summary is that multiculturalism has had real but incomplete citizening effects. Can we imagine a form of multiculturalism that is more effective in countering these hierarchies of worthiness? For some commentators, the crucial limit of multiculturalism is its failure to address the problem of dehumanizing racial prejudice. This raises important questions about how we understand the relationship between multiculturalism and anti-racism, and whether we can develop a more robustly anti-racist multiculturalism. Since this is discussed in the chapter by Debra Thompson, I will focus on the other dimension of worthiness—namely, perceptions of Canadian-ness, and whether minorities are seen as insufficiently Canadian. In my view, this is perhaps the most distinctive promise of multiculturalism: it promised not only to recognize the humanity of minorities, but also to recognize their Canadian-ness. Multiculturalism said not only that there were many ways of being human, but that there were many ways of being Canadian, and so offered a new and more pluralistic and inclusive conception of "we-ness."

Has this message taken root? Do Canadian-born, English-speaking Canadians in fact recognize minorities as sharing in a mutual commitment to Canada, as opposed to simply being Canadians of convenience? Do members of the majority view minorities as having a sense of attachment and affiliation to Canada and a sense of solidarity and concern for fellow Canadians? Do members of the majority see minorities as complying with an ethics of membership?

Surprisingly, majority perceptions of minority commitment have not really been studied. We know a lot about how majorities think of their own national identity, but surprisingly little about how majorities perceive minorities' attachment to the nation. In order to fill this gap, my colleagues, Allison Harell and Keith Banting, and I devised a battery of survey questions intended to tap whether respondents believe that members of minority groups are committed to the larger society. For example, one of our questions—which proved to be highly informative—is a simple "Cares" question: *How much do you think immigrants care about the concerns and needs of other Canadians?* Another question was "Sacrifice:" *How willing do you think immigrants are to make sacrifices for other Canadians?* These questions were included in a broader online survey of 2100 Canadians fielded in August 2017 in both English and French (see Table 1.1 for the full wording of all eight questions; and see Harell et al. 2021 for details of the 2017 survey methodology).

The results were striking. On all eight criteria, members of the Canadian-born English-speaking majority perceived immigrants to be significantly less committed to Canada (Figure 1.1).

Some readers may think that this is just the inevitable result of the fact that immigrants are new arrivals in the country, and that these perceptions of lack of commitment will diminish over time. But our survey revealed the same pattern in relation to Canada's long-standing "national" groups—namely,

TABLE 1.1 Membership Commitment Questions

BETTER PLACE	Do demands made by each of the following groups makes Canada a better place to live or a worse place to live?
PATRIOTIC	Where would you rate [group] on the following dimension: Unpatriotic–Patriotic
IDENTITY	How much do you think each of the following groups identifies with Canada?
CARES	How much do you think each group cares about the concerns and needs of other Canadians?
THANKFUL	The government provides various programs and benefits that seek to help various communities in Canada. How thankful do you think each group is to receive these benefits?
SACRIFICE	How willing do you think the following groups are to make sacrifices for other Canadians?
FAIR SHARE	One way citizens contribute to society is by working and paying taxes. Given the resources available in each community, do you think the following groups are contributing their fair share, or more or less than their fair share?
FIGHT	If Canada was involved in a war, how willing do you think people from each of the following groups would be to volunteer to fight for Canada?

Note: The eight items for each of the four groups load into a single dimension. Cronbach's alpha scores, when excluding ingroup members, are 0.86 (Immigrant scale), 0.82 (Aboriginal peoples scale), 0.84 (French-speaking Québécois scale) and 0.71 (English-speaking Canadians).

28 Will Kymlicka

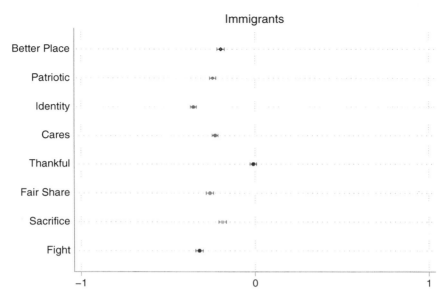

FIGURE 1.1   Immigrants

Note: Scores indicate difference in mean score for each target group compared to English-speaking Canadians, with bars indicating 95% confidence intervals. 0 indicates no difference between the two scores.

Source: Harell et al. 2021a.

Francophone Québécois and Indigenous peoples. Discussions of diversity in Canada often distinguish its historic "nations within"—the Québécois and Indigenous peoples who formed self-governing societies prior to British colonization—from later "ethnic groups" formed through migration to Canada as a British colony or independent country. The former have a sense of separate "nationhood," and have fought historically to retain or regain powers of self-government. In principle, Canada's constitutional framework accepts the aspirations of these "national minorities" or "nations within:" Canada's framework of bilingualism and federalism says that the Québécois should not have to hide or renounce their sense of nationhood to participate fully in Canadian public life; and Canada's framework of treaty rights, Aboriginal rights and reconciliation says that Indigenous peoples should not have to hide or renounce their sense of peoplehood in order to participate fully in Canadian public life.[12] Our surveys suggest, however, that whenever the Québécois or Aboriginal peoples exercise their rights under these frameworks, they are perceived as showing a lack of commitment to Canada and to Canadians (Figures 1.2 and 1.3).

These results are striking and discouraging. Multiculturalism as a policy and an ideology says that members of ethnic minorities should not have to hide or

Multiculturalism as Citizenization 29

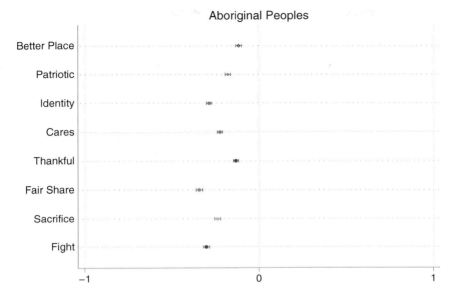

FIGURE 1.2 Aboriginal Peoples Source: Harell et al. 2021a.

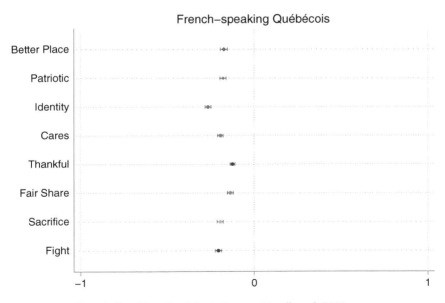

FIGURE 1.3 French-Speaking Québécois Source: Harell et al. 2021a.

renounce their identities in order to particulate fully in Canadian public life. It seems clear, however, that many majority Canadians view the maintenance of minority identities—whether immigrant-origin, Québécois or Indigenous—as evidence of a lack of a commitment to Canada. The findings suggest that members of the Canadian-born, English-speaking majority in Canada operate, implicitly or explicitly, with a "story of peoplehood" that privileges their own way of belonging to Canada, and which pathologizes minority forms and modes of belonging as deficient.[13] And this perception matters. Our survey showed that when majorities view minorities as less committed to Canada, they are less likely to support minorities' access to the welfare state, to cultural accommodations or to political claims-making—and again, this holds true not just for immigrants, but also for Aboriginal peoples and for Francophone Québécois (Harell et al., 2021a).[14] In short, minorities in Canada suffer from systemic "membership penalties:" they are seen as less committed members of the larger society, and as a result, are seen as less deserving of both recognition and redistribution.

These are sobering results, and we might indeed view them as evidence of the failure of multiculturalism. Before jumping to that conclusion, however, it is worth asking how these Canadian results compare with other countries. Perhaps these membership penalties are even larger in other countries? And that indeed is what we found when added our questions to a recent eight-country European study: immigrants in all eight countries are much more likely to be seen as lacking in membership commitment (Table 1.2).

Viewed in this comparative perspective, Canadian multiculturalism seems like a relative success: membership penalties faced by immigrants are lower in Canada compared to other Western countries. Of course, there may be many reasons for this, beyond the presence of multiculturalism. But we might

TABLE 1.2 Perceptions of Immigrants' Membership Commitment Source: Harell et al. 2021b.

	Perceptions of Immigrants' Membership Commitment
Canada	−0.168
United Kingdom	−0.279
Romania	−0.331
Spain	−0.363
Poland	−0.438
Germany	−0.441
Italy	−0.442
Netherlands	−0.442
France	−0.481

speculate that the "story of peoplehood" advanced by Canadian multiculturalism provides more space for minorities to stake claims to belonging. There is certainly nothing in these findings to suggest that rejecting multiculturalism (as in France) or retreating from multiculturalism (as in the Netherlands) is a better option for citizenization: these countries in fact exhibited the highest membership penalties.

Still, even if the membership penalties faced by immigrants are smaller in Canada compared to many other countries, they remain sizeable. And if 50 years of multiculturalism has not eliminated these membership penalties, then perhaps the idea of a truly inclusive "multicultural citizenship" is a mirage. Perhaps, at the end of the day, the official "story of peoplehood" told by the majority controlling the state can only be pushed so far to include minorities, even with an explicit commitment to multiculturalism. Perhaps a conception of multiculturalism that is citizenist will always put minorities in an impossible position: it grants minorities the right to assert their difference, but whenever they actually do so, their commitment to the larger society is questioned.

We might put the problem this way: stories of peoplehood seem to operate in a way that differentially locates majorities and minorities. Whenever majorities engage in political mobilization and make political claims—for or against increased taxes, say, or for or against building pipelines—this is taken as evidence of their concern for and commitment to the country and its future. They are seen as carrying forward the story of peoplehood, for which they are the natural (prototypical) bearers. By contrast, when minorities engage in political mobilization for the recognition of their differences, they are often seen, not as expressing a commitment to the larger society, but as engaging in selfish behavior, as a form of group egoism. Majorities see themselves as acting from a commitment to the collective "we," whereas minorities are seen as more likely to be acting upon group egoism rather than concern for others.[15] It seems that citizenist multiculturalism can at best diminish this penalty but not remove it.

If so, then perhaps a truly liberatory conception of multiculturalism should cut the link with citizenship entirely. Perhaps we should not ask or expect minorities to situate themselves in relation to categories of citizenship, "Canadian-ness," or "stories of peoplehood." Perhaps a truly liberatory multiculturalism would be more unbounded and cosmopolitan, focusing on our humanity, not our citizenship.

Multiculturalism beyond Citizenship?

And this brings us back to the debate I started with, over the role of citizenship in progressive politics. An increasing number of progressive thinkers argue that our goal should not be to pluralize conceptions of citizenship—as citizenist multiculturalism has tried to do—but rather to dissolve or abolish the status of citizenship entirely. Our fundamental rights and claims of justice—including multicultural claims—should attach to us simply as human beings, which we carry with us as we move around the world, rather than attach to us in virtue of our status in some regime of state citizenship.

Some defenders of this post-citizenship view argue that state-based citizenship was always illegitimate. Others argue that citizenship played a valuable role historically, when the vast majority of people were sedentary and/or when migration was one-way and permanent, but the current realities of global mobility require moving it. This latter view often draws a distinction between an earlier "age of migration" and our new "age of mobility." During the era of migration, immigrants were seen as settling permanently in their new country and becoming future citizens. This assumption of permanent settlement made citizenist politics—including citizenist multiculturalism—coherent. Permanent residents and future citizens have a self-interest in investing in society, becoming members and contributing to it, just as native-born citizens have a self-interest in ensuring that long-term immigrants develop a sense of belonging. So, in principle, one could imagine a "story of peoplehood" that did genuinely make room for immigrants to stake full claims to membership.

In the "age of migration," however, migration is increasingly temporary or circular, not permanent. Of course, temporary migration is not entirely new. Even in the 1970s and 1980s, there were temporary migrants in Canada with no right to long-term residence, including business visitors, international students and temporary foreign workers (TFWs), such as the Mexican farm laborers who come to Canada on a seasonal basis. Such temporary migrants do not fit in "citizenist" models of multiculturalism, and indeed, as I noted earlier, they have been excluded from the federal multiculturalism policy, as they are excluded from other integration policies (such as language training), which are reserved for permanent residents.

Until recently, this exclusion was not a matter of public debate in Canada, perhaps because the number of people in these temporary categories was relatively small. But starting in 2002, the government radically increased the number of TFWs, such that by 2007, the number of TFWs admitted annually to Canada exceeded the number of permanent residents being admitted. Moreover, a dizzying array of programs and procedures exist by which some—but not all—temporary workers and students can gain a more secure permanent residency, even as other policies generate the risk that they will descend from legal temporary residency into illegality.[16]

As a result, old assumptions that there is a clear separation between temporary and permanent immigrants, and that the former are a just a small group, are no longer tenable. Nor is Canada unique in this respect. Many people believe that the very distinction between permanent and temporary migration is breaking down around the world. Hence the familiar trope that we now live in an "age of mobility" rather than "an age of migration." Observers suggest that we will soon be living in a world of "superdiversity" with a multitude of legal statuses that are neither wholly temporary nor wholly permanent, but rather have varying degrees of conditionality and precariousness (Vertovec, 2015). And one consequence of this, many commentators argue, is that old models of multicultural citizenship are increasingly obsolete.

We can find various expressions of this argument in Canada:

- "how relevant is a bounded and managed multiculturalism as a national governance framework (physically circumscribed, culturally specific, and spatially exclusive national identity) in a relatively unbounded and unmanaged world of transmigratory movements, translocal linkages, hyperdiverse identities, cosmopolitan yearnings, and deterritorialized belongings?" (Fleras, 2015: 312);
- whereas multiculturalism privileges national identifications, we should instead seek "fluid" solidarity "capable of forming new forms of social relationships based on cooperation through and against existing national borders" (Sharma, 2011: 100);
- whereas multiculturalism "as an ideology of state-building reveals the state as being very careful to prescribe the type of belonging and the extent of inclusion," these restrictions "are constantly challenged by transnational migrants" with their own ideas of community and belonging (Walton-Roberts, 2011: 120).

In each case, the proposed alternative involves some form of "post-national" multiculturalism, in which state citizenship is decentered.

What should we make of these claims? In these passages, we are offered a series of rhetorical contrasts: bounded, managed and circumscribed multicultural citizenship versus unbounded, mobile, fluid and deterritorialized cosmopolitan solidarities. The rhetoric is clear, but what does this mean in practice? How exactly does multicultural citizenship "bind" people, and what would it mean concretely to unbind them? Elsewhere, I have tried to unpack different versions of this argument and explain why I think they are overstated (Kymlicka, 2017). However, for now, let me just flag two general reasons why I think there may yet be a future for multicultural citizenship.

First, the contrast between "an age of migration" and an "age of mobility" is overstated. Many immigrants still think of themselves as settling and making a life in a new country. And for those who do have this identity and project of permanent settlement, it may be very important to be recognized as a (committed) member of their new country. Long-settled immigrant groups typically want to be recognized, not just as fully human, but as fully Canadian. They want to be recognized as belonging and as committed to, participating in and contributing to a shared society. To be sure, we all have "cosmopolitan yearning and deterritorialized belongings," but (permanent) immigrants also have national yearnings and territorialized belongings. They want to be accepted as full members of Canadian society, not seen as mobile visitors passing through. Critics argue that multicultural citizenship involves the state prescribing or imposing ideas of national membership on immigrants, but the evidence suggests that immigrants and native-born citizens often share very similar views about the legitimacy and desirability of inculcating expectations of moral commitment to the larger society.[17] Permanent immigrants do not want to be exempted from expectations of moral commitment, they simply want a fair opportunity to meet these expectations. And this is what multicultural citizenship promised.[18]

Of course, as we've seen, multiculturalism has not in fact created a level playing field in relation to membership evaluations, and immigrant-origin ethnic groups face significant "membership penalties." But responding to membership penalties by negating the entire category of membership claims is a Pyrrhic victory. We need to find a way to enable immigrants (and other non-dominant groups) to fulfill their aspirations to membership, rather than pretending that these aspirations do not exist.

This only applies to long-settled immigrants and their descendants, and we need a different story about those migrants who are genuinely transient and temporary, such as TFWs. For them, something like "returnist multiculturalism" might be appropriate. This is explored in Terri-Anne Teo's chapter in this volume (see also Teo, 2021). But it would be a mistake to suppose that returnist multiculturalism (for temporary workers) or deterritorialized multiculturalism (for the hypermobile) can take the place of citizenist multiculturalism (for settled immigrants).

So, I think that citizenist multiculturalism matches the aspirations and yearnings of at least some immigrant groups. But there is a deeper reason for worrying about the post-citizenship approach to multiculturalism. Ideas of bounded membership may in fact play an indispensable role in underpinning progressive politics.

Political philosophers often distinguish two grounds on which we can make claims of justice on each other. First, there are claims we can make simply on the basis of our shared humanity, often articulated in the language of universal human rights. These claims are grounded in ideas of respect for "human dignity" or respect for "human personhood." To be denied these rights is to be treated as less-than-fully human, to be dehumanized. These rights are universal and portable—we take them with us as we move around the face of the world—and are not owed solely to our co-citizens. Everyone—whatever their legal or political status as tourists, refugees or native-born citizens—must be treated in ways that respect our common humanity and human dignity.

Second, there are claims we can make on the basis of our shared membership in a specific society, often articulated in the language of citizenship rights. These claims are grounded in the idea that people who have made their life in a particular society—the long-term, non-transient residents who have set down roots in a society—have a distinctive stake in that society that gives them distinctive rights to share in the fruits of society's scheme of cooperation as well as distinctive responsibilities towards the future of that society. Citizenship rights, in TH Marshall's famous and evocative words, rest on "a direct sense of community membership based on loyalty to a civilisation that is a common possession" (Marshall, 1950: 96). This metaphor of society as a "common possession" is vague, but we can think of it in terms of bi-directional belonging. If someone is a member of society, then they belong here, but equally society belongs to them, and they become the rightful custodians or stakeholders of this common possession. Citizenship rights are tied to this role or status.

Note how different this is from the moral logic of humanitarianism. It is not a response to suffering or to the denial of human dignity, but rather seeks to enable members to see society as a "common possession." The assumption is that we form a community, and that the function of the welfare state is to ensure that everyone feels equally at home in the community, that everyone can equally partake in the social and cultural life of the community and enjoy its civilization, and that everyone can feel that they belong to the community and that the community belongs to them. In this sense, we can say that one key function of the welfare state is to distribute membership goods or *membership stakes*: the welfare state secures what people need to flourish as members of a shared society. Whereas universal human rights recognize and respect us as human beings with inherent dignity, the welfare state empowers us as members of a particular society to enjoy our shared society as a common possession. This idea that politics should seek to create a shared society as a common possession of its members has been vital to the politics of social democracy in the 20th century, and to the "citizenship struggles" that have helped to build social democracy (Kymlicka, 2015, 2022).

In my view, progressive politics requires both a humanitarian track and a membership track.[19] The elaboration of universal human rights tied to respect for common humanity has been a profound moral accomplishment, which needs to be continuously reaffirmed and strengthened. But the elaboration of social-democratic welfare states tied to the idea of membership in society as a common possession has also been a profound moral accomplishment. If we lose the ability to appeal to this idea of society as a common possession, and can only appeal to ideas of shared humanity, we will have a much weaker basis for progressive politics.

Of course, as we've seen, the membership track comes at a price. Membership rights, unlike universal human rights, presuppose allegiance to some bounded "we." My obligations to you as a fellow member depend on the perception that we both share an allegiance or "loyalty," in Marshall's words, to a shared society. And as our survey results reveal, these perceptions are deeply biased and skewed against minorities. As a result, the membership track creates membership penalties for minorities, and to date at least, 50 years of multiculturalism has failed to fully remedy those penalties.

This suggests we are stuck between a rock and a hard place. We need membership rights for progressive politics, but any scheme of membership-based politics is likely to create unfair membership penalties. In my view, this dilemma is an enduring one, and we need to confront it head on, rather than wishing it away. Some cosmopolitans try to avoid the dilemma by denying the need for membership politics. Others try to avoid the dilemma by denying that membership politics creates membership penalties. Many liberal nationalists, for example, argue that a "civic" or "color-blind" approach to membership would not penalize minorities. But neither view is plausible: we need membership politics, and even "civic" nations create membership penalties for minorities. In my view, we need to acknowledge that membership penalties are a chronic feature of liberal-democratic politics, even in "civic" nations, and we need to take proactive steps to identify and remedy them. And this, I think, is the promise of a distinctly multicultural citizenship. Progressive politics requires membership politics, but all too often, membership politics has been built on the backs of minorities. At its best, citizenist multiculturalism is an acknowledgement of that dilemma, and a commitment to do better.[20]

Notes

1 A fuller review would require distinguishing different dimensions of this dispute, including a statist–anarchist dimension, and a nationalist–cosmopolitan dimension, and within the cosmopolitan strand, a further subdivision between those who are most concerned with how citizenship reproduces global inequality and those who think citizenship is a betrayal of our humanity even when not associated with global inequalities.
2 Habermas famously argued that while democracy could only have emerged in tandem with ideas of nationhood, it is now time to cut the umbilical cord and shift to a post-national form of democracy (Habermas, 2001). A parallel argument has been made about multiculturalism: it could only have emerged in tandem with state citizenship but must now transcend it (Fleras, 2015).
3 Like other settler states, one of Canada's long-standing national myths is about the "settling" of "wilderness" by intrepid Europeans, a myth that rendered invisible the violent displacement and dispossession of the Indigenous peoples whose homelands were being colonized. As the myth is increasingly criticized by Indigenous voices, ethnic groups today are less likely to celebrate the fact their members were "pioneer" settlers. But historically—and certainly in the 1960s—white ethnic groups in Canada actively embraced this myth of settlement, celebrated their role in it, and invoked it as grounds for multicultural recognition. See Ladner's chapter in this volume for discussion of this dynamic.
4 This already casts doubt on some familiar versions of the claim that multiculturalism undermines citizenship. Neil Bissoondath, for example, argued that multiculturalism encourages immigrants (and their children) to think of themselves as foreigners, not Canadians, to "see Canada with the eyes of foreigners. Multiculturalism, with its emphasis on the importance of holding on to the former or ancestral homeland, with its insistence that There is more important than Here,

encourages such attitudes" (Bissoondath, 1994: 133). His account simply ignores the fundamental differences between returnist multiculturalism and citizenship-based multiculturalism.
5 As Martin Gilens famously put it, "Politics is often viewed, by elites at least, as a process centered on the question 'who gets what.' For ordinary Americans, however, politics is more often about 'who *deserves* what'" (Gilens, 1999: 2). His study focused on how white Americans view Blacks as less deserving, but subsequent research has confirmed that (a) ordinary citizens everywhere care about who deserves what; and (b) majorities everywhere tend to view minorities as less deserving. The "politics of deservingness" is not uniquely American, or uniquely tied to white–Black race relations.
6 This often involves tropes of animality: viewing members of a minority as lacking "distinctly human" qualities of moral self-regulation, and hence as being closer to animals in terms of impulsiveness, aggression, laziness.
7 On "citizens of convenience," and the antipathy towards them in Canada, see Park 2013.
8 On the idea of an "ethics of membership," and its role in shaping judgements of deservingness, see Kymlicka 2022.
9 Not everyone reads the evidence this way. Some commentators argue there is evidence that multiculturalism has negative effects (e.g., Koopmans, 2010), while others argue that we simply lack the evidence that would allow us to draw confident conclusions one way or the other (e.g., Reitz, 2009).
10 Triadafilopoulos and Rasheed (2020) suggest that Canada exhibits an "Islamophobic multiculturalism," where generalized support for multiculturalism co-exists with antipathy towards Muslims. See also Kymlicka 2021.
11 On the securitization of multiculturalism, see Dhamoon, 2012.
12 On the similarities and differences between these three "pillars" or "silos" of diversity policy in Canada, and how they interact with each other, see Kymlicka, 2007.
13 On the idea that all modern states operate with "stories of peoplehood," see Smith, 2003. For an interpretation of multiculturalism as an attempt to rewrite this story of peoplehood, see Kymlicka, 2022.
14 It is worth noting that these results hold even when controlling for outgroup antipathy. As noted earlier, the absence of racial prejudice does not entail a sense of "we-ness" (Harell, 2021a).
15 See Amarasingham et al., 2016 and Thurairajah, 2017 for two of many recent examples where the public expression of minority identities is interpreted as lack of concern for the country. For further elaboration of how stories of peoplehood generate this effect, see Kymlicka, 2022.
16 See Goldring and Landolt, 2013 for the "ladders and chutes" by which temporary residents can either ascend to secure status or descend to illegality.
17 Midtbøen, 2020; Osipovič, 2015; Reeskens and Van Oorschot, 2015; Kremer, 2016.
18 In my view, the deeper ethical dilemmas raised by expectations of compliance with an ethics of membership are not actually in relation to immigrants, but rather in relation to historic substate nations and Indigenous peoples. Expecting those who have been conquered or colonized by the state to show membership commitment is obviously normatively problematic, and existing policy frameworks around federalism/bilingualism (for French-Canadians) and treaty rights/reconciliation (for Aboriginal peoples) do not fully square the circle. For further discussion, see Kymlicka, 2022. My focus in this chapter however is on the link between citizenship and immigration-origin multiculturalism.
19 There are of course other grounds for claims-making, including the rectification of historic injustice and the fulfillment of international treaties and agreements, which generate distinctive obligations alongside both humanitarian and membership claims. But I would argue that these simply strengthen the importance of

membership politics. Without the idea of society as a common possession of its members, it would be difficult to make sense of either the authors or addresses of obligations arising from historic injustices or treaties.

20 I've emphasized the role that citizenist multiculturalism plays in promoting the membership track, but of course it can and should advance the humanitarian track as well. Membership politics can and should be embedded in a larger story about respect for universal human rights, and multiculturalism can and should encourage an ethos and practice of intercultural exchange that resists tendencies towards dehumanization. At its best, citizenist multiculturalism not only addresses membership penalties, but does so in a way that synchronizes with efforts to strengthen universal human rights.

References

Amarasingam, Amarnath, Gayathri Naganathan and Jennifer Hyndman. 2016. "Canadian Multiculturalism as Banal Nationalism: Understanding Everyday Meanings Among Sri Lankan Tamils in Toronto." *Canadian Ethnic Studies 48* (2): 119–141.

Baines, Donna and Nandita Sharma. 2002. "Migrant Workers as Non-Citizens: The Case Against Citizenship as a Social Policy Concept." *Studies in Political Economy 69* (1): 75–107.

Bissoondath, Neil. 1994. *Selling Illusions: The Cult of Multiculturalism in Canada.* Toronto: Penguin.

Bloom, Tendayi. 2017. *Noncitizenism: Recognising Noncitizen Capabilities in a World of Citizens.* London: Routledge.

Bosniak, Linda. 1998. "The Citizenship of Aliens." *Social Text 56*: 29–35.

Dahrendorf, Ralf. 1974. "Citizenship and Beyond: The Social Dynamics of an Idea." *Social Research 41* (4): 673–701.

Dhamoon, Rita. 2012. "Security Warning: Multiculturalism Alert." In *Ashgate Research Companion to Multiculturalism*, Duncan Ivison (ed.) Aldershot: Ashgate.

Favell, Adrian. 2019. "Integration: Twelve Propositions after Schinkel." *Comparative Migration Studies 7*: 21.

Fleras, Augie. 2015. "Beyond Multiculturalism." In *Revisiting Multiculturalism in Canada*, S. Guo and L. Wong (eds.) Rotterdam: Sense, 311–334.

Fraser, Nancy. 1995. "From Redistribution to Recognition? Dilemmas of Justice in a "Postsocialist" Age." *New Left Review 212*: 68–68.

Fraser, Nancy and Linda Gordon. 1994. "Civic Citizenship against Social Citizenship." In *The Condition of Citizenship*, B. van Steenburgen (ed.) London: Sage, 90–107.

Gilens, Martin. 1999. *Why Americans Hate Welfare.* Chicago: University of Chicago Press.

Goldring, Luin and Patricia Landolt. 2013. *Producing and Negotiating Non-Citizenship: Precarious Legal Status in Canada.* Toronto: University of Toronto Press.

Habermas, Jürgen. 2001. *Postnational Constellation.* Cambridge, MA: MIT Press.

Harell, Allison, Keith Banting and Will Kymlicka. 2021b. "The Boundaries of Generosity: Membership, Inclusion and Redistribution." In *The Edward Elgar Handbook on Migration and Welfare*, Markus Crepaz (ed.) Cheltenham: Elgar, 102–117.

Harell, Allison, Keith Banting, Will Kymlicka and Rebecca Wallace. 2021a. "Shared Membership Beyond National Identity: Deservingness and Solidarity in Diverse Societies." *Political Studies*, early view.

Kremer, Monique. 2016. "Earned Citizenship: Labour Migrants' Views on the Welfare State." *Journal of Social Policy* 45 (3): 395.

Kochenov, Dimitry. 2019. *Citizenship*. Boston: MIT Press.

Koopmans, Ruud. 2010. "Trade-Offs Between Equality and Difference: Immigrant Integration, Multiculturalism and the Welfare State in Cross-National Perspective." *Journal of Ethnic and Migration Studies* 36 (1): 1–26. http://www.informaworld.com/smpp/title~db=all~content=t713433350~tab=issueslist~branches=36-v36.

Kymlicka, Will. 2007. "Ethnocultural Diversity in a Liberal State: Making Sense of the Canadian Model(s)." In *Belonging? Diversity, Recognition and Shared Citizenship in Canada*, Keith Banting, Thomas Courchene and Leslie Seidle (eds.) Montreal: Institute for Research on Public Policy, 39–86.

Kymlicka, Will. 2012. "Multiculturalism: Success, Failure, and the Future." In *Rethinking National Identity in the Age of Migration*, Migration Policy Institute (ed.) Berlin: Verlag Bertelsmann Stiftung, 33–78.

Kymlicka, Will. 2015a. "Solidarity in Diverse Societies." *Comparative Migration Studies* 3 (1): 1–19.

Kymlicka, Will. 2015b. "The Three Lives of Multiculturalism." In *Revisiting Multiculturalism in Canada: Theories, Policies, and Debates*, Shibao Guo and Lloyd Wong (eds.) Rotterdam: Sense Publishers, 17–35.

Kymlicka, Will. 2017. "Multiculturalism Without Citizenship?" In *Multicultural Governance in a Mobile World*, A. Triandafyllidou (ed.) Edinburgh: Edinburgh University Press, 139–161.

Kymlicka, Will. 2021. "The Precarious Resilience of Multiculturalism in Canada." *American Review of Canadian Studies* 51 (1): 122–142.

Kymlicka, Will. 2022. "Nationhood, Multiculturalism and the Ethics of Membership." In *Majorities, Minorities, and the Future of Nationhood*, Liav Orgad and Ruud Koopmans (eds.) Cambridge: Cambridge University Press, 87–128.

Marshall, T. H. 1950. *Sociology at the Crossroads*. London: Heinemann.

Midtbøen, Arnfinn, et al. 2020. "Assessments of Citizenship Criteria: Are Immigrants More Liberal?." *Journal of Ethnic and Migration Studies* 46 (13): 2625–2646.

Osipovič, Dorota. 2015. "Conceptualisations of Welfare Deservingness by Polish Migrants in the UK." *Journal of Social Policy* 44 (4): 729–746.

Park, Augustine. 2013. "Racial-nationalism and Representations of Citizenship: The Recalcitrant Alien, the Citizen of Convenience and the Fraudulent Citizen." *Canadian Journal of Sociology* 38 (4): 579–600.

Reeskens, Tim and Wim Van Oorschot. 2015. "Immigrants' Attitudes Towards Welfare Redistribution. An Exploration of Role of Government Preferences Among Immigrants and Natives Across 18 European Welfare States." *European Sociological Review* 31 (4): 433–445.

Reitz, Jeffrey. 2009. "Assessing Multiculturalism as a Behavioural Theory." In *Multiculturalism and Social Cohesion*, Jeffrey Reitz et al. (eds.) Dordrecht: Springer, 1–47.

Ryan, Phil. 2010. *Multicultiphobia*. Toronto: University of Toronto Press.

Schönwälder, Karen. 2010. "Germany: integration policy and pluralism in a self-conscious country of immigration." In *The Multiculturalism Backlash*, Steven Vertovec and Susanne Wessendorf (eds.), London: Routledge, 152–169.

Scott, James. 1998. *Seeing Like a State: How Certain Schemes to Improve the Human Condition have Failed*. New Haven: Yale University Press.

Sharma, Nandita. 2011. "Canadian Multiculturalism and Its Nationalisms." In *Home and Native Land*, May Chazan et al. (eds.) Toronto: Between the Lines, 85–101.
Smith, Rogers. 2003. *Stories of Peoplehood: The Politics and Morals of Political Membership*. Cambridge: Cambridge University Press.
Teo, Terri-Anne. 2021. "Multiculturalism Beyond Citizenship: The Inclusion of Non-Citizens." *Ethnicities 21* (1): 165–191.
Thurairajah, Kalyani. 2017. "The Jagged Edges of Multiculturalism in Canada and the Suspect Canadian." *Journal of Multicultural Discourses 12* (2): 134–148.
Triadafilopoulos, T. and J. Rasheed. 2020. "A Religion like No Other: Islam and the Limits of Multiculturalism in Canada." Working Paper No. 2020/14, Ryerson Centre for Immigration and Settlement.
Tully, James. 2001. "Introduction." In *Multinational Democracies*, Alain Gagnon and James Tully (eds.), 1–34. Cambridge: Cambridge University Press.
Vertovec, Steven. 2015. *Super-diversity*. London: Routledge.
Walton-Roberts, Margaret. 2011. "Multiculturalism Already Unbound." In *Home and Native Land*, May Chazan et al. (eds.) Toronto: Between the Lines, 102–122.

2
MULTICULTURALISM AND INCLUSIVE DEMOCRACY

Canadian Multiculturalism and Immigrant Citizenship

Irene Bloemraad

In the summer of 1994, I worked as a parliamentary guide in Ottawa, walking Canadian and international tourists through the architectural beauty of the parliament buildings and teaching them the basics of the federal political system. The security screenings now standard in many government buildings did not exist, and Members of Parliament (MPs) would walk the same halls as the visitors. More than once, a foreign tour group would comment on a few particular MPs. "Who is that?" More bluntly, "What is that man wearing on his head?" one French woman asked. She was referring to Gurbax Singh Malhi, elected to federal office in 1993 from Ontario. He had the distinction of being the first turban-wearing Sikh to be elected to Canada's House of Commons. Twenty-five years later, during the 2019 federal election campaign, my American colleagues expressed amazement that a leader of a major Canadian political party, Jasmeet Singh of the New Democratic Party, had achieved such a prominent position while retaining his turban as a practicing Sikh and embracing his Punjabi heritage. Malhi and Singh not only embody demographic diversity in Canadian politics, but their success suggests that many Canadian voters do not see public displays of diversity as problematic in their national representatives. In contrast, citizens of other countries appear to have a harder time imagining such multiculturalism among their office holders.

These snapshots of political diversity inspire this chapter, which considers whether and how government policy and political leaders' pronouncements on multiculturalism foster democratic inclusion for those of immigrant origin. Proponents of multiculturalism contend that when discourse and policy valorize and accommodate cultural specificity, members of minority communities will feel increased connection to and engagement in the polity

DOI: 10.4324/9781003197485-5

and society. Critics argue that, as a normative ideal and public discourse, multiculturalism contributes to a divided citizenry lacking a common identity and that, as a government policy, multiculturalism impedes immigrant integration and promotes cultural isolation to produce siloed communities. Sometimes these debates are thoughtful and help to clarify the moral stakes that guide public decision-making. But more often such debates degenerate into polemic pronouncements by politicians and media commentators. Advocates and critics latch onto shining examples of success (e.g., the former refugee, now a millionaire) or egregious examples of harmful behavior (e.g., a deadly, isolated terrorist attack by an immigrant-origin Canadian) to draw broad conclusions about multiculturalism. Such claims are divorced from systematic data. In this chapter, I consider the assertions of proponents and critics of multiculturalism and put them in dialogue with existing empirical evidence.

In examining immigrant incorporation, I argue that multiculturalism likely has limited effect, positive or negative, on some outcomes such as economic integration, but that, at least in Canada, we find solid evidence of positive political incorporation, which in turn fosters democratic inclusion.[1] Comparative research suggests that immigrants in Canada acquire citizenship at very high levels and very rapidly compared to other Western democracies; this rapid move to citizenship is due in part to the instrumental assistance and symbolic impact of policies such as multiculturalism. Similarly, politicians of immigrant origin have been very successful in running for federal office, rendering the Canadian House of Commons much more representative of immigrant diversity than other rich democracies. Part of this success is due to a reimagined narrative of (Anglo) Canadian identity that is understood as inherently multicultural.

In the conclusion, I consider whether these outcomes are unique to Canada, and whether the positive relationship between multiculturalism and inclusive democracy will continue. I am cautiously optimistic. For many in Canada, multiculturalism has become part of collective identification as a Canadian and a point of pride vis-à-vis other countries. Further, the very success of incorporating immigrant-origin residents into civic and political life—by, for example, becoming voters—makes it hard for far-right political parties to garner significant support. This does not mean, however, that other actions to advance inclusive democracy, especially around racial inequities and Indigenous voice, are not needed. We also need further diversification of political representation at provincial and municipal levels of government. While multiculturalism is no magic elixir that eliminates the challenges of making democracy work for a diverse citizenry, it has certainly done much to transform Canada from a self-styled British dominion to a pluralist country where most residents celebrate diversity and multiculturalism as part of national identity.

The Rise of "Multiculturalism:" Concept, Policy and Discourse

If you type "multiculturalism" into Google's Ngram viewer, you find that virtually no book in the English language used this term up to the late 1960s.[2] The Canadian federal government's announcement of a multiculturalism policy in 1971 occurs very early in an increase in the term's frequency, raising the possibility that the announcement spurred the use of and interest in the word (see Figure 2.1). Usage grows slowly through to the late 1980s then, around 1988, just as Canada's parliament passes the Multiculturalism Act, the popularity of "multiculturalism" in books increases rapidly for a decade. In the late 1990s, the term's usage continues to grow, albeit at a slower rate. We find an apparent inflection point around 2013. Since then, there has been a slight decrease in the relative use of "multiculturalism" compared to other words.

Serious scholars of word usage know that there are important limitations to relying on the Google book corpus and that a nuanced understanding of a word's prominence and evolution requires more than simple "plug and play" into a web-based search engine. And yet the trend line in Figure 2.1 maps well onto researchers' and observers' sense of the rise—and possible fall—of multiculturalism's popularity. Canadian government actions seem to be at the leading edge of key moment of change.

Of course, what is precisely meant by "multiculturalism" can vary widely across this immense corpus of books. In some cases, authors use the term "multiculturalism" to describe demographic pluralism. While Statistics Canada no longer uses "multicultural" in reporting on population diversity—the preferred heading is now "Immigration and Ethnocultural Diversity"—the "key indicators" of diversity for Statistics Canada include counts of the immigrant population (those born outside of Canada), the second generation (those who have at least one foreign-born parent) and the "visible minority population."[3] We learn that almost 22% of Canadian residents were foreign-born in 2016, that the second generation makes up another 18% of the population, and that more than 1 in 5 people (22%) self-identify as visible minorities. There are also data about citizenship, ethnicity, mother tongue and religious affiliation. Canada has clearly become much more demographically "multicultural" since Confederation: in 1871, the first census of the new Canadian Confederation reported that over 9 in 10 residents had origins in the British Isles (60.5%) or France (31.1%). By 2016 only a third of Canadian residents said that they had at least one origin from the British Isles (32.5%) and just under 1 in 7 (13.6%) reported French origins (Statistics Canada 2017).

In other countries, and for some Canadians, "multiculturalism" might also include Indigenous populations, the descendants of those forcibly transported as slaves and long-standing minority groups that see themselves as distinct nations, such as the descendants of French colonists in Quebec or Francophone communities

44 Irene Bloemraad

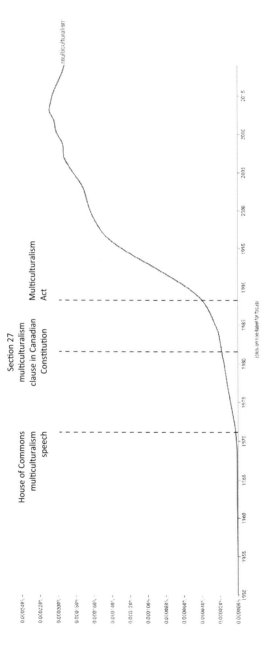

FIGURE 2.1 Relative Prevalence of the Word "Multiculturalism" in English-Language Books, 1950–2019

in other Canadian provinces. For the purposes of this chapter, I consider multiculturalism in the context of immigrant-generated diversity. This usage has animated some of the strongest calls to abandon multiculturalism in favor of alternative policies of "color-blind" integration and republican assimilation or, conversely, to focus instead on tackling systemic racism rather than recognizing "culture."

"Multiculturalism" covers far more that demographic diversity, however. Key to this chapter, multiculturalism also encompasses a range of policies that aim to recognize and accommodate ethno-racial and religious diversity and it is a public discourse that affirms and valorizes diversity in origins, cultures and religions. Multiculturalism as public discourse began well before philosophical theories of multiculturalism were elaborated, as Prime Minister Pierre Trudeau's 1971 speech in the House of Commons shows. Policies and discourse can be advanced by a wide range of social institutions, from schools to private businesses. For example, school and work cafeterias might offer diverse foods to take into account students' and employees' dietary restrictions, including religious restrictions, while uniforms might be modified to accommodate religious or cultural traditions, from wearing turbans or headscarves to braiding one's hair in cornrows.

Schools, businesses and other institutions can advance multiculturalism, but scholarly attention has tended to focus on public policy and government pronouncements, often at the national level, although also increasingly at sub-national and local levels. To measure policy, researchers have categorized countries—mostly Western democracies—as being more or less multicultural (e.g., Koopmans et al., 2005; Banting and Kymlicka, 2013; Helbling and Vink, 2013). The Multicultural Policy Index, one of the most prominent of these measures, reports on eight indicators of policy accommodation for immigrant-origin minorities, finding that Canada scores among the highest (with Australia) in multiculturalism, whereas countries such as Denmark and Japan have no evidence of any state-led multicultural policies from 1980 through to 2010.[4]

Multiculturalism as public discourse is harder to quantify or measure for impact. Yet, as I argue below, it carries real consequences. We get a sense of this when contrasting multicultural discourse to older tropes of Anglo-conformity that dominated in North America previously (or "Americanization" in the United States), or contrasting multiculturalism to contemporary rhetoric of universalist, ethno-racial "blind" republicanism in countries such as France. The discussion below focuses on government policy and political leaders' pronouncements on multiculturalism, investigating whether and how multiculturalism as policy and discourse may foster democratic inclusion.

Why Might Multiculturalism Work, or Fail? Collective Identification and Socio-Economic Integration

The early proponents of multiculturalism, whether political leaders or political philosophers, almost uniformly viewed multicultural ideas and policy as mechanisms for minority incorporation. Prime Minister Pierre Trudeau's 1971 speech emphasized the twin goal of "full participation" in Canadian society by Canadians of all backgrounds and of "national unity." Canadian-based philosophers, whether communitarian-oriented or liberal theorists, argued that cultural recognition does not divide a polity but rather generates connection to and engagement with the political collective (Taylor, 1994; Kymlicka, 1995). The mechanisms of this connection and engagement were not clear—the focus was on moral principles, not on-the-ground social processes—but presumably the causal link between multicultural policy and discourse, on the one hand, and "full participation" or "unity," on the other, lies in feelings of belonging and psychological identification with the country and to fellow citizens. For advocates, the danger lay in failing to adopt pluralism and diversity policies, since the status quo, largely built on a combination of assimilation, private individualism or Anglo conformity, alienated minorities from the nation's political life and would presumably continue to do so as new immigrants joined the polity.

Critics of multiculturalism raise a range of concerns in response. A common worry is that emphasizing diversity reifies differences, and that this undermines rather than promotes collective national identity (Barry, 2002; Miller, 1995). A key empirical question, then, is the effect of pluralism discourse and policy on people's sense of attachment or belonging. Is it integrative (the multicultural argument) or isolating (the critics' claim)? Critics also argued that without a somewhat homogenous collective identity, countries would have trouble advancing collective political projects, such as recruiting people to join the military or convincing voters to support taxes for redistributive spending (Scheffer, 2011). The empirical hypothesis is that color-blind republicanism or assimilation to a majority culture will create greater solidarity, which in turn will facilitate collective projects of sacrifice, whether with one's life or one's tax dollars. In a slightly different vein, some scholars claim that promoting diversity encourages minorities to live in self-segregated communities, inhibiting their adoption of the majority language and preventing social ties with people outside their ethnic enclave (Huntington, 2004). Such "parallel" societies might not only hinder collective political projects but would also hurt the socio-economic integration of immigrants. Isolated in "ethnic ghettos," immigrants will have higher unemployment, lower wages and greater reliance on welfare programs, while their children will be at a disadvantage in school because of poor majority language skills, impeding their educational attainment (Borjas, 2001; Koopmans, 2010). Critics of multiculturalism argue that such outcomes are problematic for immigrants and for the societies in which they reside.

Do the research data support or contradict such claims? We should first note that the critique of multiculturalism that links collective identity to solidarity presumes a zero-sum trade-off: that recognizing or promoting multiple and diverse origins will undermine social cohesion. But the empirical evidence shows that such a trade-off is not automatic, and at times it is demonstrably false. Canadian social psychologist John Berry (2005, 2013) has argued that hyphenated or nested identities produce greater social psychological benefits than a unitary attachment to only the majority society or only the minority community (see also Phan and Breton, 2009). Those who integrate heritage and national identities exhibit greater tolerance and self-assessed wellbeing, Berry reports, a finding bolstered by Nguyen and Benet-Martínez's (2013) meta-analysis of over 50 psychology studies. They conclude that bicultural individuals show better psychological adjustment, as measured by higher life satisfaction and self-esteem, and lower alienation, anxiety, depression and loneliness. Berry (2005) argues that a positive dual identity is easier to achieve in multicultural countries. Indeed, in Canada, when asked how important their ethnicity and "the nation" are to their sense of who they are, immigrant respondents in Canada are more likely to report a high salience of their ethnic identity compared to US residents and, in addition, those in Canada also express the same or higher national attachment than counterparts in the United States (Bloemraad and Wright, 2014; Berry, 2013). In comparisons between multicultural Canada and republican France, researchers find that Muslim immigrants in France are more socially isolated from the mainstream than their Canadian counterparts when it comes to friendship, although trends in national identification are similar, albeit for different reasons (i.e., longer residence in France, more education among immigrants in Canada) (Reitz, Simon and Laxer, 2017). In short, strong ethnic identity does not necessarily come at the cost of national identification with Canada.

What about the claim that cultural recognition and accommodation impedes socio-economic integration? Here we see some differences in the conclusions drawn by North American and European social scientists. In the United States, scholars who believe that immigrant integration is "segmented" by race and class (the segmented assimilation model) contend that "selective acculturation" (i.e., biculturalism) is protective: it helps the children of immigrants do well in school, get along with parents, and stay out of trouble by avoiding "downward" assimilation to a minority, urban American culture (Portes and Zhou, 1993; Portes and Rumbaut, 2001). Others, who identify a mostly "straight-line" (rather than segmented) process of integration into mainstream American society also consider immigrant culture beneficial for socio-economic incorporation: cultural hybridity—combining the best of US and heritage cultures—correlates with higher educational attainment (Kasinitz et al., 2008). The meta-analysis noted above also concludes that biculturalism is positively correlated with academic achievement, career success and reduced delinquency (Nguyen and Benet-Martínez, 2013). It is rarer to read European accounts of how migrant culture fosters economic mobility; the presumption seems to be that immigrants' culture is an obstacle. Ruud Koopmans (2010) has argued that multicultural policies, when accompanied by a generous welfare state, produce greater welfare dependency among immigrants. The evidence is far from settled in Europe, however. Other research finds that second generation residents' educational attainment, occupational prestige and residential diversity appear higher in countries such as the Netherlands, Sweden and the UK (all of which score high on multiculturalism) compared to countries hostile to public multiculturalism such as Austria, Germany, France and Switzerland (Alba and Foner, 2015; Bean et al., 2012).

As it stands, there is no clear evidence of a negative impact of multicultural policies on immigrants' socio-economic integration, and some suggestive evidence of positive effects, although it is hard to come to conclusive findings. It is extremely difficult to compile cross-national, comparative metrics to test the effects of variation in policy contexts and to control adequately for differences in time periods, immigrants' background characteristics and other policy effects beyond multiculturalism (e.g., welfare programs, labor protections). Conceptually, too, the posited causal chain linking multiculturalism policies to socio-economic integration is complex. For example, we would need to know, empirically, whether the presence of multicultural policies has an effect on immigrants' majority language competency, and then we would need to evaluate how much majority language competency matters for securing a better-paying job, all else equal, as well as whether or not multicultural policies reduce employer discrimination in hiring. Further, we would need to separate out the possible effect of multiculturalism from the multitude of other factors that influence economic success, such as immigration selection policy, the organization of the educational system, legal employment protections and so forth. Recognition of cultural diversity might be far less important to socio-economic outcomes than racial minority status. Reitz and Banerjee (2009) find, for example, a clear division in income trajectories and poverty between racial minority residents of Canada and those of European origins. It is worth observing that those countries most reluctant or averse to multicultural policies have not demonstrated remarkably better socio-economic or educational incorporation than countries that have embraced multicultural policies. Immigrant-origin youth in non-multicultural, republican France are not doing better in the labor market than similar immigrant-origin youth in multicultural Canada.

Inclusive Citizenship: Political and Civic Incorporation

There is a stronger evidentiary case for the argument that multicultural policies and discourse facilitate political and civic incorporation. Immigrants acquire citizenship more quickly and at higher levels in countries with more multicultural policies (Bloemraad and Wright, 2014). For example, Canada, Sweden and Australia rank, internationally, as countries with high commitment to multiculturalism. These three countries also have very high naturalization levels. Among working age (15–64) foreign-born residents with at least 10 years of residence, 89% had taken out citizenship in Canada in 2007, 82% had done so in Sweden and 81% had acquired Australian citizenship (Liebig and Von Haaren 2010: 27–28). Conversely, naturalization levels were low among countries with few multicultural policies, such as Switzerland (35%) or Germany (37%). It is, of course, possible that countries with more multicultural policies also adopt more liberal citizenship policies or are characterized by other immigrant-friendly legislation or programs, so higher citizenship levels are not just thanks to multiculturalism, but clearly they do not hurt, either.

In most countries, acquiring citizenship opens the door to greater political rights, such as being able to cast a ballot in the electoral system. Not surprisingly, then, immigrant-origin citizens appear to have more success in winning national office in more multicultural countries, in both first-past-the-post and proportional representation voting systems (Bloemraad, 2013; Griffith, 2019). Beyond electoral politics, data on public claims-making indicate that immigrant-origin minorities in more multicultural countries are more likely to engage in a range of non-violent political activities than those in more "monocultural" societies, and that the activism of the former is more likely to be directed at the country of residence than the homeland (Koopmans et al., 2005: 128, 137). In other analyses, researchers find no effect, positive or negative, between living in a multicultural country and indicators of political integration. Wright and Bloemraad (2012) find no statistically significant relationship between the prevalence of multicultural policies and the political behaviors of immigrants and their children across six indicators of political participation, ranging from contacting a public official to signing a petition, as well as trust in or attachment to political institutions (Bloemraad and Wright, 2014). In short, the evidence of multiculturalism's effect on political incorporation tends to be positive or nil. Countries embracing stronger multicultural policies do not experience greater political fragmentation or political apathy among immigrant-origin residents than countries that reject diversity policy and discourse.

Among countries more supportive of multiculturalism, Canada does stand out for the high degree of immigrant political incorporation, whether we consider citizenship or the representation of visible minority and immigrant elected officials in federal parliament. In 2019, 14% of seats in the House of Commons were held by foreign-born representatives (Griffith, 2019). This is not at parity with the proportion in the general population (22%), but quite high, comparatively. In Australia, where over 28% of the general population was born abroad, immigrants counted for just under 10% of all those sitting in either house of parliament (Blakkarly, 2019). In the United States, 14% of residents were foreign-born, but only 3% of those serving in Congress (House and Senate) in 2019 were immigrants (Geiger, 2019). To achieve parity, the share of foreign-born elected officials would have to increase by 57% in Canada, 180% in Australia and 367% in the United States. Canada's relative success is striking. Is there something unique in Canadian multiculturalism?

How Does Multiculturalism Promote Civic and Political Incorporation?

The research data summarized above challenge the direst claims of multiculturalism's critics, but they leave open the questions of how and why multiculturalism produces political and civic incorporation. Is it a simple story of psychology? We can imagine that, by promoting diversity and legitimizing pluralism, immigrants feel that they belong, and thus they feel motivated to acquire citizenship and participate in politics. This is often the implicit claim in the normative political philosophy arguing for multiculturalism.

Based on my research, such "interpretative pathways" are not the whole story, but they are very important (Bloemraad, 2006). Government policies generate cognitive maps, cultural meanings and emotive understandings of membership, politics and who has legitimate political standing in a country. Some scholars call this a country's "discursive opportunity structure." For immigrants, the discursive opportunity structure includes a country's articulation of political membership (based either on ancestry or on civic bonds) and a country's tolerance of cultural plurality (or its belief in a singular national culture) (Koopmans et al., 2005). A country might embrace civic citizenship but reject public cultural pluralism (e.g., France), it might advance some cultural pluralism but within an ancestry-based political membership (e.g., Switzerland), it might articulate an ancestry-based membership of a singular national culture (e.g., Germany up to 2000) or it might adopt civic citizenship with cultural pluralism (e.g., Canada). These symbolic representations have real power by setting up—or undermining—hierarchical distinctions of political and social legitimacy and deservingness.

The integration mechanisms of multiculturalism are not just about symbolic or discursive politics, however. They also involve a more complex process of structured mobilization. Government policies, including but not limited to multiculturalism, distribute symbolic and material resources, and these in turn influence political and civic incorporation through interpretative and instrumental mechanisms. On the instrumental side, the material resources that public policies provide to immigrant and non-immigrant actors affect groups' and people's ability to participate and mobilize. In the Canadian context, these policies include multiculturalism but also immigrant integration and settlement programs, which also distribute public funding to individuals, community-based groups and non-profit immigrant service providers.[5] Such financial assistance allows community organizations to provide collective help—such as language training, legal assistance or other services—as well as resources for collective mobilization. The instrumental and symbolic effects of public policy can also reinforce each other. When immigrant-serving organizations benefit from multicultural or integration policy by receiving grants and providing services, this has effects at a cognitive and affective level, communicating the deservingness of these communities and building a sense of political legitimacy and membership. A lack of such policies may, conversely, send immigrants the message that they are second-class residents or that their political membership is irrelevant or unwelcome.

Consider, for instance, Canada–US differences in multicultural and integration discourse and programming. The federal Canadian government adopted an official policy of multiculturalism in 1971, an idea that was written into the 1982 Canadian Constitution, and also enshrined in the 1988 Multiculturalism Act. In the United States, while multicultural curricula are readily found in various schools, there is no similar diversity policy at the federal level, especially one directed at immigrant communities. Indeed, under the Trump administration, the United States Citizenship and Immigration Service (USCIS) changed its mission to eliminate a passage that describes the country as a "nation of immigrants," instead adopting language to underscore USCIS's duty in "securing the homeland" and administering "the nation's lawful immigration system" (Gonzales, 2018).

Such public rhetoric matters. Canadian multiculturalism policy signals that immigrants have legitimate membership and standing in the national community. As one Vietnamese-Canadian senior explained during my field research in Toronto,

> The Canadian government listens to the voice of the people's will, the requests, and helps to respond. They not only respect the cultures of the different community backgrounds, but they always try to develop the culture and tradition of that community more.
> *(reported in Bloemraad 2006b: 683)*[6]

This senior voted regularly even though his language skills were limited. In contrast, Manuela, an immigrant in the United States who had limited education and worked as a cleaner in the Boston area, felt shut out of the political system,

> It is tough. But they [the government] don't know how it is … You can't say, "Sir, sir, send people that care about the immigrants, because they are the people who can't speak up." There is nowhere to complain to, and we can't complain.
> *(Bloemraad 2006a: 1)*

The policy differences also have instrumental impact. In Canada, the federal government provides significant funding for language training, job assistance and other integration and settlement services, programs that are often provided by non-profit community organizations. In the 2010–2011 fiscal year, Citizenship and Immigration Canada projected spending $1.1 billion CAD on immigrant integration, for a total population of almost seven million foreign born (Seidle, 2010: 4). Often this federal support is complemented by additional provincial, and even municipal, programs, part of the federalization of immigration in Canada since 1990 (Paquet, 2019). In comparison, there is no federal US integration program and USCIS provides virtually no settlement funding. In 2011, USCIS gave out only $9 million USD for naturalization activities for a population of 22 million non-citizens living in the country (US Citizenship and Immigration Services, 2011).

Greater funding in Canada eases the process of acquiring citizenship, especially for those with modest resources and less human capital. Drawing again on my field research in Toronto, I interviewed Tilla, who had immigrated to Canada with limited schooling and no knowledge of English. Reflecting on becoming a citizen years later, she recounted,

> Oh, I want[ed] to vote, I want[ed] to vote … [It is] very difficult because my income is not much and my husband's income is not very much. Manuel, he's the one who taught us to get [citizenship] papers. He applied for a supplement from [the] government to pay him to teach us.
>
> *(Bloemraad 2006a: 1)*

In comparison, when Tung, a Vietnamese refugee in Boston, sought help to prepare for the naturalization language and civic tests, he ended up paying for assistance, "I studied from a book and I also took a course in Chinatown. I had to pay. … My friends who had already took the course told me about it" (Bloemraad, 2006a: 86). In considering how public policies affect people, we must consider both the symbolic and instrumental effects.

Multicultural Backlash? Populism, Feedback Loops and a Reimagined (Anglo) Canada

Early in the 21st century, observers within and outside academia noted a "backlash" against multiculturalism (Brubaker, 2001; Joppke, 2004). In important ways, the turn against multiculturalism played out more in public discourse, especially by right-of-center and far-right political parties, rather than in actual national policy (Banting and Kymlicka, 2013) or in the on-the-ground relations between ethno-racial communities and sub-national government agencies (Korteweg and Triadafilopoulos, 2015). Thus, instead of "retreat," the operative word is probably multicultural "polarization:" many people have accepted or embraced diversity discourse and policies, but others have been emboldened to oppose multicultural ideals, sometimes violently and in racist or Islamophobic ways. The election of Donald Trump in the United States and the popularity of anti-immigrant politicians such as Marine Le Pen, Geert Wilders and others in Europe are both a consequence and further cause of this polarization. Canada is not immune. Reviewing data on Canadian public opinion toward cultural diversity, Besco and Tolley (2018) report that up to a third of Canadians have negative attitudes toward multiculturalism and that perhaps another third are "conditional multiculturalists." In a few horrific cases, anti-diversity views have translated into murder, such as the attack on the Islamic Cultural Centre in Quebec City in 2017 in which six people were killed, or the 2021 homicides of a Muslim family walking along a residential street in London, Ontario when a man purposely hit them with his truck. Such incidents underscore the need to stay vigilant in protecting, recognizing and celebrating all Canadians, regardless of background and beliefs.

At the same time, anti-diversity views have had a harder time finding formal purchase in the Canadian political system as compared to many other liberal democracies. The loss of Conservative Party leader Stephen Harper to Justin Trudeau's Liberal Party in 2015 was in part over ideals of multiculturalism. The Conservative government promoted a traditional history, including Canadians' military engagement in the War of 1812 and Canada's ties to the British crown, and it downplayed or outright challenged diversity, especially the legitimacy of Muslim minorities. In contrast, Trudeau ran an election platform that included the promise to resettle tens of thousands of Syrian refugees in Canada. More recently, politician Maxime Bernier, after failing in his bid to lead the Conservative party, created the populist right People's Party of Canada, which ran on an anti-immigrant, anti-diversity platform in 2019. No one from the party was elected to office, not even its leader, who garnered 28% of the vote in his riding of Beauce, Quebec. When Bernier subsequently ran for a vacated seat in York Centre, Ontario, he came in fourth with less than 4% of the vote.

Why have populist, anti-immigrant politicians had a harder time getting a toehold in Canada? One important reason is the feedback loops that come from the successful political incorporation of immigrants. The symbolic and material resources of Canadian policies encourage immigrants to acquire citizenship and, once they hold citizenship, they can vote in local, provincial and federal elections. While immigrants are not necessarily pro-immigrant—indeed, there is a long tradition of earlier waves of immigrants opposing new arrivals "fresh off the boat" (or the plane)—they are, all else equal, more likely to support immigration and diversity policies (Bilodeau et al., 2021). This changes the political calculation for those wanting to win elections. We can look to the changes in the Canadian political right for an illustration of some of those pressures. At its founding in 1987, the right-wing, Prairie-based Reform Party was antagonistic to multiculturalism and suspicious of immigration. In its 1991 "Blue Book," which outlined the party's platform, the party committed itself to opposing "the current concept of multiculturalism and hyphenated Canadianism" and to abolishing the program and ministry dedicated to multiculturalism. Twenty years later, in 2011, when key actors from the old Reform Party had become members of a new Conservative Party and gained a majority in federal Parliament, they did not rescind the 1988 Multiculturalism Act. Indeed, for a number of years, the minister in charge of immigration, Jason Kenney, would jokingly attribute his weight gain to all of the ethnic festivals and multicultural events he attended in advancing his portfolio. Thus, while there is some evidence that those who identify strongly as Albertans (and from Saskatchewan) hold more negative views of immigration and multiculturalism, this is not the case in other provinces (Bilodeau et al., 2021). As a result, in Canada, an anti-immigrant regional party has limited ability to succeed nationally. Further, without a proportional representation electoral system, regional anti-immigrant sentiments have a hard time being amplified through legislative seats.

The relative lack of multicultural backlash in Canada goes deeper than hard political calculations. Multiculturalism policies affect non-immigrant Canadians, too. Some Canadians might feel threatened by immigration or prefer a discourse of homogeneity. But many others have grown up living everyday multiculturalism in their communities. They embrace a narrative of Canadian national identity that includes multiculturalism. In a 2015 Focus Canada opinion poll by Environics, over half of respondents identify multiculturalism as an "important symbol" of Canadian identity, more than the proportion who named the CBC, the Queen or even hockey as key to national identity. Indeed, unlike many other Western democracies, in Canada, those with a stronger sense of attachment to the Canadian nation are also more likely to support immigration and multiculturalism (Citrin, Johnston and Wright, 2012; Bilodeau et al., 2021).

The identification of "Canadian-ness" with multiculturalism might be somewhat stronger in English Canada since it is a particularly potent way for those living in English-speaking Canada to distinguish themselves from Americans, a British heritage and, possibly, from Francophones in Quebec. Elke Winter (2015) argues that Francophone Québécois nationalism in the 1990s and the province's 1995 vote on independence made English-speaking Canadians more amenable to multiculturalism. It not only helped to integrate a diverse English-speaking population in places like Toronto and Vancouver, but it also served as a counter-narrative to Québécois nationalism. At the same time, including multiculturalism and diversity as part of the (imagined) Canadian psyche allows all Canadians, regardless of language and province, to assert a pride in their country compared to other nations. In a 2018 public opinion poll, when asked about the issue on which Canada can be "most effective as an international role model," the two most popular answers were, first, on multiculturalism, immigration and refugees, and second, on support for human rights. Other issues, including environmental policy, the healthcare system and even peacekeeping (a traditional source of diplomatic pride in Canada), were much less prominent. Whether they live in Quebec or another province, those who express the most attachment to Canada are also the most likely to support multiculturalism and immigration (Bilodeau et al., 2021).

Of course, past practice and opinion offer no guarantees for the future. Winter (2015) suggests that, as the constitutional crises of the 1990s receded in the early 21st century, the tenor of multiculturalism shifted to be somewhat less about "us" as Canadians and more about "them" as minorities. A recent analysis by Banting and Soroka (2020) argues that Canadians' support for immigration may well lie more in the economic selection criteria of the Canadian system than in any particular Canadian value or pro-diversity cultural orientation. The success of immigrant-origin politicians in the federal parliament is, perhaps surprisingly, not necessarily mirrored on municipal councils or in provincial legislatures (Andrew, Biles, Siemiatycki and Tolley, 2009). Critically, multicultural discourse and policy are likely weak instruments to tackle racial inequalities or experiences of discrimination among some ethno-racial minority communities (Reitz, 2009). In an era where African-Americans' cries that "Black Lives Matter" have echoed around the globe and demands for reparations to the countries' Indigenous communities continue to grow stronger, Canada must move beyond thinking multiculturalism, by itself, will ensure equity and full inclusion.

Still, it is striking to contrast the recent Canadian and US Supreme Court nominations as we consider the ripples of multiculturalism. These nominations capture something important about the institutionalization of multiculturalism in Canadian practice and worldview. On the Canadian side, in 2021, the Prime Minister nominated Mahmud Jamal to the Supreme Court of Canada—a lawyer who was born in Kenya to Indian-origin parents, raised in the Ismaili community and now a practicing Bahá'í. In the United States, the most proximate nominations to the highest judicial bench were those of Brent Kavanaugh and Amy Coney Barrett, two people whose immigrant roots lie in the 19th century with Irish and French ancestors and whose religious beliefs are firmly embedded in traditional American Christianity. Canada still has a lot of work to do—Jamal is the first person of color nominated to the court—but credit for the progress that the country has made certainly includes the adoption and continued support for multicultural policy and discourse.

Notes

1 I use the term "political incorporation" to refer to the process by which foreign-born migrants become part of the political community, which can be measured by acquisition of citizenship, participation in electoral politics and winning elections, among other indicators. I use the term "democratic inclusion" to refer to the incorporation of not just those of immigrant origins, but all individuals and groups, especially those marginalized historically.
2 The Ngram viewer tracks the prevalence of words and phrases in all published books that Google has digitized. The Google corpus skews to scholarly and scientific books but includes popular work. My description of the trend line relies on modest smoothing of the data. See https://books.google.com/ngrams/info for more information.
3 See https://www.statcan.gc.ca/eng/subjects-start/immigration_and_ethnocultural_diversity, last accessed May 18, 2021.

4 See the Multiculturalism Policies in Contemporary Democracies project at Queen's University, https://www.queensu.ca/mcp/immigrant-minorities, last accessed May 18, 2021. The eight indicators are an official affirmation of multiculturalism; multiculturalism in school curriculum; inclusion of ethnic representation/sensitivity in public media and licensing; exemptions from dress codes in public laws; acceptance of dual citizenship; funding of ethnic organizations to support cultural activities; funding of bilingual and mother-tongue instruction; and affirmative action for immigrant-origin groups.
5 Immigrant-serving organizations can access a wide range of grants and contracts at the federal, provincial and municipal levels. The goals and contours of "multiculturalism" programs have changed substantially over the last half-century, from supporting heritage language retention and cultural events in the early decades to advancing anti-racism and intercultural understanding efforts in recent decades. For immigrant communities, such efforts can be complemented by integration and settlement grants, which tend to focus on economic, linguistic and social inclusion by, for example, providing grants or contracts to teach immigrants English or French or provide job-readiness classes.
6 The interview quotes come from field research I conducted in the Toronto and Boston metropolitan areas between 1998 and 2001, reported in Bloemraad (2006a, 2006b). Below, I draw on more recent research to specify continuities and changes since then.

References

Alba, Richard and Nancy Foner. 2015. *Strangers No More: Immigration and the Challenges of Integration in North America and Western Europe.* Princeton, NJ: Princeton University Press.

Andrew, Caroline, John Biles, Myer Siemiatycki and Erin Tolley, eds. 2009. *Electing a Diverse Canada: The Representation of Immigrants, Minorities, and Women.* Vancouver, BC: University of British Columbia Press.

Banting, Keith and Will Kymlicka. 2013. "Is There Really a Retreat from Multiculturalism Policies? New Evidence from the Multiculturalism Policy Index." *Comparative European Politics* 11 (5): 577–598.

Banting, Keith and Stuart Soroka. 2020. "A Distinctive Culture? The Sources of Public Support for Immigration in Canada, 1980–2019." *Canadian Journal of Political Science* 53 (4): 821–838.

Barry, Brian. 2002. *Culture and Equality: An Egalitarian Critique of Multiculturalism.* Cambridge, MA: Harvard University Press.

Bean, Frank D., Susan K. Brown, James D. Bachmeier, Tineke Fokkema and Laurence Lessard-Phillips. 2012. "The Dimensions and Degree of Second-Generation Incorporation in US and European Cities: A Comparative Study of Inclusion and Exclusion." *International Journal of Comparative Sociology* 53 (3): 181–209.

Berry, John W. 2005. "Acculturation: Living Successfully in two Cultures." *International Journal of Intercultural Relations* 29 (6): 697–712.

Berry, John W. 2013 "Research on Multiculturalism in Canada." *International Journal of Intercultural Relations* 37 (6): 663–675.

Besco, Randy and Erin Tolley. 2018. "*Does Everyone Cheer? The Politics of Immigration and Multiculturalism in Canada.*" In *Federalism and the Welfare State in a Multicultural World*, Elizabeth Goodyear-Grant, Richard Johnston, Will Kymlicka and John Myles (eds.) Kingston: McGill-Queen's University Press, 291–318.

Bilodeau, Antoine, Audrey Gagnon, Stephen E. White, Luc Turgeon and Ailsa Henderson. 2021. "Attitudes toward Ethnocultural Diversity in Multilevel Political Communities: Comparing the Effect of National and Subnational Attachments in Canada." *Publius: The Journal of Federalism* 51 (1): 27–53.

Blakkarly, Jarni. 2019. "Australia's New Parliament is No More Multicultural than the Last One." *SBS News*, May 21, 2019. https://www.sbs.com.au/news/australia-s-new-parliament-is-no-more-multicultural-than-the-last-one, last accessed May 18, 2021.

Bloemraad, Irene. 2006. *Becoming a Citizen: Incorporating Immigrants and Refugees in the United States and Canada*. Berkeley, CA: University of California Press.

Bloemraad, Irene. 2013. "Accessing the Corridors of Power: Puzzles and Pathways to Understanding Minority Representation." *West European Politics* 36 (3): 652–670.

Bloemraad, Irene and Matthew Wright. 2014. "'Utter Failure' or Unity out of Diversity? Debating and Evaluating Policies of Multiculturalism." *International Migration Review* 48 (S1): S292–S334.

Borjas, George J. 2001. *Heaven's Door: Immigration Policy and the American Economy*. Princeton, NJ: Princeton University Press.

Brubaker, Rogers. 2001. "The Return of Assimilation ? Changing Perspectives on Immigration and its Sequel in France, Germany, and the United States." *Ethnic and Racial Studies* 24 (4): 531–548.

Citrin, Jack, Richard Johnston and Matthew Wright. 2012. "Do 'Patriotism' and 'Multiculturalism' Collide? Competing Perspectives From the U.S. and Canada." *Canadian Journal of Political Science* 45 (3): 531–552.

Geiger, A.W. 2019. "In 116th Congress, at Least 13% of Lawmakers are Immigrants or the Children of Immigrants." Pew Research Center, January 24, 2019. https://www.pewresearch.org/fact-tank/2019/01/24/in-116th-congress-at-least-13-of-lawmakers-are-immigrants-or-the-children-of-immigrants/, last accessed May 18, 2021.

Griffith, Andrew. 2019. "House of Commons Becoming More Reflective of Diverse Population." *Policy Options Politiques*, November 5, 2019. https://policyoptions.irpp.org/magazines/november-2019/house-of-commons-becoming-more-reflective-of-diverse-population/, last accessed May 18, 2021.

Gonzales, Richard. 2018. "America No Longer a "Nation of Immigrants," USCIS Says." *National Public Radio*, February 22. https://www.npr.org/sections/thetwo-way/2018/02/22/588097749/america-no-longer-a-nation-of-immigrants-uscis-says, last accessed May 18, 2021.

Helbling, Marc and Maarten P. Vink. 2013. "The Use and Misuse of Policy Indices in the Domain of Citizenship and Integration." *Comparative European Politics* 11 (5): 551–554.

Huntington, Samuel P. 2004. *Who are We? The Challenges to America's National Identity*. New York: Simon and Schuster.

Joppke, Christian. 2004 "The Retreat of Multiculturalism in the Liberal State: Theory and Policy." *British Journal of Sociology* 55 (2): 237–257.

Kasinitz, Philip, John H. Mollenkopf, Mary C. Waters and Jennifer Holdaway. 2008. *Inheriting the City: The Children of Immigrants Come of Age*. Cambridge, MA: Harvard University Press.

Koopmans, Ruud. 2010. "Trade-Offs Between Equality and Difference: Immigrant Integration, Multiculturalism and the Welfare State in Cross-National Perspective." *Journal of Ethnic and Migration Studies* 36 (1):1–26.

Koopmans, Ruud, Paul Statham, Marco Giugni and Florence Passy. 2005. *Contested Citizenship: Immigration and Cultural Diversity in Europe*. Minneapolis, MN: University of Minnesota Press.

Korteweg, Anna C. and Triadafilos Triadafilopoulos. 2015. "Is Multiculturalism Dead? Groups, Governments and the "Real Work of Integration"." *Ethnic and Racial Studies* 38 (5): 663–680.

Kymlicka, Will. 1995. *Multicultural Citizenship*. New York: Oxford University Press.

Liebig, T. and F. Von Haaren. 2010. "Citizenship and the Socio-Economic Integration of Immigrants and Their Children: An Overview Across EU and OECD Countries." In *Naturalisation: A Passport for the Better Integration of Immigrants?* 23–64 Paris: OECD Publishing. doi: 10.1787/9789264099104-en.

Nguyen, Angela-MinhTu D., and Verónica Benet-Martínez. 2013. "Biculturalism and Adjustment: A Meta-Analysis." *Journal of Cross Cultural Psychology* 44 (1): 122–159.

Miller, David. 1995. *On Nationality*. New York: Oxford University Press.

Paquet, Mireille. 2019. *Province Building and the Federalization of Immigration in Canada*. Translated by Howard Scott. Toronto: University of Toronto Press.

Phan, Mai B. and Raymond Breton. 2009. "Inequalities and Patterns of Social Attachments in Quebec and the Rest of Canada." In *Multiculturalism and Social Cohesion: Potentials and Challenges of Diversity*, Jeffrey G. Reitz, Raymond Breton, Karen K. Dion and Kenneth L. Dion (eds.) New York: Springer Publishing, 89–121.

Portes, Alejandro and Ruben G. Rumbaut. 2001. *Legacies: The Story of the Immigrant Second Generation*. Berkeley, CA: University of California Press.

Portes, Alejandro and Min Zhou. 1993. "The New Second Generation: Segmented Assimilation and Its Variants." *Annals of the American Academy of Political and Social Science* 530: 74–96.

Reitz, Jeffrey G. 2009. "Behavioural Precepts of Multiculturalism: Empirical Validity and Policy Implications." In *Multiculturalism and Social Cohesion: Potentials and Challenges of Diversity*, Jeffrey G. Reitz, Raymond Breton, Karen K. Dion and Kenneth L. Dion (eds.) New York: Springer Publishing, 157–171.

Reitz, Jeffrey G. and Rupa Banerjee. 2009. "Racial Inequality and Social Integration." In *Multiculturalism and Social Cohesion: Potentials and Challenges of Diversity*, Jeffrey G. Reitz, Raymond Breton, Karen K. Dion and Kenneth L. Dion (eds.) New York: Springer Publishing, 123–155.

Reitz, Jeffrey G., Patrick Simon and Emily Laxer. 2017. "Muslims' Social Inclusion and Exclusion in France, Québec, and Canada: Does National Context Matter?" *Journal of Ethnic and Migration Studies* 43 (15): 2473–2498.

Scheffer, Paul. 2011. *Immigrant Nations*. Cambridge: Polity Press.

Seidle, F. Leslie. 2010. *The Canada-Ontario Immigration Agreement: Assessment and Options for Renewal*. Toronto: Mowat Center for Policy Innovation. Available at: https://tspace.library.utoronto.ca/handle/1807/96198, last accessed 19 May 2021.

Statistics Canada. 2017. "Census in Brief: Ethnic and Cultural Origins of Canadians: Portrait of a Rich Heritage." Ottawa: Ministry of Industry. https://www12.statcan.gc.ca/census-recensement/2016/as-sa/98-200-x/2016016/98-200-x2016016-eng.cfm, last accessed May 18, 2021.

Taylor, Charles. 1994. "The Politics of Recognition." In *Multiculturalism and the Politics of Recognition*, Amy Gutmann (ed.) Princeton, NJ: Princeton University Press, 25–73.

United States Citizenship and Immigration Services. 2011. "USCIS Announces FY 2011 Citizenship and Integration Grant Program Recipients $9 Million Awarded to Expand Citizenship Preparation Programs for Permanent Residents." Washington, DC. https://www.uscis.gov/archive/uscis-announces-fy-2011-citizenship-and-integration-grant-program-recipients-9-million-awarded-to, last accessed October 10, 2022.

Winter, Elke. 2015. "Rethinking Multiculturalism After its "Retreat": Lessons From Canada." *American Behavioral Scientist* 59 (6): 637–657.
Wright, Matthew and Irene Bloemraad. 2012. "Is There a Trade-off Between Multiculturalism and Socio-Political Integration? Policy Regimes and Immigrant Incorporation in Comparative Perspective." *Perspectives on Politics* 10 (1): 77–95.

3
MULTICULTURAL CITIZENSHIP IN SINGAPORE

Terri-Anne Teo

Proponents of multicultural citizenship, such as Bhikhu Parekh (2000) and Tariq Modood (2013), argue that citizenship as status and identity must represent and recognize cultural differences within a given population. Theoretical justifications of equality and justice have resulted in various frameworks of multicultural citizenship. While there are variances in emphases placed on liberal values and the value of culture across theories of multicultural citizenship (Kymlicka, 1995; Parekh, 2000), they are anchored in the recognition of group-specific differences based on the equal treatment of culturally differentiated citizens. In questioning if multiculturalism hinders or helps citizenship, this chapter considers both multiculturalism and citizenship as operating relationally, rather than as a binary relationship. This relationship occurs where multiculturalism enables citizenship to be more inclusive for citizens and at times, non-citizens as well. However, multiculturalism's reliance on citizenship can also hinder the latter's inclusiveness if it neglects how citizenship, as a legal status, is built on an "us/them" relationship where non-citizen residents are automatically excluded from a set of rights and privileges.

In practice, multiculturalism is not mutually exclusive from citizenship; indeed, we have seen how these two concepts work rather well together, whether as an independent policy or where it is part of networks of governance. As a policy framework, multicultural citizenship is expansive and elaborate in its engagement with other arms of government. How multiculturalism is interwoven with networks of governance can at its best offer citizens and even non-citizens some avenues for integration and the accommodation of group-differentiated needs. Multicultural policies may inform or be informed by migration policies, wider integration policies and labor policies that, depending on countries, operate within or beyond multiculturalism programs. For

DOI: 10.4324/9781003197485-6

instance, the inclusive nature of Canadian multiculturalism policy explains at least in part Canada's higher naturalization rate compared to the assimilative variant in the US (Bloemraad, 2006: 10). The inverse—where wider citizenship policies affect multicultural integration, also occurs when non-citizens, such as permanent residents, are offered voting rights, which are a step forward in the inclusion of minority interests (Nagy, 2013: 169).

In principle, multicultural citizenship as a theory seeks both redistribution and recognition as a matter of respect for cultural difference (Kymlicka, 2002: 151). However, taking multicultural citizenship for granted as a path leading to inclusion could inadvertently hinder the development of citizenship as a vehicle for inclusiveness across cultural groups, unless multiculturalism finds flexibility within itself to mitigate the exclusions of citizenship. Where I have suggested how this may be done elsewhere (Teo, 2019), this chapter takes an empirical approach to illustrate in a specific case how the lines of multiculturalism become exclusionary when affixed to citizenship.

Here, I illustrate through the case of Singapore how multiculturalism in practice can have problematic outcomes when principles of fair treatment and group recognition are tied to citizenship. This chapter focuses on the tensions in a society that defines itself as "multiracial." In Singapore, multiculturalist ideas of cultural recognition and group-specific needs are sewn within the identity of the Singaporean citizen. Citizenship is tied to racial diversity and inclusion, with the nation declared a "constitutionally multiracial state" by the ruling party upon independence in 1965 (Chua, 2003: 60). This creed finds resonance in Canada's own position on inclusion, where Prime Minister Justin Trudeau described Canadians as "taking diversity for granted: In so many ways, it's the air we breathe" (Trudeau, cited in Abu-Laban and Nath, 2020).

Although Singapore's state ideology of multiracialism is often conflated with the term multiculturalism, the two are distinct. Confusion between the terms may be attributed to the popular use of "multiculturalism" where it denotes the existence of multiple cultures, rather than the academic, theoretical understanding of multiculturalism. Similarly, the terms multiculturalism and multiracialism are often used in Singapore within political rhetoric and media reports without much explanation as to their specific meaning (MOE, 2000; Chan, 2013). The conflation of "race," "culture" and "ethnicity" in Singapore adds to the confusion, where racial classifications include presumptions of religious and linguistic associations as well as stereotypes and physical features.

Singapore's multiracial framework, which emphasizes the relationship between race and citizenship appears to encourage inclusivity. However, their interwovenness also binds citizens to fixed obligations and raced identities. Curated narratives of multiracialism, constructed through themes of "racial harmony," conflict with the tensions in Singapore's "multiracial" reality. Within this curated fantasy, the Singaporean citizen is constructed as a racial subject obliged to comply to racial norms. This chapter shows how minorities are included within a certain framework of accommodation in the form of "multiracialism" but are at the same time doubly minoritized through categories of race that structure this very framework. After outlining the context of Singapore, I argue that the practice of multicultural citizenship while extending some forms of accommodation to citizens, hinders membership among them through the exclusions of multicultural horizons. This exclusion applies to varying groups of citizenship statuses, including Singaporean citizens who fall beyond the multiracial norm, and non-citizens who are still expected to conform to certain ideals of Singaporean multiracialism.

Multicultural Citizenship in Singapore

On the surface, Singapore is an exemplary case of multiculturalism if we take multicultural policies, such as group-specific provisions, as a hallmark of a multicultural society. Such provisions offered to the three main "races"[1]—the Chinese, Malay and Indian ethnic groups—include official recognition within Singapore's constitution, and a raft of policies include language rights and public holidays recognizing days of significance across several cultures and religions. Singapore is certainly not representative of multiculturalism as an ideal theory. Groups are not all fairly represented and recognized, and minorities are still subject to institutional and everyday discrimination (e.g., Rahim, 2012; Velayutham, 2016). While Singapore is not exceptional in this way, it illustrates how multiculturalism, when taken as inextricable with citizenship, can in practice divide and exclude, limiting its inclusive agenda.

An inclusive national identity is central to various multiculturalist leanings, specifically to the Bristol School of Multiculturalism as compared to other variants such as those seen in the Canadian school of thought (Levey, 2019). To create a "multiculturally constituted common culture," national identity should extend a sense of belonging and security to groups so that the nation "is a place where their culture is free from threat" (Modood, 2013: 118; Parekh, 2000: 219; Uberoi, 2007: 152). This sense of belonging "is about full acceptance and feeling at home, and justice, which is about rights and interests, satisfies only one of its preconditions" (Parekh, 2006: 237). Alongside formal citizenship, national identity reflects the diversity of thought, memory and concepts of the good life that a multiculturalist society represents (Parekh, 1995; Triandafyllidou, 2013).

Singapore's multiracial framework speaks directly to such a practice of multicultural citizenship. Multiracialism drives national narratives, rhetoric and policies to the extent that being "multicultural" has become key to the identity of the Singaporean citizen. The narrative of multiracialism permeates Singapore's landscape, bearing both demographic and political significance. Multiracialism refers to the practice of cultural tolerance and provision of equal opportunity for advancement in Singapore (Hill and Lian, 1995: 31).

Singapore's ruling party, the People's Action Party (PAP), fosters multiracialism as a national ideology and within that, racial and religious harmony as its key components. The import of maintaining a narrative of multiracialism is linked to Singapore's national survival as a multi-ethnic nation with a large migrant population. Singapore's population of 5.637 million consists of 3.55 million citizens and 0.52 million Permanent Residents (PRs) (Singapore Government, 2022). Non-residents form 1.56 million of Singapore's total population, including non-citizens who are working, studying or living in Singapore but are not granted Permanent Resident status, excluding tourists and short-term visitors. According to the national census, they include a majority of Chinese (75.9%), followed by Malays (15%), Indians (7.5%) and "Others" (1.6%), with the latter category including individuals who do not fall within the primary "racial" categories (Singapore Government, 2020). These categories are referred to with the acronym "CMIO" in mainstream media, political rhetoric and public discourse.

In itself, "race" is a defining character of Singaporean citizenship, where the very conception of the Singaporean identity is one that is hyphenated "because this is simultaneously ethnic and national" (Hill and Lian, 1995: 107). The lived experience of the racialized Singaporean citizen has early beginnings, with race determining policies including that of language, education curricula, financial aid, housing and electoral politics specific to citizens. This framework is premised on the equal treatment of citizens through fair representation and a meritocratic system. The constitution establishes English as one of Singapore's four official languages alongside Mandarin, Bahasa Melayu and Tamil, which represent *de jure* equality of treatment among the Chinese, Malay and Indian racialized groups where these languages are assumed to be their "mother tongues" (C Tan, 2005: 42).[2] Citizenship by registration requires applicants to fulfil several conditions, including residence in Singapore for a minimum of ten years, the intention to reside permanently in Singapore and an "elementary knowledge" of any of the four official languages, namely Malay, English, Mandarin and Tamil.

Today, multiracialism prevails as rhetoric and policy justifications. For instance, Singapore's turbulent history is often revisited in order to reiterate the continual threat faced by a multiracial country, despite the relative peace that has ensued since the 1970s (Chua, 2009: 243). Reminders of the racial discord in Singapore's history recur in political rhetoric, emphasizing the need for racial and religious harmony (Aljunied, 2009: 20; Rahim, 2012). The 1964 race riots are often rehashed. They include two incidents involving Chinese and Malay groups in July and September. Various factors contributed to the riots, including rising tensions amidst political tensions. Prior to the separation of Singapore from Malaysia, the PAP and the United Malays National Organisation (UMNO) disagreed on several areas of governance, including affirmative action for Malays in Singapore. While political and ethnic issues were deeply intertwined, the riots are often portrayed as being racially motivated alone, rather than politically or ideologically (Milne, 1966).[3]

While acknowledging the presence of racism in society, there remains an underlying message that racial harmony is still the defining cornerstone of Singapore's progress. As Education Minister Lawrence Wong said in January 2021, "It is a big issue [...] But is the situation today better than it was 10 years ago, 20 years ago? I would say it is too" (Ong, 2021). Maintaining racial harmony in Singapore is further identified as the collective obligation of responsible citizens. Conceptualized as a "communitarian model of multiculturalism," such an approach "assumes that the individual is simultaneously a member of a larger social unit, to which he has obligations and responsibilities towards" (Lian, 2016: 3). Faltering as a single member therefore has a manifold effect on social cohesion. Through political rhetoric and public policy, multiracialism was and is conveyed as a pragmatic need, forming part of a political and economic agenda to maintain territorial loyalty and a sense of nationhood in place of then-perceived racially divided loyalties. As then-Prime Minister Lee Kuan Yew (cited in Hill and Lian, 1995) put it in gendered terms in 1979,

> The litmus test of a good education is whether it nurtures good citizens who can live, work, contend and cooperate in a civilised way [...] Is he filial, respectful to elders, law-abiding, humane and responsible? [...] Is he tolerant of Singaporeans of different races and religions?

Education is a key component of citizenship building. National Education (NE) was deemed as a necessary component of the national curriculum for citizens in the public schooling system in Singapore in 1997. Within NE, "Social Studies" and "Civic and Moral Education" are mandatory courses in Singapore's public schooling system and have a central role in the dissemination of dominant ideologies to citizens (Lim, 2016). These courses extol multiracialism as a core part of being a Singaporean citizen, emphasizing the importance of respecting "different races in Singapore," "unity in diversity" and building "community spirit," appealing to a sense of patriotism and belonging, in line with racial harmony. In this way, NE programs aim to provide a Singapore-centric curriculum about the "Singapore Story," which narrates the nation's history, challenges, vulnerabilities, and the importance of developing a Singaporean national identity and core values based on meritocracy and racial harmony.

A shared past characterized by rife racial tensions anchors citizenship at the nexus of national loyalty and a commitment to fulfil the goals of national survival and development. Racial Harmony Day is celebrated on July 21st every year to commemorate the 1964 race riots, as described above, where students dress in cultural attire associated with another "race" and participate in cultural exchange exercises to commemorate the value of racial harmony—a performative experience that is both celebrated and critiqued in Singapore as a form of statecraft that produces a certain narrative of multiracialism (MOE, 2013; Sim, 2005). This same performativity reinforces the identity of the Singaporean citizen as one embedded in a racialized landscape, which should be protected collectively as responsible citizens.

Multiracialism, as a national ideology, is an acknowledgment that culture is composed of various beliefs, values and practices. This ideology forms the backbone of policies such as "self-help groups" (or more precisely, group-help groups). These groups are ethnic-based welfare bodies and were founded with the objective of encouraging Singapore citizens to assist the socially advantaged among their ethnic communities. These include the Chinese Development Assistance Council (CDAC), Mendaki for the Malays, Singaporean Indian Development Association (SINDA) and the Eurasian Association. These organizations are described as "self-help groups" within political rhetoric, government websites, state media and by the organizations themselves (e.g., Lee, 2014b; MCCY, 2014; SINDA, n.d.; WDA, n.d.). While the term "self" implies individual help, each organization is responsible for its designated members as a racialized group. Other racialized policies include the Ethnic Integration Policy (EIP) and the Group Representation Constituency (GRC) system that respectively seek to eradicate ethnic ghettos and ensure the political representation of ethnic groups in the political system (Sin, 2003; Vasu, 2012). In theory, these policies should ensure the equal treatment of Singaporeans regardless of race, religion, gender or creed.

Yet, whether inadvertently or not, they entrench the marginalization of "other" groups in Singapore. For instance, the self-help system, which is premised on fair treatment across all racial groups, inherently favors the majority and disadvantages ethnic minorities. Theoretically, all citizens have equal opportunities to succeed through the financial aid and scholarships that community-based funds provide. While they are useful to a degree, these groups conceal structural disadvantages. With the institutionalization of ethnic-based welfare bodies, the responsibility of socio-economic mobility is placed on the individual and ethnic community rather than the state. Contrary to its intent, the ethnicized welfare system is subject to the proportionate distribution of resources that favor the ethnic majority. Consequently, other groups do not benefit from additional funding received from the Chinese as a numeric majority (Moore 2000: 348).

Within scholarship on race in Singapore, much has been said about how the fixity of racial identities in Singapore belies the complexity of group recognition. Criticisms of multiculturalism find bearing in Singapore, where recognition of ethnic identity "fixes" group lines, limiting the fluidity of self-identification and religious freedom (Rahim, 2012; Sin, 2003). Over the years, the practice of categorizing "race" has come under criticism and its oversights highlighted (e.g., EKB Tan, 2005; Teo, 2019; Velayutham, 2016). In turn, the public has raised various suggestions ranging from expanding the categories to include multiple identities, to doing away with them completely in the pursuit of a race-blind society (Kurohi, 2020; Ong, 2020).

Narratives of racial harmony are used to define citizens and by default the "other," in the image of the "non-multicultural" outsider. The next section explores how multiracialism as a fixed identity creates us/them divisions between groups. First, I highlight how non-citizens are "othered" through multiracialism. Second, I show how citizens who are not seen to comply with multiracialism are cast as "irresponsible" citizens.

The Irresponsible "Other"

The dominance of multiracialism as a state ideology in Singapore fixes citizenship as a multiracial identity, with state-constructed multicultural norms as its parameters. Critiquing representations of "multicultural Britain," Anne-Marie Fortier shows how "multicultural horizons" are an intricate web composed of "simultaneous *witnessing, questioning,* and *imagining:* witnessing that the 'we' *are* multicultural ... questioning how to achieve 'integration with diversity' ... and imagining the future of the multicultural nation" (Fortier, 2008: 3, original emphasis). This "reworking of the nation as inherently multicultural" (Fortier, 2008: 22) is apparent in histories and values (re)produced in education, rhetoric and policy frameworks. Ironically, the valorization of multiracialism creates dividing lines between those seen as cohering with what is deemed to be "multicultural," and those—both citizens and non-citizens, who are perceived as disrupting the norm.

Non-Citizens as "Othered" Multiracial Subjects

Non-citizens are also subject to norms of citizenship. Conceptualizing non-citizenship as a "membership category in its own right [... and] a positive status beyond the simple absence of citizenship" (Tonkiss and Bloom, 2016: 840) is a reminder that non-citizens include groups of different legal statuses, such as permanent residents, economic migrants on tiered work visas, as well as dependents and students from abroad. The lived experience of non-citizens varies across economic statuses, ethnicity and gender, with not all of them feeling "othered" in the same way or if at all. However, the examples below show a common thread where non-citizens are perceived as a "multiracial other," not as a raced "other," but rather as an interlocuter who does not conform to norms of racial harmony and as such threatens Singapore's national identity. They illustrate how citizenship is founded on a distinct yet subjective idea of being "multiracial," with certain expectations on newcomers for them to be accepted into the fold. A collective sense of what it means to be a citizen certainly contributes to social cohesion. However, emphasizing solidarity over difference in this way risks alienating individuals if the self-definition of a society excludes them as outsiders, which could occur because of how their differences are perceived.

Multiracialism, as constructed within Singapore's national rhetoric, has successfully created a unifying identity among citizens while also enabling a metric to which "others" are perceived. This "normative standard of judging new migrants' interactions with other members of Singapore society" is variously reported in the media, discussed in forums and harnessed as a criticism (Ortiga, 2014: 14) of the state's openness to migration. Ortiga's (Ibid) online ethnography of platforms in Singapore shows how "forums portray Chinese and Indian migrants as too bigoted and too prejudiced to interact with Singapore's diverse ethnic groups, making them inassimilable for Singapore's multicultural society." This reaction to some migrants is contrary to the long-entrenched idea in Singapore that calibrating migration to match Singapore's ethnic ratio would reduce the risk of ethnic strife. Significant to citizenship, multicultural horizons have become a difference marker between citizens and (perceived or not) non-citizens.

While it is not possible to measure the degree to which multiracialism is internalized by Singaporeans as a product of governance, instances of nationalist fervor are revealing of the exclusionary ways in which multiracialism as a way of "doing" citizenship is reproduced. In 2011, a quarrel took place between neighbors when a "China-born" family took their Singaporean-Indian neighbors to Singapore's Community Mediation Centre. The dispute began over the smell of curry, which the Indian family frequently cooked. The judge ruled that the Indian family should only cook curry when the "China-born" family was not at home, and the latter had to promise to sample curry in return. While this ruling was conducted in the spirit of racial harmony and in a "consensual way," it met with hostility from the public who perceived the "China-born" as acting in a manner contrary to Singapore's multiracialism (Fong, 2011).

Singaporeans contended that "the mediator should tell the PRC [People's Republic of China] family to adjust and adapt to Singapore's way of life and not tell the locals to adjust to the foreigner's way of life!" (Moore, 2011). In response to the incident, a Facebook event was set up inviting people to cook curry as a symbol of Singapore's multiracialism. Some 61,000 people "joined" the event. Since then, August 3rd, the day of the incident, has become "Cook and share a pot of curry" day. The media variously described the event as an "anti-immigration protest," an "anti-Chinese curry war" and a "Curry protest" (Adam, 2011; Moore, 2011; Suhartono, 2011). While trivial compared to anti-migrant protests elsewhere, the "Curry protest" illustrates how the "China-born" are constructed as different according to Singapore's multiracial norms.

Multiracial standards are raised toward outsiders. It would be remiss to neglect how practices of racism and intolerance exist among Singaporean citizens (legal status holders), toward ethnic minorities within and beyond the citizenry. In school, children hurl names at others of darker complexion using terms such as "blackie," "black coffee" (Lee et al., 2004: 128–130) and "black tofu" (Velayutham, 2009: 267). Parents influence their children through statements such as "that boy is black because he did not bathe," or "do not hold the hands of that Indian girl, otherwise your hands will also turn black" (Lee et al., 2004: 137) and that they "bathed in mud or excrement or never bathed at all" (Velayutham, 2009: 267). These statements reinforce tropes of anti-Blackness, involving a lack of hygiene and untouchability. Blackness is also associated with criminality, incivility and deviant behavior. Robbie Goh's (2005) study of Little India, a neighborhood in Singapore, portrays South Asian migrant workers as "disorderly" and "dirty." A Singaporean-Chinese man "complained about having to leave the area before dark, otherwise 'the blacks' would make it difficult or impossible for him to get to his car," and another was unhappy about the crowds of migrant workers who jaywalk and block pedestrian traffic, attributing the crowd patterns to "the way they live in villages in India," referring to the lack of rules and regulations, noise and informal way of living (Goh, 2005: 134). After an incident in Little India in 2013 that involved South Asian migrants, skin color was a trending joke. For instance, Twitter users tweeted and retweeted "Black boys black boys, what you gonna do when they come for you.[4] #LittleIndiaRiot finally some action in sg haha" (Teo, 2019: 233).

Despite the prevalence of racism, certain expectations of non-, new and/or potential citizens are reflected in various studies. One demonstrates how Singaporean youth favor stricter regulations on foreigners who "do not respect racial harmony" and who are therefore perceived as racist and "affect[ing] the safety of Singaporeans [... by] disrupt[ing] racial harmony" (Thian, 2019: 12). Being adaptable to Singapore's identity as multiracial is associated with integrating, where those who are perceived to be unwilling to integrate are those seen to be racist by respondents. These comments find resonance with another survey that shows how Singaporeans perceive new migrants from China as "more racist" than Singaporean-Chinese, Malays and Indians (Lee, 2016). In 2019, more than six in ten respondents in a survey said immigrants were not doing enough to integrate into Singapore (Yap, 2019). These findings show how citizenship, as an identity, is based on the condition of conforming to being as "multiracial." Where seen to fall short, non-"multiracial" identities are othered as different while at the same time reinforcing the unity of a "multiracial us" offered by a cohesive national identity.

The Foreclosure of Racism

The creation of "structures of feeling" is one that is powerful in uniting a nation when norms of civility become part of the "national fantasy [...] a cultural formation through which the fantasy structure of the nation is sustained and (re)formulated" (Fortier, 2008: 11). The quilted nature of multiracialism is as such where policies, national history and the future of the nation form the fabric of society, and one that should be protected and upheld. However, the insistence that "we are multicultural," and the belief that to be multicultural is central to the nation's survival, conceals the existence of racism within the dominant narrative of multiracialism.

Multiracialism as a creed and identity was held as a line of defense when a polarized discussion took place over the relevance and racial implications of brownface in Singapore. In 2019, furor over a brownface advertisement reignited debates about the normalization of racism in Singapore with polarizing discourse that at one end highlighted the marginalization of ethnic minorities and on the other denied that racial impersonation was indicative of racism in Singapore. That year, an advertisement for (Network for Electronic Transfers (NETS) EPay (a Singapore payment application) featured a male Chinese MediaCorp actor portraying four characters: a tudung (hijab)-wearing Malay woman, an Indian man (with a name tag reading "K Muthusamy") in office wear, a Chinese woman in a pink jacket and a Chinese man in blue overalls. The actor had his skin tone darkened to portray the Indian character.

Citizenship as an identity is "a relative concept always constituted through definitions of the Self and other and always subject to internal differentiations" (Matless, 1998: 17). While some defended the advertisement as an attempt at humor, others questioned the very premise of brownface and why racial minorities were not hired instead, surfacing debate about racial hierarchies and discrimination in Singapore (Stambaugh, 2020; Thanapal, 2019). The discourse that followed included criticisms of the advertisement as an example of brownface.

Two main strands of thought emerged. First, because of Singapore's multiracial creed there was the assumption that racial impersonation cannot have negative implications in the nation state. Denying this consequently reproduces the concealment of embedded racism, projecting the inaccurate impression that racial impersonation is not harmful and a rare occurrence in Singapore. There are stereotypical portrayals of ethnicities in Singapore on sitcoms, radio shows and entertainment through brownface, accents and negative stereotypes (Tan, 2004).[5] Kenneth Paul Tan's analysis of sitcoms in particular draws attention to infantile comedy that reproduce racialized, classed and gendered Malay and Indian stereotypes to reinforce the fantasy of Chinese racial homogeneity, "typical of the kind of mimetic content that reinforces a taken-for-granted simplification of complex realities" (Tan, 2008: 143). This fantasy feeds into carefully curated narratives of multiculturalism as "multiracialism" in Singapore, where there are neat categories of race, co-existing in a landscape of racial harmony.

Second, there was a cultural disconnect of blackface and minstrelsy, given its "Western" provenance in the US—which resulted in debates over the in/appropriate import of cultural values. While acknowledging that the advertisement was "ignorant" and that "sometimes, people are become less mindful of their insensitivity to others," a critic (Chan, 2019) argued in *The Straits Times* that "Brownface is not Singaporean:"

> "Brownface east" does not exist. The painted face as racist slur belongs to Western culture [...] In Singapore, to the contrary, many people are quite pleased when someone of another race is keen to dress like us, cook our favourite traditional food and join in our cultural activities.

The narrative that brownface is specifically "not Singaporean" exempts Singapore from wider discourses of race. The reliance on culturalist language reproduces the grammar of multicultural citizenship in the context of Singapore that seeks to differentiate it from other societies to keep the nation united. This is reminiscent of the "psychic glue" that Jacqueline Rose (1998: 5) observes, where fantasy has a "central, constitutive role in the modern world of states and nations" through parallel processes of elaborating, reinforcing and barring memories. That the history of minstrelsy is excluded from national education, a key component of citizenship, colors how citizenship is constructed in Singapore. The "protective fiction" of national narratives, while providing support to a nation and its citizenry, becomes problematic when it conceals rather than recognizes and heals wrong done (Freud, cited in Fortier, 2008: 11).

These narratives neglect how representations of Blackness are located within global narratives that position non-whiteness in subordination to whiteness. In the Netherlands, the figure of *Zwarte Piet*, a black helper with a curly wig and thickly colored wigs, was justified as "not a blackface but a person with a black face," and therefore of no relation to minstrels seen in the US (Erik van Muiswinkel, cited in De Beukalaer, 2019). Moreover, it was argued that the racism attached to blackface was intrinsically associated with racism in the US, and not one coherent with the "Dutch self-perception as an innocently color blind and non-racist society" (De Beukalaer, 2019: 796). This trajectory of events was also seen in Australia when in 2009, an American guest panelist Harry Connick Jr criticized a minstrel performance on Australia's *Hey Hey It's Saturday* as racist as the performers blacked their faces for the show. The show's host, Daryl Somers, argued that he "didn't think how it would be seen in your country" (Sharpe and Hynes, 2016: 91). Similar occurrences of blackface in France were brushed aside as issues not relevant for their US-centrism (Sommier, 2020).[6]

Among the plethora of factors that may have contributed to this culturalist lens, there is a stark absence of minstrelsy and Blackness within NE in relation to Singapore's history, rendering the connection to global and local narratives irrelevant to many Singaporeans. This said, there are specific connections to Blackness in Singapore's history that debunk arguments that connotations of blackface are only located in the "West."

Only associating blackface with the US reduces discourses to one that is only connected to a singular history of racism, neglecting traveling hierarchies and their transnational connections. There are wider implications here, where global discourses of Blackness meet local hierarchies of race. For example, analyses of blackface in China signal colonial economic patterns with Africa, reproducing a "white-yellow-black" hierarchy grounded in colonial discourse and colonial knowledge about the Black body (Chow-Quesada and Tesfaye, 2020; Wigfall, 2015: 236). In Australia, blackface historically relates to the portrayal of Indigenous characters including King Billy Cokebottle as well as the Indigenous Australia Rules footballer Nicky Winmar (Stratton, 2020: 172).

The "Others" among Us: Brownface

Upholding this fantasy is crucial in protecting the nation from the "real" self through the exposure to the potential for disintegration. As such, discordant voices highlighting the racism of brownface were extraordinarily accused of threatening Singapore's social fabric. Most visibly, two Singaporean siblings, Preeti and Subhash Nair, highlighted the history of media representation of Indians in Singapore, referring to a case when a Singaporean-Chinese man wore a Sikh turban as his "costume" on Deepavali, and instances of brownface in locally produced media (Rice Media, 2019).

These varying iterations and forms reflect a

> polysemic flow of signifiers and signified—that ensures the longevity of stereotypes as they are adjusted to suit social, cultural, historical and political contexts [... affecting] how those experiences are verbalized, visualized, interpreted and translated into various kinds of social performance.
>
> *(Russell, 2012: 42)*

In this sense, brownface as a racialized practice is rooted in Singapore's history. First, minstrel parties were ubiquitous during the colonial period, such as "costume races" featuring British jockeys in blackface to represent "A White Eyed Kaffir," "Malay Costume" and "A Heathen Chinese" among others (*Straits Times*, 1887). The Patriotic Concert of 1915 featured actors "in the costume of the perspiring though industrious sinkeh," (*Malaya Tribune*, 1915). Other similar events include sports games, concerts and balls (*The Singapore Free Press and Mercantile Advertiser*, 1894, 1895; *The Singapore Free Press and Mercantile Advertiser* (Weekly), 1908; *The Straits Times*, 1937; also see Kaur, 2019). Second, these phenotypical stereotypes continue to permeate contemporary society. Other occasions of racial impersonation in the form of brownface and blackface include costume parties such as workplace events or at Halloween.[7] Twitter user, @RubyThiagarajan, whose tweet was retweeted 4,000 times as of writing said, "Brownface in a Singaporean ad in 2019. I thought we already went over this ..." Another Twitter user @visakanv said, "it's time for a history of Singaporean-Chinese people in Brownface," with a thread that included references to blackface at workplace parties, a Singaporean-Chinese actor in a blackface role on a sitcom, and a Singaporean-Chinese actor who made a Deepavali greeting on Instagram (a post that has now been removed) in blackface.[8]

Some of those offended by the video lodged police reports against the siblings for inciting racial disharmony in Singapore. Eventually, the Singapore government ordered the video to be taken down and expressed concern that it might upset racial harmony in Singapore (Rice Media, 2019; Wong, 2019). The siblings were also given a 24-month conditional warning by the police (Ng, 2019). As explained by K Shanmugam, Minister of Home Affairs and Minister of Law, "[i]f we allow the line to be crossed ... then it's free for all, the Chinese can be equally offensive, and the minorities will be the losers in such a conversation" (Lim, 2019). Critics of the video argued that in making "numerous allegations that there exists widespread systemic discrimination in Singapore" are "sweeping allegations aimed at an entire racial group," a claim that was in itself racist that should warrant charges of "sedition, and inciting ethnic ill-will" (Hong, 2019).

These narratives reproduce constructed exemplars of multiracial citizens and concomitant practices such as "racial harmony day" that act as governing parameters for how to be multicultural. Rather than encouraging dialogue about race, citizens are instead coaxed into conforming to the state-sanctioned notion of multiracialism, which sanitizes racism as absent or innocuous in Singapore.

Similar incidents have occurred, with the most recent incident being a political candidate from an opposition party, Raeesah Khan, who was vilified for pointing out discrimination on social media in Singapore during the lead-up to the general elections in 2020. Khan's remarks included criticism of how ethnic minorities are not treated equally in Singapore, compared to other groups such as wealthy Singaporean-Chinese, Christians and Caucasians. Two police reports were lodged by members of the public against Khan, who allegedly contravened Section 298 of the Penal Code through remarks on social media two years earlier that promoted "enmity between different groups on grounds of religion or race" (Chow, 2020; CNA, 2020). She apologized for her remarks that were allegedly discriminatory and cooperated with police investigations.

This example shows how the logic of multiracialism forecloses the possibility of racism. When Khan pointed to systemic racism in "multiracial" Singapore, she was accused of inciting racial disharmony. The erasure of racism here has a double layer, where both the occurrence of racism and those speaking about racism are censored. This process speaks to a form of "symbolic violence by making particular interests and invested understandings and social relations of the world appear universal, natural, and true," legitimizing sense-making narratives (Hancock, 2008: 798). It is striking that multiracialism's code of conduct on one hand polices the behavior of racism based on norms of integration and civility, while at the same time polices the calling out of racism when it rears its head. The survival of the multicultural nation is as such contingent on the survival of what it means to be a multicultural citizen, whether imagined or not.

Various practices of multicultural citizenship in Singapore build upon a narrative of identity politics intrinsically tied to national identity and an ideology of what it means to be a citizen. While the advertisement and reactions to it may initially appear out of sorts with this portrayal of Singaporean society, it is perhaps not that surprising that cracks that have always existed are becoming more visible. Fixed understandings of race and racial harmony contribute to a certain identity politics that is so rooted in "stability, homogeneity, closure, pre-ordained boundaries and in general a neat, fixed self-coherence" that unravels simply with the acknowledgement that "any such political identity […] will have none of these features" (Calder, 2011: 111). In a society like Singapore where multiracialism relies on categorizations of race and a fixed understanding of racial harmony, it is perhaps unsurprising that the brownface advertisement unsheathed racial divides and polarizing views.

Conclusion

The thorny boundaries of Singapore's multicultural citizenship framework prick at both citizens and non-citizens. The case of Singapore demonstrates how being a Singaporean citizen shows how citizenship is both a legal status and an identity, as it requires citizens to fulfil the obligations of a multiracial framework. The ambivalence of this distinction is made evident through the various conditions of citizenship for citizens and non-citizens, where being "'good citizens' has become a prerequisite for becoming a citizen" (Joppke, 2021: 202) whether they are to be neoliberal subjects or in this case also multiracial subjects.

The case of Singapore shows how the nation's implementation of multicultural citizenship blurs the line between inclusionary promises and exclusionary potentials. This paradoxical quality resonates with observations of how "inclusive policies do not address exclusion, […] where] the presence of inclusive policies is often performing the management of diversity" (Lee and Johnstone, 2021: 11). Singapore illustrates how the state's formulaic conception of multiracialism are demarcations of how citizens should or should not act, and how society should or should not be. This identity is coupled with a framework of citizenship policies that govern how groups are recognized through language rights, cultural accommodations and inter-religious dialogue. Whether multiculturalism helps or hinders citizenship is, as such, a path where inclusion and exclusion co-exist, rather than being mutually exclusive.

Notes

1 I use the term "race" where I refer to how groups are referenced and categorized in Singapore by the state. Racial classifications in Singapore include presumptions of religious and linguistic associations as well as stereotypes and physical features.
2 Contrary to its name, "mother tongue" refers to an individual's patrilineal ancestry. Mother tongue languages are taught to students of a specific racial group, such as Mandarin for Chinese students and Bahasa Melayu for Malay students.
3 These include, for instance, the Maria Hertogh riots of the 1950s that occurred when Catholic parents of a Dutch girl claimed custody from a Muslim woman who had adopted her during World War Two, culminating in violent conflict between the Malay Muslim and European communities in Singapore (Aljunied, 2009: 20).
4 A reference to the song "Bad Boys" by Inner Circle, which was the theme song to *Cops*, an American documentary reality show. Somewhat apt in the context of this chapter, a study by (Monk-Turner et al., 2007) showed how *Cops* overrepresented perpetuators of crime as Black African-American males (93%), while police officers were more likely to be portrayed as white Caucasians (67%). These numbers were found to be inaccurate in their shaping of public perception through racialised myths.
5 Similar incidences in the past were disputed for the same reasons. For instance, the Singaporean-Indian actor Shrey Bhagarva reported being asked to speak in an "Indian accent" for a role, a request that reflects deeply embedded racial stereotypes within media representations and society at large. Similarly, these claims, while supported by some, were rejected by others on the basis that Singapore is a multiracial society and even if it were racist, racism could not have been intentional (Lay and Lee, 2017).
6 This approach is taken by critiques of male characterizations and representations of Japanese girls in Japan, where the "cute, childlike and sometimes comically inept" are related to the "sentimental and reassuring appeal of the humble, simple-minded 'southern darkie'" (Kinsella, 2006: 83). While they are grounded in a racial cultural language, they find common ground in the power relations embedded within the production and consumption of caricatures.
7 Beyond Singapore, brownface has also been used as a form of comedy or mockery in Asia, such as Hong Kong, Malaysia and Taiwan to portray stereotypes of ethnic minority groups (Cheung, 2020; Editorial Staff, 2021; Kuruvilla, 2016).
8 See for instance "It's time for a History of Singaporean Chinese people in Brownface," Twitter, 30 July 2019, https://twitter.com/visakanv/status/1156122999042404352?lang=en.

References

Abu-Laban, Y. and N. Nath. 2020. "Citizenship, Multiculturalism, and Immigration: Mapping the Complexities of Inclusion and Exclusion Through Intersectionality." In *The Palgrave Handbook of Gender, Sexuality, and Canadian Politics*, M. Tremblay and J. Everitt (eds) Switzerland: Palgrave, 507–527.

Adam, S. 2011. "Curry Protest Heats Up Vote with Facebook Campaign." *Bloomberg*, 19 August. Business. Available at: Singapore Curry Protest Heats Up Vote With Facebook Campaign (accessed 14 July 2015).

Aljunied, S.M.K. 2009. "British Discourses and Malay Identity in Colonial Singapore." *Indonesia and the Malay World* 37 (107): 1–21.

Bloemraad, I. 2006. *Becoming a Citizen: Incorporating Immigrants and Refugees in the United States and Canada*. Berkeley: University of California Press.

Calder, G. 2011. "Disability and Misrecognition." In *The Politics of Misrecognition*, S. Thompson and M. Yar (eds) Surrey and Burlington: Ashgate Publishing Company, 105–124.

Chan, M. 2019. "'Brownface' is Not Singaporean." *The Straits Times*, 7 August. Available at: https://www.straitstimes.com/opinion/brownface-is-not-singaporean (accessed 5 March 2021).

Chan, R. 2013. "Two Hong Lim Park Events, One Singapore." Available at: http://www.asiaone.com/News/Latest%2BNews/Singapore/Story/A1Story20130505-420422.html (accessed 5 May 2013).

Cheung, H. 2020. "Blackface Rears Its Ugly Face in Taiwan." *Taipei Times*, 4 June. Available at: https://www.taipeitimes.com/News/feat/archives/2020/06/04/2003737585 (accessed 2 February 2021).

Chow, B. 2020. "GE 2020: How 298A Of S'pore's Penal Code Failed Raeesah Khan." *Vulcan Post*, July. Available at: https://vulcanpost.com/703901/raeesah-khan-penal-code-singapore/ (accessed 20 August 2020).

Chow-Quesada, S.M.E. and F. Tesfaye. 2020. "(Re)mediating 'Blackness' in Hong Kong Chinese Medium Newspapers: Representations of African Cultures in Relation to Hong Kong." *Asian Ethnicity 21* (4): 384–406.

Chua, B.H. 2003. "Multiculturalism in Singapore: An Instrument of Social Control." *Race and Class 44* (3): 58–77.

Chua, V. 2009. "Kinship, Ethnic Segregation and Multiculturalism in Singapore: A Relational Study." *Asian Journal of Social Science 37* (4): 677–698.

CNA. 2020. "Police Investigating WP Candidate Raeesah Khan Over Alleged Online Comments on Race, Religion." *Channel NewsAsia*, 5 July. Available at: https://www.channelnewsasia.com/news/singapore/raeesah-khan-workers-party-police-reports-race-ge2020-sengkang-12903248?cid=h3_referral_inarticlelinks_24082018_cna (accessed 25 September 2020).

De Beukalaer, C. 2019. "Ordinary Culture in a World of Strangers: Toward Cosmopolitan Cultural Policy." *International Journal of Cultural Policy 25* (6): 792–805.

Editorial Staff. 2021. "Singer Resorts to Using Brownface in Music Video for Skin Whitening Product." *Yahoo Entertainment*, 26 January. Available at: https://www.yahoo.com/entertainment/singer-resorts-using-brownface-music-174335893.html (accessed 2 February 2021).

Fong, K. 2011. "Shanmugam Clarifies 'Curry Issue'." *Yahoo News*, 17 August. SingaporeScene. Available at: https://sg.news.yahoo.com/blogs/singaporescene/shanmugam-clarifies-curry-issue-050053270.html (accessed 14 July 2015).

Fortier, A-M. 2008. *Multicultural Horizons: Diversities and the Limits of the Civil Nation*. Abingdon, Oxon and New York: Routledge.

Goh, R.B.H. 2005. *Contours of Culture: Space and Social Difference in Singapore*. Hong Kong: Hong Kong University Press.

Hancock, B.H. 2008. "Put a Little Color on That!" *Sociological Perspectives 51* (4): 783–802.

Hill, M. and K.F. Lian. 1995. *The Politics of Nation Building and Citizenship in Singapore*. Politics in Asia series. London and New York: Routledge.

Hong, I. 2019. "Preetipls Should be Charged for Inciting Ethnic Ill-Will. Here's Why." Available at: https://medium.com/@ivanhong_25005/preetipls-should-be-charged-for-inciting-ethnic-ill-will-heres-why-a0c1b579b84e.

Joppke, C. 2021. *Neoliberal Nationalism: Immigration and the Rise of the Populist Right.* Cambridge: Cambridge University Press.

Kaur, S. 2019. "Everything Old is New Again." *Coconuts Singapore*, 16 August. Available at: https://coconuts.co/singapore/features/everything-old-is-new-again-singapores-long-history-with-blackface/ (accessed 10 March 2021).

Kinsella, S. 2006. "Minstrelized Girls: Male Performers of Japan's Lolita Complex." *Japan Forum 18* (1): 65–87.

Kurohi, R. 2020. "Parliament: WP's Sylvia Lim Calls for Open Review of Race-Based Policies." *The Straits Times*, 1 September. Available at: https://www.straitstimes.com/politics/parliament-wps-sylvia-lim-calls-for-open-review-of-race-based-policies (accessed 2 October 2020).

Kuruvilla, C. 2016. "Hong Kong Actor Wears 'Brown Face,' Highlights Prejudice Among Asians." *Huffington Post*, 11 January. Available at: https://www.huffpost.com/entry/derek-wong-ppap-indian-auntie_n_5817722ee4b0990edc326acc (accessed 2 February 2021).

Kymlicka, W. 1995. *Multicultural Citizenship: A Liberal Theory of Minority Rights.* Oxford and New York: Clarendon Press; Oxford University Press.

Kymlicka, W. 2002. *Politics in the Vernacular: Nationalism, Multiculturalism and Citizenship.* Oxford: Oxford University Press.

Lay, B. and J. Lee. 2017. "Ah Boys To Men 4 Audition Accused of Being Racist, Debate Ensues, Nation Clearly Divided." *Mothership*, 28 May. Available at: https://mothership.sg/2017/05/ah-boys-to-men-4-audition-accused-of-being-racist-debate-ensues-nation-clearly-divided/ (accessed 8 November 2017).

Lee, C., M. Cherian, R. Ismail, M. Ng, J. Sim and M.F. Chee. 2004. "Children's Experiences of Multiracial Relationships in Informal Primary School Settings." In *Beyond Rituals and Riots: Ethnic Pluralism and Social Cohesion in Singapore.* Singapore: Eastern University Press, 114–145.

Lee, E and M. Johnstone. 2021. "Lest We Forget: Politics of Multiculturalism in Canada Revisited during COVID-19." *Critical Sociology* OnlineFirst: 1–15.

Lee, H.L. 2014. "Speech by Prime Minister Lee Hsien Loong at CDAC 20th Anniversary Celebrations." Available at: http://www.pmo.gov.sg/mediacentre/speech-prime-minister-lee-hsien-loong-cdac-20th-anniversary-celebrations-english (accessed 1 August 2015).

Lee, P. 2016. "New Migrants from China Perceived as More Racist." *The Straits Times*, 20 August. Available at: https://www.straitstimes.com/singapore/new-migrants-from-china-perceived-as-more-racist (accessed 2 May 2021).

Levey, G.B. 2019. "The Bristol School of Multiculturalism." *Ethnicities 19* (1): 200–226.

Lian, K.F. (ed.) 2016. *Multiculturalism, Migration, and the Politics of Identity.* Singapore, Heidelberg, New York, Dordrecht and London: Springer.

Lim, A. 2019. "Rap Video by Local YouTube Star Preetipls on 'Brownface' ad Crosses the Line, Not Acceptable: Shanmugam." *The Straits Times*, 3 August. Available at: https://www.straitstimes.com/politics/rap-video-by-local-youtube-star-preetipls-on-brownface-ad-crosses-the-line-not-acceptable (accessed 29 October 2020).

Lim, L. 2016. "Analysing Meritocratic (In)equality in Singapore: Ideology, Curriculum and Reproduction." *Critical Studies in Education 57* (2): 160–174.

Malaya Tribune. 1915. "Patriotic Concert." *Malaya Tribune*, 3 May.

Matless, D.S. 1998. *Landscape and Englishness*. London: Reaktion.
MCCY. 2014. "Government Increases Matching Grant for Self-help Groups." Available at: http://www.mccy.gov.sg/news/press-releases/2014/Government-increases-matching-grant-for-Self-Help-Groups.aspx (accessed 1 August 2015).
Milne, R. 1966. "Singapore's Exit from Malaysia; the Consequences of Ambiguity." *Asian Survey* 6 (3): 175–184.
Modood, T. 2013. *Multiculturalism*. 2nd edition. Cambridge and Malden: Polity Press.
MOE. 2000. "Education in a Multicultural Setting – The Singapore Experience." Available at: http://www.moe.gov.sg/media/speeches/2000/sp24112000_print.htm (accessed 1 May 2013).
MOE. 2013. "Racial Harmony Day Celebrations 2013: 'Celebrating Singapore'." Available at: http://www.moe.gov.sg/media/press/2013/07/racial-harmony-day-celebrations-2013.php (accessed 2 February 2014).
Monk-Turner, E., H. Martinez, J. Holbrook, et al. 2007. "Are Reality TV Crime Shows Continuing to Perpetuate Crime Myths?" *Internet Journal of Criminology* 1–15.
Moore, M. 2011. "Singapore's 'Anti-Chinese Curry War'." *Telegraph*, 16 August. Available at: http://www.telegraph.co.uk/news/worldnews/asia/singapore/8704107/Singapores-anti-Chinese-curry-war.html (accessed 14 July 2015).
Moore, Q.R. 2000. "Multiracialism and Meritocracy: Singapore's Approach to Race and Inequality." *Review of Social Economy* 58 (3): 339–360.
Nagy, S.R. 2013. "Politics of Multiculturalism in East Asia: Reinterpreting Multiculturalism." *Ethnicities* 0 (0): 1–17.
Ng, H. 2019. "YouTuber Preetipls and Brother Subhas Given Conditional Warning by Police Over Rap Video on 'Brownface' AD." *The Straits Times*, 14 August. Available at: https://www.straitstimes.com/singapore/youtuber-preetipls-and-brother-subhas-given-conditional-warning-by-police-over-rap-video.
Ong, J. 2020. "Race in Singapore: What Topics are Due for Discussion, and How?" *The Straits Times*, 5 December. Available at: https://www.straitstimes.com/singapore/politics/race-in-singapore-what-topics-are-due-for-discussion-and-how (accessed 3 March 2021).
Ong, J. 2021. "Racism Still Exists in Singapore, But Identity Politics Must Not Take Root, Says Lawrence Wong." *The Straits Times*, 25 January. Available at: https://www.straitstimes.com/singapore/racism-still-exists-in-singapore-but-identity-politics-must-not-take-root-says-lawrence (accessed 2 February 2021).
Ortiga, Y.Y. 2015. "Multiculturalism on its Head: Unexpected Boundaries and New Migration in Singapore." *International Migration and Integration* 16: 947–963.
Parekh, B. 1995. "The Concept of National Identity." *Journal of Ethnic and Migration Studies* 21 (2): 255–268.
Parekh, B. 2000. *Rethinking Multiculturalism: Cultural Diversity and Political Theory*. London: Macmillan.
Parekh, B. 2006. *Rethinking Multiculturalism: Cultural Diversity and Political Theory*. London: Palgrave-Macmillan.
Rahim, L.Z. 2012. "Governing Muslims in Singapore's Secular Authoritarian State." *Australian Journal of International Affairs* 66 (2): 169–185.
Rice Media. 2019. "If the Preetipls Video Caused any Damage, It was Only by Revealing How Stupid Chinese People Are." 1 August. Available at: https://www.ricemedia.co/current-affairs-commentary-preetipls-epay-brownface/ (accessed 26 August 2020).
Rose, J. 1998. *States of Fantasy*. Oxford: Oxford University Press.

Russell, J.G. 2012. "Playing with Race/Authenticating Alterity: Authenticity, Mimesis, and Racial Performance in the Transcultural Diaspora." *The New Centennial Review* 12 (1): 41–92.

Sharpe, S. and M. Hynes. 2016. "Black-Faced, Red Faces: The Potentials of Humour for Anti-Racist Action." *Ethnic and Racial Studies* 39(1): 87–104.

Sim, J.B-Y. 2005. "Citizenship Education and Social Studies in Singapore: A National Agenda." *International Journal of Citizenship and Teacher Education* 1(1): 58–73.

Sin, C.H. 2003. "The Politics of Ethnic Integration in Singapore: Malay 'Regrouping' as an Ideological Construct." *International Journal of Urban and Regional Research* 27(3): 527–544.

SINDA. n.d. "Collaborative Tuition Programme." Available at: http://www.sinda.org.sg/students/collaborative-tuition-programme/ (accessed 1 August 2015).

Singapore Government. 2020. "Population in Brief 2020." Available at: https://www.strategygroup.gov.sg/files/media-centre/publications/population-in-brief-2020.pdf (accessed 29 April 2021).

Sommier, M. 2020. "'How ELSE are You Supposed to Dress Up Like a Black Guy??': Negotiating Accusations of Blackface in Online Newspaper Comments." *Ethnic and Racial Studies* 43 (16): 57–75.

Stambaugh, A. 2020. "Singapore Advertisement Sparks 'Brownface' Controversy." *CNN*, 30 July. Available at: https://edition.cnn.com/2019/07/30/asia/singapore-brownface-ad-sparks-controversy-intl-hnk-trnd/index.html (accessed 26 August 2020).

Straits Times. 1887. "The Jubilee." *Straits Times*, 6 July. Straits Times Weekly Issue.

Stratton, J. 2020. *Multiculturalism, Whiteness and Otherness in Australia*. Switzerland: Palgrave Macmillan.

Suhartono, H. 2011. "Singaporeans' Culinary Anti-immigration Protest: Curry." *Reuters*, 22 August. Singapore. Available at: http://www.reuters.com/article/2011/08/22/uk-singapore-curry-idUSLNE77L01020110822 (accessed 15 July 2015).

Tan, C. 2005. "Change and Continuity: Chinese Language Policy in Singapore." *Language Policy* 5 (1): 41–62.

Tan, E.K.B. 2005. "Multiracialism Engineered: The Limits of Electoral and Spatial Integration in Singapore." *Ethnopolitics* 4 (4): 413–428.

Tan, K.P. 2004. "Ethnic Representation on Singapore Film and Television." In *Beyond Rituals and Riots: Ethnic Pluralism and Social Cohesion in Singapore*, A.E. Lai (ed.) Singapore: Eastern University Press, 289–315.

Tan, K.P. 2008. *Cinema and Television in Singapore: Resistance in One Dimension*. The Netherlands: Koninklijke Brill NV.

Teo, T-A. 2019. *Civic Multiculturalism in Singapore: Revisiting Citizenship, Rights and Recognition*. Cham, Switzerland: Palgrave Macmillan.

Thanapal, S. 2019. "The Backlash to "Brownface" in Singapore." *The Interpreter*, 8 August. Available at: https://www.lowyinstitute.org/the-interpreter/backlash-brownface-singapore (accessed 26 August 2020).

The Singapore Free Press and Mercantile Advertiser. 1894. "The Magpie Minstrels." *The Singapore Free Press and Mercantile Advertiser (Weekly)*, 28 August. Available at: https://eresources.nlb.gov.sg/newspapers/Digitised/Article/singfreepresswk18940828-1.2.48?ST=1&AT=search&k=minstrel%20costume&QT=minstrel,costume&oref=article (accessed 10 March 2021).

The Singapore Free Press and Mercantile Advertiser. 1895. "Masonic Smoking Concert." *The Singapore Free Press and Mercantile Advertiser*, 30 September. Available at: https://

eresources.nlb.gov.sg/newspapers/Digitised/Article/singfreepressb18950930-1.2.6?ST=1&AT=search&k=minstrel%20costume&QT=minstrel,costume&oref=article (accessed 10 March 2021).
The Singapore Free Press and Mercantile Advertiser (Weekly). 1908. "The Calico Ball." *The Singapore Free Press and Mercantile Advertiser (Weekly)*, 9 January.
The Straits Times. 1937. "Ceylon Sports Club's Hockey Gala Game." *The Straits Times*, 31 October.
Thian, W.L. 2019. "How to be Singaporean: Becoming Global National Citizens and the National Dimension in Cosmopolitan Openness." Available at: https://ink.library.smu.edu.sg/cgi/viewcontent.cgi?article=4108&context=soss_research (accessed 8 May 2021).
Tonkiss, K. and T. Bloom. 2016. "Theorising Noncitizenship: Concepts, Debates and Challenges." *Citizenship Studies* 19 (8): 837–852.
Triandafyllidou, A. 2013. "National Identity and Diversity: Towards Plural Nationalism." In *Tolerance, Intolerance and Respect*, J. Dobbernack and T. Modood (eds) Basingstoke and New York: Palgrave Macmillan, 159–185.
Uberoi, V. 2007. "Social Unity in Britain." *Journal of Ethnic and Migration Studies* 33 (1): 141–157.
Vasu, N. 2012. "Governing Through Difference in Singapore." *Asian Survey* 52 (4): 734–753.
Velayutham, S. 2009. "Everyday Racism in Singapore." In *Everyday Multiculturalism*, S. Velayutham and A. Wise (eds) Hampshire and New York: Palgrave Macmillan, 255–273.
Velayutham, S. 2016. "Races Without Racism?: Everyday Race Relations in Singapore." *Identities: Global Studies in Culture and Power* 24 (4): 455–473.
WDA. n.d. "Funding for Individuals." Available at: http://www.wda.gov.sg/content/wdawebsite/L101-ForIndividuals/L702-WorkerBasedFund.html (accessed 1 August 2015).
Wigfall, J. 2015. "Four Seasons of Race, Color, and Representation in China." *Glocal Colloquies* 1 (1): 234–245.
Wong, T. 2019. "Singapore Government Accuses YouTuber Preetipls of 'Blatant Racism' Over Rap." *BBC*, 3 August. Available at: https://www.bbc.com/news/world-asia-49205225 (accessed 5 November 2020).
Yap, J. 2019. "More than 6 in 10 Feel Immigrants Not Doing Enough to Integrate into Singapore: Survey." *Channel NewsAsia*, 3 August. Singapore. Available at: https://www.channelnewsasia.com/news/singapore/more-than-6-in-10-feel-immigrants-not-doing-enough-to-integrate-11778888 (accessed 12 May 2021).

PART 2
Multiculturalism, History and Intersectionality

4
MULTICULTURALISM AND DECOLONIZATION

Avigail Eisenberg

Introduction

Over the last five decades, Canadian multiculturalism has been celebrated for transforming public attitudes and government policies towards cultural minorities. Multiculturalism has incentivized public and private actors to develop institutional practices, such as rules of cultural accommodation and employment equity, in order to eliminate obstacles that minorities face when they seek to participate in the public sphere or access public resources. To be sure, the public sphere in Canada continues to favor dominant groups. And minorities today battle backlash and stigma, which have been considered side effects of these policies.[1] Nevertheless, multiculturalism has established a set of public ideals that aim to eliminate minority marginalization and a set of (albeit imperfect) institutional practices by which these ideals can be attained.

Yet even these limited kinds of success are not evident in the policies and practices that aim at improving state relations with Indigenous peoples. On one hand, international and domestic efforts have led to several noteworthy policy reforms, predominantly, the United Nations Declaration of the Rights of Indigenous Peoples (UNDRIP) and various initiatives to address the historical injustices of colonialism (see, e.g., Canada, 2015; also see Lu, 2017). On the other hand, none of these initiatives has so far transformed the relations between Indigenous and settler populations. On the contrary, Canada, like many colonizing states, has recently witnessed intense conflict between Indigenous communities, industry and state actors over projects for land development and resource exploitation. In many corners of the world, governments and developers treat Indigenous rights as obstacles to economic development. In some cases, a colonial mindset has licensed the use of coercion against Indigenous peoples and their supporters who resist mining, logging and pipeline projects that encroach on their territories (Imai, 2017). Despite well-publicized reports of this coercion and Indigenous resistance to it, openly hostile publics continue to deny their responsibility for addressing the wrongs of colonialism today.

With an eye to these conflicts and to the recent scholarship about decolonization, this chapter considers the role of multiculturalism in colonial states such as Canada. I focus on a central tension between the ideals of multiculturalism and decolonization. Whereas multiculturalism is premised on the public accommodation of minorities, decolonization requires that states and publics recognize the political authority of Indigenous peoples. This tension, between accommodating identity and recognizing authority, is explored in the sections to follow. I argue that Indigenous claims have been distorted due to a failure on the part of state actors to distinguish between claims of cultural identity and claims of authority. The difference between accommodating Indigenous cultural identity and recognizing Indigenous legal and political authority ought to be central to decolonization efforts today. The final section considers three approaches that aim to furnish a genuine decolonized or postcolonial alternative to conventional state authority.

Identity versus Authority

In the 1990s, advocates for liberal multiculturalism argued that individuals require a secure cultural context in order to live autonomous lives. They pointed out that cultural identity anchors how people understand themselves and is tied to their sense of dignity and self-respect (Avineri and Halbertal, 1994; Kymlicka, 1995: 89–90). Multiculturalism was defended as a means to protect minority cultural practices in order to ensure that minorities have access to the benefits available in the public sphere on terms that do not require them to give up practices important to their identities. As Kymlicka argued, multiculturalism helps to provide a "secure cultural context" in which no individual suffers unfair disadvantages because of their cultural or linguistic identity (see Kymlicka, 1995: Ch. 5).

Western states have encountered several challenges when attempting to protect minority cultural practices. One challenge has been how to distinguish between cases about cultural difference, which require accommodation, and cases about cultural domination, which require changing relations of authority or power. It is well known by now that dominant groups have used culture, language and religion to wield authority over minorities, for example, by excluding and marginalizing groups from mainstream institutions and opportunities based on language, religion or ethnicity. In Canada, French settlers and Indigenous peoples were both subject to this kind of cultural domination. For instance, until language laws were enforced to protect the French language in Quebec, English dominated commercial relations and marginalized French speakers who constituted a majority of the population. Both French and British settlers also imposed policies of assimilation on Indigenous peoples, which targeted them through their cultural practices and traditional livelihoods, by prohibiting the use of native languages, and, in some cases, mandating the removal of Indigenous children from their families to residential schools to be raised in the language and values of the colonizing group. These policies are remembered today as examples of coercive cultural assimilation.

Canadian multiculturalism is not designed to respond to these histories of coercive assimilation. It is not intended as a policy meant to integrate French-Canadians and Indigenous peoples, who most Canadians consider "founding peoples," not cultural minorities. At the same time, like some other minorities, both French-Canadians and Indigenous peoples, have been targets of discrimination due to their cultures and have suffered disadvantages because of this. In Canada, cultural discrimination has been used against both national minorities and more recent immigrant groups to secure the political authority of the dominant group.

In one sense, the connection between cultural injustice and colonial subjugation is widely recognized today. We recognize, for instance, that policies that sought to alter the culture or language of Indigenous communities were not merely aimed at reshaping Indigenous culture. Instead, their intent was to pacify Indigenous communities, which actively resisted the imposition of state authority. This pacification sometimes involved undermining familial, political and economic structures of authority by which Indigenous peoples organized their communities. Structures of authority could be undermined by prohibiting the "cultural" practices that sustained them. On the west coast of North America, practices such as the Potlach, Spirit Dancing and whale hunting were means by which political leadership, authority and governance within Indigenous communities was established and managed. Colonial authorities restricted these cultural practices in order to replace Indigenous structures of authority with colonial structures. Restrictions successfully undermined Indigenous governance practices, breaking ties between the Indigenous community and its traditional territories, weakening kinship networks and family bonds, and rendering communities financially dependent on state governments.

One legacy of this history is that, today, state policies that intentionally or unintentionally restrict particular Indigenous cultural practices become contentious in broader struggles between the state and Indigenous peoples over where final authority over the governance of Indigenous communities, territories and interests lies. Some of the cultural practices important to Indigenous communities today give content and meaning to the internal structures of Indigenous law-making and governance which these communities seek to rebuild. These practices are the means through which community political authority is manifested.

And yet, state attempts to protect Indigenous "culture" can obscure rather than illuminate the important connection between culture and political authority. This is especially the case where policies that aim to protect culture fail to challenge or change relations of political authority. For example, states can sanction the revitalization of Indigenous languages and cultural practices without altering colonial relations of political authority.

In this regard, courts are careful to distinguish in their decisions between the accommodation of Indigenous cultural identity and the recognition of Indigenous governing authority, and to sanction only the protection of cultural identity. Domestic courts in Canada, the United States and Australia typically shift disputes about territory or resources away from questions about Indigenous jurisdictional authority towards questions about the role of a particular territory or resource in a community's cultural identity. Such shifts transform disputes about jurisdictional authority into questions about narrow legal exemptions for cultural practices. For instance, courts will consider whether an Indigenous community's distinctive identity requires exemption from a state licensing requirement to hunt or fish in a particular way or in a particular place (*R v Sparrow* [1990] 1SCR 1075; also see Ross, 2006).[2] But they will not consider the question of whether Indigenous jurisdiction over the resource *is* the practice that makes the culture distinctive (see Borrows, 2017). An Indigenous community's right to manage a resource, which has been central and definitive of the community's distinctive way of life, is thus transformed into a right to have access to the resource as deemed necessary by the court for distinctive and limited cultural purposes.

To be sure, decisions made along such narrow lines can nonetheless be helpful at securing important legal exemptions for Indigenous communities. But such narrow exemptions sometimes do more to reinforce the authority of the state than to recognize Indigenous authority over the resource in question. Courts are often clear about their aims in this respect and have required Indigenous claimants to prove their case by showing that a disputed cultural practice made their community culturally distinctive before the state declared sovereign authority over the Indigenous community's territory (see *R v Vanderpeet* [1996] 2 SCR 507; also see Borrows, 1997–1998; Eisenberg, 2011). This carries a message that, once the state declares sovereignty, Indigenous communities no longer have authority over the resources and territories they traditionally used even though they might still have a state-protected right of access for limited "cultural" purposes.

In one sense, multiculturalism is irrelevant to these colonial disputes. Today, multiculturalists and their critics debate whether states, primarily in Europe, have given up too much political power to minorities and left majority cultures under-protected. Some critics argue that generous policies of cultural accommodation and lenient immigration rules have allowed minorities to take over the public sphere where they change rules about the workplace, public education, public holidays, etc. in the name of (a misconceived and illiberal) group-based equality (Orgad, 2014; Kaufman, 2018). Against these charges, multiculturalists point out that cultural accommodation aims at the inclusion of all groups under one political authority (that of the liberal multicultural state). They argue that rather than giving up too much authority to minorities, the challenge has been to ensure that states do not overextend their authority and become the arbiters of the cultural and religious practices of minority groups. From their point of view, the critics' contention that multiculturalism licenses minoritarian politics and causes social fragmentation is misplaced.

Even though multiculturalism is usually considered an approach that responds to conflicts between majority groups and immigrant minorities, in its initial iteration, multiculturalism was defended in the context of thinking about the wrongs of colonialism. In Canada, multiculturalism's advocates, including myself, examined Canada's history of colonial injustice partly in terms of its impact on the cultural distinctiveness of Indigenous peoples (Eisenberg, 2009: Ch. 6; Kymlicka, 1995; Taylor, 1994: 26, 39–40). In his 1995 book, *Multicultural Citizenship*, Will Kymlicka anchored Indigenous rights in the broader project of improving the ways in which states respect cultural diversity. As Kymlicka described it, cultural communities that are incorporated into a larger state, "typically wish to maintain themselves as distinctive societies alongside the majority culture, and demand various forms of autonomy and self-government in order to ensure their survival as distinct societies" (10). In the United States, advocates and critics of multiculturalism pointed to the ways in which the cultural assumptions of dominant groups distort legal decisions about Native American tribal membership rules and religious practices (Rentln, 2004: 79–84; Song, 2009: Ch. 5). In Latin America and the Arab world, multiculturalism has been conventionally used to refer to the claims of Indigenous peoples (Ennaji, 2014; Kymlicka and Pföstl, 2014; Siedler, 2002). In all of these contexts, rights to cultural protection are considered to be one kind of remedy to colonial policies which historically sought to assimilate Indigenous peoples coercively.

By contrast, today, one of the driving forces behind decolonization efforts is to re-establish the authority of Indigenous peoples to govern themselves and their communities using their own laws and governance structures regardless of whether or not this helps to secure lost cultural practices. In fact, some scholars go so far as to condemn cultural recognition and intercultural dialogue as pernicious forms of recolonization (see Coulthard, 2014a; also see Rollo, 2004). Glen Coulthard explains that Indigenous peoples are sometimes caught in a cultural "no win" situation when they refuse to situate themselves in relation to values associated with Western progress, capitalist development, modernization and globalization in the same ways that settler populations typically do. Indigenous "difference" in these values and dispositions are then carried into interactions with the state over land development negotiations, or in court cases and intercultural dialogue, where Indigenous perspectives end up being viewed by settlers as incomprehensible, unpersuasive or as confirming that communities are backward and unable to govern themselves today (Coulthard, 2014b. Also see Nichols, 2013; Rollo, 2004). Some of those sympathetic with Coulthard's view also point to the lasting effects of colonialism that have distorted identities by leading Indigenous peoples to internalize attitudes of inferiority and ambivalence towards their traditional governing institutions and practices (Tully, 2010: 244). In these respects, colonialism is linked to distorting Indigenous identity in ways that impact self-respect and dignity.

Yet, it would be misleading to diagnose these concerns as matters requiring cultural protection even if cultural differences are implicated in how disputes unfold. Today, Indigenous scholars, including Coulthard, John Borrows, Val Napoleon and many others, argue that decolonization requires re-establishing Indigenous authority by rebuilding Indigenous political and legal orders and reintroducing traditional practices, customs and languages to community members. For some communities, these are daunting projects that require reconstituting Indigenous legal traditions and governance structures and revitalizing Indigenous languages. Obviously, this requires that states agree to protect and help to rebuild some Indigenous cultural practices. But the purpose of these efforts is not only to protect cultural identity. Instead, the hope is that these efforts will reconstitute Indigenous political and legal orders as legitimate sources of governance, sometimes even if this requires departing from traditional practices and values. For this reason, reforms that subordinate Indigenous legal orders to state authority, such as proposals to use federal and municipal government structures as templates for Indigenous self-government, are often considered unsatisfactory. It should come as no surprise when Indigenous communities reject such reforms or consider them temporary weigh stations on the road to more genuine forms of self-determination. More genuine forms of self-determination require recognition of Indigenous political orders as distinct political entities with legitimate law-making authority over communities and traditional territories independently of state concession or the delegation by states of constitutional authority to them (see Napoleon, 2012).

To re-establish Indigenous authority structures, in the sense I have described, poses significant challenges to contemporary state governance and raises many difficult questions. One question is how can Indigenous legal orders, which directly contest the authority of the state, coexist with the state? Is the sovereign legal authority of contemporary states compatible with Indigenous legal authority? If it is compatible, what measures are required to secure the coexistence of legal orders in ways that make sense to populations throughout the world who live on territories where these authorities overlap? If these different authority structures are incompatible, how far can either order go in successfully addressing colonial injustice? These are some of the pressing questions states face today. They are different from the questions addressed by multiculturalism. They implicate cultural difference but, at the same time, are sensitive to the fact that state-based cultural protections can be an obstacle to decolonization.

Restructuring Political Authority

Despite the significant challenges of decolonization, one response to the concerns raised above has been to rely on sovereign states to reform in ways that better protect Indigenous communities. There are several moral and pragmatic reasons why the state, as an ideal political framework, is considered well-suited to address some of the deep and complex challenges of colonial injustice. One reason is the capacity of states to secure their borders, which smaller communities lack. This capacity fulfills one of the leading promises of liberal democracy, which is to provide a secure and stable context in which people can lead their lives well. States can sustain a complete set of institutions for national majorities and some national minorities to live in their language and according to their cultural values and practices. Beyond these groups, the state can also accommodate linguistic, ethnic and religious minorities. In these ways, states have capacities and resources to provide a context for minorities and majorities to enjoy cultural security. The point of multiculturalism is to provide a set of ideals to guide states in these aims and to ensure smaller, ethnic minorities have access to the same benefits of citizenship as national majorities and minorities do.

In relation to these different groups and strategies, Indigenous communities are anomalous. On one hand, Indigenous peoples are similar to national minorities because they seek linguistic and cultural security and the right to self-determination on their traditional territories. On the other hand, many Indigenous communities are often too small to sustain a complete set of societal institutions on their own. They would need access to some of the state's resources. In a world in which states have a monopoly over legitimate political authority, Indigenous communities, at best, could enjoy limited forms of self-government. Otherwise, they require the protection and accommodation of sovereign states.

That being the case, over the last 30 years, several models of governance better suited to Indigenous self-determination, self-governance and collective autonomy have been proposed. Below, I examine three alternative approaches that advance post-colonial or decolonized alternatives to conventional state-centric approaches to governance. First, internationalism proposes international institutions as the means to empowering Indigenous communities. Second, legal and political pluralism offer institutional accounts of governance that directly challenge state-centric accounts of political authority. Third, radical pluralism or "pluriversal" approaches propose an ethics to decolonize relations of authority.

Internationalism

Internationalism employs the oversight of international institutions to sway state decision-making over matters important to Indigenous communities. The United Nations Declaration of the Rights and Indigenous Peoples (UNDRIP), the International Labor Convention 169 and the International Covenant on Civil and Political Rights are leading examples of conventions that have empowered Indigenous peoples to secure their rights and interests against states. The aim of these conventions, according to Patrick Macklem, is to "mitigate the adverse effects of the structure and operation of the international legal order" by providing Indigenous peoples (and other minorities) with leverage against states (2015: 15). James Anaya, the former United Nations Special Rapporteur on (the Situation of Human rights and Fundamental Freedoms of) Indigenous People and one of the chief architects of UNDRIP, echoes Macklem's assessment in the case of UNDRIP. UNDRIP creates opportunities for Indigenous peoples to mobilize around issues that affect them and to use the leverage of the international community and domestic advocates to keep state authority in check.

UNDRIP is designed to mediate between the state and the human rights of Indigenous peoples while incentivizing substantive institutional change. These incentives are operationalized through the mandates of the convention, which require signatory states to develop internal institutions to fulfill their obligations. For instance, UNDRIP mandates a duty of states to consult with Indigenous peoples over projects that implicate the interests of Indigenous communities or territories (Anaya and Puig, 2017: 437). In order to fulfill this duty, states must create institutions competent to carry out consultations. These newly created institutions then contribute to a state infrastructure that enhances the likelihood of state accountability and transparency in dealings with Indigenous peoples while also providing a means to publicize state failures to abide by the terms which states agree to. In this way, international conventions can change the configuration of state institutions and alter the distribution of political power within states.

To be sure, international institutions are beset with all sorts of difficulties when it comes to altering the behavior of states towards Indigenous peoples, including their failure to offer coherent principles for distinguishing between the claims of Indigenous peoples and non-Indigenous stateless national minorities (see Corntassel, 2003; Kymlicka, 2007a: 265–291). Yet, at the same time, the virtues of internationalism, as an addendum to state-centric governance, are significant. International institutions have provided opportunities for Indigenous peoples to organize, mobilize and develop counter-narratives to Euro-modern views that otherwise dominate international and domestic law. In particular, UNDRIP has been a productive site for Indigenous mobilization around matters important for self-determination. It has incentivized states to sign agreements with Indigenous communities and to create institutions that advance values and interests which post-colonial states ought to protect. That said, international institutions, including UNDRIP, do not fundamentally alter the basic institutions of the state system or how state authority is understood. On the contrary, internationalism relies on the continuity of the international system of states. Its aim is to create better states. But it does so without disturbing how legal and political authority is understood and practiced.

Legal and Political Pluralism

Approaches to governance that recognize plural authorities are a natural fit for decolonization efforts because they challenge the sovereignty idea according to which the state is the final and absolute authority within its borders. Pluralists recognize states as one amongst a possible multiplicity of authorities. The aim of pluralism is to show how legitimate political authority can originate from sources other than the state (see, e.g., Cover, 1983; Griffiths, 2015; Merry, 1988; Muniz-Fraticelli, 2014). By displacing the state as the final source of law and authority, pluralism can give direct recognition to Indigenous legal orders. For this reason, Indigenous legal scholars have drawn on the principles of legal pluralism to argue that Indigenous communities have internally recognized legal orders that can be legitimized independently of state recognition.[3] These arguments contribute to the more general observation that colonial injustice is rooted in the unjust suppression of Indigenous legal traditions and governance practices. According to this view, current international legal norms perpetuate colonialism when they deny recognition to Indigenous legal orders (Rajagopal, 2003: 263–266). By providing arguments for the legitimacy of Indigenous legal and political orders, pluralist arguments are proposed today as a helpful corrective to colonial injustice (see Griffiths, 1986).

One of pluralism's chief claims is that a plurality of legitimate authorities can exist within a single domain. By recognizing plural legal authorities, pluralism is said to offer a less distorted understanding of legal authority than conventional accounts of authority, which recognize only the legitimacy of state law. According to both statist and pluralist accounts, law is legitimate where it consists of a system of rules that community members recognize as legitimate and to which they defer and where communities recognize a set of officials as the legitimate source of creating and interpreting legal rules. Based on this view of law, pluralists argue that customary law, transnational law, religious law and Indigenous law can all count as legitimate law independently of whether sovereign states recognize their legitimacy. From the pluralist vantage, when states dismiss the legal authority of Indigenous law and governance, they misinterpret the criteria by which their own law is considered legitimate.

Pluralism has potentially significant implications for Indigenous communities, but it suffers from some practical problems. Legal pluralists are criticized for "finding legality everywhere" and for advancing a theory that allows for the proliferation of conflict amongst multiple, incommensurable authorities while providing no means to settle conflict (see Griffiths, 1986). To recognize the legitimacy of Indigenous law might seem like a Pyrrhic victory if it is accompanied by recognition of the legitimacy of conflicting laws of the colonial state. Some pluralists "grasp the nettle" by arguing that conflict and especially the "incommensurability of authorities" is a virtue of pluralism because it indicates pluralism's commitment to offer an approach compatible with the deep diversity of approaches to governance, including approaches associated with Indigenous perspectives (see, e.g., Muniz-Fraticelli, 2014).

However, the incommensurability of different authorities also points to a troubling feature of pluralism. Multiple authorities, each of which is properly constituted, can occupy the same legal domain and assert authority over the same physical space with no obvious means to resolve conflicts that arise between them. The difficulty to which pluralism points is that any definitive means of resolving conflicts amongst multiple authorities, would, *ipso facto*, diminish the authority of these multiple authorities and, would, in effect, reproduce a legal centrism akin to state sovereign rule. If, for instance, a state court is charged with resolving conflicts between plural authorities, then it is the state, via its own institution, that has final authority. With multiple authorities comes conflict, to which pluralists offer no unique "pluralist" solutions.

Nonetheless, in the context of colonialism, a pluralist framework can be helpful. It clarifies that one of the wrongs of colonialism is the domination of one legitimately constituted legal and political order by another and, through this, the disempowerment of a community, which is prohibited from living according to the legal and political order to which it is committed. To understand colonial conflict in this way suggests that many Indigenous legal and political practices have been rendered invisible by colonial legal frameworks which have supplanted them. Efforts to decolonize may require helping communities rebuild their orders. But often these orders, and the practices which constitute them don't need to be rebuilt because they already exist, albeit in the shadow of state law and governance (Eisenberg, 2022).

Decolonization requires a framework in which the authority of an Indigenous community, and the practices by which its authority is manifested, can be rendered visible to those within and outside Indigenous communities. This suggests again that colonialism is not adequately addressed through state-initiated protections for Indigenous cultural rights. From a pluralist point of view, cultural rights often miss that facet of colonial injustice that lies in the attempt to erase sources of authority asserted through the cultural practices of colonized peoples.[4] State recognition of Indigenous rights and self-determination and the conventions of internationalism may provide some of the tools required for recovering how Indigenous political authority has been obscured. But like other state-based approaches, cultural rights and internationalism see solutions to colonialism in reforms that help states govern Indigenous peoples more legitimately, whereas pluralists see solutions in reforms that treat sovereign state authority over Indigenous people as illegitimate and unjust.

Radical Pluralism and the Pluriverse

Cultural rights, internationalism and legal pluralism each propose institutional solutions to the problem of colonial relations. In contrast, radical pluralism is an ethical approach, albeit one with institutional implications. Like legal and political pluralists, radical pluralists recognize a multiplicity of different and potentially incommensurable normative orders. They deny that a single order exists which provides a universal standpoint from which all others can be understood or legitimately governed (see Allard-Tremblay, 2018). Some radical pluralists advocate for a pluriverse, an idea that draws on the radical empiricist philosophy of William James who was interested in finding ways to maintain the validity of claims about supernatural phenomena. James was interested in the sort of claims which do not make sense within frameworks of scientific rationalism and naturalism (James, [1909] 1943; also see Hutchings, 2019: 116). His concept of "pluriverse" or "multiverse" was meant to grapple with a multiplicity of ontologically distinct worldviews. Today, the concept is used to understand and reassess approaches that Indigenous movements take to urbanization, industrialization and land development (see Escobar, 2016; Tully, 2018; Zúñiga, 2020). The pluriverse refers to movements that "understand themselves as located in worlds that are radically different to modern ways of being, that provide an alternative place and time from which to mobilize resistance to modernity" (Hutchings, 2019: 116). Where Euro-modern perspectives consider Indigenous movements to be "backward" or "uncivilized" when they oppose development projects, pluriverse arguments consider alternative explanations grounded in the existence of different ontologies. According to Arturo Escobar, the pluriverse provides a tool "to make alternatives to one world plausible to one-worlders" (2016: 22).

Pluriversal arguments have been used to reassess interactions between states and Indigenous peoples. They challenge modes of thinking and acting that presuppose a universal standpoint or insist that a single set of standards and principles can be fairly applied to all groups (see Conway and Singh, 2011). The "pluriverse" creates spaces for recognizing multiple ontologies that are not subsumed to one hegemonic way of being. For these reasons, the pluriverse is helpful when thinking about what decolonizing global ethics requires. As Kimberly Hutchings notes, it is a means to reconsider the "imperial reach" of our ethical commitments to other peoples and to revalue ethical capacities such as self-restraint and humility in dealing with others (2019: 122).

Pluriverse arguments have been applied to reexamine how to collaborate and coexist with others without subsuming them into one world or another. Its advocates seek forms of interaction that foreground relations of "being with" rather than principles that ought to be adopted by all peoples (see Dunford, 2017; Hutchings, 2019: 124). Pluriversality is about accepting that sometimes no agreed-upon set of values exists, even about core interests. We sometimes must accept "the limitation of our own rectitude in light of the commitment to work with others toward a particular goal" even if this means putting "one's own sense of self and entitlement to one side" (Hutchings, 2019: 122).

As Hutchings makes clear, pluriverse arguments are ethical arguments rather than approaches to institutionalized governance. In other words, these arguments do not replace state-based decision-making but rather prescribe a radical rethinking of how interaction and collaboration should proceed in a decolonized world. They foreground humility, self-restraint, negotiation and agreeing to disagree, in hopes that these values will be productive avenues by which to build a decolonized coexistence. At the same time, the idea of the pluriverse can provide a critical vantage from which to assess the space that exists for claims that do not fit within hegemonic and state-centric frameworks of governance.[5]

Conclusion

Since its inception, Canadian multiculturalists have insisted on a strict separation of claims of Indigenous peoples from the claims of other cultural minorities. They have argued that policies governing Canadian diversity regarding ethnic minorities, Quebec and Indigenous peoples have different origins, are embodied in different legislation, refer to different parts of the constitution, are administered by different government departments and are guided by different concepts and principles: "each forms its own discrete silo, and there is very little interaction between them" (Kymlicka, 2007b: 39–40).

Here, I have tried to show that Indigenous claims have been distorted and conflated with claims for cultural accommodation. In Canada, multiculturalism has exerted something like a gravitational force, pulling different kinds of claims into its orbit, and transforming them into claims of culture, which are less radical and more manageable from the perspective of a colonial state. Not only have Indigenous claims been thus distorted, so has the manner in which the Canadian public understands what is at stake in Indigenous-state conflicts (see Eisenberg, 2022). Transposing claims for the recognition of Indigenous political authority into claims about cultural accommodation, which are comparatively more innocuous, has led to hollow victories for Indigenous peoples who seem to "win" policy battles and court cases and yet continue to resist state authority. On the account I offer here, the problem is that some of these victories amount to no more authority for Indigenous peoples over their traditional territories or communities. Instead, so-called victories often involve courts urging the state to recognize the distinctive cultural practices and interests of

Indigenous peoples. Insofar as these distortions inform the current landscape of Indigenous-state relations in Canada, multiculturalism has helped to shore up the power of a colonial state.

At the same time, it is important to recognize that multiculturalism and decolonization are different projects. On one hand, multicultural principles can inform the governance of a decolonized state even if they cannot be deployed to bring about decolonization. From this perspective, radical ethical pluralism, political and legal pluralism, post-colonial political orders and multiculturalism ought to be considered complementary solutions to the challenges of diversity.

On the other hand, multiculturalism offers an approach to governance that relies on a unified, albeit diverse, sovereign state. Legal pluralists, radical pluralists and even some advocates of internationalism have contested this vision in different ways and for good reason. They consider the challenges of colonialism, self-determination and ecological sustainability, rather than cultural accommodation, to be the appropriate central preoccupations of political theories of diversity (see Zúñiga, 2021). They point out that questions about cultural diversity have become confused with questions about political authority. And they insist, minimally, on distinguishing between injustices that stem from cultural disadvantage and those that stem from the subjugation and domination of Indigenous peoples.

Notes

1 On backlash, see Orgad 2014; Vertovec and Wessendorf 2010. On the connection between stigma and "affirmative multicultural remedies," see Fraser 1995: 82–85. Canadian multiculturalism has also been criticized for neglecting racism (see Bannerji, 2000) and facilitating neoliberal integration because it aims, primarily, at integrating minorities in the market economy (see Abu-Laban and Gabriel, 2002).
2 For instance, in *R v Sparrow* ([1990] 1SCR 1075) the Court held that the state-mandated drift net size requirements, imposed on all fishers in British Columbia, violated the fishing rights of Ronald Sparrow who was a member of the Musqueam First Nation when he fished with a large drift net in Canoe Passage on the Fraser River. The Court decided that, in the absence of a treaty, Sparrow's right to fish in Canoe Passage was based on cultural traditions exercised by the Musqueam in the area since time immemorial. The worry generated by the decision is that, when Indigenous rights are tied to culture, they will only be protected narrowly and only when practiced in the specific manner that reflects how the court understands the Indigenous cultural tradition.
3 Essays by leading Indigenous scholars have been collected in the Special Issue on Indigenous Law and Legal Pluralism, *McGill Law Journal* 2016, 61: 4.
4 For this reason, John Borrows argues that Indigenous claims to authority are nested within Indigenous cultural interests. See Borrows 1997–1998. Also see Pasternak, 2017 for an account of Indigenous cultural practices that establish jurisdictional authority.
5 See Hutchings 2019 for examples of how pluriversal ethics apply to conflict management in Latin America. I outline an institutional account of plural political authority and apply it to the recent conflict over land development on Wet'suwet'en territory in British Columbia in Eisenberg, 2022.

References

Abu-Laban, Yasmeen and Christina Gabriel. 2002. *Selling Diversity: Immigration, Multiculturalism, Employment Equity and Globalization*. Peterborough, ON: Broadview Press.
Allard-Tremblay, Yann. 2018. "The Modernist and the Political Pluralist Perspectives on Political Authorities." *Review of Politics* 80 (4): 675–700.
Anaya, S. James and Sergio Puig. 2017. "Mitigating State Sovereignty: The Duty to Consult with Indigenous Peoples." *University of Toronto Law Journal* 67 (4): 435–464.
Bannerji, Himani. 2000. *The Dark Side of Nation: Essays on Multiculturalism, Nationalism and Gender*. Toronto, ON: Canadian Scholars.
Borrows, John. 1997–8. "Frozen Rights in Canada: Constitutional Interpretation and the Trickster." *American Indian Law Review* 22: 37–64.
Borrows, John. 2017. "Challenging Historical Frameworks: Aboriginal Rights, The Trickster, and Originalism." *Canadian Historical Review* 98 (1 March): 114–135.
Canada. 2015. "Truth and Reconciliation Commission of Canada." http://www.trc.ca/
Conway, Janet and Jakeet Singh. 2011. "Radical Democracy in Global Perspective: Notes from the Pluriverse." *Third World Quarterly* 32 (4): 689–706.
Corntassel, Jeff. 2003. "Who is Indigenous? 'Peoplehood' and Ethnonationalist Approaches to Rearticulating Indigenous Identity." *Nationalism and Ethnic Politics* 9 (1): 75–100.
Coulthard, Glen. 2014a. *Red Skins, White Masks: Rejecting the Colonial Politics of Recognition*. Minneapolis, MN: University of Minnesota Press.
Coulthard, Glen. 2014b. "Place Against Empire: The Dene Nation, Land Claims and the Politics of Recognition in the North." In *Self-determination versus Recognition*, Avigail Eisenberg, Jeremy Webber, Glen Coulthard and Andree Boisselle (eds.) Vancouver, BC: UBC Press, 147–173.
Cover, Robert. 1983. "Nomos and Narrative." *Harvard Law Review* 97 (4): 4–65.
Dunford, Robin. 2017. "Toward a Decolonial Global Ethics." *Journal of Global Ethics* 13 (3): 380–397.
Eisenberg, Avigail. 2009. *Reasons of Identity: A Guide to the Political and Legal Assessment of Identity Claims*. Oxford: Oxford University Press.
Eisenberg, Avigail. 2011. "Domestic and International Norms for the Assessment of Indigenous Identity." In *Identity Politics in the Public Realm*, A. Eisenberg and W. Kymlicka (eds.) Vancouver, BC: University of British Columbia Press, 2011, 137–162.
Eisenberg, Avigail. 2022. "Decolonizing Political Authority: The Conflict on Wet'suwet'en Territory." *Canadian Journal of Political Science* 55 (1): 40–58.
Ennaji, Moha ed. 2014. *Multiculturalism and Democracy in North Africa: Aftermath of the Arab Spring*. London: Routledge.
Escobar, Arturo. 2016. "Thinking and Feeling with the Earth: Territorial Struggles and the Ontological Dimension of the Epistemologies of the South." *Revista de antropologia Iberoamericana* 11 (1): 11–32.
Fraser, Nancy. 1995. "From Redistribution to Recognition? Dilemmas of Justice in a "Post-Socialist" Age." *New Left Review* 1 (212): 68–93.
Griffiths, John. 1986. "What is Legal Pluralism?" *Journal of Legal Pluralism and Unofficial Law* 24: 1–55.
Griffiths, John. 2015. "Legal Pluralism." In *International Encyclopedia of the Social and Behavioural Sciences*, 2nd ed, vol. 13, James Wright (ed.) Amsterdam/Boston, MA: Elsevier, 757–761.

Hutchings, Kimberly. 2019. "Decolonizing Global Ethics: Thinking with the Pluriverse." *Ethics and International Affairs 33* (2): 115–125.

Imai, Shin. 2017. "Consult, Consent, and Veto: International Norms and Canadian Treaties." In *The Right Relationship*, M. Coyle and J. Borrows (eds.) Toronto, ON: University of Toronto Press, 370–408.

James, Willliam [1909] 1943. *Radical Empiricism and the Pluralistic Universe*. New York: Longmans, Green and Co.

Kaufmann, Eric. 2018. *White Shift: Populism, Immigration and the Future of White Majorities*. New York: Abrams Press.

Kymlicka, Will. 1995. *Multicultural Citizenship*. Oxford: Oxford University Press.

Kymlicka, Will. 2007a. *Multicultural Odysseys*. Oxford: Oxford University Press.

Kymlicka, Will. 2007b. "Ethnocultural Diversity in a Liberal State: Making Sense of the Canadian Model(s)." In *Belonging? Diversity, Recognition and Shared Citizenship in Canada*, Keith Banting, Tom Courchene and Leslie Seidle (eds.) Montreal: Institute for Research in Public Policy, 39–86.

Kymlicka, Will and Eva Pföstl (eds.). 2014. *Multiculturalism and Minority Rights in the Arab World*. Oxford: Oxford University Press.

Lu, Catherine. 2017. *Justice and Reconciliation in World Politics*. Cambridge: Cambridge University Press.

Macklem, Patrick. 2015. *The Sovereignty of Human Rights*. Oxford: Oxford University Press.

Margalit, Avishai and Moshe Halbertal. 1994. "Liberalism and the Right to Culture." *Social Research 61* (3): 491–510.

Merry, Sally Engle. 1988. "Legal Pluralism." *Law and Society Review 22*: 869–896.

Muniz-Fraticelli, Victor. 2014. *The Structure of Pluralism*. Oxford: Oxford University Press.

Napoleon, Val. 2012. "Thinking about Indigenous Legal Orders." In *Dialogues on Human Rights and Legal Pluralism*, René Provost and Colleen Sheppard (eds.) New York and London: Springer, 229–245.

Nichols, Robert. 2013. "Indigeneity and the Settler Contract Today." *Philosophy and Social Criticism 39* (2): 165–186.

Orgad, Liav. 2014. *The Cultural Defense of Nations: A Liberal Theory of Majority Rights*. Oxford: Oxford University Press.

Pasternak, Shiri. 2017. *Grounded Authority*. Minneapolis, MN: University of Minnesota Press.

Rajagopal, Balakrishnan. 2003. *International Law from Below*. Cambridge: Cambridge University Press.

Renteln, Alison Dundes. 2004. *The Cultural Defense*. Oxford: Oxford University Press.

Rollo, Toby. 2004. "Mandates of the State: Canadian Sovereignty, Democracy and Indigenous Claims." *Canadian Journal of Law and Jurisprudence XXVII* (1): 225–238.

Ross, Michael Lee. 2006. *First Nations, Sacred Sites*. Vancouver, BC: University of British Columbia Press.

Siedler, Rachel (ed.). 2002. *Multiculturalism in Latin America: Indigenous Rights, Diversity and Democracy*. Houndmills, Basingstoke: Palgrave/Macmillan.

Song, Sarah. 2009. *Justice Gender and the Politics of Multiculturalism*. Cambridge, MA: Cambridge University Press.

Taylor, Charles. 1994. "The Politics of Recognition." In *Multiculturalism and the Politics of Recognition*, Amy Gutmann (ed.) Princeton, NJ: Princeton University Press, 25–75.

Tully, James. 2018. "Reconciliation Here on Earth." In *Resurgence and Reconciliation: Indigenous-Settler Relations and Earth Teachings*, James Tully, John Borrows and Michael Asch (eds.) Toronto, ON: University of Toronto Press, 83–129.

Tully, James. 2010. "Consent, Hegemony and Dissent in Treaty Relations." In *Between Consenting Peoples*, Jeremy Webber and Colin M. Macleod (eds.) Vancouver, BC: University of British Columbia Press, 233–256.

Vertovec, Steven and Susanne Wessendorf. 2010. *Multiculturalism Backlash: European Discourses, Policies and Practices*. London: Routledge.

Zúñiga, Didier. 2020. 'Nature's Relations: Ontology, Vulnerability, Agency." *Hypatia* 35 (2): 298–316.

Zúñiga, Didier. 2021 "To Think and Act Ecologically: The Environment, Human Animality, Nature." *Critical Review of Internatiownal Social and Political Philosophy*. doi: 10.1080/13698230.2020.1772605.

5

MULTICULTURALISM IN THE POST-COLONY

Shadows of Agamben in South Africa

Amanda Gouws

Introduction

The concept multiculturalism has never really applied to South Africa, even though the country meets the requirements of cultural pluralism that includes a diversity of ethnic, language and religious groups. The imposition of racial/ethnic identities by the apartheid government may have prevented ethnic conflict (something that is common in some other African countries) through its spatial segregation into ten ethnic enclaves (Bantustans), but it created the desire for a nation-building process that would not be focused on identities, but rather on unity. The unity that was supposed to be created through the democratic transition was captured in the notion of the "Rainbow Nation." Unity constituted by different cultural groups was the model chosen to reinforce the liberation struggle's goal of non-racialism. Therefore, multicultural policy frameworks have never been developed for South Africa by the post-apartheid government.

In other multicultural societies like Canada and Australia there is one dominant culture that is embedded in liberal-democratic forms of governance. In these societies multiculturalism is seen as providing every individual with a cultural reference point and sense of belonging to a particular ethnic community (McAllister, 1997: 61). This often disguises an assimilationist agenda, because as Bradley (2013: 2) articulates it the dominant culture is not part of the cultural mosaic. In South Africa there is no one dominant group which could establish the core values of the society, even though all ten African ethnic groups form an African majority of 80.9 % of the population. Whites are 7.8%, mixed race (called colored) 8.8% and Indian 2.5%.[1] In multicultural societies cultural diversity is valued and celebrated through dress, cuisine and art with the focus on difference, rather than commonalities (Baines, 1998). It is constitutive of the nation, not a threat to it (McAllister, 1996: 74). The fear in South Africa was that a focus on multiculturalism could easily lead to identity politics that is counterproductive for nation-building (Baines, 1998) when it becomes a basis for political mobilization, competition and domination (McAllister, 1996: 74).

While non-racialism was the rhetoric of the ruling African National Congress (ANC) after transition, affirmative action policies to correct the disadvantage of different non-white groups as a consequence of apartheid, put the government in a bind. In order to keep track of successes with affirmative action it had to keep the imposed apartheid racial identities intact (white, colored, Black and Indian). As a consequence, it galvanized differences among the different race groups, hampering the formation of a non-racial society.

Twenty-eight years after democratic transition, South Africa is experiencing similar global trends as Europe and North America with the rise of populism, embodied by the populist political party, the Economic Freedom Fighters (EFF), that exploits racial divisions, for its own political goals, especially around land reform. This has led to serious racial polarization. As in other countries in the Global North, South Africa also has a huge influx of migrants from other African countries, triggering a backlash from many Black South Africans who see their presence as a competition for scarce resources.

Nearly three decades after transition the pernicious effects of being the most unequal society in the world with nearly 50% of the population living under the upper bound poverty line of $79 per month, with unemployment of nearly 45% if the expanded definition of unemployment is used[2] and chronic landlessness, social marginalization and exclusion have become the norm for a majority of the African population. These conditions have been aggravated and deepened by the COVID-19 pandemic.

While these conditions can be attributed to bad governance, endemic corruption and the lack of political imaginary to implement an "imagined community" this criticism will be too harsh if we do not understand how multiculturalism in post-colonial societies is being undone by the legacies of colonialism (and in the case of South Africa combined with the legacies of apartheid). What multicultural liberal democracies do is to erase colonial legacies and the violent operations of power, without being able to undo the racism of colonial settlement, the ghosts of which stalk the boundaries of the newly formed political community. Exclusions from the polity are aggravated by the constitution of the liberal subject as an individual rights bearer without accounting for the relationship of the liberal subject with its community (Gouws, 2016). Rights are often juxtaposed with culture in a way that positions culture as inferior to rights.

Identity is not only dependent on cultural resources, but there is a strong connection between identity and place or land, because land is a marker of belonging and citizenship (Sharp, 1999). The significant pushback against recent waves of influx of migrants into multicultural societies in Europe relates directly to contestation over place and the destabilization of the core values of the dominant culture threatening to uproot multiculturalism. In post-colonial societies landlessness is a stark reminder of colonial dispossession.

The transition to democracy in 1994 ensured sovereignty and an end to apartheid with the promise of freedom and an end to land dispossession. Sovereignty in post-colonial African societies is closely related to state formation and the inclusion of fragmented territories under one single authority. The political community in settler states was created through subdividing land into territorial homelands (fragmented sovereignty) that were made subject to separate legal regimes with cultural and ethnic distinctions, transforming these groups into administrative-political units, called tribes or ethnic groups (Mamdani, 2021: 11).

Forging multicultural societies out of territorially segregated communities, plural legal systems (civil and customary law) and uniting colonially imposed identity groups in a bounded territory also entailed a redetermination of who are considered minorities and majorities and who are included as citizens and subjects. In this regard processes of decolonization have to address the challenges of embodiment—or racialization—the construction of colonial subjects as backward, barbaric and uncivilized that informs identity formation of the settler and the subject, since identities exist in relation to each other. Embodiment also determines gender identities and gender relations that were made more static and immutable through the codification of customs and tradition. The particularity of codified customs and oral traditions becomes a point of contention when they come into conflict with the universalism of human rights of multicultural societies that would consider them (i.e., customs) illiberal and harmful, especially in relation to women and LGBTIQ communities (Gouws and Stasiulis, 2016). Sovereignty, land and embodiment are therefore crucial to understand the limits of multiculturalism in the post-colony.

Theories of multicultural accommodation fail to explain the impact of the legacies of colonialism in post-colonial societies like South Africa. Below I will show how the issue of territory or land constitutes a crucial dimension of sovereignty without which citizens are still excluded from citizenship as rights bearers. In South Africa the slow processes of land reform have contributed to the precarious lives of rural farm dwellers and rural landless people, resulting in what Agamben calls "bare life." Rather than drawing on liberal theories of multiculturalism I want to draw on Agamben's theory of the *homo sacer*, analyzing post-colonial sovereignty through the state of exception and bare life which are the antitheses of multicultural sovereignty, to illustrate how processes of marginalization and exclusion continue despite post-colonial sovereignty. I will also show how the shift from majority to minority status, allows white farmers, who own the biggest portion of agricultural land, to claim that they have become the victims of a white genocide due to the murders of white farmers, at the same time that landless Africans struggle for access to land. These claims of genocide echo Mahmood Mamdani's[3] analysis of the genocide in Rwanda of "victims [in this case those oppressed under apartheid] who have become killers." The violent operations of power and land dispossession are also deeply raced and gendered.

Sovereignty after Settler-Colonialism

Agamben's theorization of the precarious lives of those who are socially marginalized without their lives having political significance is very applicable to the South African society because of the large number of people who are socially excluded, landless and living in poverty with a disconnect from the liberal-democratic ("multicultural") society.

Giorgio Agamben's (1998) theory of the *homo sacer* has been very influential in explaining purportedly exceptional phenomena, such as Nazi concentration camps, refugee conditions caused by mass migration in late modernity. Agamben makes a distinction between life in general (*zoe*) and political life (*bios*), because he is interested in the difference between mere life and a life of political significance. A bare life is a life devoid of political significance and is inhabited by the *homini sacri*, who can be exposed to unlimited violence that is not considered a crime and those who kill the *homo sacer* will not be prosecuted. Bare life arises in a state of exception where the *homini sacri* are still exposed to the functioning of the law but not protected by the law (Lemke, 2005: 5). The main feature of modern biopolitics therefore is the state of exception that arises because of the suspension of law, something that has become the rule in late modernity. In this zone of indistinction the *homo sacer* is included in the very act of being excluded from the law. Banishment and the suspension of law go to the heart of sovereignty because this can only be done by sovereign power.

Agamben's theorization does not consider colonies and specifically, settler colonial societies, where bare life shows a continuation in the post-colonial state that has gained sovereignty. The dynamics of race and gender, two dimensions on which Agamben is silent, also need to be included in this theorization. The racial and sexual nature of national power arose in settler colonies rather than being something that was transposed from Europe (Morgensen, 2012: 68), but it has deeply influenced liberal governance in previous colonial centers such as Europe and North America.

At the heart of Agamben's theory is the understanding of sovereignty as a decision over life and death (who gets banished to bare life and who has the power to suspend the law to create a state of exception). The state of exception has hardly been a state of exception for colonialized peoples, where race and coloniality are central to the constitution of modernity and the making of its sovereignty (Thobani, 2012: 3). The racial logic of power (of lives that are racially distinct, less-than-human and subjected to exceptional violence) is inherent in the global order that universalizes the Western experience and is foundational to sovereignty. This logic continues in the post-colony where the state of exception can be considered the rule (Thobani, 2012: 6).

Settlers in settler colonial societies treated Indigenous populations through the creation of racial embodiment that functioned according to a logic of elimination or displacement, while at the same time they universalized Western law and liberal governance. This is why Patrick Wolfe calls settler colonialism a structure not an event, a structure that amalgamated Indigenous peoples, cultures and lands into the body of the settler nation through the exercise of biopolitics that is a persistent activity in settler states (Morgensen, 2011: 53–56). Sovereignty assumes a citizen with membership in a sovereign state. In post-colonial settler societies Western law is validated by incorporating Indigenous peoples into settler nations through a new subjectivity that embraces multiculturalism that is the pluralist, deracialized ideal that is empirically unattainable, because it has to oppose the internalized colonial subjectivity forged through the exclusion of the racial other (Thobani, 2012: 17).

Agamben does not engage sovereignty in relation to territory. Sovereignty relates to bounded, territorial jurisdiction and how political authority is exercised over this territory (Calarco and DeCaroli, 2007: 47). The relationship between authority and bodies determines membership in the political community. Sovereignty, therefore, is a relational concept—the relation between the rulers and the ruled and is context-dependent (e.g., the context of the settler colonial state). State territory *precedes* law, creating a form of governing of life that the law codifies and preserves. It is also a process of boundary-making through establishing a relationship between the legal and non-legal as a way to determine who is a citizen and who is the exile (Calarco and DeCaroli, 2007: 49). The state of exception enters between the legal and non-legal and establishes the boundary between law and non-law that makes banishment possible (54). Sovereignty cannot be thought without territory. The colonial project incited the need to define the terms of territorial ownership and political belonging, in order to make a distinction between savages and the civilized, citizens and subjects, as well as between incorporation and inclusion (Bonilla, 2017: 332). Mbembe (2016: 79) puts it as follows, "Colonial occupation itself consisted in seizing, delimiting and asserting control over a geographical area—of writing a new set of social and spatial relations on the ground." Colonial settlement defined who matters for inclusion and who are disposable bodies, what Mbembe calls the work of death or necropolitcs. Becoming a colonial subject meant upholding the work of death (Mbembe, 2016: 68).

Rifkin (2009) extends the argument about territory by arguing that biopolitics comes at the expense of a discussion of geopolitics and the production of race and space in the operation of sovereignty (Rifkin, 2009: 90). In settler states certain types of embodiment, or the biopolitical project of defining the proper body (i.e., the raced body), is connected to the geopolitical project that regulates the politics of collectivity and occupancy, resulting in what he calls "bare habitance." The ideal body will be recognized as citizen, while "others" will be subjects who can be relegated to bare life and excluded from meaningful political participation (Rifkin, 2009: 93). The biopolitical project cannot exist without the geopolitical project of defining the territoriality of the nation, that through sovereign violence naturalizes national space. Rifkin (2009: 109) views sovereignty itself as an empty concept, or a place holder to displace or contain the paradox of asserting domestic authority over populations whose existence as people precede the existence of the state. The struggle for sovereignty in settler states is not about policy, but about the meta-political authority of defining the content and scope of law and politics, that will determine who will be recognized as citizens and who will be consigned to bare life. It will also determine what modes of inhabitance of territory will be considered legitimate and who will be able to determine this (Rifkin, 2009: 93–94). Agamben locates this biopower in the very nucleus of the concept of sovereignty (Genel, 2006).

In processes of decolonization, many settler states have embraced liberal-democratic sovereignty and human rights regimes, and incorporated fragmented groups of Indigenous peoples into multicultural societies, but as Gundogdu (2012: 3) argues human rights are inextricably tied to the logic of biopolitical sovereignty and that human rights struggles will reproduce the sovereign violence that it aims to contest. Agamben's notion of sovereignty as decisions over life and death and the creation of the biopolitical body challenges the social contractarian myth that conceals sovereign power. Legal norms, rights and the rule of law are grounded in the originary violence and therefore reinscribes legal (and land) dispossession as an inescapable condition in the post-colony (Gundogdu, 2012: 12–13).

Settler Colonialism

Settler colonialism needs to be distinguished from other forms of colonialism because it is a land-centered project that in many settler colonies led to genocide through the logic of elimination (e.g., Indigenous populations in the USA and Canada) (Morgensen, 2011:55). The focus on land in settler colonies was to ensure livelihoods, but also to extend capitalism through the possibilities of extraction from land (Wolfe, 2006: 394), thus leading to land deprivation with violence in proportion to the amount of settlement (Mamdani, 2001: 10).

Settler colonial identities are also directly related to land as an agricultural project, a potent symbol of settlers' permanence, coupled with the discursive construction of the native as non-agricultural, nomadic and rootless (Wolfe, 2006: 396). To acknowledge the natives as agriculturalists would confirm the permanence of their presence. In many settler colonies this prevention of permanence led to genocide. In the South African case it led to displacement of the natives from the land, confining them to very small pieces of land. Mamdani (2001: 14) calls this the "genocidal logic of colonial pacification." According to him, it is violence that binds the settler and the native together in a chain of violence that becomes bigger than both of them.

Settler post-colonial multicultural societies have to be forged from fragmented sovereignties of different (ethnic) groups whose identities and bounded territories were created or imposed through processes of colonization that created permanent majority–minority distinctions (Mamdani, 2021: 7).

Colonial indirect rule therefore has defined the relation between the national majority and minority (even though the majority in the South African case was a numerical minority). The nation state in Africa that was imposed on Indigenous populations foisted upon them a national political subjectivity, even though they did not think of themselves as members of a nation state (Mamdani, 2021:3). Indirect rule therefore produced in the Indigenous population a national political subjectivity that created permanent majorities and minorities, through which ethnic differences were made to appear natural. These majority and minority statuses were fixed in place through violent nationalisms on the one hand, and through tolerance that made liberal democracy possible on the other hand. As long as minorities were non-threatening and accepted their status, through which they sacrificed sovereignty, they were accepted in the nation state which justifies sovereignty through the extension of human rights (Mamdani, 2021: 7–8). Decolonization of settler states involved dislocating permanent majority and minority identities that define the contours of the nation state and determine the political community and political belonging (Mamdani 2021: 19).

South Africa as a Post-Colonial Settler State

South African colonial state formation conformed to the processes that Crais (2006) identifies as necessary in order to create administrative units for colonial governmentality. The invention of sovereignty through colonial settlement relied on four processes: (1) embodiment which allows political principles to inhere in persons as holders of office (i.e., traditional leaders or chiefs), (2) spatialization or the territorialization of culture (i.e., space and culture became coterminous), (3) codification (of oral laws), jurisdiction and policing (of adherence to law and territorial boundaries) and (4) sovereignty naturalized some political principles such as rule through chiefship, at the same time as it fragments and marginalized forms of power not recognized by the colonial state (Crais, 2006: 730).

As a settler colonial state, settler colonists in South Africa relied on the logic of displacement, rather than the logic of elimination (Patrick Wolfe's term in Morgensen (2011)) that makes land a central focus for decolonization. Land was settled through processes of movement into the interior and claiming "empty land" or acquiring it through conquest, as well as through law making. Forced removals of Black people in South Africa started with the 1913 Land Act and was accelerated under apartheid, conjoining land and identity that contributes to contestation around belonging in the political community.

The small tribal homelands (i.e., Bantustans) that were created to accommodate the ten ethnic groups were colonial and apartheid expressions of power. These homelands were too small for sustainable livelihoods, creating a class of people whose lives were precarious and without political significance. Prior to the transition to democracy the settler colonialists exploited the conquered land through the labor (or racial capitalism) of defeated communities contributing to Eurocentric modernity (Reddy, 2016: 59). The administration of the Indigenous populations occurred through the organization of space, institutions and social relations (Reddy, 2016: 72), that determined the boundaries of the political community in South Africa.

As Reddy (2016: 38) argues, the Indigenous population was historically not included in the political community and remained rights-less, reduced to bare life and their conditions hardly improved under liberal democracy. They only attained a semblance of political significance. The majority of Black South Africans still live in the margins of society, in informal settlements and impoverished townships where women are continuously exposed to gender-based violence. As he states: "Under democratic conditions, South Africa's *homo sacer* battles daily against vulnerability, hence extraordinary politics [the politics of constant protest against social exclusion and marginalization] is normalized." The majority of Black South Africans therefore live in a state of exception where legal protection has limited meaning, and violence and death are normal occurrences. Resistance against these conditions takes the form of protests, sometimes violent clashes with the police or the violent destruction of infrastructure such as schools and libraries—symbols of colonial mastery.

Land Reform in South Africa

One of the biggest challenges for post-apartheid South Africa is the redistribution of land in a fair and equitable way that would also be representative of justice for colonial and apartheid land dispossession. The 1913 Land Act ensured 86% of land ownership by the white minority and only 14% for the Black majority. The transition to liberal multicultural democracy in South Africa meant the granting of sovereignty in a bounded territory where the new citizens could lay claim to land. This shift in sovereignty also redetermined majority and minority status. The redistribution of land therefore also became one of the ways to reverse colonial and apartheid landlessness, in order to create a new political community. For these reasons land reform was one of the contentious issues in the negotiation process during democratic transition, leading to a balancing act of giving direction to the redistribution of land while at the same time protecting existing property rights of white (settler) citizens.

Part of the negotiated settlement land reform was included in Clause 25 of the Bill of Rights in the Constitution. This clause reads as follows:

Property: (1) No one may be deprived of property except in terms of law of general application, and no law may permit arbitrary deprivation of property.
(2) Property may be expropriated only in terms of law of general application –
  (a) For a public purpose or in the public interest; and
  (b) subject to compensation, the amount of which and the time and manner of payment of which have either been agreed to by those affected or decided or approved by a court.
(3) The amount of the compensation and the time and manner of payment must be just and equitable, reflecting an equitable balance between the public interest and the interest of those affected, having regard to all relevant circumstances.

(The South African constitution)

Land redistribution aims at dealing with the very unequal distribution of land as a consequence of the 1913 Land Act. The Land Reform Process focused on three areas: land restitution, land tenure reform and land redistribution. Restitution aimed at redressing the injustice of apartheid forced removals through a process of returning land or property. Land tenure reform recognizes people's right to own land with a focus, inter alia, on farm dwellers, who live and work on farms but do not own land. Land redistribution entails a more equitable distribution of land from the owners of land to the landless. All three processes have been very slow and dissatisfying to the Black majority.

By the end of 1998, the cutoff point to lodge land claims, nearly 64,000 claims were filed. By 2000 less than 1% of the claims were finalized, leading to predictions that it may take another 20 years to settle all claims (Walker, 2008: 15). But by 2007, 74,417 claims or 93% of the 79,696 claims were settled, with the majority of settlements for land in urban areas. Many urban claimants accepted payment as compensation, while in the rural areas there was a greater demand for the return of the land.

As Walker (2008) points out, the master narrative of land redistribution was one of colonial land dispossession and that restoration was possible to dispossessed households, communities and their descendants, *without* (my emphasis) also highlighting that ownership of land in the hands of the majority would not easily overcome entrenched poverty, suffering, alienation, ignorance and conflict as part of the history of colonialism and apartheid. For Walker, there is a disjuncture between the symbolic importance of land on the level of the state and local levels of commitment to the process on the ground. Far more attention was paid to land restitution in urban areas rather than rural areas where the need for land is palpable. In a national survey, in 2003, 53% of farm dwellers indicated that they needed more land. Land itself became the symbol for restitution and justice on many levels. In the same survey, 85% of Black respondents indicated that land was taken away by white settlers in an unjust manner and that they (whites) do not have any rights to land (Walker, 2008: 24).

The policy for land reform that the South African government has used up to the present is "willing buyer, willing seller," relying on a market mechanism to encourage property owners to sell land at market value, a process through which the state could remain hands-off. The "willing buyer, willing seller" policy is costly to the state (through its subsidization of acquired land) and it prevents the state from addressing land dispossession in a timely fashion (De Vos, 2013). Using the market compounded the problem of landlessness and marginality by those who cannot access the market (Hall, 2004: 225), an inability that is embedded in the history of agrarian formation. South Africa's agrarian structure is dualistic, with previous white farmers involved in capital-intensive commercial farming and large-scale production linked to export and global value chains, while the impoverished areas of the Black homelands depend on low-input, labor-intensive subsistence production (Hall, 2004: 213). Black farm dwellers who work on the land had lived on white farming land for generations but have no claim to the land and in most cases live lives of poverty and marginalization. Under the Reconstruction and Development Plan, the macroeconomic policy under President Mandela, the aim was to redistribute 30% of agricultural land to the poor and landless. This amounted to about 26 million hectares out of 86 million hectares owned by commercial farmers (Hall, 2004: 214).

Twenty-seven years after democratic transition, about 72% of privately owned farmland belongs to white farmers and only 4% to Black African farmers, something that is completely disproportional to the racial composition of the South African population—80.9% African and 7.8% white. These numbers speak to the injustice of colonial land dispossession, the impoverishment of Black farm dwellers and their dependency on the goodwill of white farmers for their livelihoods.

Where white farmers have become hostile toward the process of land reform it encouraged evictions of Black farm dwellers, turning many into squatters without access to land. This led to job losses, and the casualization of labor, promoting the process of proletarianization, intensifying land dispossession by separating rural workers from access to the land (Hall, 2004: 218). The South African Black proletariat's lives since 1994 have become more precarious as a consequence of poverty and marginalization that exposes them to bare life.

Given the slow pace of reform[4] and the frustration of the landless, the issue of land reform has become increasingly politicized. The "left-leaning" populist opposition party, the Economic Freedom Fighters (EFF), started to demand land expropriation without compensation, mobilizing the landless and encouraging land grabs.[5/6] Under this pressure, parliament passed a motion in February 2018 to start a process of considering land expropriation without compensation through an amendment to Clause 25 of the Constitution, because the Constitution prohibits the arbitrary deprivation of property. Currently expropriation has to be made subject to the payment of compensation. This compensation must conform to "the amount of which and the time and manner of payment of which have either been agreed to by those affected or decided or approved by a court" (De Vos, 2013). Yet, there is widespread support for land expropriation in the state, because of the settler history of land confiscation. For those who own land it raises the specter of land expropriation Zimbabwean style where white farmers lost their land and their livelihoods and many had to flee Zimbabwe. Land grabs and illegal occupations are deeply threatening to the white minority.[7] The frustration of those waiting for land, facing struggles of survival, has escalated into illegal acts such as the occupation of private and state-owned land, murders of white farmers and in some cases their Black farm workers, as well as increasing cases of stock theft (Hall, 2004: 222–223).

A report by the Institute for Security Studies (ISS), drawing on statistics from the South African Police Services (SAPS) (whose statistics are incomplete) and the Transvaal Agricultural Union of South Africa (TAU SA) show that between 1991 and 2001 there were 6,122 violent farm attacks, resulting in 1,254 deaths. During the 2001 farm attacks there were 1,398 victims of various crimes including murder, rape, robbery, assault and others, of whom 61.6% was white, 33.3% Black, 4.4% Asian and 0.7% colored, resulting in 147 deaths. According to TAU SA statistics for the period 1990 to 2017, taking into consideration murder only, a total of 1,938 people was killed on farms. Of these, 1,697 (87.6%) were white and 241 (137 farm workers) (12.4%) were Black (Burger, 2018). Violent deaths on farms belonging to white farmers are therefore disproportionate to other deaths in rural areas and not insignificant but comparing statistics for 2017/2018 farm murders of 62 out of 800,000 farm residents it is 7.75 per 100,000, versus the national homicide rate of 35.8 per 100,000. The farm murder statistics are therefore dwarfed by the rate for national homicides.[8] Farm murders are, however, exceptionally violent, brutal and often include torture (see Akinola, 2020). This has led to analyses that farm murders are racially motivated and that this is the revenge of "the native" or in Mamdani's (2001) words "killings by yesterday's victims" for centuries of sub-human conditions on farms.

A study on rural safety has shown that despite the increase in farm murders the Rural Safety Plan that was supposed to safeguard rural areas against crime was not properly implemented, it was not satisfactorily explained to communities, and there was little interaction between the SAPS and those they have to protect (Sonjani and Snyman, 2018). While (white) farmers ensured their own protection through the use of commandos these were phased out in 2003 in favor of sector policing and the recruitment of reservists that had limited success (Sonjani and Snyman, 2018: 85).

It was #BlackLivesMatter and the death of George Floyd in the USA (as discussed in Chapter 12 by Debra Thompson) that clearly showed how complicated issues of race and land are in South Africa. Solidarity with #BlackLivesMatter became polarized between a majority of Black South Africans and small minority of whites who discursively constructed the murders of white farmers as a white genocide, in a pushback against BLM.

In a response to a video about BLM that went viral on WhatsApp in which a white editor of News24 and Network24, said that "if you are white and you don't know the name of George Floyd you are part of the problem," a nameless white man ranted: "do you know the names of [white] farmers who have been killed?" According to him, if you don't you are part of the problem. In the months after Floyd's death the racialized nature of the debate around BLM was the most visible in the arena of sport. Lungi Ngidi, a Black cricketer expressed the need for the South African cricketers and cricket board to take a solid stand on the BLM movement because South Africa's painful history with apartheid and racial discrimination mandated this. In response to this Rudi Steyn, a white cricketer, said in an online post: "I believe the Proteas (South Africa's cricket team) should make a stand against racism, but if they stand up for 'Black lives matter' while ignoring the way white farmers are daily being 'slaughtered' like animals, they have lost my vote."[9] This post discursively constructs white farmers as victims of racial violence to the extent that it constitutes a white genocide, obscuring the historically grounded nature and specificity of settler colonial power relations around land.

Akinola (2020) argues that the non-categorization of farm murders as a special crime aggravates the racialization which found expression in racism to the effect that the rhetoric of "white genocide" depicts farm murders as systematic acts orchestrated by the Black race, supported by a Black majority government. There is a belief among whites that there is a specific racial and gender dynamic to farm murders that condemn white farmers to bare life. This discourse is steeped in setter colonial tropes and the racial logic resonates with Whitley's (2017: 14) critique of Agamben: "Agamben's theory screens out the particularities, and the differential distributions of power which would mean that race and racism are not experiences which come later, but are essential modes through which power functions."

Simon Roche of Die Suidlanders (a white right-wing group that claims thousands of supporters) warned, in an interview with James Pogue of *Harpers Magazine* (2019)[10], about Black Africans' propensity for killing women and children that according to him predates white settlement in the interior and was worse than anything that happened in the great wars of Europe. He confided: "It is not about the land. It has got nothing to do with the land." It was about a plot to destroy whites.[11] In the same interview, another Suidlander said: "[No] one will come to rape our women four at a time here, they know we'd f--- them up." The counter discourse to this is that of Black activist, Andile Mngxitama of the radical Black First Land First,[12] who told Pogue (2019) that "[T]he project here is essentially a race problem. The confrontation is going to be racialized." According to him, South Africa is a racial war zone of which farm murders is just another day on the battlefield. As he put it to Pogue:

> "We kill small ones. We kill old ones, we kill white people—of course, because we're killing ourselves. And why do we kill ourselves? Because we're put in subhuman conditions. Life means nothing. Why the f--- must I care for your life? Life is meaningless.On both sides there is racial and gender rhetoric—on the side of whites the colonial tropes of Black people as barbaric and prone to extreme violence and rape—the "barbarians at the gate," while on the side of Blacks structural violence of colonial settlement that caused bare life and dehumanization for Africans is raised.
>
> *(Pogue, 2019)*

White people and white farmers are not unaware of these sentiments that have fueled angst around land issues (see e.g., Falkof, 2022). The Afrikaans word for farmer is *boer*, which is also the derogatory term for white Afrikaners, captured in a liberation struggle song "Kill the Boer, Kill the Farmer." This very song was sung by young Black anti-apartheid activists when they dragged the white American exchange student, Amy Biehl,[13] from her car and stabbed her to death during the violence of the last days of apartheid in 1993. This song is still sung today with the encouragement of the EFF, even though its leader, Julius Malema, was found guilty of hate speech in the Equality Court that determined the song may not be sung anymore. Judge Collin Lamont specifically referred to the naming of people as cockroaches during the Rwandan genocide and how the use of derogatory terms may contribute to genocide.[14]

The subjectivity of the colonizer and the colonized are linked in deep unconscious processes, of which fear is one. The colonial settlers never stop fearing the Other, even before they had to relinquish power, they manage the fear through violence (Mbembe, 2016: 134–135). Now that they do not have political power anymore the fear is aggravated and expressed in the fear of the rape of white women by the "savage other" that becomes a motivation for violent retaliation, even before any transgressions have happened.

The Suidlanders also relied on (right-wing) populism for their cause. Between March and September 2018 they sent a delegation to the USA to lobby alt right groups for money for their cause, causing President Trump to tweet about the large scale killing of white farmers that resembles a white genocide, instructing Mike Pompeo to investigate this.[15] The outcry about farm murders by the Suidlanders and other right-wing groups led to the Australian government fast-tracking visas for white farmers who wanted to leave South Africa, so that they could flee their "horrific circumstances."

Processes of colonization and settlement are deeply gendered. Stoler (2010) argues that gender and sexuality, just as race, were produced and mobilized in "the intimacies of empire" through the regulation of women's sexuality, through violence, in the colonies. While the victimization through sexual violence of white women is raised by the Suidlanders, there is a silence on the victimization of Black women. Just like any other women in South Africa, women on farms are exposed to very high levels of gender-based violence (GBV) and sexual assault. Most intervention centers or shelters are located in urban areas, so that GBV on farms goes unnoticed. Often the police refuse to drive to farms or do not want to intervene, because of the complicated situation of getting farm owners to open electronic gates. Often, women who complain about GBV to farm owners are evicted along with their families. The NGO, Women on Farms, has regular intervention programs against domestic and sexual violence on farms. Women farm dwellers are the most likely not to have permanent work, doing seasonal work, or lower paying jobs. They also do not have independent tenure rights from their husbands, making them economically dependent on male farm workers, unable to leave abusive relationships. Farm women in general do not get assistance from the police, even if they manage to get to a police station, which is often not possible due to a lack of public transport.[16] Rapes of Black women farm dwellers, therefore, have a far greater probability than the rape of the wives and daughters of white farmers (even though marital rape goes unreported). Even though the intersectionality of race, gender, rurality and farm ownership position of Black and white women on farms, differentially both groups are vulnerable to sexual violence, given the very high rates of rape in South Africa.

Mamdani (2021: 191) singles out two groups of post-apartheid beneficiaries—white farmers and traditional leaders of the former Bantustans that continue to benefit from land ownership. They both resist land reform. In recognizing traditional authorities, more power was granted to them after democratic transition, especially in relation to land management. The Communal Land Rights Act (CLRA) give traditional leaders significant power to manage and distribute communal land. The CLRA was aimed at protecting communal land rights and securing Indigenous entitlement to land. What the act does, however, is to continue colonial distortions of land possession by not taking into consideration how land is owned by families and the family-based nature of land rights under customary law that has given women access to land (Claassens and Mnisi, 2011: 95). This has deepened women's insecurity around land (Gouws, 2016: 43). Unmarried rural women living on family land are the worst affected, as are widows and divorcees, because land is distributed to men. These women are relegated to a zone of indistinction because they are included in the law, but in relation to land do not benefit from it. Decisions are taken on their behalf, not through their participation.

Conclusion

Landless Africans in South Africa suffer from bare life due to their precarious conditions as farm dwellers and/or rural marginalization. While liberal democracy has included them in the law but they are still excluded from its protection, and as *homini sacri* they live in the zone of indistinction. Applying Agamben's theory to the political context in South Africa shows the limits of liberal multiculturalism in the post-colony. Liberal multiculturalism constructs the subject as an individual with self-making and self-regulating agency, as bearers of rights that have an equal standing before the law. By individualizing claims for land and regulating it through market mechanisms it obscures the origins of land claims of the collectivity that also has an imaginary of the political community that cannot be located in the individual. Without land, political community is stifled in the post-colony. Sovereignty in the post-colony is therefore not related to rights-bearing as such, but in Agamben's terms, to a decision over inclusion and exclusion in the polity. Yet, Agamben's theory also needs adjustment for the post-colony.

In the case of land reform, the South African state is not enabling the Black landless to access land, nor is it protecting white farmers through the police service. Cooper-Knock (2018), who has applied Agamben's theory to policing in South Africa, argues that his theory is too state-centric, constructing the state as undifferentiated, disregarding Foucault's view of power as dispersed in the state. On the other hand, there are theorists who argue that Agamben gives too much agency to the state because bare life happens when the state abandons citizens, rather than deliberately rendering them into bare life (see Pratt, 2005; Sanchez, 2004; Savarese, 2010 and Gouws, 2021).

It may also be the case that abandonment is too totalizing a notion for state action. Cooper-Knock's (2018: 2–29) use of the concept "permissive space" is helpful here to apply to the state's actions in relation to land reform. As she argues, we should not focus on the exception but on how sovereignty gets constructed in everyday life. It is not about the "one" who decides the exception but about the multiple layers and practices involved in sovereignty. In situations that can be considered the present day "camp," such as the biopolitical project of border control, or the policing of cultural practices of minority groups (in the USA, for example) it is easier to recognize racial and racist treatment of subjects, because there is a clear demarcation of the disposable body and how violent relations of power are constituted. In the post-colony, where the legacies of colonization have condemned the majority of subjects to the zone of indistinction, it is harder to see the violent (racist) operations of power, because bare life is everyday life (Whitely, 2017: 8–9).

In practice, sovereignty operates in spaces that are shaped by social, political and economic forces where the violence of social exclusion and marginalization operates. Permissive space, however, allows for flexibility, avoids state-centric approaches and therefore can be constituted, contracted, collapsed, closed or expanded (34). Agamben fails to investigate the underlying reasons, political interests and the power relations that demand certain measures that through their complexity and layeredness constitutes a regime of governmentality (Erlenbusch, 2013: 54).

Sovereignty is therefore not only related to the law and how the law can be used as a blunt instrument but is kept in place through perceptions of the state's legitimacy. The state desires the legitimacy of both the rural landless (to do justice to its transformation agenda), as well as white farmers who ensure food security and make a significant economic contribution. With "willing buyer, willing seller" there was a permissive space for negotiation around land, but this space has now contracted. The populist demands of the EFF opened another space that enables the state to take on board the demands of the rural landless and gives legitimacy to land expropriation without compensation. This action, however, confirms the fears of white farmers that they may lose their land.

It is therefore possible for both a Black majority and white minority to claim that they have been relegated to bare life at the same time. If land expropriation continues, it may change the bare habitance of Black farm dwellers to territorially grounded citizenship. On the other hand, white farmers may demand more negotiation on land redistribution in a counter claim, because permissive space is not imposed unilaterally but shaped in ongoing exchange and connected to sovereignty that is as fragile as the negotiated space itself (Cooper-Knock, 2018: 29–30). As the research of Walker (2008) has shown there is always a discrepancy between the symbolic value of land and policy implementation on the ground. What land restitution looks like is "a kaleidoscope of generally messy, always locality-specific, often conflictual and personality-inflected projects" (231).

Multiculturalism as a mechanism to foster a broad consensus among diverse cultural groups to prevent conflict can only succeed where there are core values that the majority of citizens agree with. These core values are usually established through the acceptance of constitutional liberal democracy that creates the space for citizens to exercise cultural rights as long as they do not undermine the core values. In conditions of extreme inequality, social marginalization and land dispossession, such as the case in the South African post-colony, neither rights nor culture protect some citizens from living a bare life in a zone of indistinction. They are not contesting the core values, but rather find them meaningless to change their lives.

Notes

1 [https://www.indexmundi.com/south_africa/demographics_profile.html] (accessed August 23, 2021).
2 The expanded definition includes people who have stopped looking for work.
3 See Mamdani on the Rwanda genocide—"When Victims Become Killers," Princeton, Princeton University Press, 2001.
4 The Department of Rural Development performs particularly poorly—it spent 100% of its budget (R3.6 billion) with land reform as a priority, but only met 37% of its targets 2019/2020 (Merten, 2021). Merten points out the tardiness of the government with the Expropriation Bill that has appeared in front of parliament three times since 2008 and was withdrawn because it was unconstitutional the first time. It was tabled in 2013 and again in 2017 and still has not been passed by parliament.
5 Julius Malema, the leader of the EFF, said the following in parliament: "Van Riebeeck, a first descendent of the Dutch to arrive in the Cape would later lead a full blown colonial genocide, anti-Black land dispossession criminal project, arguing that simply because our people could not produce title deeds, this land, that they have been living in (sic) for more than a thousand years, was not their own" (Hansard, National Assembly, February 27, 2017: 25–26).
6 EFF leader in the Free State, Mandisa Makesini, e.g., asked followers to grab and expropriate 70 farms for the 70 EFF councillors. [https://www.polity.org.za/article/eff-land-grab-threats-in-the-free-state-are-illegal-and-irresponsible-2020-02-11] (accessed May 23, 2021). In 2018, 5 areas in the province of Gauteng were singled out for land grabs [https://businesstech.co.za/news/government/231543/5-areas-in-gauteng-that-are-currently-subject-to-the-effs-land-grabs/] (accessed May 23, 2021).
7 AfriForum, an interest group that mobilizes for the protection of interests of white Afrikaners, makes the following argument: "The South African government's push for expropriation without compensation is founded in racist sentiment and a distortion of history. It is also clear that the so-called hunger for land is largely non-existent—particularly with regard to agricultural land." Also "Expropriation without compensation—a disaster in waiting" (6). The same article makes the argument that most farmland owned by white farmers was acquired by settling on empty land and that land conquest was rare (AfriForum, 2019) [https://afriforum.co.za/afriforum-memorandum_expropriation-without-compensation_a-disaster-in-waiting/] (accessed May 23, 2021).
8 [https://www.washingtonpost.com/politics/2019/05/15/tucker-carlson-those-south-african-white-rights-activists-arent-telling-you-whole-truth/] (accessed September 9, 2020).
9 [https://tfipost.com/2020/07/white-farmers-are-slaughtered-daily-former-south-african-cricketers-slam-lungi-ngidi-over-Black-lives-matter/] (accessed September 8, 2020).
10 James Pogue (2019) "The Myth of White Genocide" *Harpers Magazine* [https://harpers.org/archive/2019/03/the-myth-of-white-genocide-in-south-africa/] (accessed September 19, 2020).
11 [https://pulitzercenter.org/reporting/myth-white-genocide] (accessed September 9, 2020).
12 Black First Land First calls itself a revolutionary socialist, Pan-African movement, with the aim of getting African land back through expropriation, even if it entails violence. It also registered as a political party and has some support.
13 South Africa History Online [https://www.sahistory.org.za/sites/default/files/archive-files/ApOct93.1684.4459.000.049.Oct1993.4.pdf] (accessed May 21, 2021).

14 Stephen Grootes "Kill the Boer" ruling—Malema's Loss is also SA Freedom's Loss" https://www.dailymaverick.co.za/article/2011-09-13-kill-the-boer-judgement-malemas-loss-is-also-sa-freedoms-loss/ (accessed May 21, 2021).
15 [https://www.abc.net.au/news/2021-05-25/trump-wants-pompeo-to-study-killing-of-farmers/10158114] (accessed May 24, 2021).
16 [https://www.dailymaverick.co.za/article/2020-12-09-women-on-farms-need-more-government-assistance-in-fight-against-gbv-report-finds/] (accessed August 23, 2021).

References

AfriForum. "Afriforum Memorandum – Expropriation without compensation – A disaster in waiting." AfriForum.co.za. November 30, 2019. https://afriforum.co.za/afriforum-memorandum_expropriation-without-compensation_a-disaster-in-waiting/. (accessed May 23, 2021).
Agamben, Giorgio. 1998. *Homo Sacer: Sovereign Power and Bare Life*. Stanford: Stanford University Press.
Akinola, Adeoye. 2020. "Farm Attacks, or "White Genocide"? Interrogating the Unresolved Land Question in South Africa." *Accord*, [https://www.accord.org.za/ajcr-issues/farm-attacks-or-white-genocide-interrogating-the-unresolved-land-question-in-south-africa/] (accessed 21 May 2021).
Baines, G. 1998. "The Rainbow Nation? Identity and Nation Building in Post-Apartheid South Africa." *Mots Pluriels* 7: 1–12.
Bonilla, Yarimar. 2017. "Unsettling Sovereignty." *Cultural Anthropology 32* (3): 330–339.
Bradley, William. 2013. "Is There a Post-Multiculturalism?" Working Paper Series, Studies on Multicultural Societies, No 19.
Burger, Johan. 2018. "Violent Crime on Farm and Small Holdings in South Africa." Report for the Institute of Security Studies, September. [https://issafrica.org/research/policy-brief/violent-crime-on-farms-and-smallholdings-in-south-africa] (accessed 24 May 2021).
Calarco, Matthew and Steven DeCaroli. 2007. *Boundary Stones – Giorgio Agamben and the Field of Sovereignty*. Stanford: Stanford University Press.
Claassens, Aninka and Sindiso Mnisi. 2011. "Rural Women Redefining Land Rights in the Context of Living Customary Law." In *Women's Social and Economic Rights*, B. Goldblatt and K. McClean (eds.) Cape Town: Juta, 80–104.
Cooper-Knock, Sarah-Jane. 2018. "Beyond Agamben: Sovereignty, Policing and "Permissive Space" in South Africa, and Beyond." *Theoretical Criminology 22* (1): 22–41.
Crais, Clifton. 2006 "Custom and the Politics of Sovereignty in South Africa." *Journal of Social History 39* (3): 721–740.
De Vos, Pierre. 2013 "Willing Buyer, Willing Seller Works…If you have a Life Time to Wait." *Constitutionally Speaking*, 13 June [https://constitutionallyspeaking.co.za/willing-buyer-willing-seller-works-if-you-have-a-lifetime-to-wait/] (accessed 20 May 2021).
Erlenbusch, Verena. 2013. "The Place of Sovereignty: Mapping Power with Agamben, Butler and Foucault." *Critical Horizons 14* (1): 44–69.
Falkof, Nicky. 2022. *Warrior State – Risk, Anxiety and Moral Panic in South Africa*. Johannesburg: Wits University Press.

Genel, Katia. 2006. "The Question of Biopower: Foucault and Agamben." *Rethinking Marxism* 18 (1): 43–62.

Gouws, Amanda. 2016. "Multiculturalism in South Africa: Dislodging the Binary between Universal Human Rights and Culture/Tradition." In *Gender and Multiculturalism – North/South Perspectives*, A. Gouws and D. Stasiulis (eds.) Scottsville: UKZN Press, 35–55.

Gouws, Amanda. 2021. "Reducing Women to Bare Life: Sexual Violence in South Africa." *Feminist Encounters* 5 (1): 1–12.

Gouws, Amanda and Daiva Stasiulis. 2016. "Gender and Multiculturalism – Dislodging the Binary between Universal Human right and Culture/Tradition: North South Perspectives." In *Gender and Multiculturalism – North/South Perspectives*, A. Gouws and D. Stasiulis (eds.) Scottsville: UKZN Press, 1–13.

Gundogdu, Ayten. 2012. "Potentialities of Human Rights: Agamben and the Narrative of Fated Necessity." *Contemporary Political Theory* 11 (1): 2–22.

Hall, Ruth. 2004. "A Political Economy of Land Reform in South Africa." *Review of African Political Economy* 100: 213–227.

Lemke, Thomas. 2005 ""A Zone of Indistinction" – A Critique of Giorgio Agamben's Concept of Biopolitics." *Outlines* 1: 3–13.

Mamdani, Mahmood. 2001. *When Victims Becomes Killers*. Princeton: Princeton University Press.

Mamdani, Mahmood. 2021. *Neither Settler, Nor Native*. Johannesburg: Wits University Press.

Mbembe, Achille. 2016. *Necropolitics*. Johannesburg: Wits University Press.

McAllister, Patrick. 1996. "Australian Multiculturalism: Lessons for South Africa?" *Indicator SA* 13 (2): 72–78.

McAllister, Patrick. (1997). "Cultural Diversity and Public Policy in Australia and South Africa – the Implications of "Multiculturalism"." *African Sociological Review* 1 (2): 60–78.

Merten, Marianne. 2021. "The Politics of Expropriation without Compensation – When Rhetoric and Reality Clash." *Daily Maverick*, 25 March.

Morgensen, Scott Lauria. 2011. "The Biopolitics of Settler Colonialism: Right Here, Right Now." *Settler Colonial Studies* 1 (1): 52–76.

Morgensen, Scott Lauria. 2012. "Theorising Gender, Sexuality and Settler Colonialism: An Introduction." *Settler Colonial Studies* 2 (2): 2–22.

Pogue, James. 2019. "The Myth of White Genocide." *Harpers Magazine*. [https:// harpers .org /archive /2019 /03 /the -myth -of -white -genocide -in -south -africa/] (accessed September 19, 2020).

Pratt, Geraldine. 2005. "Abandoned Women and Spaces of Exception." *The 2005 Antipode Lecture*. Editorial Board of Antipode, pp 1052–1078. [https://onlinelibrary.wiley.com/ doi/pdf/10.1111/j.0066-4812.2005.00556.x?casa_token=U9PURMWAG1oAAAAA :2oERz1N38hg7levZRF60JHt-61rWRgE0GyMOEZMHRuiyd5oAbJA9Gb75E3g 74i9sGXZsFymw98FMN4Md] (Accessed 20 May 2021).

Reddy, Thiven. 2016. *South Africa, Settler Colonialism and the Failures of Liberal Democracy*. Johannesburg: Wits University Press.

Rifkin, Mark. 2009. "Indigenizing Agamben: Rethinking Sovereignty in Light of the "Peculiar" Status of Native Peoples." *Cultural Critique* 73: 88–124.

Sanchez, Lisa. 2004. "The Global E-Rotic Subject, the Ban and the Prostitute-Free Zone: Sex Work and the Theory of Differential Exclusion." *Environment and Planning D: Society and Space* 22 (6): 861–883.

Savarese, Josephine. 2010. "Doing No Violence to the Sentence Imposed: Racialized Sex Worker Complainants, Racialized Offenders and twhe Feminization of the *Homo Sacer* in Two Sexual Assault Cases." *Canadain Journal of Women and the Law* 22 (2): 365–396.

Sharp, John. 1999. "Culture, Identity and Nation in South Africa." In *Between Unity and Diversity*, Githanjali Maharaj (ed.) Cape Town: David Philip Publisher.

Sonjani, T. B. and H. F. Snyman. 2018. "Making Rural Areas Safer: Potential Benefits of the Rural Safety Plan." *Acta Criminologica: Southern African Journal of Criminology* 31 (4): 84–96.

Stoler, Ann. 2010. *Carnal Knowledge and Imperial Power: Race and the Intimate in Colonial Rule*. Berkeley, CA: University of California Press.

Thobani, Sunera. 2012. "Empire, Bare Life and the Constitution of Whiteness." *Borderlands* 11 (1): 1–29.

Walker, Cheryl. 2008. *Landmarked – Land Claims and Land Restitution in South Africa*. Johannesburg: Jacana.

Whitley, Leila. 2017. "The Disappearance of Race: A Critique of the Use of Agamben in Border and Migration Scholarship." *Borderlands* 16 (1): 1–23.

Wolfe, Patrick. 2006. "Settler Colonialism and the Elimination of the Native." *Journal of Genocide Research* 8 (4): 387–409.

6
LANGUAGE AND MULTICULTURALISM IN THE UNITED STATES

Dan Freeman-Maloy and Raymond Tatalovich

A rose by any other name might, as Shakespeare wrote, smell as sweet, but in politics, one cannot credibly dissociate power from the power to name (Bannerji, 2000). Popular challenges to "the callers of names" (Trudell, 2016) thus find strong footing in social scientific theory and practice. The implications are particularly salient in the discussion of language policy.

"Metaphor," in all cases, "plays an essential role in establishing links between scientific language and the world," as Thomas Kuhn (1993: 539) helped to establish. An example from past legislative debates concerning US civic culture illustrates the point. On February 2, 1993, ten Republican members of the House of Representatives cosponsored a Declaration of Official Languages Act (House Resolution 739). It opened with the statement "America is no longer the melting pot; America is becoming more like a patch quilt" (Tatalovich, 1995: 16). To which of these images does the term *multiculturalism* correspond?

Some have argued that it is a matter of interpretation. This was the position of Arthur Schlesinger, reputed as a critic of multiculturalism. Schlesinger's *The Disuniting of America* (1992) warned against multiculturalist trends that were in his analysis eroding the strength of a unitary American civic culture. The future sponsors of the Official Languages Act were among those calling for a unified national focus on the English language to arrest perceived civic fragmentation. Schlesinger took a different tack but likewise urged a return to the US civic commitment captured by the Latin phrase *E pluribus unum*, or "Out of many, one."

The pedigree of this phrase is well established. For Schlesinger, it spoke, along with the melting pot metaphor, to Frederick Jackson Turner's classical vision of the American Republic as home to a new "composite nationality" (Schlesinger, 1992: 30). But this returns us to the basic question: does

DOI: 10.4324/9781003197485-10

defending this tradition mean opposing multiculturalism or upholding it? Schlesinger was not alone in suggesting that it could mean either (Glazer, 1991). While the pursuit of traditional civic unity could be counterposed to multiculturalism, Schlesinger wrote, it could just as well mean the defense of a pluralism inclusive of multiculturalism's most responsible forms. One lesson from Schlesinger's analysis concerns the substantive importance of turns of phrase. He wrote: "'Paradoxical though it may seem,' Diane Ravitch has well said, 'the United States has a common culture that is multicultural'" (Schlesinger, 1992: 135).

Now, the fact that this terminological debate can get stuck on semantics is precisely the point. Where language is at issue, the terms of discussion are always part of what the discussion is about. If, to borrow a final phrase from Schlesinger, the United States developed as "a society that was inescapably English in language, ideals, and institutions" (14), what this means has been a subject of debate ever since the establishment of the republic. To the question of the civic status of other European languages, from Spanish to German, were added questions of "race" that were also discussed in terms of English or other language categories (notably, "Anglo-Saxon"). US scholars and jurists have for centuries agreed that the meanings beneath the surface of language are matters of crucial political substance.

This chapter reviews the trajectory of US multiculturalism under the legislative and judicial surface. Legislatively, efforts to give the de facto predominance of the English language in US public life a sharpened de jure significance peaked in the immediate aftermath of World War I. In the late 20th century, advocates of Official English returned to this effort with uneven results (Tatalovich, 1995). More recently, the verbal endorsement of Official English by President Donald J Trump seemed to create circumstances propitious for the passage of new federal language legislation (Tremblay, 2021). The failure of the Republican Party to seize this opportunity suggests that this legislative track is, for the foreseeable future, stalled.

Judicially, the relationship between language and voter access remains a subject of heated controversy (Higgins, 2015). This has brought world attention to an old debate about US voting rights, reframed for a new century. Matters of language are at its surface in two principal respects. First, literacy tests worked to circumscribe voter access in certain US jurisdictions following the collapse of Reconstruction (Bryce, 1908). When the US franchise was expanded in the 1960s and 1970s, the legislation expanding voting rights was written in dialogue with this legacy, which continues to define the debate over civic inclusion. Second, language assistance in voting was attached to the Voting Rights Act (VRA) of 1965 by means of a 1975 amendment. At the beginning of this century, Executive Order 13166 attached further language assistance provisions to Title VI of the Civil Rights Act of 1964, which prohibits discrimination on the grounds of race, color and national origin (Tremblay, 2019).

The question of US language policy, however, also strikes deeper, amid an old challenge of what the Rand Corporation now represents as a crisis of "truth decay" (Kakutani, 2018: 13). Following the presidential elections of 2020 and the profound partisan cleavage that marked them, the prospects for multiculturalism in the United States continue to hinge on the debate over contested meanings. "There has been a tendency to decry phrases and phrase-making," wrote James M Beck (1918: vi), amid the campaign for English language unity that marked World War I. This chapter explores how and why the force of language in the United States has kept this tendency in check, maintaining language as a paramount political concern.

Most notably, many observers suggest that beneath the contemporary Republican Party slogan "Stop the Steal" lies a challenge to the US franchise expansion of the 1960s and 1970s (SPLC, 2021). Yet even at their sharpest, proposals to give cultural primacy to white or "legacy Americans"—a 2021 coinage—remain the stuff of linguistic elision. In sum, there is in the United States no official multiculturalism as such. But the debates about which multiplicity of cultures has primacy in US politics have always defined the language of the republic.

Speaking English or Talking American?

Language is one surface expression of the political meanings that shape a social order. A phrase from the single most influential US style guide thus provides a useful point of departure for analysis of the cultural and language politics of the United States. "Do not be tempted by a twenty-dollar word when there is a ten-center handy," the authors propose. "Anglo-Saxon is a livelier tongue than Latin, so use Anglo-Saxon words" (Strunk and White, 1979: 76–77). To unpack these phrases is to get at the core of traditional US language politics.

The United States was established by the Thirteen Colonies that broke away from the First British Empire to found an American Republic. At that stage, more than a century before Frederick Jackson Turner, Britain itself was already home to a kind of "composite nationality." To this day, the concept of British nationality encompasses English, Scottish, Welsh and Irish sub-nationalities. This heritage, whether described as English, British or "Anglo-Saxon," was traditionally imagined as the core of the US *demos*. Twelve of the Thirteen Colonies were, at their point of origin, "settled colonies" of Britain, in the language of English law. The 13th, New York, had previously been Dutch, and its capture was to some extent analogous to the later capture of Canada from France (Hancock, 1937: 9). In its turn, the United States was all but officially shaped as a composite fragment of Europe (Hartz, 1955), pan-European (or "white") in naturalized demography but "inescapably English" in heritage and cultural trajectory.

Strunk and White's injunction for American writers to prefer the "ten-center" to the "twenty-dollar word" should not be taken as hostility to high commerce. Rather, it codifies fidelity to the English fragment from which US cultural leadership emerged. Where Latin was the traditional language of English court and clergy, the English vernacular is a West Germanic language whose mythological links with Saxon antiquity were recast in early modern times as timelessly Anglo-Saxon (Blake, 1996). In the England of the 17th and 18th centuries, the invocation of an Anglo-Saxon past provided a populist platform for supporters of parliamentary authority, who were in recurring competition with the authority of the Crown and the old aristocracy (MacDougall, 1982). In the United States, the abolition of hereditary feudal titles sharpened this anti-Latinizing trend.

On the one hand, the pioneering expert on American English, Noah Webster, sharpened the presumed distinction between the Germanic simplicity of the English vernacular and the Latin pomposity of aristocratic English norms. The most prestigious norms of metropolitan English at the time were those spelled out by Samuel Johnson. Webster (1789: 32) took aim at Johnson directly, deriding his "intolerable composition of Latinity, affected smoothness, scholastic accuracy and roundness of periods." The predominant US English story was that Latinized pretension must go the way of hereditary aristocratic titles. The enduring effects of this linguistic populism can be gauged by a comparison between the language register of a British conservative politician like Boris Johnson and that of a conservative US politician like Donald J Trump—or, for that matter, Joseph R Biden.

Johnson speaks a dialect that is distinctively Etonian or "posh." Even its populism is expressed with a sort of aristocratic flair. The British Broadcasting Corporation (BBC) identified this aristocratic populism at its plainest in the language of the traditionalist English Tory Jacob Rees-Mogg. "I'm a man of the people; *Vox populi, vox Dei*," Rees-Mogg winked (BBC, 2011). It would be unthinkable for a US populist to resort in this way to Latin phraseology. The US *Vox populi*, or "voice of the people," always affects a working-class aesthetic. In this respect, the paradox of a Donald J Trump was anticipated nearly two centuries ago by Alexis de Tocqueville. "No European noble is more exclusive in his pleasures" than the American businessman, wrote de Tocqueville, "or more jealous of the smallest advantages which his privileged position confers upon him." But surrounding this exclusivity is a levelling aesthetic: "His dress is plain, his demeanor unassuming" (de Tocqueville, 1841: 192)

On the other hand, while distancing American English from the English of England, Webster urged American language unity as a practical political imperative. Concerning the surface of civic life, Webster called attention to "the influence which a uniformity in speech may have on national attachments." Concerning deeper cognition, he insisted upon "the connection between language and logic." To forge a community cohesive in purpose and thought was, in Webster's view, to shape its terms of expression. As a cohesive nation, the United States would need to "destroy the differences of dialect which our ancestors brought from their native countries." And as an independent nation, it would need to look to "a future separation of the American tongue from the English" (ibid.: 18–22). It is through the articulation of these basic tensions that US language debates have since evolved.

Legislative efforts to give de jure status to the de facto predominance of English in the United States peaked after World War I. Near to the core of US cultural leadership, two small splits at that moment can usefully be identified. From the patrician far right of the northeastern United States, Madison Grant—"intellectually the most important nativist" of the century (Higham, 1983: 155)—restated the link between US language populism and the old commercial challenge to nobility. He rejected both (Grant, 1921: 6). For Grant, the simplification of American English signaled a slippage of class and racial standards. Officials of some influence agreed that English language assimilation could only go so far when dealing with diverse European immigrants, some of whom George Creel, of the US Committee on Public Information, derided as "so much slag in the melting-pot" (Higham, 1983: 277).

From an opposing angle, however, the concept not only of Anglo-Saxon but even of *English* heritage was challenged as regressively narrow. The plainest wrinkle in the language of American Anglo-Saxonism was the Irish, against whom metropolitan Anglo-Saxonism had traditionally been articulated—but who were close to the core of US language unity. The terms of inclusion were relative: "An Irishman might be described as a lazy, dirty Celt when he landed in New York," records Reginald Horsman (1981: 4), "but if his children settled in California they might well be praised as part of the vanguard of the energetic Anglo-Saxon people poised for the plunge into Asia." After World War I, some argued that US language unity was better articulated in a language that could strike native roots in American soil.

The legislative push toward what would later be known as Official English was in the first instance anticipated by Nebraska. During World War I, federal and state officials, in close coordination with business and civic groups, pushed for English-language assimilation in the name of the Americanization that wartime unity was said to require. In 1919, the Republican majority in the Nebraska state senate passed three measures to give English-language predominance de jure expression. First, Nebraska ended the requirement that county board proceedings and land sales by county treasurers be published in German, Swedish and Czech (Bohemian) as well as in English. Second, it required that all public meetings be held in English. And third, it circumscribed the teaching of any language other than English to any students who failed to meet standards of English proficiency, in order to break perceived patterns of cultural insularity among non-anglophone immigrants (Tatalovich, 1995: 34–35).

Then, in 1923, the Illinois state senate passed its own legislation—signaling a break with the American English mainstream and restating a traditional tension within it. The preamble to the legislation invoked the need for the United States "to weld the racial units into a solid American nation in the sense that England, France and Germany are nations." Significantly, the language of the senate defined this position not in opposition to non-anglophone immigrants, but rather in opposition to what it represented as the local fragment of English Toryism. Senator Rodney B Swift (R-Lake Co.) proposed that in London, he had discovered that "I didn't speak the English language. We do talk the American language, … a language that we call the language of this continent, of the Western hemisphere." Illinois thus legislated to establish "American" rather than English as the state's official language.

Rarely have the linguistic presuppositions of settler "nativism" been spelled out as plainly as they were by Congressman Washington J McCormick (R-Mont.), who wanted the federal government to follow Illinois's lead. McCormick hoped that the House of Representatives could join in insisting upon the need for a civic culture that *talked American*. His language evokes memories of the Boston Tea Party, a protest against the British Crown by Americans some of whom famously wore Indigenous-themed clothing. "Let our writers drop their top-coats, spats, and swagger-sticks," McCormick proposed to the House, "and assume occasionally their buckskin, moccasins, and tomahawks." With a de jure commitment to talking American, McCormick declared, the US government could "supplement the political emancipation of '76 by the mental emancipation of '23" (Tatalovich, 1995: 65–70).

Illinois proved distinctive, not to say eccentric, in its proposal for a declaration of linguistic independence. To date, however, 32 states have passed operative legislation designating English as their official language. In contradistinction to this trend, only three states, Oregon (1989), Rhode Island (1992) and Washington (1989), have passed "English Plus" legislation, with subsidiary recognition of minority language rights. McCormick's proposal went nowhere; and federal efforts in the intervening century to establish English as an official language have failed, suggesting the impracticability of new federal legislation in this area (Tremblay, 2021). But this only goes so far in determining the future prospects for American multiculturalism as such. Debate continues to rage under the surface.

"A Common Culture That Is Multicultural"

What Gabriel Almond and Sidney Verba (1963) described as the "civic culture" of the United States emphasizes synthesis over antithesis, favoring the ironing of wrinkles over their abstract interrogation. The pursuit of consensus is systemic. In thinking through the local politics of multiculturalism, therefore, it is important to recall that even narrow language categories like *English* or *Anglo-Saxon* were never fleshed out with monocultural meanings.

Nothing, argued the classical advocates of English or Anglo-Saxon leadership, was more responsibly pluralistic than what came to be known as the melting pot. This sentiment was particularly strong in the early decades after the Civil War of 1861–1865. As John Higham wrote in his seminal study *Strangers in the Land* (1983: 33), "Anglo-Saxon and cosmopolitan nationalisms merged in a happy belief that the Anglo-Saxon has a marvelous capacity for assimilating kindred races, absorbing their valuable qualities, yet remaining basically unchanged." By "kindred" was meant all whom Congress juridically defined as "free white persons" (Jacobson, 1999). Higham notes that Anglo-Saxonism in its narrowest form was strongest in the northeastern United States. Farther west, the bounds of composite European identity were more inclusively defined against an East Asian foil. To the south, the influence and heritage of the plantation economy meanwhile riveted attention on the African/European color dichotomy, the effects of which radiated outwards and influenced all regional subcultures.

Crucially, this color dichotomy in Black and white was a classical object of US linguistic elision. Thus, in the drafting of the US Constitution of 1787, the terms slave and slavery were side-stepped. Article I, enumerating the population for purposes of representation in Congress, counts all "free persons" and "three-fifths of *other persons*," the reference to enslaved Africans hovering just between the implicit and the explicit (Wilentz, 2018). In turn, the first naturalization legislation passed by Congress defined the core of the US *demos* as comprising "free white persons," beginning more than a century of judicial confusion concerning the term "white"—including court debates over East Asian skin tone (Jacobson, 1999). Outside of courtrooms, language categories like Anglo-Saxon, Teutonic and Indo-European or Aryan continued to stand in for race in the most prestigious doctrines (Poliakov, 1974).

In a comparative volume, it bears mentioning that the United States did not propound these doctrines alone. The African/European color dichotomy was never as central to the political life of British colonies of settlement in Loyalist North America and Australasia as it was in the United States. In Canada, the surface language of Anglo-Saxonism was classically directed against French-Canadians, and early intellectual references to "race" problems were as likely as not to relate to what in the US were ethnic tensions internal to whiteness. In the early 20th century, however, the New York precedent partly repeated itself when Britain took hold of formerly Dutch colonies in South Africa. John Buchan, a prominent British theorist of multiculturalism and future Governor-General of Canada (Henshaw, 2007), took the occasion to sharpen the distinction between differences of ethnicity and differences of race.

The historian Peter Henshaw (2007) is not alone in identifying Buchan as a symbol of what he calls "the British imperial origins of Canadian multiculturalism." Immigrants to Canada are today still made to study a citizenship guide which features a portrait of Buchan "in Blood (Kainai First Nation) headdress" under the heading "Unity in Diversity" (Citizenship and Immigration Canada, 2021: 11). This is a legacy of Buchan's openly racialistic version of *E pluribus unum*, which built outward from the British Empire's cultural union between English and Scottish.

Just as Scottish, Welsh and Ulster sub-nationalities became British within a framework of overall English predominance, so too, Buchan argued, could other Europeans be organized around a composite British core. After the British victory over the Boers in the South African War of 1899–1902, Buchan made one of the most detailed arguments on record for a composite white supremacy. Buchan was first and foremost a British race patriot: "The last word in all matters," he wrote in his *Studies of the Reconstruction* (1908: 338), "must rest with us—that is, with the people of British blood and British sympathies." But he proposed an ecumenical white supremacy with the following metaphor: "An two men ride of a horse, one must ride behind." Buchan insisted that Boer ride behind Briton, but also that they cooperate the better to treat Black South African society as the brute (Magubane, 1996).

The basic principle was plain: "it is the white man's interests which must decide" (Buchan, 1908: 294). But so too was the commitment to linguistic elision. Buchan explained:

> The root distinction between types of franchise lies in the method employed to exclude an undesirable class, whether a direct one, by disqualifying in so many words, or an indirect, by setting one standard of qualification for all, to which, as a matter of fact, the undesirable class cannot attain.
>
> *(Buchan: 339–340, 1908)*

Buchan favored the use of indirect language in order to establish the vaguest and so most durable possible color-bar franchise.

In the United States, the *federal* government had by this time rejected linguistic elision of the "other persons" type, gone to war with the South, and seen slavery abolished. After the Civil War, Congress passed three constitutional amendments designed to safeguard the rights of emancipated slaves from the formerly slave-holding states. The 13th amendment abolished forced labor in the absence of criminal conviction. The 14th prohibited states from denying "to any person within its jurisdiction the equal protection of the laws," thus banning state discrimination. And the 15th extended the franchise regardless of race. But by the turn of the 20th century, literacy tests had become the instrument of a new elision.

From the northeastern United States, advocates of a more restrictive immigration policy lobbied for literacy tests to filter out European immigrants of suspect ethnicity (Tatalovich, 1995: 64). But only between the world wars did the federal government follow this program for discriminating among

European ethnicities as a matter of law. In 1897, President Grover Cleveland vetoed an immigrant literacy test with which Congress aimed to filter Euro-ethnics (Higham, 1983: 105). At the state level, however, discriminatory language tests thrived.

This returns us to the former Confederacy. For 11 years following the Civil War, an attempt at Reconstruction moved in the direction of fulfilling the promise of emancipation (Du Bois, 1992). The establishment of the Freedman's Bureaus was one of the most conspicuous features of this attempt to reconfigure post-slavery social and political life. But ultimately, the withdrawal of federal troops from the South following the presidential election of 1876 cleared the way for the return of an official policy of white primacy. The imposition of "Jim Crow" racial segregation was brazen. The resonant fact (SPLC, 2021) is that the constitutional amendments of the Reconstruction era endured on paper but were not enforced.

James Bryce, British ambassador to the United States and president of the American Political Science Association (APSA), singled out the state of Mississippi for the means by which it crafted a color-bar franchise that dare not speak its name. This was done with a provision that left a prospective voter's eligibility to the discretion of state officials. Officials were empowered to interpret as a condition of voting a citizen's capacity "to read any section of the Constitution or be able to understand the same when read to him, or give a reasonable interpretation thereof." Elasticity of meaning provided the necessary room for interpretation. Bryce (1908: 485) explained that the point was "to furnish a peaceful method of excluding illiterate negroes and including illiterate whites: a result which has been in fact attained." The southern United States model of white-power politics was the proximate inspiration for Buchan's South African *Studies in the Reconstruction*.

In turn, the US franchise expansion of the 1960s and 1970s was legislated in dialogue with this legacy: congressional legislation was crafted to foreclose the interpretative mischief to which lax enforcement mechanisms had given rise. The results have been described as a Second Reconstruction, even a "second founding" of the union (Foner, 2019). Key pieces of the new legislative architecture included the Civil Rights Acts of 1964, the Voting Rights Act of 1965 and the Fair Housing Act of 1968. In further recognition of the importance of language to voter access, a 1975 amendment to the Voting Rights Act prohibited any state whose electorate comprised a certain percentage (5%) of voters with Limited English Proficiency (LEP) "from providing English-Only 'voting material' in any election." Today, the debate is once more structured around problems of compliance and enforcement (Higgins, 2015).

Problems of ethnic discrimination in the United States have, since the mid-20th century, given way to an increasingly flattened whiteness captured by the nebulous term "Caucasian" (Jacobson, 1999). The intra-European distinction between Anglo-Saxon and other is no longer a salient divide. Yet while the

African/European color dichotomy is not as such linguistic, its articulation has been bound up with language debates at their most heated.

Contestation concerning language differences *as such* meanwhile finds its most direct legislative and judicial expression in the interplay between state-level recognition of English predominance, calls for federal legislation to the same end, and the judiciability of LEP voters' claims. While there has been conspicuous focus on Indigenous, East Asian and other linguistic minorities, the public debate concerning Spanish speakers looms largest. It underscores the challenge of terminological complexity. Although European hispanophones were among those whom earlier restrictionists represented as "slag in the melting pot," US courts from the outset classed hispanophone Europeans as "free white persons." Hemispheric migration, however, complicated matters, with early US immigration officials distinguishing between a "Spanish race" of European extraction and a "Mexican race" of mixed European and Indigenous descent. Prohibitions on discrimination by national origin have since upended these terms of reference. In practice, however, "Hispanic" remains an ambiguous cultural marker, hovering between language, ethnicity and race, depending on location and circumstance (Foley, 2004).

In the 21st century, "race" is the most judiciable marker of difference in the United States (Tofighbakhsh, 2020), and the debate over language policy is most heated where contending allegations of racism arise (Tatalovich, 1995). Social scientists should not, however, confuse what is judiciable with what is conceptually precise. In the final analysis, the point is not so much that language can be a proxy for race, but that "race," as a will-to-power sleight of hand, was elaborated as a politico-literary proxy for language—the Latin versus the Teutonic, the Anglo-Saxon within the Indo-European, etc.—through a series of physiological stories that predated credible physiological study and were then debunked by it (Poliakov, 1974; Gould, 1996). The debates about language, race and civic inclusion which history has bequeathed us will evolve along established trajectories for the foreseeable future. The challenge for scholarship is to lend perspective and precision to terms of reference whose full meanings are never self-evident.

Conclusion: Thin Reeds and Uncertain Prospects

The "power in words," to borrow the title of a volume concerning the public leadership of Barack Obama (Berry and Gottheimer, 2010), is universally understood to shape US politics. Polling data shows that large majorities of Americans support the predominance of English as the language of US public life. Yet phrases like Donald Trump's "Stop the Steal" point to profound disagreements beneath simple-sounding English phraseology.

While there is wide support for the English language as a normative marker of American identity—a support which extends across the most conspicuous

US demographic divides (Citrin et al., 1994)—calls for an "English Only" policy face three main official obstacles. First, where the franchise is concerned, the Voting Rights Act of 1965 expressly prohibits states from circumscribing voting rights based on voters' "inability to read, write, understand, or interpret any matter in the English language." The 1975 amendment mandating language assistance for LEP voters additionally constrains the implementation of states' Official English policies.

Second, executive action since the Carter administration has extended the interpretation of Title VI of the Civil Rights Act of 1964, which prohibits discrimination on the grounds of race, color and national origin, to include minority language access to Title VI information. President Bill Clinton's Executive Order 13166 of August 11, 2000 (Tremblay, 2019: 192–194) built on this precedent, interpreting Title IV as including a duty "to improve access to federally conducted and federally assisted programs and activities for persons who, as a result of national origin, are limited in their English proficiency."

While the predominance of English in US civic culture is uncontested, a third countervailing pressure is federal spending on bilingual education. The Elementary and Secondary Education Act of 1965 (ESEA) provided federal funds to educational agencies in low-income areas. During congressional hearings in 1967–1968 to reauthorize this program, Senator Ralph Yarborough (D-Tex) added an amendment designed to reduce the gap in levels of educational achievement between Spanish-speaking and other majority and minority students. It was enacted as the Bilingual Education Act of 1968 (BEA) and broadened the ESEA's definition of students with special needs to include "the large numbers of children of limited English-speaking ability in the United States." Since then, the BEA was reauthorized in 1974, 1978, 1984, 1988 and 1994 but failed to be reauthorized from 1997–2001 (Tremblay, 2019: 201). Under newly elected President George W Bush, the BEA was absorbed and renamed the English Language Acquisition, Language Enhancement and Academic Achievement Act of 2002 as one provision of the No Child Left Behind Act (NCLB) of that year. Now the emphasis was on English acquisition rather than teaching a child in their native tongue while transitioning to English.

As pillars of linguistic multiculturalism go, these are thin reeds. In the shaping of US civic culture, official educational policies have always been supplemented by "other channels of political socialization," and the intergenerational "development of a structure of voluntary associations" (Almond and Verba, 1963: 502) has contributed to the social and cultural foundations of the US polity even when governmental involvement has fallen short of the civic interventionism of early 20h-century Americanization campaigns. One open question is how and to what extent associational diversity will evolve in the years ahead. Prior to World War I, there was more language diversity in US civic life: Americanization campaigns then focused on the German-language press as a danger to civic unity and pushed the main European ethnic groups into increasingly English-only civic exchange. But as early as the 1920s, Spanish-language radio began to establish its North American presence, buoyed by the regional proximity of Mexico and Puerto Rico (Paxman, 2018). Today, the most associationally robust language communities in the United States other than anglophone ones are those that speak Spanish.

In any case, it is mainly in the English language that US debates about cultural diversity are conducted. In an educational report whose release coincided with the "Stop the Steal" challenge to the 2020 presidential election result, the outgoing Trump administration urged new Americanization campaigns to address what the President (Trump, 2020) described as a critique culture of "toxic propaganda, ideological poison that, if not removed, will dissolve the civic bonds that tie us together." Anticipating the establishment of a new media platform, Truth Social, the *1776 Report* argued that founding US documents should be seen not as objects of interrogation but as the source of "claims that are true for all time" (Arnn et al., 2021: 31). This speaks to one controversial but powerful approach to US civic life.

The foil against which the *1776 Report* was presented is also contested. The foil is not linguistic fragmentation as such but race-focused critique in the English language. President Trump and his advisory team took aim in particular at the *New York Times*'s 1619 Project. This project most substantively alleges that the American Revolution was motivated by a defense of slavery, a historical position often associated with leftist critique. 1776 marked the declaration of US independence from Britain, but left critics marshal considerable evidence to argue that one cannot "supplement the political emancipation of '76," in Washington McCormick's phrasing, because it was not emancipation in the first place (Horne, 2014).

As a hook for this debate, the year 1619 is mainly symbolic; but it has formed a conspicuous part of the Canadian view of the US educational imagination. The reference is to the arrival of enslaved Africans in the English colony of Jamestown, in what became Virginia. In the days when normative whiteness openly framed English-Canadian classroom material, hostility to the presence of people of African descent (Asaka, 2017) latched onto the memory of 1619 in Canada. A 1968 Canadian textbook read: "What a lot of trouble that first ship that carried slaves to Jamestown in 1619 brought with it!" (McDiarmid and Pratt, 1971: 75). Educators in the 1619 Project mold aim to center Black political history as neither vice or sidebar, but as an elemental feature of North American life in its totality.

The details of this debate are for another place. Suffice it here to underline how confusions can arise when debates are conducted in the language of scholarly inquiry and of public mobilization at one and the same time. Words spoken at one language register can have different meanings at another. This is especially challenging for analysts of contending claims concerning the integrity of the 2020 presidential elections and the electoral contests to come. Once again, where cultural inclusivity is concerned, some layered meanings result from the consensual tenor of American political language and the value it places upon synthesis.

Most conspicuously, a language of opposition to racism is universal within the American cultural mainstream. So, when even traditional voices of the US civic culture contended that Donald Trump had "overtly declared himself the candidate of white America" (Baker, 2020), the *1776 Project* rebuttal was that it was affirmative action advocates on the left who are discriminatory, having "revers[ed] the promise of color-blind civil rights" (Arnn, Swain, and Spalding, 2021: 15). This reverse racism charge was neatly anticipated by Buchan. "If your opponent has a sword," Buchan (1906: 171) taught, "it is wiser to annex if for your own use than to destroy it." The transformation of discussions of "white supremacy" into discussions of "woke supremacy" shows nothing but the fungibility of political surface language (Baltimore, 2021). Too often, however, it is power rather than conceptual rigor that defines the language of US politics.

The implications are global as well as domestic, inasmuch as the United States is the undisputed center of global English as a medium of verbal exchange. Comparative volumes like this one offer valuable occasions to consider where that leaves us. Multicultural roses of one and another kind are as flourishing in one context as in the next. But perspective and precision are imperative if we hope to work through the terms with which their social substance is defined.

References

Almond, Gabriel A. and Sidney Verba. 1963. *The Civic Culture: Political Attitudes and Democracy in Five Nations*. Princeton, NJ: Princeton University Press.
Arnn, Larry P., Carol Swain, and Matthew Spalding. 2021. *The 1776 Report: The President's Advisory 1776 Commission*. Washington, DC: President's Advisory 1776 Commission.
Asaka, Ikuko. 2017. *Tropical Freedom: Climate, Settler Colonialism, and Black Exclusion in the Age of Emancipation*. Durham, NC: Duke University Press.
Baker, Peter. 2020. (September 6). "More Than Ever, Trump Casts Himself as the Defender of White America." *New York Times*.
Baltimore, Thad. 2021. (November 23). "White America's Latest Fear Mongering Code Language: CRT and Wokeness." *Black Agenda Report*.
Bannerji, Himani. 2000. *The Dark Side of the Nation: Essays on Multiculturalism, Nationalism and Gender*. Toronto: Canadian Scholars' Press Inc.
Beck, James M. 1918. *The Reckoning*. New York: G.P. Putnam's Sons.
Berry, Mary Frances and Josh Ottheimer. *Power in Words: The Story Behind Barack Obama's Speeches, from the State House to the White House*. Boston, MA: Beacon Press.
Blake, N.F. 1996. *A History of the English Language*. New York: New York University Press.

British Broadcasting Corporation (BBC). 2011. "Jacob Rees-Mogg MP – Posh and Posher: Why Public School Boys Run Britain." YouTube short by BBC Two, January 24, 2011.
Bryce, James. 1908. *The American Commonwealth, Vol. I.* New York: The Macmillan Company.
Buchan, John. 1906. *A Lodge in the Wilderness.* London: Thomas Nelson and Sons.
Buchan, John. 1908. *The African Colony: Studies in the Reconstruction.* Edinburgh: William Blackwood and Sons.
Citizenship and Immigration Canada. 2021. *Discover Canada: The Rights and Responsibilities of Citizenship.* Ottawa: Her Majesty the Queen in Right of Canada, represented by the Minister of Citizenship and Immigration Canada <https://www.canada.ca/content/dam/ircc/migration/ircc/english/pdf/pub/discover.pdf>.
Citrin, Jack, Ernst B. Haas, Christopher Muste and Beth Reingold. 1994. "Is American Nationalism Changing? Implications for Foreign Policy." *International Studies Quarterly 38* (1): 1–31.
De Tocqueville, Alexis, translated by John C. Spencer. 1841. *Democracy in America, Vol I.* New York: J & H. G. Langley.
Du Bois, W.E.B. 1992. *Black Reconstruction in America, 1860–1880.* New York: The Free Press.
Foley, Neil. 2004. "Straddling the Color Line: The Legal Construction of Hispanic Identity in Texas." In *Not Just Black and White: Historical and Contemporary Perspectives on Immigration, Race, and Ethnicity in the United States,* Nancy Foner and George M. Fredrickson (eds.) New York: Russell Sage Foundation, 341–357.
Foner, Eric. 2019. *The Second Founding: How the Civil War and Reconstruction Made the Constitution.* New York: W.W. Norton and Company, Inc.
Glazer, Nathan. 1991. "In Defense of Multiculturalism." *The New Republic 205*: 18–20.
Gould, Stephen Jay. 1996. *The Mismeasure of Man.* New York: W.W. Norton & Co.
Grant, Madison. 1921. *The Passing of the Great Race.* New York: Charles Scribner's Sons.
Hartz, Louis. 1955. *The Liberal Tradition in America.* New York: Harcourt, Brace and World.
Hancock, W.K. 1937. *Survey of British Commonwealth Affairs, Vol. I.* London: Oxford University Press.
Henshaw, Peter. 2007. "John Buchan and the British Imperial Origins of Canadian Multiculturalism." In *Canadas of the Mind: The Making of Unmaking of Canadian Nationalism in the Twentieth Century,* Norman Hillmer and Adam Chapnik (eds.) Montreal: McGill-Queen's University Press, 191–213.
Higgins, Matthew. 2015. "Language Accommodations and Section 203 of the Voting Rights Act: Reporting Requirements as a Potential Solution to the Compliance Gap." *Stanford Law Review 67* (4): 917–960.
Higham, John. 1983. *Strangers in the Land: Patterns of American Nativism, 1860–1925.* London: Rutgers University Press.
Horne, Gerald. 2014. *The Counter-Revolution of 1776: Slave Resistance and the Origins of the United States of America.* New York: New York University Press.
Horsman, Reginald. 1981. *Race and Manifest Destiny: The Origins of American Racial Anglo-Saxonism.* Cambridge, MA: Harvard University Press.
Jacobson, Matthew Frye. 1999. *Whiteness of a Different Color: European Immigrants and the Alchemy of Race.* Cambridge, MA: Harvard University Press.
Kakutani, Michiko. 2018. *The Death of Truth.* New York: Tim Duggan Books.

Kuhn, Thomas S. 1993. "Metaphor in Science." In *Metaphor and Thought*, Andrew Ortony (eds.) Cambridge: Cambridge University Press, 533–542.

MacDougall, Hugh A. 1982. *Racial Myth in English History: Trojans, Teutons, and Anglo-Saxons*. Hanover, NH: University Press of New England.

Magubane, Bernard M. 1996. *The Making of a Racist State: British Imperialism and the Union of South Africa, 1875–1910*. Asmara, Eritrea and Trenton, NJ: Africa World Press.

McDiarmid, Garnet and David Pratt. 1971. *Teaching Prejudice: A Content Analysis of Social Studies Textbooks Authorized for Use in Ontario*. Toronto: Ontario Institute for the Studies in Education for the Ontario Human Rights Commission.

Paredes, Mari Castañeda. 2003. "The Transformation of Spanish-Language Radio in the U.S." *Journal of Radio Studies 10* (1): 5–16.

Paxman, Andrew. 2018. "The Rise of US Spanish-Language Radio From "Dead Airtime" to Consolidated Ownership." *Journalism History 44* (3): 174–186.

Poliakov, Léon. 1974. *The Aryan Myth: A History of Racist and Nationalist Ideas in Europe*, translated by Edmund Howard. London: Chatto Heinemann.

Schlesinger, Arthur. 1992. *The Disuniting of America*. New York: W.W. Norton & Company.

Southern Poverty Law Center (SPLC) 2021. *Overcoming the Unprecedented: Southern Voters' Battle Against Voter Suppression, Intimidation, and a Virus*. Montgomery: SPLC.

Strunk, William Jr. and E.B. White. 1979. *The Elements of Style*. New York: Macmillan Publishing Co. Inc.

Tatalovich, Raymond. 1995. *Nativism Reborn? The Official English Language Movement and the American States*. Lexington, KY: University Press of Kentucky.

Tofighbakhsh, Sara. 2020. "Racial Gerrymandering After Rucho v. Common Cause." *Columbia Law Review 120* (7): 1885–1928.

Tremblay, Arjun. 2019. *Diversity in Decline? The Rise of the Political Right and the Fate of Multiculturalism*. Cham, Switzerland: Palgrave Macmillan/Springer Nature.

Tremblay, Arjun. 2021. "Are There "Sources of Resilience" When the Separation of Powers Breaks Down?" *Constitutional Forum 30*: 25–36.

Trudell, John. 2016. "We Are the Halluci Nation." In *The Halluci Nation*, Track 1. Toronto: Radicalized Records.

Trump, Donald J. 2020 (September 17). "Remarks by President Trump at the White House Conference on American History." White House Press Releases and Documents.

Webster, Noah. 1789. *Dissertations on the English Language*. Boston, MA: Isaiah Thomas and Company.

Wilentz, Sean. 2018. *No Property in Man*. Cambridge, MA: Harvard University Press.

Wilkinson, Kenton T. 2016. *Spanishw-Language Television in the United States: Fifty Years of Development*. New York: Routledge.

7
FRAMING DIVERSITIES

European Approaches to Minorities within Minorities

Dolores Morondo Taramundi

Introduction

Cultural diversity has grown in importance as a topic of study within the field of human rights. To be sure, some form of acknowledgement and protection of cultural diversity was enshrined in the 1948 Universal Declaration of Human Rights as part of the right to participate freely in cultural life (Article 27), and so to was the right to enjoy this right without discrimination (Article 2). However, minority rights as such were excluded from the Declaration (UN General Assembly 1948) and came to occupy a separate, self-contained place in human rights literature and debates. Beyond antidiscrimination issues, mainstream human rights scholarship paid little attention to "minority group" status; the convergence of debates has been burdened with difficulties related to the idea of group entitlement under human rights law.

Recent decades have seen an increasing interest in ethno-cultural diversity from a human rights perspective (Pentassuglia, 2014). This interest has brought to the forefront debates on the potential conflict between minority cultural and social norms and practices on the one hand, and human rights standards, on the other. One potential conflict concerns cases described as minorities within minorities. These cases typically have two main features. They involve a minority group whose power to apply a traditional rule or practice has been recognized by the state with a view to preserve the self-autonomy and cultural specificity of the group. And they also involve a member of the minority group who considers that such a rule or practice violates individual rights recognized by the state, as preference is accorded to the rights of the group over the person's individual entitlement.

During the 1990s and 2000s, a discussion on the tensions between minority rights and the protection of the human rights of groups and individuals identified as minorities within minorities (or internal minorities) developed and took hold in the United States and in Canada. Concern over a potential conflict between these two rights' imperatives was first raised by Leslie Green (1995) but the debate really took off when Susan Moller Okin (1997, 1998) pointed to the potential inadvertent effects of multicultural policies on maintaining women's subordinated status within cultural minority groups. By the mid-2000s, it was widely accepted that there was indeed a conflict between accommodating cultural differences and protecting historically disadvantaged groups within cultural minorities, with focus largely on protecting women's rights within minority groups (Eisenberg and Spinner-Halev, 2004). To be absolutely clear, the growing literature on minorities within minorities did not specifically take issue with the principles of multiculturalism itself, but rather it articulated a concern of who does and should carry the costs of multicultural arrangements (Phillips, 2007); this concern was called "the paradox of multicultural vulnerability" (Shachar, 2000). By the end of the 2000s, the discussion revolved around what could be called hard choices. That is to say, cases concerning minorities within minorities were largely conceived of as involving a clash between two incommensurable or conflicting rights: the collective right to culture vs the individual right to freedom or equality. Any resolution to this seemingly intractable situation consisted in either considering the minority within a minorities' right to exit or proposing that the minority itself leave the rights framework altogether in order to embrace forms of "negotiation" or political processes that would lead to joint forms of governance and some protection for vulnerable internal groups (Morondo Taramundi, 2018).

Compared to what has occurred in the United States or Canada, Europe—and especially continental Europe—has yet to witness a fully engaged discussion on minorities within minorities. This does not mean, however, that the delicate situation of individuals who qualify as members of minorities within minorities in other places is completely unknown to Europeans, nor does it mean that minorities within minorities' access to rights and their opportunities are not being discussed in Europe. But it is critically important to point out that these discussions have emerged in far different contexts and that they have been framed quite differently.

Accordingly, this chapter's main aim is to highlight some of the key issues and concerns emerging from the discussion on minorities within minorities in Europe, and to assess their frames of reference. Some of the issues relating to minorities within minorities in Europe are not so different than those being discussed in North America. For example, there are issues related to the treatment of second or subsequent wives involved in polygynous marriages in migrant communities in France and the UK. There are also issues related to the application of Islamic rules to marriage and inheritance under private international law, to homosexual persons employed by religious associations or churches and to children in Roma communities and in religious families. These cases have generally been studied either in relation either to the domestic law of European states or from a comparative perspective in relation to the solutions offered by private international law and domestic accommodation mechanisms in other countries (Foblets, Gaudreault-DesBiens and Dundes Renteln, 2010). The history and the individual peculiarities of different European countries' dealings with cultural diversity and minority groups are far too heterogeneous to be fully addressed in this chapter. It is for this reason that I have decided here to focus on the far more manageable discussion on diversity at the European supranational level. As this chapter will show, both the Council of Europe (CoE) and the European Union (EU) have dealt with cultural diversity in their specific spheres of action for a long time. Although their contributions have been less studied than domestic laws and policies, both have accumulated considerable experience in the frames of reference of European multiculturalism and the related issue of minorities within minorities.

As a point of clarification before proceeding, the term "cultural diversity," while holding a very important place in the CoE's and the EU's political and policy rhetoric, has been used to serve different functions and has been deployed to serve different political goals. It has been noted (Kraus, 2006) that both supranational European institutions and European national states usually celebrate cultural diversity in abstract terms and in different ways across policy fields. The ways in which "cultural diversity" has been used has expanded since the 1970s (Calligaro, 2014). In Europe, the term "cultural diversity" was initially used to describe the diversity among the cultures of the CoE's member states (Council of Europe, 1954), but its usage gradually changed to refer to the different subnational cultures in the EU member states (Council of Europe, 2005).[1] From the 2000s, "cultural diversity" has also come to be used in reference to subnational and transnational issues related to the governance of the European multicultural societies that have resulted from the dual trends of migration and globalization (Council of Europe, 2015). Consequently, "cultural diversity" has now come to be associated with a range of different policy instruments and concepts, such as European cultural heritage, intercultural dialogue, migration governance, integration and social cohesion and equality and human rights protection.

In what follows I will firstly dissect the different approaches to and conceptions of "cultural diversity" that have influenced the debate on multiculturalism in Europe. The subsequent sections will focus on the analysis of three different frameworks that European supranational institutions have adopted in their response to multicultural challenges. In so doing, this chapter focuses specifically on how minorities within minorities situations are being treated under these frameworks.

The Multicultural Debate in Europe

Approaches to minorities within minorities in Europe have mainly been determined by how relevant actors have understood and treated cultural diversity and multiculturalism.

For example, the European Commission (EC) defines multiculturalism as

> A policy that endorses the principle of cultural diversity and supports the right of different cultural and ethnic groups to retain distinctive cultural identities ensuring their equitable access to society, encompassing constitutional principles and commonly shared values prevailing in the society.
> *(European Commission N.B.)*

And yet, since 2010, several political leaders of important EU member states have considered that multiculturalism had failed[2] in Europe. This disjuncture raises a key question: are the EC and European leaders critical of multiculturalism referring to the same thing? After all, Europe has significant cultural diversity, more so if its relatively reduced geographical space is taken into account. One can hardly travel a couple of hundred miles (and in some latitudes, not even that) without observing changes in languages, religious affiliations, legal culture, gastronomy and political histories and allegiances. Furthermore, European states have been known to fiercely defend their cultural differences and even efforts to build a European identity have had to emphasize common values which are deemed to be universal, since references to common ethno-cultural traits were met with considerable resistance (Calligaro, 2014).[3]

The paradox of clinging to European ethno-cultural diversity while condemning multiculturalism must be assessed in relation to two variables: first, the different meanings that the expression "cultural diversity" has acquired in Europe; second, the different policy frameworks that have been applied to various "cultural difference" questions. The particular combinations of these variables have determined the specificities of the different approaches to minorities within minorities in Europe.

The expression "cultural diversity" is used to address different issues in Europe. Historically, most European states were created by introducing strong patterns of cultural homogenization (Kraus and Sciortino, 2014). The processes of state formation involved changing borders until the second post-war period in Western Europe, and until much more recently, in Central and Eastern Europe. This produced three "cultural diversity" issues:

- the first was an **interstate** cultural diversity issue, whereby European states identified with their homogeneous national identity vis-à-vis other European national states;

- the second was a **transstate** cultural diversity issue, which consisted in border changes leading to the emergence of minority groups that were ethnically, linguistically or religiously connected to a neighboring nation state;
- and the third was an **intrastate** cultural diversity issue, in which the patterns of cultural homogenization, based on the cultural characteristics of a majority or politically powerful groups, resulted in the identification of cultural minorities (national minorities, linguistic minorities, religious minorities, indigenous groups, Roma peoples, etc.) within European states;
- a fourth cultural diversity issue, unrelated to the process of state formation but relevant to this chapter's discussion, is associated with immigration flows and the processes of globalization.

These different "cultural diversity" issues have elicited different responses by European states and European regional institutions. The issue of interstate cultural diversity is viewed today in terms of the equal recognition and status of European states as parties to supranational institutions. For example, the linguistic policy of the EU has evolved from the more traditional role of French and English as the two languages of diplomacy to a more flexible (and costly) mechanism of translation into the officially designated languages of the member states.[4] Ironically, we can also see this diversity issue manifest itself in the promotion of a European (supranational) identity, which is intended to agglutinate the European political space but that has been systematically associated with the concept of cultural diversity both by the CoE and the EU; from the 1954 European Cultural Convention to the 2005 Convention on the Value of Cultural Heritage for Society, cultural diversity has been invoked to prevent criticism of and resistance to homogenizing temptations.

The EU motto "unity in diversity," or the concept of European cultural heritage, has come to include not only interstate cultural diversity, but also cultural variations within European states; what I refer to above as trans- and intrastate forms of cultural diversity. Intrastate cultural diversity is very common in Europe regarding language, cultural heritage, religious affiliation and customary law. In addition to constitutional provisions embodying varying degrees of recognition and protection across European states, this kind of cultural diversity has also been addressed at the level of the CoE and the EU.

The CoE adopted the European Charter for Regional or Minority Languages (ECRML) in 1992 and the Framework Convention for the Protection of National Minorities (FCPNM) in 1995. Both instruments were intended to preserve and promote diversity and the European cultural heritage. However, they left the decision as to what specifically is to be protected (and to what extent) to the member states. Each state decides which languages are regional or minority languages in its territory and must therefore be protected. Each state also defines what a "national minority" is, and which groups must be protected as national minorities.

Since minorities must be first recognized as such by a state and the rights to be granted are also decided by the state in question, the instruments of the CoE therefore do not create group rights available to ethno-cultural minorities. These instruments are consistent with the departure from the traditional approach to minority rights which had been applied to national minorities (generally, transstate minorities) in Europe before the Second World War. In fact, the minority protection system of the League of Nations, based on international treaties and declarations, was not followed up by the United Nations after the Second World War.[5] Rather, it was thought that people belonging to minorities would be better protected by fundamental rights, varied forms of constitutional recognition and by antidiscrimination provisions (UN Secretary-General, 1950). Transstate cultural diversity, which had previously been addressed by international minority rights documents, was now part of constitutional arrangements that included *inter alia* different degrees of territorial self-autonomy[6] and constitutional guarantees for the protection of religious, linguistic and national minorities (De Witte, 2004), and for the protection of indigenous populations.[7] Minorities protected on the basis of international treaties, such as the Greek Muslim minority of Western Thrace, thus became an exception.

When the question of national minorities reemerged in the 1990s with the collapse of communism in Central and Eastern Europe and the enlargement of the European Union, international instruments referred to cultural diversity and cultural richness yet focused on member states' political and territorial stability. Minority protection was therefore considered a constitutional and legislative issue for the new post-communist states. It had to be aligned through constitutional arrangements, respect for fundamental rights and antidiscrimination provisions in the light of international standards set by the FCPNM and the ECRML. Furthermore, states could use these instruments to address both the issues of national minorities resulting from shifting borders and the claims made by internal minorities—such as the Basques and the Catalans in Spain, or the Sardinians and Sicilians in Italy—that had resisted cultural homogenization in their states.

While the EU does not have specific powers to protect minorities, EU action has strengthened an intrastate approach to cultural diversity within the member states. In the context of the EU enlargement process, and fearing the political instability associated with national minority issues, the protection of minorities was included as a value in Article 2 of the Treaty on European Union (1992).[8] This value was subsequently incorporated into the 1993 Copenhagen criteria for the accession of the candidate countries from Central and Eastern Europe seeking to join the EU. It is important to note, however, that Article 2 did not recognize minority rights as such, but the rights of individuals belonging to minorities. And, as the Copenhagen criteria did not establish benchmark indicators for minority protection, the CoE's instruments were used as a reference.

The frame of reference for intrastate cultural diversity in Europe thus became firmly rooted in the constitutional arrangements of each state. These constitutional arrangements range from the assimilationist to the pluralist, while a broad margin of appreciation[9] is applicable at the supranational level. The preeminence given to states has led to very few group rights being granted to minority groups, unless they are characterized as part of the territorial organization of the state (for example, in the recognition of linguistic rights or customary law in certain regions of an individual state). Yet, in these cases, residence—and not "belonging" to the minority group—is generally the main requirement for the exercise of these rights.

Although the intrastate approach to minority protection rests mainly on the guarantee of fundamental rights of individuals belonging to minorities and on antidiscrimination clauses, no reference has been made to the cultural diversity associated with migrant groups. In determining which minority groups could qualify as national minorities under the FCPNM, or which languages would be protected by the ECRML, European states drew noticeably clear lines around citizenship, territoriality, and historical membership of the state and excluded the application of these instruments to the cultural heritage of migrant communities.

Thus, for the most part, the cultural diversity associated with immigration has been treated separately (Eide, 2010). This is significant because, as already mentioned, the main European approach to cultural diversity lies in fundamental rights and antidiscrimination clauses; hence the cultural diversity associated with the dual trends of migration and globalization can be easily encompassed within it. Yet, some particularities and nuances in applying this framework to cultural diversity related to migrants' groups should be underlined. The measures adopted to protect or promote intrastate cultural identity have been largely discussed under the frameworks for identity, heritage and pluralism. These differentiated frames of reference can still be noticed in the Minimum Standards for Minorities in the EU issued by the European Parliament in 2018 (European Parliament, 2018). This document excluded forms of cultural diversity associated with migration and advocated a "mosaic of cultures, languages, religions, traditions and history forming a community of diverse citizens united by their common core values," and described a cultural heritage also by "persons belonging to minorities that have been living in Europe for centuries."

By consequence, cultural diversity when it refers to migrant communities[10] has different theoretical and regulatory frameworks. For example, the theoretical and regulatory frameworks associated with multiculturalism, interculturalism and more recently, superdiversity, have been used (almost) exclusively in relation to immigration.[11] This is clearly illustrated by the White Paper on Intercultural Dialogue "Living Together as Equals in Dignity," launched by the CoE in 2008 in an attempt to find a solution to the growing criticism of multiculturalism. In this document's introduction, intercultural dialogue is considered a "means of promoting awareness, understanding, reconciliation and tolerance, as well as preventing conflicts and ensuring integration and the cohesion of society." The White Paper on Intercultural Dialogue includes more than 40 references to migrants or migration, unlike the documents on national minorities and cultural heritage which contain none.

In addition to being embedded within distinct theoretical and regulatory frameworks, migration-associated diversity is mobilized across different policy areas. Whereas fundamental rights and antidiscrimination (together with the promotion of European cultural heritage) are the main instruments in dealing with "traditional" European cultural minorities, these instruments have been sidelined in favor of references to integration and inclusion in the case of migrant-associated cultural diversity. In fact, the European leaders who criticized multiculturalism as a failure were pointing to the perceived cultural differences related to immigrants from outside the EU. It is when addressing migrant communities and their cultural heritage that multiculturalism and support for cultural diversity are counterbalanced by, and opposed to, integration into "our" societies. As delicate as questions regarding national and linguistic minorities are for some European states,[12] cultural diversity associated with immigration has caused the debate on multiculturalism in Europe to heat up, especially as it concerns Muslim communities. In the policy fields of integration and inclusion, people belonging to minority groups tend to be considered in terms of vulnerable groups or vulnerable situations, rather than in terms of hierarchies of social groups. The notion of vulnerability has seen a remarkable development in the last decade in Europe, including in the case-law of the European Court of Human Rights (ECtHR) (Burgorgue-Larsen, 2014). However, the use of this notion has long raised concerns regarding its potential to stigmatize, stereotype and disempower individuals within vulnerable groups (Peroni and Timmer, 2013), and in relation to its limitations to pinpoint and to address structural forms of inequality. The combination of the notion of vulnerability with antidiscrimination clauses operates in the framework of integration policies to strengthen the individualistic response to cultural diversity associated to migration, thus driving the discussion even further away from recognition of group rights.

European Frameworks for Minorities within Minorities Situations

The main difficulty in drawing a parallel between the case of minorities within minorities in Canada and the United States, on the one hand, and the case of minorities within minorities in Europe, on the other, is, therefore due to the absence in the latter of equivalent minority group rights which can conflict with the individual rights of minority group members. Cases in Canada or the United States typically feature the right to decide on certain matters granted to a minority group on criteria that may not respect rights or principles that group members have as citizens, such as in the classic example of Audrey Martinez.[13]

It is rare to find this kind of legal arrangement for minority groups in Europe, be it for European intrastate cultural minority groups or—even more rarely— for cultural minorities resulting from migration and contemporary globalization.[14] In general, minority rights in Europe do not give power to minority groups (or acknowledge the social or religious power they might have) that may supersede the rights of their individual members. Protection is afforded to "individuals belonging to minorities" rather than to minority groups themselves. Notwithstanding the warnings of the European Parliament and the scholarship (Ahmed, 2015; Ringelheim, 2010; De Schutter, 2010; Malloy, 2010) regarding the limitations of antidiscrimination approaches in supporting minority cultures and avoiding assimilation, antidiscrimination and fundamental rights guarantees are still the predominant binding tool for minority protection in Europe. There are, nonetheless, some cases where tensions exist between legal arrangements intended to guarantee intrastate cultural diversity (even if they are not strictly minority rights) and the claims of individuals who consider that those arrangements violate some of their fundamental rights.

One such case concerns linguistic diversity. Most European states have minority and regional languages, and several European states have legal arrangements to protect the use of those languages. While, at the domestic level, there have been various cases of non-speakers of a regional language who have considered themselves wronged by the legal arrangements protecting the use of that language in their region,[15] a similar situation has emerged only once at the supranational level. In the case, "Relating to certain aspects of the laws on the use of languages in education in Belgium," the ECtHR was confronted with a complaint from several French-speaking Belgian families who wished to see their children educated in that language. The families, however, lived a region regarded by law as Dutch-speaking. The ECtHR ruled that the rights under the European Convention of Human Rights did not "have the effect of guaranteeing to a child or to his parent the right to obtain instruction in a language of his choice" (*Case relating to certain aspects of the laws on the use of languages in education in Belgium v. Belgium*, [1968] 1474/62 and 5 Others: 32). The Court hereby highlighted that the right to education enshrined in Article 2 of the Protocol, even if read together with the prohibition of discrimination under Article 14, was not the right of a minority or of a group, but the subjective right of every individual regardless of nationality, race or ethnic origin. Furthermore, the Court stressed its deference towards the constitutional and organizational choices of state parties in arranging their intrastate linguistic diversity, granting those choices with a very wide margin of appreciation.[16]

There are cases, revolving around religion in the European Union, that raise a similar tension. To be clear, these cases are not *sensu stricto* concerned with minorities within minorities. As we will see in the examples below, these cases differ from those concerning linguistic rights (which are of a territorial nature) in that, while they feature group rights or collective rights, they are not minority rights. These are rights that have been recognized to exist for all religious groups, be they of the majority or be they minority groups. Furthermore, they are not founded on multiculturalism, but rather on the guarantee of the human right to religious freedom.

For example, the Equal Treatment Directive (Council Directive, 2000) allows member states to introduce an exception to the prohibition of discrimination in the case of churches and other public or private ethos organizations, whereby differences of treatment based on a person's religion or belief shall not be considered discrimination where a person's religion or belief constitutes a genuine, legitimate and justified occupation requirement. In *IR v. JQ*, [2018] C-68/17, the Court of Justice of the European Union (CJEU) decided on the dismissal of a divorced and subsequently remarried Catholic doctor employed by a hospital run by a Catholic organization. The employer argued that the dismissal was fair because the employee had violated his contractual duty of loyalty to the ethos of the Catholic Church. The employee contended that, had he not been a Catholic, he would not have been fired for remarrying, since German law allows employers to establish different degrees of loyalty. In this case, it was deemed that Catholic employees were required to observe the principles of Catholic doctrinal and moral teachings, whereas other Christian employees were expected to respect the truths and values of the gospel. Therefore, if the doctor had been a Protestant engaged in the same conduct, his actions would have not led to his dismissal. Unlike in Canadian or US cases, where courts have refrained from interfering with the autonomy of minority groups and assessing the legitimacy or justifiability of their rules or decisions, the CJEU ruled that the determination of what constitutes a "genuine, legitimate and justified occupational requirement" within an organization is for the courts, and not for the employer, to determine. The CJEU also found that, notwithstanding the aim of the rule intending to protect the autonomy of religious organizations, violations of the principle of equality can only be justified when there is a "probable and substantial risk" to either the organization's right to autonomy or its ethos. According to the Court, the ability to provide medical care is not related to the employee's religion and, thus, non-compliance with religious norms by such an employee cannot pose a substantial risk to the organization.

It is interesting to compare the abovementioned decision by the CJEU with an ECtHR judgement on a similar case, *Fernández Martínez* (*Fernández Martínez v. Spain* [2014] 56030/07). Fernández Martínez was a Catholic priest involved in the movement for optional celibacy of the clergy and who was also married and a father, in the literal and not in the doctrinal sense. He was employed as a teacher of religious education and ethics in a state-run school in Spain, a position for which the consent of the bishop is required under the terms of the international agreement signed between Spain and the Holy See. He was dismissed after the bishop refused to renew his consent on the grounds that Martínez had revealed in public that he was married with children and, thus, had caused "scandal." In what proved to be a very close decision, the Grand Chamber of the ECtHR found that there was no violation of Article 8 of the European Convention of Human Rights (right to privacy and family life) in this dismissal. The Court considered that religious communities can demand a certain degree of loyalty and that it is not unreasonable to impose it on persons who might appear as representatives of the Church, such as religious education teachers.

Therefore, in Europe, group rights such as the rights of religious organizations or churches to self-government and autonomy are recognized, but they are counterbalanced by fundamental rights and the principle of non-discrimination. Furthermore, the balancing act between the autonomy of the group and the protection of fundamental rights falls within the jurisdiction of the courts and it is not left to the sole discretion of the minority group. Other rights, especially those referring to minority or regional languages or customary law, tend to be linked to territories and applied on the basis of residence and not on the basis of self-identification nor on the basis of membership in the group. In these cases, supranational courts have allowed a wide margin of appreciation to states in terms of organizing and managing intrastate cultural plurality.

The collective or group dimension is even less apparent in the approach that has been adopted for cultural diversity associated with migration, migrant communities and globalization (especially as it concerns transnational families). As explained above, these are the topics around which the debate on multiculturalism was structured and were also the real target of the criticism of multiculturalism. In these debates, there are more requests made on the basis of "European values" or on the counterbalance of fundamental rights and the principle of equality regarding group or on the collective rights of minority groups than in cases of the intrastate cultural diversity that survived the European states' national identity building processes. This is clearly evidenced in the emphasis placed by both the CoE and the EU on ideas of integration, inclusion, and intercultural dialogue when they have discussed cultural pluralism related to migration or to non-European cultures. In most of these cases, fundamental rights and antidiscrimination clauses test the relationship between the majority's culture (or common values) and the treatment of minority members (not necessarily minorities within minorities). It must be taken into account that Europe has a very limited and restrictive development of antidiscrimination case law on grounds of race or ethnic origin and concerning minority religions (Ringelheim 2010). In this constrained context, which operates under the differentiated frame of reference of integration as "our values/our societies," minorities within minorities cases have been addressed through the notions of "vulnerability" or "vulnerable groups." However, as already mentioned, vulnerability has been criticized as patronizing and disempowering. It generally focuses on the individual and has shown a very limited capacity to deal with collective dimensions of inequality and discrimination.

For example, in *DH and Others v. The Czech Republic*, [2007] 57325/00, the ECtHR condemned the school segregation of Roma children and remarked on the historical vulnerability of Roma minority in Europe. However, in the judgment the Court disqualified the capacity of Roma parents to take informed decisions in relation to their children's education precisely because they belong to this vulnerable minority (instead of, for example, emphasizing the lack of conditions for giving real consent). Additionally, in *BS v. Spain*, [2012] 47159/08,[17] the racialized sexism of the treatment of the plaintiff by the Spanish police was re-interpreted by the Court as a particularly vulnerable position due solely to the victim's migrant status and her engagement in sex work.

As we can see in both these cases, the ECtHR and the CJEU are reluctant to acknowledge group hierarchies and structural dimensions in equality and non-discrimination cases, preferring to focus on the specific situation of the individual or individuals before them. This individualistic approach regarding the vulnerable position of people belonging to cultural minorities associated with migration does not allow to distinguish the compounded vulnerability that the individual might suffer: because of her double membership in the migrant minority and a subordinated social group (such as women or homosexuals) or the forms of vulnerability that this individual might suffer because of the way her migrant minority group treats her particular group (women or homosexuals). This can also be seen in the treatment given to cases of Muslim women wearing religious headwear (*Sahin v. Turkey*, [2004], 44774/98; *SA. v. France*, [2014] 43835/11; *Dakir v. Belgium*, [2017] 4619/12; *Belcacemi and Oussar v. Belgium*, [2017] 37798/13; *Lachiri v. Belgium*, [2018] 3413/09), where discussions have raged around whether this was a case of compounded discrimination, since these women were discriminated on the grounds of religion and on the grounds of sex, or whether it was a gendered and discriminatory religious practice that could not be understood under human rights or antidiscrimination standards (Morondo Taramundi, 2015).

Conclusion

As has been demonstrated in the foregoing analysis, minorities within minorities cases in Europe cannot be compared to their counterparts in the United States or Canada. In the European context, minorities within minorities have very few and very limited group rights. There is also a major cleavage between traditional European national and linguistic minorities and the treatment reserved to migrant communities in all policies regarding cultural diversity. We have also seen that European supranational institutions have opted to adopt and implement very individualistic frameworks, regarding both the protection of the rights of persons belonging to minorities and in their approaches to the most vulnerable groups. Unfortunately, I do not believe that these approaches are likely either to stop assimilation or to upend group inequality and hierarchies that affect minority groups, social groups and individual members of minority groups.

Notes

1 The EU Culture, MEDIA and MEDIA Mundus programs, with the support of the cultural and creative sectors, played a role in promoting Europe's cultural and linguistic diversity. They were brought together and replaced by the CREATIVE EUROPE program in 2013.
2 Angela Merkel in October 2010, David Cameron in 2011, Angela Merkel again in 2015 and Nicolas Sarkozy in 2016 (Mikelatou and Arvanitis, 2019).
3 Most notably, the dispute over the inclusion of the Judeo-Christian identity was rooted in the failed attempt to have a European Constitution in 2005.
4 The EU has 24 official languages, three of which (English, French and German) have status as "procedural" or working languages for the European Commission. For the European Council and the European Parliament, all official languages are working languages. EU nationals have the right to use any of the 24 official languages to communicate with the EU institutions, and the institutions must reply in the same language. Legal acts are available in all official EU languages. The rules regarding the use of languages in the EU are laid down by the Council Regulation No. 1 determining the languages to be used by the European Economic Community, that was amended last in 2013 to introduce Irish as an official language.
5 Although the League of Nations ended in "embarrassment and silence," and is regarded as a failure, some authors have noted the significant expertise developed by the organization in the field of legal protection of minorities and the continuity of many of its contributions in current international human rights law (Scheu, 2022).
6 Such as in the Italian regions of Val D'Aosta, Friuli Venezia-Giulia and Trentino Alto Adige, or the Bonn-Copenhagen Declarations regarding the minorities in Schleswig-Holstein.
7 For example, the constitutional guarantees for the Sami indigenous population in Finland and Sweden.
8 Article 2: the Union is founded on the values of respect for human dignity, freedom, democracy, equality, the rule of law and respect for human rights, including the rights of persons belonging to minorities. These values are common to the member states in a society in which pluralism, non-discrimination, tolerance, justice, solidarity and equality between women and men prevail.
9 The margin of appreciation is a technical term used by the European Court of Human Rights to refer to the room for *maneuvering* accorded to national authorities in the fulfillment of their obligations under the ECtHR. It derives from the French term "marge d'appréciation" and it has been noted that it might be more helpful if the term was translated as "margin of assessment/appraisal/estimation" (Greer, 2000).
10 The expression "migrant communities" is sometimes coupled with "religious groups or leaders," as if migrant cultural diversity and religious pluralism were

somewhat part of the same continuum. In fact, intercultural dialogue is often juxtaposed with interreligious dialogue.
11 There is a debate in Europe whether multiculturalism and interculturalism are really different theoretical frameworks (Levrau and Loobuyck, 2018; Sealy, 2018) or whether it is just a "war of words" (Joppke, 2018) and interculturalism is just a new term introduced as a remedy to the backlash against multiculturalism. While this may be, it is clear that migrant communities and their diversity figure prominently in the European debates on multi- and interculturalism, and that migrant-related cultural diversity is discussed mostly through these frameworks, as opposed to other frameworks that appeared related to European intrastate diversity, such as pluralism, cultural heritage or even fundamental rights.
12 See, for example, the extremely serious constitutional developments in Catalonia, Spain, since 2006, which further escalated with the attempt to hold a referendum on independence in 2017.
13 *Santa Clara Pueblo v. Martinez*, [1978] 436 US 49. Julia Martinez, a US citizen and full-blooded member of the Santa Clara Pueblo tribe, residing in the Santa Clara Reservation had married a non-tribal man and had a child by him. The girl was brought up on the Pueblo and was, culturally speaking, a Santa Clara Indian. However, according to the laws of the Pueblo, children born to marriages with non-members would acquire the status of members if their father was a member, thus excluding children of female members that married outside. In 1978, the US Supreme Court, on grounds of "non-intervention," rejected the equal protection claim raised by Julia Martinez and her daughter.
14 There are some exceptions. Muslims in Western Thrace in Greece, for example, are subjected to religious personal law, which could create cases of sex discrimination on issues such as divorce, inheritance or parental rights. No such case has been discussed by the ECtHR, however. The proposal to allow Sharia law to be applied in family arbitration also caused considerable stir in the UK.
15 In Spain, for example, the legal provisions for the use of co-official regional languages have been contended before the courts for some time now, see for example the Judgements of the Spanish Supreme Court, [2019] 190/2019, or [2020] 634/2020.
16 The Court did not find Belgian legislation discriminatory because it considered that Belgium had a legitimate, necessary and proportionate reason to support it: "the Belgian legislative power thought a just settlement of the violent linguistic dispute between Flemings and Walloons could be achieved if the language boundary were drawn immutably once and for all, territorial unilingualism being introduced at the same time." The Court did not enter to debate this settlement but left it to the margin of appreciation recognized to the State.
17 It is interesting to notice that the plaintiff had presented her claim using the language of intersectionality, not of "vulnerability." Intersectionality (Crenshaw, 1989), as a perspective that allows for a more complex understanding of the interaction between different social hierarchies, could shed some light in minorities within minorities cases (Morondo Taramundi, 2018). However, the CJEU and the ECtHR have not used this concept for dealing with subordinated groups within minority groups.

References

Ahmed, T. 2015. "The EU's Relationship with Minority Rights." In *Cultural Governance and the European Union*, E. Psychogiopoulou (ed.) London: Palgrave Macmillan, 177–191. https://doi.org/10.1057/9781137453754_14.

Belcacemi and Oussar v. Belgium, Application No. 37798/13, Judgement of 11 July 2017.
B.S. v. Spain, Application No. 47159/08, Judgment of 24 July 2012.
Burgorgue-Larsen, L. (ed.). 2014. *La vulnerabilité saisie par les juges en Europe*. Paris: Pedone.
Calligaro, O. 2014. "From "European Cultural Heritage" to "Cultural Diversity"? The Changing Core Values of European Cultural Policy." *Politique Européenne 45* (3): 60–85. https://doi.org/10.3917/poeu.045.0060.
Case *Relating* to *Certain Aspects* of the *Laws* on the *Use* of *Languages* in *Education* in Belgium v. Belgium, Case 1474/62, 1677/62, 1691/62, 1769/63, 1994/63, and 2126/64, Judgement of the Court (Plenary) of 23 July 1968, ECLI:CE:ECHR:196 8:0723JUD000147462.
Council Directive 2000/78/EC of November 2000 establishing a general framework for equal treatment in employment and occupation [2000] OJ L303/16. https://eur-lex.europa.eu/legal-content/EN/TXT/PDF/?uri=CELEX:32000L0078&from=EN
Council of Europe. 1954. European Cultural Convention (Paris Convention).
Council of Europe. 2005. Convention on the Value of Cultural Heritage for Society (Faro Convention). https://www.coe.int/en/web/conventions/full-list/-/conventions/rms/0900001680083746. Since 2006
Council of Europe. 2015. Recommendation CM/Rec(2015)1 of the Committee of Ministers to Member States on intercultural integration.
Crenshaw, K. 1989. "Demarginalizing the Intersection of Race and Sex: A Black Feminist Critique of Antidiscrimination Doctrine, Feminist Theory and Antiracist Politics." *University of Chicago Legal Forum 140*: 139–167.
Dakir v. Belgium, Application 4619/12, Judgment of 11 July 2017.
De Schutter, O. 2010. "The Framework Convention on the Protection of National Minorities and the Law of the European Union." In *Double Standards Pertaining to Minority Protection*, K. Henrard (ed.) Leiden: Brill, 71–115. https://doi.org/10.1163/ej.9789004185791.i-440.21.
De Witte, B. 2004. "The Constitutional Resources for an EU Minority Policy." In *Minority Protection and the Enlarged European Union. The Way Forward*, G.N. Toggenburg (ed.), Budapest: LGI Books, 109–124.
D.H. and Others v. The Czech Republic, Application No. 57325/00, Judgment of 13 November 2007.
Eide, A. 2010. "The Rights of "New" Minorities: Scope and Restrictions." In *Double Standards Pertaining to Minority Protection*, K. Henrard (ed.) Leiden: Brill, 163–193. https://doi.org/10.1163/ej.9789004185791.i-440.42.
Eisenberg, A. and J. Spinner-Halev (eds.). 2004. *Minorities within Minorities. Equality, Rights and Diversity*, Cambridge: Cambridge University Press.
European Commission. N.B. "Multiculturalism", *Migration and Home Affairs, Open Glossary of the European Migration Network*. https://ec.europa.eu/home-affairs/pages/glossary/multiculturalism_en.
European Parliament. 2018. European Parliament Resolution of 13 November 2018 on Minimum Standards for Minorities in the EU, 2018/2036(INI).
European Union, *Treaty on European Union (Consolidated Version), Treaty of Maastricht*, 7 February 1992, Official Journal of the European Communities C 325/5; 24 December 2002, available at: https://www.refworld.org/docid/3ae6b39218.html [accessed 7 November 2022].

Fernández Martínez v. Spain, Application no. 56030/07, Judgement of 12 June 2014.
Foblets, M-C., J-F. Gaudreault-DesBiens and A. Dundes Renteln (eds.). 2010. *Cultural Diversity and the Law. State Responses from Around the World*, Brussels: Bruylant.
Green, L. 1995. "Internal Minorities and their Rights." In *Group Rights*, J. Baker (ed.), Toronto: University of Toronto Press, 257–272.
Greer, S. 2000. *The* Margin *of Appreciation: Interpretation and Discretion under the European Convention of Human Rights*, Strasbourg: Council of Europe Publishing. https://www.echr.coe.int/librarydocs/dg2/hrfiles/dg2-en-hrfiles-17(2000).pdf.
IR v. JQ, Case C-68/17, Judgment of the Court (Grand Chamber) of 11 September 2018, ECLI:EU:C:2018:696.
Joppke, C. 2018. "War of Words: Interculturalism v. Multiculturalism." *Comparative Migration Studies 6*: 11. https://doi.org/10.1186/s40878-018-0079-1.
Kraus, P.A. 2006. "Legitimacy, Democracy and Diversity in the European Union." *International Journal of Multicultural Societies 8* (2): 203–224. www.unesco.org/shs/ijms/vol8/issue2/art4.
Kraus, P.A. and G. Sciortino. 2014. "The Diversities of Europe: From European Modernity to the Making of the European Union." *Ethnicities 14* (4): 485–497. https://doi.org/10.1177/1468796814528696.
Lachiri v. Belgium, Application 3413/09, Judgment 18 September 2018.
Levrau, F. and P. Loobuyck. 2018. "Introduction: Mapping the Multiculturalism-Interculturalism Debate." *Comparative Migration Studies 6*: 13. https://doi.org/10.1186/s40878-018-0080-8.
Malloy, T.H. 2010. "Standards to Eliminate Compounded Discrimination: The Case of the Intersectionality of 'Minorities Within Minorities' or, Why Universal Legal Standards Must Engage with the Concept of Culture." In *Double Standards Pertaining to Minority Protection*, K. Henrard (ed.) Leiden: Brill, 259–296. https://doi.org/10.1163/ej.9789004185791.i-440.72.
Mikelatou, A. and E. Arvanitis. 2019. "wMulticulturalism in the European Union: A Failure beyond Redemption?" *International Journal of Diversity in Organisations 19* (1): 1–18. https://doi.org/10.18848/1447-9532/CGP/v19i01/1-18.
Morondo Taramundi, D. 2015. "Between Islamophobia and Post-Feminist Agency: Intersectional Trouble in the European Face-Veil Bans." *Feminist Review 110*: 55–67. https://doi.org/10.1057/fr.2015.13.
Morondo Taramundi, D. 2018. "Minorities-within-Minorities Frameworks, Intersectionality and Human Rights: Overlapping Concerns or Ships Passing in the Night?" In *Ethno-Cultural Diversity and Human Rights*, G. Pentassuglia (ed.) Leiden: Martinus Nijhoff Publishers, 256–285. https://doi.org/10.1163/9789004328785_010.
Okin, S.M. 1997. "Is Multiculturalism Bad for Women?" *Boston Forum Review*. https://bostonreview.net/archives/BR22.5/okin.html.
Pentassuglia, G. 2014. "Ethno-cultural Diversity and Human Rights: Legal Categories, Claims and the Hybridity of Group Protection." *The Yearbook of Polar Law VI*: 250–317. https://doi.org/10.1163/1876-8814_010.
Peroni, L. and A. Timmer. 2013. "Vulnerable Groups: The Promise of an Emerging Concept in European Human Rights Convention Law." *I·CON 11* (4): 1056–1085. https://doi.org/10.1093/icon/mot042.
Phillips, A. 2007. *Multiculturalism Without Culture*, Princeton: Princeton University Press.

Ringelheim, J. 2010. "Minority Rights in a Time of Multiculturalism – The Evolving Scope of the Framework Convention on the Protection of National Minorities." *Human Rights Law Review* 10 (1): 99–128. https://doi.org/10.1093/hrlr/ngp038.

Sahin v. Turkey, Application No. 44774/98, Judgment of 29 June 2004.

Santa Clara Pueblo v. Martinez, 436 U.S. 49 (1978).

S.A.S. v. France, Application No. 43835/11, Judgment of 1 July 2014.

Scheu, H.C. 2022. "The Heritage of the League of Nations' Minority Protection System." *Hungarian Journal of Legal Studies* 61 (4): 356–371. https://doi.org/10.1556/2052.2021.00224.

Sealy, T. 2018. "Multiculturalism, Interculturalism, 'Multiculture' and Super-Diversity: Of Zombies, Shadows and Other Ways of Being." *Ethnicities* 18 (5): 692–716. https://doi.org/10.1177/1468796817751575.

Shachar, A. 2000. "The Puzzle of Interlocking Power Hierarchies: Sharing the Pieces of Jurisdictional Authority." *Harvard Civil Rights-Civil Liberties Law Review* 35: 385–426.

Spanish Supreme Court Ruling No. 190/2019 of 19 February 2019.

Spanish Supreme Court Ruling No. 634/2020 of 2 June 2020.

UN General Assembly. 1948. Universal Declaration of Human Rights, A/RES/217 (III)C Fate of Minorities.

UN Secretary-General. 1950. Study of the Legal Validity of the Undertakings Concerning Minorities, E/CN.4/367.

PART 3
Multiculturalism, Religion and Secularism

8
INTERCULTURALISM AND THE FAIR MANAGEMENT OF DIVERSITY IN MULTINATIONAL DEMOCRACIES

The Contribution of Quebec–Canada Dynamics

Félix Mathieu

Multinational democracies are polities in which at least two national communities coexist within the realm of a single sovereign state.[1] Hence, democracies such as Canada are not only composed "of many cultures (multicultural) but also of two or more nations (multinational)" (Tully, 2001: 1). Up to a certain extent, the complex socio-political fabric that is characteristic of Canada and many other contemporary liberal democracies (e.g., Belgium, Italy, Spain, the UK, etc.) poses serious challenges to the theory and practice of multiculturalism. For instance, can multiculturalism in general, and the Canadian Multiculturalism Policy (CMP) in particular, fairly treat both the multicultural and multinational reality of the Canadian federation? Put differently, is this model fit to appropriately address the typical issues (recognition, institutional self-rule, political self-determination) associated with national diversity as much as it is towards dealing with ethnocultural minorities?

Even though there is no straightforward answer to these questions (see the chapters of Dolores Morondo Taramundi, Yasmeen Abu-Laban, Alain-G Gagnon and Arjun Tremblay, and Tariq Modood in this volume), and even though one should keep in mind that various theories of multiculturalism exist (see Crowder, 2013; May, 2016), prominent scholars and political actors in Quebec have suggested that the CMP is not fit to treat minority nations fairly (see Lamy and Mathieu, 2020). Presented as an alternative to the CMP, interculturalism has appeared to many in Quebec as a better, fairer model (Gagnon, 2000; Bouchard, 2011). On the other hand, critics have suggested that as far as interculturalism may help to ensure the sustainability of the cultural majority—which in this situation is also a minority within the sovereign state—it does so at the expense of treating fairly its own internal ethnocultural diversity (see Rocher and White, 2014; Frozzini, 2014).

This critical perspective must be considered and addressed. Nevertheless, I argue that interculturalism represents a model of pluralism that is of great value for Quebec and most minority nations evolving in multinational democracies. In the end, I contend that this shall be the case *if and only if* the reach and scope of the principles associated with interculturalism are defined in such a way that due consideration is given to the legitimate demands stemming from both *societal* and *ethnocultural* diversity. I suggest that fairness towards the various types of minorities in multinational democracies must not be understood through the prism of a zero-sum game, and that interculturalism is a well-balanced model that can help reach this goal.

The chapter opens with a short discussion on the connection between minority nations and ethnocultural minorities in multinational democracies when reflecting on theories of pluralism. Then, it moves to a brief examination of how and why interculturalism was developed from a policy perspective as a response to the CMP, which the political elite in Quebec was prompt to reject. With these Quebec-Canada dynamics in mind, I further advance the discussion to a more theoretical and normative level and present the main features that are associated with interculturalism. At this point, while focusing on the work carried out by scholars such as Gérard Bouchard, Alain-G. Gagnon and Raffaele Iacovino, I distinguish interculturalism from both multiculturalism and the most common European conception of interculturalism. Finally, the chapter presents different analytical frameworks with the objective of finding a set of general principles which would contribute to defining the legitimate scope and reach of interculturalism so that it leads to a fair treatment of both national and ethnocultural minorities.

On Managing Diversity in Multinational Democracies

To avoid any conceptual ambiguity, let us clarify first that a "nation" shall refer to a *societal community*, that is "a human group conscious of forming a community, sharing a common culture, attached to a clearly demarcated territory, having a common past and a common project for the future and claiming the right to rule itself" (Guibernau, 1999: 47; see also Kymlicka, 1995). Inevitably, multinational democracies are home to at least one *minority* nation.

In a nutshell, there is no fundamental distinction between "majority" and "minority" nations (*cf.* Gagnon, 2014); that is, the former is not necessarily "civic" and "individualistic" whereas the latter would be "ethnic" and "collectivistic" (*cf.* Greenfeld, 1992: 9–12; Lluch, 2014). These two types of national communities mostly differ from one another as a result of historical contingencies; some have become the bearer of a sovereign state while others have not. Henceforth, minority nations simply characterize such national communities whose inhabitants do not represent the majority of the population within a given sovereign state.

Irrespective of their majority or minority status, national communities are either the holders of a "societal culture" or aspire to develop and to consolidate a societal culture: that is to say they hold or aspire to develop a dynamic institutional and political framework "which provides its members with meaningful ways of life across the full range of human activities, including social, educational, religious, recreational and economic life, encompassing both public and private spheres" (Kymlicka, 1995: 76).[2] A societal culture represents this territorially concentrated institutional nexus upon which is founded any "host society" that is welcoming and integrating ethnocultural minorities—a type of diversity which results mostly (but not exclusively) from immigration.

The core argument in favor of multinational models of democracy is that "normal" modern sovereign states are not neutral *vis-à-vis* (national) diversity: states tend to promote the legitimacy of only one societal culture within their midst; usually the one associated with the most dominant national group (i.e., the majority nation). As Will Kymlicka puts it:

> A multinational state which accords universal individual rights to all its citizens, regardless of group membership, may appear to be "neutral" between the various national groups. But in fact it can (and often does) systematically privilege the majority nation in certain fundamental ways – for example, the drawing of internal boundaries; the language of schools, courts, and government services; the choice of public holidays; and the division of legislative power between central and local governments. All of these decisions can dramatically reduce the political power and cultural viability of a national minority, while enhancing that of the majority culture.
>
> *(Kymlicka, 1995: 51–52; see also Abu-Laban, 463–464)*

This argument implies that a majoritarian conception of democracy which only considers individual rights leads to unfair treatment of minority societal communities in a multinational polity, as it will not be welcoming towards their usual requests. To put it in a nutshell, a minority national community typically demands that the sovereign state accommodate its desire to be recognized as the bearer of a singular societal culture, i.e., as being legitimate to self-govern and self-determinate (Keating, 2001; Nootens, 2013; Guénette and Mathieu, 2018). The consequences of not addressing these demands properly can lead minority nations to express some kind of collective feeling of fragility or insecurity, which in turn can amplify tensions and worsen the relationship between the cultural majority and its internal ethnocultural minorities (Bouchard and Taylor, 2008; Laforest, 2015; Guénette and Mathieu, 2018: 899–900).

As for ethnocultural minorities *per se*, irrespective of their evolution in the midst of a minority or majority societal culture, they advance other kinds of political requests (Kymlicka, 1995; Tremblay, 2019). Of course, a multinational democracy should not overlook these claims either. Typically, ethnocultural minorities demand that the state develop specific policies to provide assistance in the complex and multifaceted process of their integration within the host society. In so doing, these are intended to help ethnocultural minorities "express their cultural particularity and pride without it hampering their success in the economic and political institutions of the dominant society" (Kymlicka, 1995: 31). For instance, echoing the Canadian debate, this may be concretely translated in public authorities implementing "reasonable accommodation practices" when an individual is facing discrimination as a result of her ethnocultural background.[3]

To sum up, theories of pluralism that focus on multinational democracies should reflect on how minority nations may possess the institutional levers necessary for them to be able to consolidate their respective societal culture. Nevertheless, one should not ignore the impact of these institutional settings on ethnocultural minorities. The legitimate yet differentiated claims made by societal communities and ethnocultural minorities should indeed be balanced rather than opposed.

Canadian Multiculturalism v. *La Société Distincte*

While interculturalism can now be depicted as a coherent normative political theory, its theoretical development was preceded by the unfolding of a specific institutional framework to manage diversity in Quebec. Looking back at these policy initiatives will help to better understand both the origins and further development of key normative features that are associated today with the theory of interculturalism.

The first milestone consisted in the creation in 1968 of the Quebec Ministry of Immigration. The Act to create the Quebec Ministry of Immigration provides that the new ministry "has the function of promoting the settlement in Quebec of immigrants who are likely to contribute to its development and participate in its progress; it also has the function of promoting the adaptation of immigrants to the Quebec environment"[4] (Assemblée législative du Québec, 1968). Therefore, the Act announced the desire for Quebec to use the full potential of its constitutional powers (taking into account that immigration is a shared jurisdiction between the orders of government in the Canadian federation; see Art. 95 of the Constitution Act, 1867) to implement its own internal citizenship regime, distinct from that of Canada as a whole.

In the spirit of the establishment of this new ministry, Quebec then rejected the CMP that Prime Minister Pierre Trudeau presented to the House of Commons on October 8, 1971. Indeed, on November 11, of the same year, Robert Bourassa, then Premier of Quebec, sent a letter to his federal counterpart announcing that Quebec would not endorse the CMP. Bourassa wrote that "[t]his notion [of multiculturalism] seems difficult to reconcile with Quebec's reality" (Bourassa, quoted in Bloc Québécois, 2007: 14). By that, he deplored that the CMP does not recognize Quebec as a *societal* minority distinct from the rest of the Canadian multicultural mosaic. Without exception, all successive governments in the Quebec National Assembly maintained the concerns expressed by Robert Bourassa with respect to Canadian multiculturalism.

A series of bilateral intergovernmental administrative agreements between Quebec and Ottawa on immigration and diversity management followed which extended Quebec's responsibilities on the matter. On the policy level, in 1981 the government of Quebec also formalized the adoption of its first "policy of integration" for the management of its internal ethnocultural minorities: *Autant de façons d'être Québécois* ("So many ways of being Quebecer"). A decade later, the Quebec government further developed its policy of integration with the adoption of the 1990 Policy Statement on Immigration and Integration, *Au Québec pour bâtir ensemble* ("In Quebec to build together"). Adopting the political grammar of a certain "duality" to express the relationship between the cultural majority and ethnocultural minorities, the policy insisted on the broad outlines of a "moral contract" between the former and the latter:

> the sharing of French as the common language of public life in Quebec society; the right and duty of all citizens, regardless of their origin, to participate in and contribute fully to the economic, social, cultural and political life of Quebec; the commitment to build together a pluralist Quebec where citizens of all cultures and origins can identify and be recognized as full-fledged Quebecers.
>
> *(Quebec, 1990: 50)*

Starting in the 1990s, scholars and political thinkers began to engage more actively with interculturalism with the goal of presenting it as a coherent model of pluralism, and one that can compete with the powerful narrative provided by Canadian multiculturalism (see Lamy and Mathieu, 2020). In doing so, the theorization of interculturalism has been closely associated with some of the guiding principles to be found in the aforementioned public policies, most importantly the "moral contract." Therefore, a scholar such as Gérard Bouchard (2015) refers to interculturalism as a typical "view from Quebec." However, I believe this is a bit shortsighted, as I contend that the value of interculturalism should not be restricted to *La Belle Province*.

Interculturalism as a Model of Pluralism

Over the past few decades, interculturalism has been mobilized by various political thinkers and actors without all of them having a common understanding of the term. While this is not specific to interculturalism—one needs only to think of multiculturalism or democracy—it has nonetheless led to significant confusion between its supporters and detractors. But one thing that many promoters of interculturalism share is their tendency to overemphasize how different it is from multiculturalism (Modood, 2017). In doing so, multiculturalism tends to be presented in a caricatural way, as a model that would accept cultural relativism, discards human rights and that necessarily leads to "ghettoization" (see, for instance, Wilson, 2009: 231).

First of all, a brief examination into some of multiculturalism's main theorists (*cf.* Taylor, 1992; Kymlicka, 1995; Parekh, 2006; Phillips, 2007; Modood, 2013) should suffice to reject the claim that multiculturalism—at least from a theoretical and normative point of view—discards human rights and accepts moral relativism while tacitly accepting ghettoization. In fact, the contrary could easily be argued (*cf.* Crowder, 2013; May, 2016; Mathieu, 2017: 115–130). In addition, it should be stressed that a variety of theories of multiculturalism exist. While, clearly, some theories can be reconciled with many of the principles associated with interculturalism—such as Will Kymlicka's (1995, 2001) or James Tully's (1995) approaches (see May, 2016: 180; Mathieu, 2017: 220–227)—most do not consider the differentiated nature of the demands made by societal communities and ethnocultural minorities (Gagnon and Iacovino, 2007; Crowder, 2013). In the end, the CMP should be associated with the latter category.

Also, it is crucial to distinguish between interculturalism as promoted notably (but not exclusively) by scholars from Quebec (*cf.* Gagnon, 2000; Bouchard, 2015; Rocher, 2015; Gagnon and Iacovino, 2016; see also Loobuyck, 2016) and "interculturality" as promoted notably by the Council of Europe (*cf.* Council of Europe, 2015; Cantle, 2012, 2016; Zapata-Barrero, 2016; see also White, 2016). The latter focuses mostly on "intercultural dialogue" within large urban cities, and therefore does not consider societal diversity.

What distinguishes the interculturalism model emerging from political and academic circles in Quebec from interculturality is its drive to advance a pluralist alternative to existing models of multiculturalism, while associating this mostly with the CMP. Interculturalism's advocates argue that it is more hospitable than multiculturalism to ensure the protection of Quebec's Francophone majority—a minority nation that presents itself as needing some kind of cultural and linguistic protections—without conflicting with ethnocultural minorities' expressed need and legitimate claim to be formally recognized and accommodated, so that its members are not discriminated against by state apparatuses.

While it is also founded on the will to foster and sustain intercultural dialogues, it nonetheless holds that this takes place in a context where there exists a cultural majority that wants to preserve what makes it a "distinct society." As a result, interculturalism is founded on a specific socio-political myth or paradigm, that of "duality," which structures "discussion and debates over diversity" (Bouchard, 2011: 443). This paradigm stems from the recognition that, in a multinational democracy, a minority nation has legitimacy to project itself as a singular host society that wishes to integrate ethnocultural minorities within its own societal culture.

As for Canadian multiculturalism in particular, it is associated not with the myth of duality, but rather with the paradigm of "diversity." Its guiding premise is that society "is composed of a collection of individuals and ethnocultural groups placed on equal footing and protected by the same laws—there is no recognition of a majority culture and, in consequence, no [societal] minorities *per se*" (Bouchard, 2011: 441).

Does this mean that interculturalism and multiculturalism are fundamentally different models? While *ceteris paribus* there exist differences between them, such as the typical "paradigm" or founding "socio-political myth" they tend to promote, interculturalism and multiculturalism are both models of pluralism that rest on a similar set of principles (*cf.* Weinstock, 2013: 107; Modood, 2020; Mansouri and Modood, 2021: 2–3). They both: (a) reject assimilationism or "anglo-conformity" (Kymlicka, 1995), (b) are in favor of a politics of recognition (Taylor, 1992) and (c) promote a fair integration of ethnocultural minorities within a given host society (Modood, 2013) or societal culture (Mathieu and Guénette, 2018).

What distinguishes interculturalism from multiculturalism is that the former is designed to be mostly appropriate for minority societal communities evolving within a multinational democracy—which tend to express a certain feeling of cultural fragility (Guénette and Mathieu, 2018)—while the latter presupposes a unique *demos* evolving within a normal nation state (*cf.* Gagnon and Iacovino, 2007: 102–103). That is why the global narrative advanced by interculturalism emphasizes more straightforwardly than multiculturalism the importance of newcomers to integrate—but not to assimilate—into a given host society (Mathieu, 2017: 195–196). This is a direct consequence of adopting the myth of duality rather than the myth of diversity.

To avoid any conceptual ambiguity, integration must not be thought of as being single-faceted. It concerns various spheres (political, institutional, economic, moral, social, etc.), and an individual may very well be economically integrated while remaining less so on the cultural level (Modood, 2013: 46). Integration is also a *process*: it is not something that happens overnight. As such, contrary to assimilation, interculturalism's conception of integration: (a) recognizes and celebrates diversity within the host society, (b) promotes cultural reciprocity and intercultural dialogue and (c) aims for a common political culture to emerge out of the dialogical interaction between minorities and the cultural majority.

Reflecting on Quebec's brand of pluralism and echoing the 1990 policy *Au Québec pour bâtir ensemble* ("In Québec to build together"), Alain-G Gagnon and Raffaele Iacovino further connect interculturalism to the idea of a "moral contract" between the cultural majority and its internal ethnocultural diversity.

Again, this line of reasoning is closely associated with the promotion of the duality paradigm:

> The moral contract is summed up as follows: a society in which French is the common language of public life; a democratic society where participation and the contribution of everyone is expected and encouraged; and a pluralist society open to multiple contributions within the limits imposed by the respect of fundamental democratic values; and the necessity of intercommunity exchange.
>
> *(Gagnon and Iacovino, 2007: 98)*

They expand upon this by stressing the idea that interculturalism aims to promote active citizenship participation and public deliberation as preferred ways to manage conflicts. Consequently, interculturalism favors "mediation, compromise and direct negotiation" over legal proceedings, even though these might be necessary as an option of last resort (Gagnon and Iacovino, 2007: 101).

Another key principle that scholars from Quebec connect to interculturalism is related to what Gérard Bouchard (2011, 2015) calls the "elements of *ad hoc* precedence for the majority culture." This principle, according to Bouchard, stresses that "while seeking an equitable interaction between continuity and diversity, interculturalism allows for the recognition of certain elements of *ad hoc* (or contextual) precedence for the majority culture" (Bouchard, 2011: 451). Bouchard then adds:

> I say *ad hoc* because it is out of the question to formalize or establish this idea as a general legal principle, which would lead to the creation of two classes of citizens. In this way, interculturalism distinguishes itself from radical republicanism that, whether directly or not, use the pretext of universalism to bestow a systematic, *a priori* precedence on what I term the majority or foundational culture. This kind of arrangement, which established a formal hierarchy, opens the door to abuses of power. That said, I think that as long as the nature and the reach of *ad hoc* precedence are carefully circumscribed it can avoid the excesses of ethnicism while giving some advantages (or the needed protections) to the majority culture.
>
> *(Bouchard, 2011: 451)*

These few features associated with this model of pluralism, which are all closely connected to Quebec–Canada dynamics, could each be expanded and nuanced. Nevertheless, I contend that they can help us in offering a general overview of what is interculturalism, and why it can be of interest for other cases of minority nations evolving in multinational democracies. In a nutshell, one may thus summarize what interculturalism stands for by pointing out to four key characteristics:

(1) interculturalism is similar to multiculturalism, since both models of pluralism reject assimilationism, advocate for politics of recognition and promote fair integration of immigrants into a given host society;
(2) interculturalism can be differentiated from most theories of multiculturalism, largely because the former is designed and mostly appropriate for minority societal communities evolving within a multinational democracy (echoing the myth of duality) while the latter generally presupposes a unique *demos* evolving within a "normal nation state" (echoing the myth of diversity). Put differently, interculturalism flourishes best in polities composed of multiple host societies or *demoi*, as it provides a valuable framework and narrative for minority societal communities to cope with their typical relative feeling of fragility;
(3) interculturalism promotes a "moral contract" based on active citizenship, participation and public deliberation for all, as a way to nurture a common political culture inspired by a perpetual intercultural dialogue;
(4) interculturalism is more transparent than multiculturalism toward intergroup power relations and does not hide the fact that the state is not neutral in the face of diversity and proposes, instead, containing this phenomenon by promoting the legitimacy of elements of *ad hoc* preferences for the cultural majority (itself a minority in the cases of minority nations).

If one accepts that these four key characteristics define what interculturalism stands for, then one also accepts the normative influence of the work carried out by Gérard Bouchard, Alain-G. Gagnon and Raffaele Iacovino. Now, the question is: can interculturalism help us to move beyond the logic of a zero-sum game in the management of societal communities and ethnocultural minorities? Focusing more specifically on these *ad hoc* preference measures for the cultural majority, can these be reconciled and balanced with providing fair treatment towards ethnocultural minorities as well?

How to Deal Properly with *ad hoc* Preference Measures?

In Quebec, this *ad hoc* preference principle has legitimated, *inter alia*, the special protection of the French language—which in the second half of the 20th century became Québécois' most cherished identity marker as the minority nation moved from an ethno-religious to a more civic, inclusive and territorial-based form of nationalism (Zubrzycki, 2016). Following the adoption in 1977 of the Quebec Charter of the French Language, commonly known as Bill 101, it is indeed required that most people living in the province of Quebec (including newcomers) send their children to the Francophone (public or semiprivate) educational system. Another impact of Bill 101 has been to require businesses to put forward a predominant French appellation when advertising.

While these and other similar measures have been qualified by many as being "illiberal" in their nature (Kymlicka, 2001: 287), they were implemented as they were perceived as being "necessary for the survival of Francophone culture" in *La Belle Province* (Bouchard, 2011: 452). In turn, as it contributed to relaxing a certain collective feeling of fragility for the majority culture, it was hoped that these measures would make the host society more welcoming towards ethnocultural minorities' typical demands for politics of recognition (Taylor, 1992; Bouchard and Taylor, 2008).

While Bill 101 may be considered today as a "great Canadian law," as former MP and cabinet minister Stéphane Dion put it, critics were very severe at the time the bill was adopted. Many believed it was creating two classes of citizens in Quebec (see the contributions gathered by Joseph Carens (1995) for nuanced perspectives on these debates).

Four decades after adopting Bill 101, the Quebec government continues to promote measures that aim at protecting the majority culture. After a decade-long, heated debate over secularization/*laïcité* in the province and the legitimate expression of minority religious symbols in public workplaces, the Coalition Avenir Québec-led government introduced new legislation that is also meant to protect the majority culture: most notably, Bill 21, *An Act Respecting the Laicity of the State*, which was formally adopted by the National Assembly of Quebec in 2019.

In a nutshell, the current government presents *laïcité* as a fundamental value of the Quebec nation. Concretely, *laïcité* is associated with four key principles: the separation of state and religion, the religious neutrality of the state, the equality of all citizens and freedom of conscience and freedom of religion (Section 2 of Bill 21). While these abstract principles may not be controversial *per se*, the way the legislature interpreted them led to significant division within the public realm. Indeed, the members of the National Assembly of Quebec voted in favor of interpreting these principles as leading to a ban on religious symbols for all public workers in a position of authority, which includes police officers, judges and prison guards as well as teachers and school principals (see Schedule II of Bill 21 for an exhaustive list). The legislature's rationale is that wearing religious symbols necessarily leads to proselytism, and that this is incompatible with the necessity for public workers in position of authority to be neutral while exercising their functions. Moreover, similar provisions are provided to require that public workers as well as "persons who present themselves to receive a [public service]" (Section 8, Bill 21)—such as public transportation—must have their face uncovered, which results *de facto* in targeting specific minority religious symbols.

In the end, what Bill 101 (1977) and Bill 21 (2019) have in common is that they are presented to the public as fitting this category of *ad hoc* precedence measures aimed to protect the majority culture. At the same time, though, these bills have been criticized as creating a toxic environment for ethnocultural minorities in Quebec (see Dabby and Leydet, 2020).

Bearing in mind that most individuals who identify with the cultural majority in Quebec no longer wear conspicuous religious symbols, one may argue that some provisions contained in Bill 21 (e.g., Sections 2 and 8) discriminate against members of specific religious minorities for whom wearing a religious symbol is not only a matter of personal preference but rather a necessary condition for them to live a "good life" (Maclure and Taylor, 2011). As a result, it can be argued that requiring them not to wear their religious symbols if they are public workers in a position of authority leads to discrimination based on religious beliefs as well as their exclusion from public spaces (The Toronto Star Editorial Board, 2021).

The question, then, is: what should be the limits to these *ad hoc* precedence measures for them not to create an unfair environment towards ethnocultural minorities while trying to secure a better, fairer environment for the minority nation? Providing a simple and definitive answer to this question may not be possible. But it is fundamental that we engage with this issue and explore the value of different analytical frameworks.

A first attempt to cope with this complex task is provided by Gérard Bouchard (2015). He suggests that these *ad hoc* measures must simply "pass the test of the tribunals." In the past, I have been quite severe in my appreciation of Bouchard's response, as I believe this legalistic approach to be a bit too simplistic to carry out this important normative task (see Mathieu, 2017: 231–240). Also, "passing the test of the tribunals" leads to a context-dependent analytical framework, which I contend is too limited if interculturalism is to be mobilized by many minority nations, not only Quebec.

Put differently, a measure which in Quebec would "pass the test of the tribunals" under the Canadian constitutional order could well be declared unconstitutional elsewhere. For example, under the Spanish constitutional order, Catalans would not be entitled to pass legislation similar to Quebec's Bill 101. It would indeed not "pass the test of the tribunals," as the Constitutional Court of Spain has held that it would be unconstitutional to restrict the right to education in Castilian to one group of Spaniards (STC 31/2010, subsection 29), which is something that the Catalonian equivalent of Bill 101 would necessarily have included.

A potential way to move beyond Bouchard's legalistic approach is proposed by Will Kymlicka (1995) when he makes a distinction between measures of "external protection" and "internal constraints." To summarize, the former refers to measures that aim at ensuring an egalitarian relationship between minority groups (societal or ethnocultural) and the majority residing in the state while the latter refers to mechanisms for limiting the individual freedom of the members of a particular group given its cultural "essence" or "authenticity." The purpose of the external protection measures that Kymlicka envisages is to (re)balance power relationships in multinational democracies and, with respect to immigrant minorities especially, to foster integration into a specific societal culture. On the other hand, the purpose of internal constraint measures is to preserve said cultural "essence" or "authenticity" from external cultural and sociopolitical dynamics. Kymlicka refers to these measures as "illiberal practices."

Relying on this analytical framework, it appears quite straightforward to argue that measures of *ad hoc* precedence for the majority culture that enters the first category are to be accepted. An "illiberal measure" should otherwise be rejected as it reveals itself as an "internal constraint" that unfairly restricts individual freedoms.

The problem with this analytical framework is that it still has a blind spot. For example, Bill 101 (1977) and Bill 21 (2019) can be seen both as external protection measures for the majority culture, and internal restrictions toward ethnocultural minorities. As Kymlicka recognizes it when reflecting on Bill 101, this framework can lead to a certain dilemma: "Many commentators commend Quebec nationalism for abandoning an ethnic definition of nationhood, but criticize it for its illiberal policies on education and commercial signs" (2001: 287). Nevertheless, the political philosopher then adds that while these *ad hoc* preference measures for the majority culture contain elements of "illiberal policies," these "are precisely what have made it possible for Quebecers to shift from an ethnic to a post-ethnic definition of nationhood" (2001: 287). As a result, we face a hard choice:

> Should we insist on a rigorous adherence to liberal norms of individual choice, knowing that this will stop and perhaps reverse the shift from an ethnic to post-ethnic definition of Québécois nationalism? Or should we accept some limited deviation from liberal norms in order to consolidate and extend the shift to a civic form of minority nationalism?
> *(Kymlicka, 2001: 287)*

Kymlicka goes on to acknowledge that he has "no definite answer to this question" (2001: 288). In an attempt to expand on Bouchard's argument and to help unpack Kymlicka's dilemma, I will conclude this section by exploring a complementary analytical framework that can help us to define the scope of legitimacy for such *ad hoc* measures.

While I maintain that relying only on the argument that a measure must "pass the test of the tribunals" is too limited to carry out the current normative task, I am now considering that it may lead, nonetheless, to a satisfactory framework. Taking Bouchard's argument seriously, I wondered what it meant concretely under the Canadian constitutional order, and I came to the conclusion that a specific Canadian legal norm could indeed serve a more general purpose. I am referring here to the 1986 Supreme Court of Canada's ruling over *R* v. *Oakes* (1 SCR 103) and what has been referred to as the "Oakes test."

As Section 1 of the Canadian Charter of Rights and Freedoms "guarantees the rights and freedoms set out in it subject only to such reasonable limits as can be demonstrably justifiable in a free and democratic society," the Court, in 1986, "established a test for determining whether a limit on a Charter right is a reasonable one" (Dodek, 2016: 155). In a nutshell, the "Oakes test" suggests that "the objective to be served by the measures limiting a *Charter* right must be sufficiently important to warrant overriding a constitutionally protected right or freedom" (*R. v. Oakes*, [1986] 1 SCR 103). Three specific criteria have been determined to examine specific situations:

> [1] To begin, the measures must be fair and not arbitrary, carefully designed to achieve the objective in question and rationally connected to that objective. [2] In addition, the means should impair the right in question as little as possible. [3] Lastly, there must be a proportionality between the effects of the limiting measure and the objective – the more severe the deleterious effects of a measure, the more important the objective must be.
>
> *(R. v. Oakes, [1986] 1 SCR 103)*

Considering these three criteria while also keeping in mind Kymlicka's distinction between "external protections" and "internal constraints," I believe one can rely on a reasonable framework to differentiate between legitimate and illegitimate measures of *ad hoc* precedence in favor of the majority culture. For instance, while I contend that this framework would lead us to accept the general ideas associated with Bill 101 and Bill 21, they would nonetheless be helpful to highlight specific features they promote that should be amended. While I lack the necessary space here to develop a more exhaustive analysis, I shall conclude this section with a brief comment regarding this issue.

Echoing the above discussion on Bill 21 it could be argued that the provision regarding the requirement that all public workers in position of authority must not wear any conspicuous religious symbols should be relaxed. On the one hand, the Oakes test would probably accept the validity of this principle for certain public workers in position of authority (judges, police officers, prison guards) because of their special degree of authority over someone's life and the need for the public to trust the religious neutrality of agents representing the state (see Bouchard and Taylor, 2008: 150). On the other hand, as long as there is no empirical evidence that wearing a religious symbol necessarily or typically leads to proselytism and hinders someone's faculty to respect the principle of religious neutrality while exercising their job, I would argue that the same prescription for teachers and school principals would not pass the Oakes test. Indeed, this illiberal practice should not be legitimated as its consequences are disproportional and somehow arbitrary, especially towards specific ethnocultural minorities.

Conclusion

This chapter sought to discuss the value of interculturalism in achieving fairness in multinational democracies. Relying mostly on Quebec-Canada dynamics, it presented how interculturalism came to be both from an institutional perspective and as a theoretical and normative framework. This led to the identification of a set of key principles to appreciate better the singularity of this model of pluralism and its potential for minority nations. In doing so, it also stressed that any measure that aims at protecting the cultural majority may only be considered as legitimate *if and only if* it does not lead to arbitrary deleterious effects on ethnocultural minorities. This is a necessary condition if one is serious about achieving fairness towards the various types of minorities in multinational democracies. Again, the legitimate yet differentiated claims advanced by societal communities and ethnocultural minorities must not be understood through the prism of a zero-sum game.

Notes

1 I would like to thank Yasmeen Abu-Laban, Alain-G Gagnon and Arjun Tremblay for their invitation to contribute to this edited volume. I would like to thank my research assistant, Paul Addison Carruthers, as well, for the precious help he provided me in the process of writing this chapter. I also wish to acknowledge that some of the arguments I advance in this manuscript build on previous research I have published (see Mathieu, 2017). In particular, the section entitled "Interculturalism as a Model of Pluralism" should be understood as a summary of Chapter 7 in *Taking Pluralism Seriously: Complex Societies Under Scrutiny* (Mathieu, 2022).
2 That is why, in this chapter, I shall use the terms "nations," "national communities," "societal groups" and "societal communities" as synonyms.
3 To avoid any conceptual ambiguity, a reasonable accommodation refers to the adaptation of a general norm or rule with the goal to attenuate or suppress the impact of the said norm on the capacity for someone to enjoy fully its rights and freedom (see Bosset, 2009: 6).
4 Translation by the author.

References

Assemblée législative du Québec. 1968. *Loi créant le ministère de l'immigration du Québec.* Loi du Québec (Chapter 68).
Bloc québécois. 2007. *Bâtir le Québec ensemble.* Mémoire du Bloc québécois à la Commission de consultation sur les pratiques d'accommodements reliées aux différences culturelles. Québec: Bibliothèque et Archives nationales du Québec.
Bosset, P. 2009. "Droits de la personne et accommodements raisonnables : le droit est-il mondialisé?" *Revue internationale d'études juridiques* 1 (1): 1–32.
Bouchard, G. 2011. "What is Interculturalism?" *McGill Law Journal* 56 (2): 395–468.
Bouchard, G. 2015. *Interculturalism: A View from Quebec.* Toronto: University of Toronto Press.
Bouchard, G. and C. Taylor. 2008. *Building the Future: A Time for Reconciliation.* Consultation Commission on Accommodation Practices Related to Cultural Differences. Québec: Bibliothèques et Archives Nationales du Québec.

Cantle, T. 2012. *Interculturalism: The New Era of Cohesion and Diversity.* New York: Palgrave Macmillan.
Cantle, T. 2016. "The Case for Interculturalism, Plural Identities and Cohesion." In *Multiculturalism and Interculturalism. Debating the Dividing Lines*, N. Meer, T. Modood and R. Zapata-Barrero (eds.) Edinburgh: Edinburgh University Press, 133–157.
Carens, J.H. (ed.). 1995. *Is Quebec Nationalism Just? Perspectives from Anglophone Canada.* Montréal and Kingston: McGill-Queen's University Press.
Council of Europe. 2015. "Intercultural Dialogue." https://pjp-eu.coe.int/en/web/youth-partnership/intercultural-dialogue (accessed 10 September 2020).
Crowder, G. 2013. *Theories of Multiculturalism. An Introduction.* Cambridge: Polity Press.
Dabby, D. and D. Leydet (eds.). 2020. *Modération ou extrémisme? Regards critiques sur la loi 21.* Québec: Presses de l'Université Laval.
Dodek, A. 2016. *The Canadian Constitution.* Second Edition. Toronto: Dundurn.
Frozzini, J. 2014. "L'interculturalisme selon Gérard Bouchard." In *L'interculturel au Québec. Rencontres historiques et enjeux politiques*, L. Emongo and B. White (eds.) Montréal: Presses de l'Université de Montréal, 91–116.
Gagnon, A-G. 2000. "Plaidoyer pour l'interculturalisme." *Possibles* 24 (1): 11–25.
Gagnon, A-G. 2014. *Minority Nations in the Age of Uncertainty. New Paths to National Emancipation and Empowerment.* Toronto: University of Toronto Press.
Gagnon, A-G. and R. Iacovino. 2007. *Federalism, Citizenship, and Quebec: Debating Multinationalism.* Toronto: University of Toronto Press.
Gagnon, A-G. and R. Iacovino. 2016. "Interculturalism and Multiculturalism: Similarities and Differences." In *Multiculturalism and Interculturalism. Debating the Dividing Lines*, N. Meer, T. Modood and R. Zapata-Barrero (eds.) Edinburgh: Edinburgh University Press, 104–132.
Guibernau, M. 1999. *Nations without States. Political Communities in a Global Age.* London: Polity.
Greenfeld, L. 1992. *Nationalism: Five Roads to Modernity.* Cambridge: Harvard University Press.
Keating, M. 2001. *Plurinational Democracy: Stateless Nations in a Post-Sovereignty Era.* Oxford: Oxford University Press.
Kymlicka, W. 1995. *Multicultural Citizenship. A Liberal Theory of Minority Rights.* New York: Oxford University Press.
Kymlicka, W. 2001. *Politics in the Vernacular. Nationalism, Multiculturalism, and Citizenship.* Oxford: Oxford University Press.
Laforest, G. 2015. *Interpreting Québec's Exile within the Federation: Selected Political Essays.* Brussels: P.I.E. Peter Lang.
Lamy, G. and F. Mathieu. 2020. "Les quatre temps de l'interculturalime au Québec." *Canadian Journal of Political Science/Revue canadienne de science politique* 53 (4): 777–799.
Lluch, J. 2014. *Versions of Sovereignty: Nationalism and Accommodation in Multinational Democracies.* Philadelphia: University of Pennsylvania Press.
Loobuyck, P. 2016. "Towards an Intercultural Sense of Belonging Together: Reflections on the Theoretical and Political Level." In *Multiculturalism and Interculturalism. Debating the Dividing Lines,* N. Meer, T. Modood and R. Zapata-Barrero (eds) Edinburgh: Edinburgh University Press, 225–245.
Maclure, J. and C. Taylor. 2011. *Secularism and Freedom of Conscience.* Cambridge: Harvard University Press.

Mansouri, F. and T. Modood. 2021. "The Complementarity of Multiculturalism and Interculturalism: Theory Backed by Australian Evidence." *Ethnic and Racial Studies* 44 (16): 1–20.

Mathieu, F. 2017. *Les défis du pluralisme à l'ère des sociétés complexes*. Québec: Presses de l'Université du Québec.

Mathieu, F. 2022. *Taking Pluralism Seriously. Complex Societies Under Scrutiny*. Montréal and Kingston: McGill-Queen's University Press.

Mathieu, F. and D. Guénette. 2018. "Introducing a Societal Culture Index to Compare Minority Nations." *Publius: The Journal of Federalism* 48 (2): 217–243.

May, P. 2016. *Philosophies du multiculturalisme*. Paris: Presses de Sciences Po.

Modood, T. 2013. *Multiculturalism*. Cambridge: Polity Press.

Modood, T. 2017. "Must Interculturalists Misrepresent Multiculturalism?" *Comparative Migration Studies* 5 (1): 1–17.

Modood, T. 2020. "Multiculturalism as a New Form of Nationalism?" *Nations and Nationalism* 26 (2): 308–313.

Nootens, G. 2013. *Popular Sovereignty in the West: Polities, Contention, and Ideas*. London: Routledge.

Parekh, B. 2006. *Rethinking Multiculturalism. Cultural Diversity and Political Theory*. Cambridge: Harvard University Press.

Phillips, A. 2007. *Multiculturalism without Culture*. Princeton: Princeton University Press.

Québec. 1990. *Au Québec pour bâtir ensemble*. Énoncé de politique en matière d'immigration et d'intégration. Québec: Ministère des Communautés culturelles et de l'Immigration du Québec.

R. v. Oakes, [1986] 1 SCR 103.

Rocher, F. 2015. "Multi et interculturalisme. Les cas canadien et québécois." *Le Débat* 4: 33–43.

Rocher, F. and B. White. 2014. "L'interculturalisme québécois dans le contexte du multiculturalisme canadien." *Étude IRPP*, Institut de recherche en politiques publiques, no 49.

Spain, Tribunal Constitucional. STC 31/2010.

Taylor, C. 1992. "The Politics of Recognition." In *Multiculturalism and 'The Politics of Recognition': An Essay*, A. Gutmann (ed.) Princeton: Princeton University Press, 25–74.

The Toronto Star Editorial Board. 2021. "Quebec's Bill 21 is Unfair and Unjust, but "legal". The Fight Againt it Must Continue." *The Toronto Star*. https://www.thestar.com/opinion/editorials/2021/04/26/quebecs-bill-21-is-unfair-and-unjust-but-legal-the-fight-against-it-must-continue.html.

Tremblay, A. 2019. *Diversity in Decline? The Rise of the Political Right and the Fate of Multiculturalim*. London: Palgrave Macmillan.

Tully, J. 1995. *Strange Multiplicity: Constitutionalism in an Age of Diversity*. Cambridge: Cambridge University Press.

Tully, J. 2001. "Introduction." In *Multinational Democracies*, A.-G. Gagnon and J. Tully (eds.) Cambridge: Cambridge University Press, 1–33.

Weinstock, D. 2013. "Interculturalism and Multiculturalism in Canada and Quebec: Situating the Debate." In *Liberal Multiculturalism and the Fair Terms of Integration*, P. Balint and S.G. Latour (eds.) London: Palgrave Macmillan, 91–108.

Wilson, R. 2009. "From Consociationalism to Interculturalism." In *Consociational Theory: McGarry and O'Leary and the Northern Ireland Conflict*, R. Taylor (ed.) London: Routledge, 221–236.

White, B. 2016. "Le vivre-ensemble comme scénario de l'interculturel au Québec." In *Pluralité et vivre-ensemble au Québec,* S. Saillant (ed.) Québec: Presses de l'Université Laval, 39–62.

Zapata-Barrero, R. 2016. "Theorizing Intercultural Citizenship." In *Multiculturalism and Interculturalism. Debating the Dividing Lines,* N. Meer, T. Modood and R. Zapata-Barrero (eds.) Edinburgh: Edinburgh University Press, 53–76.

Zubrzycki, G. 2016. *Beheading the Saint: Nationalism, Religion, and Secularism in Quebec.* Chicago: University of Chicago Press.

9

MULTICULTURALISM

The Place of Religion and State–Religion Connections

Tariq Modood

Canada has supplied several internationally prominent policy-relevant pro-diversity philosophies, which may or may not also be called "multiculturalism." The most famous is that of Will Kymlicka (1995), which I think of as "multinationalism;" another is an interculturalism which can take a majoritarian form (Bouchard and Taylor, 2008).[1] Whatever their strengths in other directions, these two both find it difficult to accept religion and religious identity on a par with say language and linguistic identity. For these reasons, whilst Canadian thinking about multiculturalism is a great resource, as a politics it is quite remote from Europe, especially the UK. I have learnt a lot from Canadian theory but am aware of how it gives low priority to or can be negligent of what for me, given my own national and regional context, indeed biography, has been central to multiculturalism today.[2]

Kymlicka's theory of multiculturalism is based on membership of "societal cultures" which cannot or should not be integrated into a national mainstream as they are nations in their own right. As with Canadian government policy, he is responding to political agitation for Québécois francophone territorial nationalism and from Indigenous peoples. As he acknowledges, migrants and their descendants do not fit this specification and so cannot benefit from the normative core of his theory. It is a theory that is best described as "multinationalism." Yet in other places—I take Western Europe and especially the UK as my main reference point—multiculturalism is centered on post-World War II immigrant settlers and their progeny and their non-assimilative inclusion in and the remaking of the national mainstream. Moreover, these settlers are marked by a shared history with the natives, albeit of colonialism, by racism and by socio-economic disadvantage (Modood, 2017a). Most relevant here is that when in Western Europe people talk of multiculturalism—whether pro

DOI: 10.4324/9781003197485-14

or anti—they are most exercised by the growing presence of Muslims and of Muslim cultural and political assertiveness. All these features are absent from Kymlicka's theory and indeed Canadian theorizing of multiculturalism. For all these reasons, Canadian philosophies of multiculturalism have a poor fit with European realities. While certainly inspired by and indebted to Canadian intellectual work and political pioneering, we on this side of the Atlantic have had to do our own customized thinking about multiculturalism; not just at the level of policies but going all the way down. One such intellectual formation has been called the Bristol School of Multiculturalism, centering on the work of Bhikhu Parekh, myself, Nasar Meer and Varun Uberoi (Levey, 2019 and the subsequent symposium). Besides centering on the political and identity features that I have just said are the key characteristics of the new settlements of Western Europe, also key to it is a bottom-up theorizing of minority politics in the region's liberal democratic polities rather than a derivation from abstract liberal theory in the style of Kymlicka. Whilst liberal democratic norms and structures (amongst others) are contextually present, liberalism is not privileged over multiculturalism (Modood, 2022). I will not further elaborate on the Bristol School and the rest of the chapter will focus on religion and secularism. I will however structure the chapter around the difference between my own views and what I take to be the relevant take of two Canadian philosophies of multiculturalism.

Kymlicka and US-style Denominationalism

Kymlicka rightly argues that the "state unavoidably promotes certain cultural identities, and thereby disadvantages others" (1995: 108; see also 2001: 24), but he excludes religion and ethnoreligious groups from "cultural identities." While his interpretation of multicultural citizenship is primarily directed toward justifying special support or differential rights in relation to language and Indigenous people, meeting needs of religious minorities seems to primarily fall within the ambit of the traditional freedoms of worship, association and conscience.[3] While Kymlicka (1995) does discuss a number of cases of religious minority claims making for exemptions and accommodations in relation to laws, policies and mainstream institutions, religious groups and religious needs were not explicitly integrated in his theory. Unlike the case of other cultural groups, minority demands for democratic participation, public resources or greater institutional representation. Kymlicka thinks that the integration of religious migrants such as Muslims has been best achieved in the United States, where no religion enjoys state support, but all denominations are allowed to flourish in equality with the rest (Kymlicka, 2009: 548).

Why should language be appropriate for multiculturalism but not for religion? Is there some categorical difference between religion and language? A state must, it is argued, use at least one language, and so choices must be made.

Which language(s)? How many languages? Complete state neutrality about language is impossible. Fairness therefore dictates that the state does not pretend to be neutral, so it should pursue an alternative strategy. Religion, on the other hand, is optional. It is not necessary to the functioning of the state, and this critique of neutrality does not extend to it. Moreover, citizens can learn several languages, but one will not be a member of several religions at the same time, so a multilingual state is an option while a multireligious state is not. That supplies a further reason why state neutrality in relation to language implies the addition of linguistic options but state neutrality concerning religion only implies disestablishment (Baubock, 2003: 43–44).

These arguments fail to save Kymlicka's theory from the charge of an antireligion bias, nor do they make practical sense. First, although Kymlicka's theory does center on language, it extends well beyond language to cover "cultural identities." His theory is meant to protect and empower ethnocultural groups and not merely languages; all cultures contain elements that are no more necessary than religion, and some cultures are centered around religion. Moreover, the idea that a multireligious state is impossible is a misunderstanding. Countries as diverse as Germany and India could be described as being quasi-multi-establishment states. The German state has various institutional and fiscal ways of supporting and working corporately with the Roman Catholic Church and the Lutheran Churches. The Indian state regulates several organized religions and incorporates their principles into law. This state recognition of faith communities is a granting of political or legal status, without meaning that state officials or citizens have to believe in any or all of these faiths.[4] States do support much that is not essential to the state's existence—the arts, science, sport and leisure—and a multiculturalist state surely is no exception.

More recently, Kymlicka has changed his mind and come to the view that 'all of the arguments for adopting multiculturalism as a way of tackling the legacies of ethnic and racial hierarchies apply to religion as well' (Kymlicka, 2015: 28). Indeed, he says this issue is 'perhaps the key question for multiculturalism in Canada at the start of the 21st century' (p. 27). That may be the case but he has not yet attempted to show how religion fits into his theory.

Open Secularism

The other Canadian multiculturalist take on religion I will look at is that of Charles Taylor and collaborators.[5] Taylor's seminal essay *The Politics of Recognition* (1994) is as influential as Kymlicka's theory and I am indebted to his concepts of recognition and the harms of misrecognition, of alienation and symbolic equality, which I have made central to my own understanding of multiculturalism (Modood, 2013 [2007]: 51–53 [47–49]) and will argue below it should be the basis of state-religion relations. This means a secularism which can be related to what Taylor calls "non-procedural liberalism" which allows that "judgement about the good life can be enshrined in laws and state action" as long as they are consistent with liberal-democratic constitutionalism, without being confined to liberal-democratic constitutionalism (Taylor, 1994). It is striking, however, that in more recent writings, and particularly under the concept of "open secularism," Taylor is no longer using the concept of recognition. "Open secularism" or "liberal pluralist secularism" (Bouchard and Taylor, 2008; Maclure and Taylor, 2011) limits itself to a focus on conscience and protection of negative liberty, of exemptions from the state rather than recognition, and advocates that fairness in a context of religious diversity can only be achieved through state neutrality. This is in stark contrast to his earlier handling of state language when he argued that Quebec's resolution to be exclusively francophone was consistent with liberal principles, which did not require linguistic neutrality by the state.

Open secularism identifies and seeks to balance four principles of secularism: i) the moral equality of persons; ii) freedom of conscience and religion; iii) the separation of church and state; and iv) state neutrality in respect of religious and deep-seated secular convictions (Bouchard and Taylor, 2008: 21). While i) and ii) form the "essential outcomes of secularism" or the *ends* of secularism (ibid.; Maclure and Taylor, 2011), iii) and iv) are given a lower status as the *means* of secularism, namely, the institutional arrangements for achieving i) and ii) (Maclure and Taylor, 2011). Although, therefore, neutrality is not posited as an essential goal for open secularism, it is posited as a structural necessity for achieving the essential goal of moral individualism. This neutrality differs from a more assertive republican secularism, as found in French *laïcité*, for instance, through its focus on a state's or state employees' *acts* (in the performance of their duties) rather than on the physical appearance of its employees or users (Bouchard and Taylor, 2008: 148, 150). In the republican conception, it is argued, the means and ends are too often confused and conflated in a "fetishism of means" such that too much importance is attached to the means (Maclure and Taylor, 2011).

For a multiculturalist it is disappointing that whilst recognizing the significance of the individual spiritual dimension so central and important for many religious adherents, there is no equivalent appreciation of the religious communities in which most individuals come to acquire and live out the significance of religion. As with Kymlicka, this appears to be a result of the concern to preserve the non-competence of the state and circumvent majority opinion within a religious group. Yet it is not clear that the desire to maintain state neutrality in relation to religious conscience can be achieved. Claims of conscience—for instance, that one's religion requires time off from work—requires the courts to adjudicate on the sincerity of a religious conviction of an individual and thus unavoidably rule on what counts as sincerity of belief based on some interpretive standards (Eisenberg, 2009; Sullivan, 2018). For Taylor, as for Kymlicka, when it comes to religion—but not language—the liberty of sovereign individuals within a state struggling to be neutral virtually wipes out the earlier significance of recognition, namely the goal of cultural group preservation.[6] State-religion connections in open secularism are judged primarily in terms of a moral individualism ignoring their role in "misrecognition" and, more positively, in developing the public good in material or symbolic terms, for example, through contributing to a sense of national identity.

Religion and Multicultural Accommodation

The shared feature in these two approaches, denominationalism as a part of a multinationalism and open secularism as part of an intercultural nationalism, is a freedom of religion based on moral individualism and state neutrality. I suggest that these conclusions have taken us a long way away from the multiculturalism that we should embrace. Namely, a bottom-up politics that seeks an egalitarian due public recognition for the minority identities important to their bearers, without exceptionalizing religion, and remaking the national identity so that all citizens can have a sense of belonging to it. In relation to religious groups this creates a challenge for all understandings of secularism based on the privatization—sometimes called "Protestantizing"—of religion, state neutrality and separatism.

So, how should multiculturalism relate to religion and religious identity? My own work has done so in two ways. Firstly, to not just think of religion as restricted to a matter of doctrine, belief and individual conscience but to keep religion firmly in the field of minorities that can suffer misrecognition and deserve recognition. Secondly, to think of normative religion-state relations not in terms of ideal theory (e.g., secularism) but work with existing normative modes of political secularism and ensure that the new religious minorities are accommodated through an application of multiculturalist concepts of equal citizenship, inclusion and national belonging. In the West, especially in European contexts, this means the recognition of the recently settled non-Christian religious minorities building on the historic adaptation of state-religion connections which have gradually extended positive recognition to Christian minorities and Jews.

How, in Western Europe, groups and controversies defined in terms of race or foreignness came to be redefined in terms of religion, and how the accommodation of Muslims came to be the dominant issue in relation to multiculturalism, has now been well established (Modood, 2005, 2007/2013). This is partly because groups can shift from say a race to a religion focus, or fuse foci, for example by combining ethnicity and religion. In tracking such group shifts it is important to not lose the concept of identity that multiculturalism entails. I mean, here, especially the dual-faceted understanding of identity, which sees that the relevant minorities can have identities ascribed to them by dominant groups in a process which can be variously described as racialization, essentialization or othering (Modood, 2019: Chapter 4). This is when a group is given negative, stereotypical, inferiorizing or hostility-expressing features such as a Black identity centered on criminal violence or a Muslim identity centered on puritanical fanaticism. In Taylor's excellent term, they are all forms of misrecognition because they make no effort to understand a group on its own terms or in ways which are not shaped by fear and domination (Taylor, 1994). Misrecognition can take many forms and cover different kinds of identities and groups (ethnoracial, ethnonational, ethnocultural, ethnoreligious and so on). They are the fundamental harm and inequality that multiculturalism addresses. The solution is recognition, namely understanding a group as it understands itself and seeks to find dignity and, typically, membership in a national citizenship. This is not just symbolic—though it will involve change in attitudes to the minority as well as how it can become part of a re-made, inclusive "We"—but also appropriate to laws, policies, distribution of resources and institutional accommodation. Broadly speaking, these policies can be divided into those of negative and those of positive equality. Negative equality here means anti-discrimination, protection against hatred and victimization and a de-othering; positive equality means the inclusion of that group and its own sense of self—which of course is always subject to some change, including during a process of recognition—into a re-formed national identity.

So, a multiculturalist approach to religious minorities consists of a program of anti-discrimination and a positive place, institutionally and symbolically, in the life of the national polity. A good example of such an ethnoreligious group which has been subject to racialization and has had to be protected against racism and included into a re-imagining of national membership are the Jews. Education and laws against antisemitism, including the outlawing of Holocaust denial,[7] the creation by the state of a national consultative body such as a Jewish Consistory, the redefining of a country from "Christian" to "Judeo-Christian" are amongst the different measures that various countries have taken even if not in the name of multiculturalism. Jews here could be understood to be followers of a religion, Judaism, but "follow" here clearly cannot mean to believe in and strictly adhere to its rules. Many proud, self-defined Jews who are recognized as Jews by fellow Jews, as well as non-Jews, are atheists and/or do not participate in approved collective worship and/or do not follow the rules of living such as keeping a kosher kitchen or covering their heads appropriately. Indeed, it is perhaps better to think of Jews as a people with a religion, such that peoplehood and religion mutually inform each other, with religion a characteristic or a possession of a people, not of individuals per se. So, while Jews would not be the people that they are without Judaism, not every individual Jew has to be religious in order to be a Jew, i.e., part of a Jewish peoplehood. Moreover, there can be sources of Jewish identity other than those that are the strictly religious, such as the Holocaust as a memory of a people or a collective commitment to the state of Israel. This is one aspect of what multiculturalism might mean in relation to the post-immigration ethnoreligious groups such Muslims, Hindus and Sikhs and so on (Modood, 2019: 5–7).

State–Religion Connections

The other aspect I wish to refer to is the inclusion of these ethnoreligious groups into the state–religion connections. This is possible and necessary because, while such connections are various, strict separation is quite exceptional. A multiculturalist who believes that a culturally neutral state is impossible will not be surprised to learn that nearly a third of all Western democracies have an official religion and more than half of all 47 democracies in the polity dataset officially or unofficially give preference to one religion. Indeed, most of the others give preference to more than one religion (Perez and Fox, 2018). To achieve greater empirical traction than political theorists usually do here, we need to work with a minimalist understanding of secularism, namely the view that there are two significant and conceptually distinct modes of authority: political and religious. This gives us the conceptual resources to observe there are two sets of institutions and activities, the political and the religious, each to some extent, sometimes to a limited extent, organizes itself in its own way, with its own conception and practice of authority, and each must be allowed to enjoy a certain autonomy within their own spheres of concern. Each actual political instantiation or normative concept will be more than this but by beginning with this minimalist concept, we will not take a particular interpretation or set of institutions to exhaust the possibilities that exist. Rather, it enables us to work with the full range of empirical cases without normatively excluding them or misdescribing them empirically.

Specifically, political secularism is the claim that religious authority should not control political authority in the sphere of government, law and citizenship. Note that this understanding of secularism does not give automatic priority to religious freedom, conscience, toleration or democracy. Of course, all of these are important but for me they are constituent features of liberal democracy and so become features of secularism in a liberal democracy. One such version of secularism, which I identify by a grounded, empirical-normative focus on the institutions and practices of countries like Britain, is what I call "moderate secularism," and it does indeed give an important place to freedom of religion. Yet, at the same time, when one considers the former Soviet Union, the People's Republic of China, the Republic of Turkey and even aspects of *laïcité*, one sees that there is no necessary connection between religious freedom and secularism, and secularists in certain times and places prize secularism above freedom of religion (as in France, see Kuru, 2009 and on the new "anti-separatism" law, Kuru, 2021; more generally, see Modood and Sealy, forthcoming, 2022).

Western European Governance of Religion

For many intellectuals, especially political theorists, (Western) secularism has been understood in terms of the religious-liberty secularism of the USA and/or the equality of citizenship secularism or *laïcité* of France (Bhargava, 2009). Yet, as a matter of fact, neither of these approaches approximates particularly closely to church-state relations amongst Western European countries beyond France, where a variety of patterns of legal constitutional and non-legal constitutional regulation and relations can be found.[8] In Germany, the Catholic and Protestant Churches are constitutionally recognized corporations, for which the state does not only collect voluntary taxes but the church welfare organizations, taken together, are the largest recipients of funding to non-state welfare providers (Lewicki, 2014). Denmark has a system of classes of recognition, producing a tiered set of rights and privileges in relation to the state (Laegaard, 2012). In Belgium, a number of religions have constitutional entitlements, and a national Council of Religions enjoys the support of the monarch. Norway, Denmark and England each have an "established" church (even if only "weakly" institutionalized), Sweden had one until 2001 and Finland has two. In Italy, Ireland and Poland the Catholic Church is powerful and influential, albeit distinct from state structures (for alternative typologies, see Koenig, 2009; Madeley, 2009; Stepan, 2011; Ferrari, 2012; Fox, 2015). Yet despite these connections between state and religion, it would be difficult to dispute that these states are not amongst the leading secular states in the world—more precisely, one could only dispute that if one had some narrow, abstract model of secularism that one insisted on applying to the varieties of empirical cases. So, we need a conception of secularism that fits this European reality.

My suggestion has been the concept of "moderate secularism" (Modood, 2010). Whilst initially conceptualized to capture a North-Western European reality and always recognizing France as a partial exception, national studies by colleagues now suggests that "moderate secularism" has considerable traction beyond that region and maybe should be understood as at least a Western European form of secularisms (Triandafyllidou and Magazzini, 2020). I characterize moderate secularism in terms of five features, which in combination lead to its distinctiveness, including from US and French models (Modood, 2017b).[9] It is important to stress that these features describe the normative character of aspects of the most liberal democratic states of contemporary Europe; that is, these are not features of an archaic or illiberal privileging of religion:

1. religious freedom based on mutual autonomy of religious and political authority, not mutual exclusion or one-sided control as explained above;
2. religion is a public not just a private good. Organized religion can play a significant role in relation to ethical voice (Habermas, 2006), general social well-being, cultural heritage, national ceremonies as well as national identity. This can take various forms, such as having input into a legislative

forum, such as the House of Lords in the UK, or on moral and welfare issues; being social partners with the state in the delivery of education, health and caring services; or more intangibly, in building social capital and the production of attitudes that create, for example, family stability, a compassionate civil society or economic hope. Of course, the public good that religion contributes is contextual; religion can, in other contexts, be socially divisive and can lead to civil and international wars. Hence, religion can also be a public harm. The point is that religion's contributions are not confined to private lives; they are socially and politically significant in many different ways and need to be addressed by the state;

3. the organizers of this public good, specifically the national church—or churches—belongs to the people and the country, not just to its religious members and clergy. The Lutheran Church in Denmark, for example, is almost universally thought by Danes to be an element, perhaps a central element of Danish national identity, even though only a minority say they believe in its doctrines and even fewer worship in the Church (Jenkins, 2011). In these and other "moderate secular" countries, even atheists feel that they have a right to use the national church for weddings and funerals. Relatedly, the Church of England's sense that it has a duty to serve the country has meant that it has in recent years often spoken up on behalf of ethnic and religious minorities. The latter have come to appreciate that its presence signifies that religious identities—including those of minorities—may be a feature of national belonging (Modood, 1997);[10]

4. it is legitimate for the state to be involved in eliciting the public good that comes from organized religion, and not just to protect the public good from dangers posed by it. If recognized as public goods, then, depending on the circumstances, it may be decided that they are best achieved through some state–religion connections rather than strict separation. This is a contingent matter, but the experience of Western Europe is that some connections are better than none;

5. moderate secularism can take different forms in different times and places, and not all forms of religious establishment should be ruled out without attending to specific cases. State-religion connections take different forms in different Western European countries depending on their histories, traditions, political cultures and religious composition, which all may change over time. One of the forms it may take is "establishment." Formal establishment is only found in a minority of countries, yet nevertheless it is one of the forms that moderate secularism takes. Even when it does so, this complex of norms and practices may be called "moderate secularism" rather than "moderate establishment" (as Dworkin, 2006 labels Britain; see also "modest establishment" of Laborde, 2013) because it is secularism, not establishment, that is in charge: the place for religion and establishment is dependent on secularist institutions and decision-makers referring

to secularist values and principles albeit open to embrace the contribution of religion to the public good. It is clear that this is what exists in practice. Both in relation to the church-state relations narrowly conceived, or in terms of an expansive sociological analysis, governing power lies with secularist institutions, networks, and individuals employing secular identities, interests and goals. Thus "the church" is a constitutive feature of moderate secularism and is a partner within it. So, moderate secularism is not something to contrast with religion; it is the governance of a particular way of relating religion with state power and politics. Moderate secularism, then, is not an abstract political theory model but is a conceptualization of a historically evolved set of arrangements and practices, formal and informal.

Multiculturalizing Moderate Secularism

A multiculturalist recognition of ethnoreligious identities is a form of equal citizenship and inclusion. It does not consist of endorsing the truth of any religion. In so far as there is an endorsement, it is an endorsement of co-membership, including the identities of the groups endorsed as belonging, not endorsement of beliefs or practices. For example, a Prime Minister attending an iftar, the eating of a meal to break the daily fast in Ramadan, is not endorsing Islam in preference to non-Islam or raising those who fast above those who do not. She is endorsing that Islam is part of the country, not asking anyone to follow it or uncritically endorsing any and every belief or practice that someone says is Islamic. It is in this sense that multiculturalism does not simply seek freedom of conscience, non-othering, non-discrimination or a religion-neutral state: equal citizenship requires positive inclusivity through identity recognition and institutional accommodation, so that all can have a sense of belonging to the national citizenship without having to privatize ethnic or religious group identities important to them.

Such a multiculturalizing accommodation of public inclusion of religious minorities is even compatible with an "established" religion as in the case of the Church of England. Given the rapidity of changes that are affecting British national identity, and the way in which religion, sometimes in a divisive way, is making a political reappearance, it would be wise not to discard lightly this historic aspect of British identity, which continues to be of importance to many even when few attend Church of England services. Yet, in my advocacy of a multiculturalized Britain, I would like to see the Church of England share these constitutional privileges—which should perhaps be extended—with other faiths. However, multiculturalism here does not mean crude "parity." My expectation is that even in the context of an explicit multifaithism the Church of England would enjoy a rightful precedence in the religious representation in the House of Lords and in the coronation of the monarch, and this would not be just a crude majoritarianism but be based on its historical contribution.

To this must be added the multiculturalist condition—namely, the Church of England's potential to play a leading role in the evolution of a multiculturalist national identity, state and society (Thompson and Modood, 2022). Both the historical and the multiculturalist contributions to national identity have a presumptive quality, and usually they qualify each other, yet where they are complementary, the case for "establishment" is enhanced—and most of all where there is simultaneously a process of inclusion of non-Anglican faith communities. It seems from King Charles' first statements on the topic on becoming king that he may have a similar vision for the Church of England and multifaith Britain (https://www.royal.uk/kings-remarks-faith-leaders).

A further illustration is about religious instruction (not merely religious education) and worship in the common school. We should not, for example, ask schools to cease Christian instruction or worship or celebrating Christmas *because* of the presence of, say, Muslims or Hindus; rather, we should extend the celebrations to include, for example, Eid and Diwali. Such separate classes and faith-specific worship needs to be balanced, however, with an approach that brings all the children together and into dialogue; indeed, without that it would be potentially divisive of the school and of society. But where that is in place, voluntary pursuit of one's own faith or philosophical tradition completes the multiculturalist approach to the place of religion in such schools. If the majority comes to the view that it no longer has a religion or does not want its religion(s) taught in common schools, fair enough. But that does not give it the right to veto the religious induction into minority faiths at school—if any minority wants to have it. Just as Christians do not have any dietary requirements at school does not give them the right to prevent the provision of kosher, halal or vegetarian options for pupils.[11]

Let me note that these two examples also illustrate an important point about multiculturalism and the national culture. The general liberal and civic nationalist approach is to say that diversity requires a "thinning" of the national culture so that minorities may feel included and do not feel that a thick majoritarian culture is imposed on them. This is also the approach of liberal multicultural nationalists. Kymlicka argues that:

> liberal states exhibit a much thinner conception of national identity. In order to make it possible for people from different ethnocultural backgrounds to become full and equal members of the nation … In so far as liberal nation-building involves diffusing a common national culture throughout the territory of the state, it is a very thin form of culture.
> *(Kymlicka 2001: 55–56)*

Yet the examples above are not a thinning of moderate secularism or of religion in state schools, they are a pluralistic thickening. Multiculturalism adds to the national culture by not disestablishing the national church but bringing other faiths into relationship with it. Indeed, in general, a multicultural society requires more state action to not just respect the diversity but to bring it together in a common sense of national belonging and that in many instances means adding to a sense of national culture, not hollowing it out. The bringing of minority faith communities into playing a role in aspects of the national or public culture alongside Christians and humanists requires us to think differently about the country and so may require an appropriate public narrative about the kind of country we now are (Commission on Multi-Ethnic Britain, 2000). In this way, multiculturalizing secularism means multiculturalizing our national identity; and conversely, multiculturalizing our national citizenship requires multiculturalizing secularism—what we might call a "multicultural nationalism" (Modood, 2018).

Conclusion

Kymlickan multinationalism and Bouchard-Taylor majoritarian interculturalism (designed for an autonomous Quebec but presumably also the philosophy for a possible independent Quebec state) have limited traction in relation to multiculturalist theory and practice in Western Europe. Features critical to multiculturalist theory and consciousness in Europe—postcolonial settlements and with it a shared history but marked by racism and racialized socio-economic disadvantage and an anti-racism politics, and, relevantly to this chapter, the centrality of religion, especially Muslims—are either absent or not treated in a multiculturalist way in their Canadian counterparts. In Kymlicka's case, from the start, religion is not given the same status as other aspects of minority group identity such as the ethnonational, ethnocultural and the ethnolinguistic, including Indigeneity, and later came to review that. In Taylor's case, the idea of recognition was withheld from religious groups when he came, with Québécois collaborators, Gerard Bouchard and Jocelyn Maclure, to develop the concept of "open secularism" as a practical proposal on how the Quebec state should or not include religious identity. I have offered an understanding of multiculturalism that has grown out of the European features mentioned above and this chapter has been dedicated to considering the implications of that for religion and secularism. I have suggested that Western Europe, with the partial exception of France, has a moderate secularism that has been progressively accommodative of Christian churches and Jewish identity, as long as accommodated religion does not interfere with political authority, and is therefore susceptible to being multiculturalized rather than thinned out. Another way of putting this is that multiculturalism seeks the sharing of the spaces for public religion and its relationship to national identity, rather than a neutral state or the imposing of majoritarian norms upon minority religious self-conceptions. It is envisaged thus that a unity in diversity is achieved, that a national citizenship is opened up to be inclusive of difference; not by reducing citizens to individuals or a religion-blindness but by remaking the national identity to include what it may have hereto excluded. Interestingly, this has been taken further in some Asian and other countries than in the West – yet they are now embracing a majoritarian nationalism even more than is found in the West. Maybe we need to learn from each other (Modood and Sealy, forthcoming, 2022).[12]

Notes

1 My interest in relation to Kymlicka is in the liberal foundations of his multiculturalism that he worked out primarily in Kymlicka 1995, not how he has developed the application of it to different contexts, regionally and temporally, nor how he has assessed different political contexts without reference to his foundational theory. Other eminent political theories I could discuss are Tully (1995) and Carens (2000) but I will confine myself to the two mentioned above as I think they are most prominent in Canada and internationally.
2 The point I am making is not confined to theory. In 2002 I was invited to a policy event in Ottawa. After I had made by presentation on what Canada might like to consider in the light of the UK experience, the most senior civil servant present politely thanked me and said the issue of religion as a part of multiculturalism was not relevant to Canada.
3 However, he is not consistent as many of the examples in his 1995 book relate to religious minorities such as the Amish, Christians, Muslims, Jews, Sabbatarians, etc. (Levey 2008).
4 For fuller examples of simultaneous state recognition of multiple religions in different ways and to different extents and their possible normative justification, see Thompson and Modood (2022).
5 This section is based on some joint work with Thomas Sealy and I am grateful for our collaboration (Modood and Sealy, forthcoming, 2022).
6 I note, however, that Bouchard and Taylor say that "open secularism resembles what Milot calls the secularism of recognition" (Bouchard and Taylor, 2008: 141). This makes no difference to my argument above.
7 Holocaust denial is punishable in 16 European countries (Austria, Belgium, Czech Republic, France, Germany, Hungary, Liechtenstein, Lithuania, Luxembourg, Netherlands, Poland, Portugal, Romania, Russia, Slovakia and Switzerland) and Israel. "Legality of Holocaust Denial," Wikipedia, https://en.wikipedia.org/wiki/Legality_of_Holocaust_denial.
8 Even in France there is the case of Alsace-Moselle, see Thompson and Modood (2022).
9 Some scholars further differentiate what I unite. Stepan (2011), for example, distinguishes between two models within what I call moderate secularism, namely "The 'Established Religion' Model" and "The 'Positive Accommodation' Model." I do not quarrel with this helpful distinction (equally useful are the other models that Stepan identifies). Moderate secularism encompasses the two and so characterises what they have in common. The same can be said of the distinctions that Bader (2017) makes.
10 See the statement by King Charles on accession to the throne and title of the Supreme Governor of the Church of England: https://www.royal.uk/kings-remarks-faith-leaders.
11 For an application of these arguments to the case of Flanders, Belgium, see Modood 2017a.

12 These matters were currently being explored in relation to 23 countries in seven world regions in an H2020-funded project, GREASE: http://grease.eui.eu/ I gratefully acknowledge the use of this funding to write this chapter. A key output of this project is Modood and Sealy (2022).

References

Bader, Veit M. 2017. "Secularisms or Liberal-Democratic Constitutionalism." In *The Oxford Handbook of Secularism*, Phillip Zuckerman and John Shook (eds.) Oxford: Oxford University Press, 333–353.
Bauböck, Rainer. 2003. "Public Culture in Societies of Immigration." In *Identity and Integration*, Rosemarie Sackmann, Bernhard Peters and Thomas Faist (eds.) Aldershot: Ashgate, 37–57.
Bhargava, Rajeev. 2009. "Political Secularism." In *Secularism, Religion and Multicultural Citizenship*, Geoffrey Brahm Levey and Tariq Modood (eds.) Cambridge: Cambridge University Press, 82–109.
Bouchard, Gérard and Charles Taylor. 2008. *Building the Future: A Time for Reconciliation*. Montreal: Gouvernement du Québec.
Carens, J.H. 2000. *Culture, Citizenship, and Community: A Contextual Exploration of Justice as Evenhandedness*. Oxford: Oxford University Press on Demand.
Commission on Multi-Ethnic Britain (The Parekh Report). 2000. *The Future of MultiEthnic Britain*. London: Profile Books.
Dworkin, Ronald. 2006. *Is Democracy Possible Here? Principles for a New Political Debate*. Princeton: Princeton University Press.
Eisenberg, Avigail. 2009. *Reasons of Identity: A Normative Guide to the Political and Legal Assessment of Identity Claims*. Oxford: Oxford University Press.
Ferrari, Silvo. 2012. "Law and Religion in a Secular World: A European Perspective." *Ecclesiastical Law Journal 14*: 355–370.
Fox, Jonathan. 2015. *Political Secularism, Religion, and the State: A Time Series Analysis of Worldwide Data*. Cambridge: Cambridge University Press.
Habermas, Jurgen. 2006. "Religion in the Public Sphere." *European Journal of Philosophy 14* (1): 1–25.
Jenkins, Richard. 2011. *Being Danish: Paradoxes of Identity in Everyday Life*. Copenhagen: Museum Tusculanum Press.
Koenig, Matthias. 2009. "How Nation-States Respond to Religious Diversity." In *International Migration and the Governance of Religious Diversity*, Paul Bramadat and Matthias Koenig (eds.) Montreal and Kingston: McGill-Queen's University Press, 293–322.
Kuru, Ahmet T. 2009. *Secularism and State Policies Toward Religion: The United States, France, and Turkey*. Cambridge: Cambridge University Press.
Kuru, Ahmet T. 2021. "France's Lower House Approves Anti-Separatism Bill to Battle Islamist Extremism." *France 24*, 23 July. https://www.france24.com/en/live-news/20210723-france-s-lower-house-approves-separatism-law-to-battle-islamist-extremism.
Kymlicka, Will. 1995. *Multicultural Citizenship: A Liberal Theory of Minority Rights*. Oxford: Clarendon Press.
Kymlicka, Will. 2001. "Western Political Theory and Ethnic Relations in Eastern Europe." In *Can Liberal Pluralism be Exported?*, Will Kymlicka and Magda Opalski (eds.) Oxford: Oxford University Press, 13–105.

Kymlicka, Will. 2009. "Historic Settlements and New Challenges: Review Symposium." *Ethnicities* 9 (4): 546–552.

Kymlicka, W. 2015 "The Three Lives of Multiculturalism." In *Revisiting Multiculturalism in Canada: Theories, Policies, Debates*, S. Guo and L. Wong (eds.) Sense Publishers, 17–35.

Laborde, Cécile. 2013. "Political Liberalism and Religion: On Separation and Establishment." *Journal of Political Philosophy* 21 (1): 67–86.

Lægaard, Sune. 2012. "Unequal Recognition, Misrecognition and Injustice: The Case of Religious Minorities in Denmark." *Ethnicities* 12 (2): 197–214.

Levey, Geoffrey Brahm. 2019. "The Bristol School of Multiculturalism." *Ethnicities* 19 (1): 200–226.

Lewicki, Aleksandra. 2014. *Social Justice Through Citizenship?: The Politics of Muslim Integration in Germany and Great Britain*. Basingstoke: Palgrave.

Maclure, Jocelyn and Taylor, Charles. 2011. *Secularism and Freedom of Conscience*. Cambridge, MA: Harvard University Press.

Madeley, John. 2009. "Unequally Yoked: The Antinomies of Church-State Separation in Europe and the USA." *European Political Science* 8: 273–288.

Modood, Tariq. 1997. "Introduction: Establishment, Reform and Multiculturalism." In *Church, State and Religious Minorities*, Tariq Modood (ed.) London: Policy Studies Institute, 3–15.

Modood, Tariq. 2005. *Multicultural Politics: Racism, Ethnicity and Muslims in Britain*. Minneapolis: University of Minnesota Press and Edinburgh: University of Edinburgh Press.

Modood, Tariq. 2013 [2007]. *Multiculturalism: A Civic Idea*. Cambridge: Polity Press.

Modood, Tariq. 2017a. "Multicultural Citizenship and New Migrations." In *Multicultural Governance in a Mobile World*, Anna Triandafyllidou (ed.) Edinburgh: Edinburgh University Press, 183–202.

Modood, Tariq. 2017b. "Multiculturalizing Secularism." In *The Oxford Handbook of Secularism*, Phillip Zuckerman and John Shook (eds.) Oxford: Oxford University Press, 354–368.

Modood, Tariq. 2018. "A Multicultural Nationalism". *Brown Journal of World Affairs 25*: 233.

Modood, Tariq. 2019. *Essays on Secularism and Multiculturalism*. London: ECPR and Rowman and Littlefield International.

Modood, Tariq. 2022. "Multiculturalism Without Privileging Liberalism." In *Majorities, Minorities and the Future of Nationhood*, Liav Orgad and Rudd Koopmans (eds.) Cambridge: Cambridge University Press, 201–224.

Modood, T. and T. Sealy. 2021. "Freedom of religion and the accommodation of religious diversity: multiculturalising secularism." *Religions* 12 (10): 868.

Modood, Tariq and Thomas Sealy (eds.). forthcoming 2022. "The Governance of Religious Diversity: Global Comparative Perspectives." Special Issue, *Religion, State and Society*.

Perez, N. and J. Fox. 2018. "Normative Theorizing and Political Data: Toward a Data-sensitive Understanding of the Separation Between Religion and State in Political Theory." *Critical Review of International Social and Political Philosophy*.

Stepan, Alfred. 2011. "The Multiple Secularisms of Modern Democratic and Non-Democratic Regimes." In *Rethinking Secularism*, Craig Calhoun, Mark Juergensmeyer and Jonathan Van Antwerpen (eds.) Oxford: Oxford University Press, 114–144.

Sullivan, Winnifred Fallers. 2018. *The Impossibility of Religious Freedom*. Princeton: Princeton University Press.
Taylor, Charles. 1994. "Multiculturalism and "The Politics of Recognition"." In *Multiculturalism and 'The Politics of Recognition*, Amy Gutmann (ed.) Princeton: Princeton University Press, 25–74.
Thompson, Simon and Tariq Modood. 2022. "The Multidimensional Recognition of Religion." *Critical Review of International Social and Political Philosophy* 1–22.
Triandafyllidou, Anna and Tina Magazzini (eds.). 2020. *Routledge Handbook on the Governance of Religious Diversity*. Abingdon: Routledge.
Tully, J. 1995. *Strange Multiplicity: Constitutionalism in an Age of Diversity (No. 1)*. Cambridge: Cambridge University Press.

10
HINDUIZING NATION

Shifting Grounds of Secularism, Diversity and Citizenship

Mohita Bhatia

Introduction

Unlike Canada or Australia where multicultural policies are well established and have official sanction from the state, India's case is different, but not incompatible with the discourse on multiculturalism and managing diversities. The Indian social landscape is marked by enormous cultural, linguistic, religious and ethnic diversities that coexist with multiple hierarchies and inequities. Here, negotiations around issues of cultural heterogeneities exist at two separate yet related levels—at the level of the state, and the everyday social level. Despite occasional social conflicts, religious Hindu–Muslim tensions, and implicit majoritarian Hindu propensities at both the levels, until recently the state, as well as societal processes, responded creatively in ways that were appreciative and accommodative of diversities. While the constitution of the Indian state is a multicultural document that recognizes the rights of different groups and has conceptualized the notion of secularism (Mahajan, 2005; Bajpai, 2017), it is at the quotidian level of social performances that heterogeneities, cultural tensions and hierarchies are lived and negotiated. Although distinct, the state and social realms mirror and complement one another in many ways. It was through these dialogues at both the levels that India had come to be defined as a diverse and secular nation state. This chapter argues that there has been a paradigmatic shift in the very idea of India since 2014 with the Narendra Modi-led Bharatiya Janata Party (BJP) coming to power. With this ruling party brazenly distancing itself from the principles of secularism and displaying a belligerent Hindu majoritarian stance, contemporary India is rejecting constitutional multicultural commitments to its minorities. The shift is not limited to the state. It is also in sync with growing anti-Muslim sentiments among the Hindu majority population, along with the popularization of terms such

DOI: 10.4324/9781003197485-15

as "sickularism" (term to ridicule secularism) or "libtards" (a disdainful term used for people holding moderate, liberal or left-leaning views). This chapter analyzes the secular crisis that underlies this shift and argues for the relevance and need of multicultural and secular perspectives in order to counter this rising intolerance against minorities.

India's Multicultural Constitution: A Reflection of Social Heterogeneities and Differentiations

The perspective on multiculturalism in India is different from that of Canada, even though the two nation states value cultural diversity and have policies in place that aim to facilitate rights and cultural practices of minorities. Within Canada and other Western countries, multicultural debates have centered around rights of ethnic and cultural minorities, mainly the immigrant population from different corners of the globe; India's integration policies are not immigrant-oriented but reflect the concerns of its own internal minorities including religious ones. As Rochana Bajpai explains, "with most followers of Islam and Christianity seen as converts from Hinduism, religious minorities are not viewed as recent migrants, unlike in Europe and North America" (Bajpai, 2017: 2). In the Indian context, rather than ethnicity or race, the diversity discourse has focused on caste, religious, linguistic and tribal minorities. Unlike Canada, India does not define itself as a multicultural state, yet its political and constitutional trajectory clearly recognizes "persons as citizens of the state as well as members of specific cultural communities" (Mahajan, 2005: 290). It is more through the idea of diversity and plurality, rather than formal use of the term multiculturalism, that the Indian state and its constitution have addressed the concerns of linguistic, caste and religious minorities (Parekh, 2017; Mahajan, 2005).

This section elaborates on the Indian context of diversities and the way that the Indian Constitution has conferred recognition to cultural minorities. This chapter focuses on the issue of religious minorities, mainly Muslims and the constitutional provision of secularism to manage religious diversities. Due to the historical legacy and trauma of partition of the Indian subcontinent in 1947[1] and Hindu–Muslim violence that accompanied it, concern for Muslim minorities becomes particularly relevant in the debates on Indian diversity.

Fluidities and overlaps between diverse cultures and religions have long existed in India. A prodigious body of work on the subject has focused specifically on Hindu–Muslim interactions and on the fusion of their local cultural practices (Uddin, 2011; Gottschalk, 2001; Khan, 2004). Contesting the idea of religion as a cohesive category, these works have illustrated intricate intermixing of religious, local and ethnic traditions that produce blurred boundaries and spaces of liminality. These local, inter-religious dialogic traditions, nevertheless, do not present an idealized picture of euphony; in fact, dialogues have coexisted with moments of tension and politics of religious mobilization. Historically, the 1947 partition of the Indian subcontinent into two nation states, India and Pakistan, was one such catastrophic incident of extreme Hindu–Muslim violence that left around 2 million people dead, and triggered the largest migration in world history (Rastogi, 2020; Zamindar, 2007; Butalia, 2015). It may be pertinent to note that 1947 was the year that represented the end of British rule over the Indian subcontinent; however, this independence came at the cost of partition of the subcontinent that resulted in communal frenzy and violence.

Although partition left an emotional scar in the minds of people and continues to influence Indian politics and society, religious and cultural communities demonstrated resilience and a willingness to move on and rebuild ties of interdependence. The fact that these communities are internally differentiated in terms of class, region, language and culture often acted as a buffer against religious polarization. In the case of Hindus, what had prevented this widely heterogeneous religious community from acting as a monolith is the internal caste competition and assertion by lower castes or Dalits against their dehumanization by the upper and middle-castes (Bhatia, 2020; Dirks, 2011). Their resistance can be traced back to caste struggles led by BR Ambedkar and other Dalit leaders who not only looked at colonial rule differently from the mainstream upper-caste-dominated Indian national movement, but also demanded adequate representation and safeguards for Dalits in the constitution of independent India (Teltumbde, 2016).[2]

The Indian Constitution was drafted keeping in mind these pluralities, hierarchies and ruptures, and therefore, was not simply a document imposed from the top. Reflecting and being shaped by on the ground realities, it successfully fused the liberal notion of individual rights with the concerns for differentiated community rights (Mahajan, 2005; Bajpai, 2017). It offered institutional and political measures for accommodation of various groups. For example, acknowledging the structural inequalities and struggles of the disadvantaged caste and tribal communities, it included affirmative action (quotas or special guarantees/protections) for Scheduled Castes, Scheduled Tribes and Other Backwards Castes in government jobs, educational institutions and the legislature.[3] Also included were provisions for the protection and freedom of religious and linguistic rights.[4] The Indian Constitution "on the one hand tried to ensure that no community is outrightly excluded or systematically disadvantaged in the public arena, on the other hand, it provided autonomy to each religious community to pursue its own way of life" (Mahajan, 1998: 4). Reflecting on the multicultural elements of the Indian society and Constitution, Rochana Bajpai argues:

> Predating Western multicultural policies by several decades, the Indian Constitution poses a challenge to the influential view that multiculturalism in Asia and Africa is a recent export from the West ... non-Western

experience of dealing with the challenges of ethno-religious pluralism is longer-standing than that of most Western democracies.

(Bajpai 2015: 1)

The protection of different religious groups, especially minorities, is best realized through the constitutional principle of secularism and secular embodiment of the Indian state. Unlike some Western secularisms such as *laïcité* in France, Indian secularism does not completely obliterate religion from the public or political sphere. It acknowledges the religious way of life of people and the impossibility of separating people's religious and public lives. This is explained by Rajeev Bhargava who states that an understanding of secularism in India has to move beyond the secular–religion dichotomy. He argues that "although that state is not identified with a particular religion … there is official and therefore public recognition granted to religious communities" (Bhargava, 2011). It is in this context that the constitution accords freedom to religious groups to regulate their internal affairs and to establish as well as to promote their educational and cultural institutions. Rather than passively tolerating religion, the Indian state provided for equal respect and neutrality towards religion. Indian secularism, thus, has been envisioned as creatively distinct as it tied well to local and cultural sensibilities (Bhargava, 2011; Tejani, 2007). This flexible secularism has been diversity-oriented, more compatible with the ideas of multiculturalism and concerned with protecting and facilitating cultural practices of religious minorities.

Despite incorporating group-differentiated rights and ethics of secularism, the Indian approach to multiculturalism has remained somewhat limited. While the Indian Constitution recognized group rights and ensured fairness for religious minorities, it did not advance the multicultural approach beyond a point due to the nation state's emphasis on citizenship equality and national unity (Parekh, 2017; Bajpai, 2017). The project of creating an Indian "nation" out of such variegated cultures and communities who before the 19th century had no common sense of belonging created insecurity among the Indian political leaders seeking to pursue the project of nation-building. Therefore, for the mainstream political leadership "[becoming] Indian involved learning to put belonging to India above belonging to any religious, linguistic, caste or tribal group" (Bajpai, 2017: 6). It was in this context that the multicultural approach to group rights was subordinated to the larger project of nationalist civilizational unity. In this sense, multiculturalism is not an official term in the Indian state's vocabulary; yet various accommodative approaches such as affirmative action—a form of group-based right integral to multiculturalism as pointed out by Will Kymlicka (Kymlicka, 1996) and Keith Banting (Banting and Kymlicka, 2006), federalism and secularism have formed the basis for negotiating issues of diversity, differences and political autonomy.

Shift in Socio-Political Dynamics: Hindu Nationalism from Fringes to the Center

While secularism, until recently, was considered a foundation and mainstay for Indian society and politics, there has been an unanticipated shift away from the secular conceptions of India. Secularism in India had never existed without contradictions. As mentioned above, the principle of secularism had always intersected with concerns of national unity. These concerns could frequently turn into a discourse of uniformity that privileges the dominant majority's cultural and religious practices (Tejani, 2007; Parekh, 2017). While the principle of secularism advocated respect for all religious practices, "unity" or "uniformity" versions of nationalist assertions created tacit cultural spaces of Hindu hegemony. A second contradiction is related to the idea of state neutrality when dealing with discords related to religious and cultural matters. Scholars have pointed out that complete state neutrality is not attainable, and there are possibilities for its subliminal, spontaneous identifications with the majority (Bhargava, 1994; Vanaik, 1997). Given the Hindu-majority context of India and the history of partition violence, on certain occasions, the state has been accused of having an implicit or explicit pro-Hindu bias (Chatterji, 2012; Teltumbde, 2016). The third challenge to secularism comes from the political parties for which religion (and/or caste) forms the easiest source of mobilization. Hindu nationalism, as articulated by right-wing organizations such as the BJP, has always existed alongside secular nationalism but had remained on the fringes before the 1980s. However, political parties at the other end of the spectrum have opportunistically invoked religion and caste as well even though they do not entirely base their politics on these lines (Jaffrelot, 1998; Hewitt, 2007). These more centrist political parties accepted secularism but simultaneously did not have qualms about using religion for electoral gain.[5] These contradictions notwithstanding, until the 1980s there remained a consensus that secularism and cultural diversities were integral to the idea of India. At both the levels, social and political, secularism was debated and critiqued; yet the principle was sacrosanct—it was unthinkable to envisage India *sans* secularism.

A shift in India's political spectrum started to take place in the 1980s and 1990s with the unexpected rise of the BJP and its deployment of Hindu nationalist ideology in the public sphere. The rise of the BJP coincided with the decline of the Congress—the party that was associated with Nehruvian secularism that was the major ruling party at the country as well as regional levels until the early 1980s.[6] The one-party monopoly of Congress was replaced by two categories of politics, one based on caste and the other based on religion (Jaffrelot, 1996). On the one hand, this period witnessed lower and lower-middle caste-based assertions[7] and the rise of political parties that represented the interests of these castes; on the other hand, this period also saw the BJP employ a politics that mobilized the upper-caste, middle-class Hindus by invoking aggressive, masculinist and religious symbols.

The upper-caste and urban basis of the BJP matched well with the new economic and cultural aspirations of expanding middle-class and privileged caste Hindus. The BJP's religious as well as market-oriented politics were viewed by this class as the new alternative to the worn-out and seemingly "socialist," "pro-poor" and "secular" politics of the Congress (Prabhu, 2020: 141–143). Thomas Blom Hansen explains that in the midst of the social flux and lower/middle-caste assertions, the rise of the BJP reflected the rising aspirations, cultural essentialism as well as caste insecurities of these upper-caste middle-class Hindus which were projected onto the minority Muslim community (Chatterji, Hansen and Jaffrelot, 2019). Religious otherness of Muslims and the projection of Muslims as "outsiders" (i.e., not original inhabitants of India) was a central discourse of the BJP and was endorsed by the upper castes. The BJP's discourse was not limited to the level of political rhetoric; the BJP made systematic public performances to reach out to the masses and engage in macro-scale campaigns, the most emotionally virulent of which was referred to as the "Rath Yatra"—a chariot tour.

The BJP's hard-liner leader LK Advani launched a countrywide campaign to build a temple in Ayodhya—the birthplace of Hindu God, "Rama"—where the Babri mosque was standing at that time. The campaign was meant to invoke religious sentiments of Hindus and organize them into a political community. Describing Advani's tour campaign, Burton Stein and David Arnold state:

> Advani, dressed as Rama (Hindu god) and armed with bow and arrow, began a ... tour of north India in a jeep dressed up as a Hindu chariot ... As his 'Rath Yatra' moved from town to town it fueled Hindu religious fervor and stirred up anti-Muslim sentiment.
>
> *(Stein and Arnold, 2010: 411)*

This militant Hindu campaign resulted in many riots, Hindu–Muslim polarization and eventually demolition of the mosque in 1992. This campaign made the BJP a nationally relevant party having a distinct political space. Its continuously growing relevance was reflected in its electoral performance as its legislative share increased from a mere two parliamentary seats in 1984 to 85 in 1989 and 119 seats in 1991 (Roy and Wallace, 2007: 68). It was set to transform the public and private discourse in India as religious nationalism or "Hindutva" became an accepted discourse not just in the political realm but also in the private familial spaces. Hindutva was now no longer the BJP's exclusive political agenda, it was imbibed by the people, initially upper caste and later even by many middle and lower-caste Hindus. Lower-caste antipathy towards the BJP's politics fizzled away to some extent at the later period when the Hindu-oriented discourse became pervasive and subsumed caste or class concerns.

Although the BJP and cultural organizations affiliated with it played an instrumental role in turning Hindu nationalism into a mass discourse,[8] this discourse did not simply emanate from the top. In fact, it was successful precisely because the party was being validated by a section of Hindus. Before the BJP became politically relevant, the collective expression of "Hindus versus Muslims" prejudices were moderated to some extent and the state did not encourage the expression of religious extremism in the public space. Blatant communal views were dampened to the extent that many of the upper-caste Hindus did not openly rationalize these expressions. Yet, even in that era of the pre-1980s, there was no strict communalism–secularism divide at the societal level, and secularism was not the only prevailing idea in this space. Processes of secularization in society were often expressed as an intricate interaction between inter-religious (and also inter-caste) coexistence, conflicts and negotiations (Tejani, 2007; Bhatia, 2013). These processes were non-linear and could move in any direction—at times fueling violence, at other moments indicating secular, syncretic relationships, and yet at other times occupying an amorphous space between these two ends. Memories of partition violence and emotional baggage from that period did create sporadic moments of mistrust and antagonism, which at times erupted in the form of small-scale communal riots. While incidents of religious prejudice were often resolved or put aside in favor of the idea of secularism, these sentiments were always present in certain segments of society. Although largely dormant, these sentiments have at times led to riots, as mentioned above. This changed with the political rise of the BJP. The party made itself politically relevant by offering a systematic coherence and legitimation to the hitherto disparate Hindu majoritarian ideas (Jaffrelot, 1996; Chatterji, Hansen and Jaffrelot, 2019). Its party workers reached out to the Hindu communities through various campaigns, eulogizing the idea of Hindu masculinity and superiority and vowing to reclaim the glorious Hindu past that was lost in history to the "barbarous" Muslim Mughal rulers or "invaders."

Even with its Hindu nationalist agenda and involvement in facilitating riots in many regions, the BJP did not completely abandon the idea of secularism. The BJP defamed secularism by labeling it "pseudo-secularism," yet during the times when it came to power as a coalition party it did not denounce or tamper with the constitutional principles of secularism and democracy (Jaffrelot, 1996). Both at the level of society and politics, there were growing signs of sectarianism; nevertheless, secularism was critiqued, not disowned. The BJP continued to uphold secular and democratic ideals, as it had to compete with a Congress party that was waning but that had not collapsed. Notwithstanding the political ascendancy of the BJP, until recently India's domestic and international image—as the most successful democracy that is inclusive of its diversity—was never questioned. The contemporary face of the BJP, as led by Narendra Modi, has marked a radical departure from this earlier soft-Hindutva position. The unmatched popularity and "larger than life" image of Modi has been a subject of analysis by various scholars (Palishkar, 2014; Gudavarthy, 2018; Chatterji, Hansen and Jaffrelot, 2019). The party is using its hegemonic political position to breach the constitutional foundations of India and institutionalize anti-secular and anti-multicultural values (Gudavarthy, 2018).

Creating a Virulent Hindu India: Citizenship Amendment Act

The BJP obtained an unexpected landslide victory in the 2014 parliamentary elections. All governments since the 1984 elections "have been dependent on coalitions and intense bargaining among partners of the ruling alliances or those who supported from outside" (Palishkar, 2014: 39). Reversing the trends of previous elections, the BJP won an absolute majority to be able to form a government on its own. Its unprecedented victory is attributed to the personality cult of Modi, his absolute control over the party, disciplined and authoritarian style of politics as well as his astute electoral strategies. Although the BJP based its election manifesto on the centrist and inclusive agenda of development for all communities, in practice it was conspicuously shifting towards extremist Hindu positions seeking to subsume or erase cultural and political diversities. Diversities were only to be accepted if their expression did not challenge Hindu supremacy (Gudavarthy, 2018). It was, however, the BJP's decisive victory in the following 2019 parliamentary elections that made the party realize its invincible position. First, no other political party in the electoral fray could provide serious competition to the BJP. Second, a large section of Hindus, across caste, class, region and ethnicity, were now unconditionally endorsing the party's aggressive agenda of national uniformity and making India a "Hindu rashtra (nation)." Many lower- and middle-caste Hindus, who previously were ambivalent, were now openly identifying with Hindu ideology (Narayan, 2021).

What is peculiar about the 2019 Modi-led government is that it is not simply attacking ideas of secularism and diversity at a discursive level but that it is using state institutions including the judiciary and police to breach the Indian Constitution and make actual changes in the socio-political fabric of India. The intent is to create India anew—one that is based on mythical ideas of Hindu civilization as opposed to a secular and plural India. In this "new India," the minorities, especially Muslims, are completely marginalized and targets of violence. It is in this pursuit that the BJP made several legal and policy changes.

For instance, the BJP has intensified its cow protection campaign that vilifies beef consumption practices among Muslims and other ethnic minorities. The cow is considered sacred by many upper-caste Hindus, and therefore the BJP amended and tightened cow protection laws to include harsher punishments against cow slaughter. Various cultural organizations affiliated with the BJP have used these laws to raid hotels, assault, beat up and in a few cases lynch

Muslim men who were accused of consuming or transporting beef (Chatterji, Hansen and Jaffrelot, 2019).[9] In its pursuit of other anti-Muslim policies, the BJP also introduced and approved the "Triple Talaq bill" to criminalize the Muslim practice of instant divorce. The BJP insisted that the bill empowers Muslim women; those critical of the bill argued that it demonizes the Muslim community and criminalizes divorce which is otherwise a civil matter (Withnall, 2019). In another move, the party suspended Article 370 of the constitution that offers political autonomy to Jammu and Kashmir, thus dispossessing the Kashmiri identity of any distinct cultural or political autonomy. Another infamous law that was passed in a few BJP-majority north Indian states is called "love Jihad" law or Prohibition of Unlawful Religious Conversion Ordinance, 2020. This law is being used to criminalize "not only Muslim men seeking to marry (or daring to have simple social interactions with) Hindu women, but also interfaith couples who had married long before the enactment of the legislation" (Apoorvanand, 2021).

Perhaps the most contentious policy and legal change is the enactment of the Citizenship Amendment Act (CAA) which triggered widespread protests by Muslims and other progressive groups. The CAA is refugee-centric and does not deal with citizens; yet it has indirect consequences for Indian citizens, especially Muslims. The Act passed by the government on December 11, 2019, amends the provisions of the 1955 Citizenship Act to fast-track Indian Citizenship for Hindu, Sikh, Christian, Buddhist, Parsi and Jain refugees who fled from some of the Muslim-majority neighboring countries due to reasons of religious persecution or fear of religious persecution, and arrived in India before December 31, 2014. The law specifically and arbitrarily leaves out Muslim refugees from eligibility for Indian citizenship and views them as "illegal migrants" (Chandrachud, 2020; Bhatia, 2021). The CAA is viewed by its opponents as anti-constitutional and violating secular principles. By drawing a distinction between Muslim and non-Muslim refugees, the Act explicitly and blatantly makes religious discrimination legal, contrary to constitutional values. Elizabeth Seshadri (2020) argued that "the CAA 2019 builds a narrative that Muslims are 'not sons of the soil.' This narrative is calculated to push the ideology of a 'Hindu rashtra (nation)'."

The Act has been strongly opposed by various political parties, religious organizations, activists and intellectuals. Although it appears to deal only with the "refugee" issue when read along with the discourse of National Register of Citizens (NRC) it has deeper implications for Muslim citizens of India. While passing the CAA, the government indicated its intention of undertaking a nationwide NRC—the exercise of registering all individuals who are Indian citizens. This exercise would require every person to prove their Indian citizenship by producing some elaborate official documents.[10] It is feared that a large segment of the Indian population that is poor or illiterate and does not possess the required documents may be stripped of citizenship, if the NRC exercise is conducted. It is here that the troubling link between CAA and NRC comes into play, as elucidated by Abhinav Chandrachud (Chandrachud, 2020: 155):

> Those left out of the NRC will include Muslims as well as non-Muslims. Many of those left out will not be migrants from across the border, but genuine Indian citizens who are unable to prove their citizenship because they lack the necessary documents. The CAA, it is argued, will save the non-Muslims who are excluded from the NRC, while disenfranchising Indian Muslims who have been left out of the list.

The CAA, that aims to make illegal non-Muslim residents (refugees) in India legal, therefore, will be used by the state to bring Hindus back on to the citizenship list in case they are excluded from the NRC, while making it impossible for many similarly placed Indian Muslims to claim back their citizenship rights. Chandrachud further explains:

> if a question arose as to whether a person was a foreigner or not, the burden was not on the government but on the person accused of being a foreigner to prove that he was, in fact, an Indian citizen … if a person's name is not listed in the National Register of Citizens, it is his responsibility to prove his citizenship, which is very difficult to do.
> *(Chandrachud, 2020: 158)*

There is a fear and panic among Muslims based on the information that the government is planning to build detention centers for illegal immigrants as well as those who would not be able to prove their citizenship (Sagar and Sircar, 2021).

The BJP has made sophisticated use of online technology and media to manufacture Hindu hyperbole and a mass anti-Muslim vocabulary. The BJP's hegemonic project is being reinforced from below, by significant sections of Hindus who hail Modi as the leader of the Hindu civilizational project—an unparalleled leader who walks the talk, who doesn't simply make empty "Hindtuva" promises but makes possible their realization. As Sonali Ranade puts it, "Where liberals like me see fibs, myths, and exaggerated claims (in Modi), his believers see sincerity, commitment, and devotion to a cause" (Ranade, 2021). Those Hindus supporting Modi are wholeheartedly embodying the process of "Hinduizing" India. Common middle-class Hindus take to social media to glorify Modi's politics; they are quick to label as "anti-national" their friends, family members, acquaintances or strangers who express online a critique of the majoritarian moves of the government. "Anti-national" is now an accepted term in the Hindu socio-political narrative that is commonly employed to defame, abuse, and wipe out any spaces of non-compliance

(Ganguly, 2019). It is not just the official IT branch of the BJP, but ordinary people who engage in online trolling and issuing of threats to stifle voices of dissent. The most recent incident was the vicious trolling of the captain of the Indian cricket team, Virat Kohli, for speaking out in support of his Muslim teammate, Mohammed Shami, who was being abused online after India lost a match to Pakistan in the T20 World Cup cricket. Kohli was subject to malicious online hate, including a rape threat issued by a young man (an engineering graduate from a top-notch Indian Institution) to his infant daughter (Mogul and Mitra, 2021).

Whether in their online or offline behavior, supporters of Modi have normalized physical and symbolic violence. "Sickulars" (for seculars) and "traitors" are the terms widely used as part of the new "Hindu" narrative, creating situations that sometimes provoke actual physical violence against the "anti-nationals." In this context, Ranade states, "Anyone who opposes the project can be vilified, demonized, excoriated, indeed extinguished. Any dissent that can be construed as hindering the 'civilizational project' is worthy of swift dissolution" (Ranade, 2021). Although much international and scholarly criticism targets Modi and the BJP, their unrestrained wrecking of the secular constitution and democratic foundations of India would not have been possible without the expanding support of the people. Many Hindus are consuming the government's propaganda, yet they are not simply being used by the government. To an extent, their newly discovered cultural aspirations and personal interests align with the BJP's ideology.

Conclusion: Resistance and Hope

The BJP's spectacular rise symbolizes a remaking of India—from a secular nation-state to a dogmatic "Hindu" India. It presents a bleak, pessimistic reality with no serious political contender to the BJP. It is expected that the BJP will retain its electoral preeminence for many years to come, thus putting at risk the democratic foundations of India. In this new India it is clear that there is increasingly shrinking space not just for Muslims and other religious minorities but also for other cultural, sexual, aesthetic or political communities that do not fit into the Hindu ideological milieu. What offers some hope is the surfacing of strands of resistance every now and then.

Although the BJP has been successful in silencing many individual and collective articulations of protest through use of force and intimidation such as job losses, etc., resistance has not completely disappeared. For instance, in a historic protest—a first-ever staged by Muslim women, the majority of whom were housewives, mothers and grandmothers—demands to abrogate the CAA were made (Bhatia and Gajjala, 2020). As a massive protest, it was also joined by activists, students, artists and intellectuals and lasted for around two months before it was quelled by the government. Another serious challenge to the BJP government is the farmers' protest from northern Indian states, mainly Punjab and Haryana. This movement started in November 2020 as the farmers were provoked by the agricultural reform laws passed by the government that seek to incentivize the corporate sector. Farmers asserted that the new laws would put them in a precarious position by opening up the

> agricultural sector of India to active commercial engagement by the big corporates, enabling them to purchase and hoard produce and sell it later at a much higher price than what they pay to the farmers for their crops. It also means these large corporates could be in charge of deciding what crops a farmer must produce (Jodhka, 2021).

Even though the government dealt harshly with the farmers, treating them as "security threats," calling them "terrorists" and "anti-nationals," one year on, the government has acceded to their demands and has repealed the farm laws.

The voices of resistance, though sporadic, often evoke the constitutional vocabulary of secularism, fundamental rights and civil liberties in asserting their demands. Notwithstanding the BJP's attempt to maneuver the constitution, this multicultural document largely remains intact, and acts as a powerful safeguard against the state's onslaught on group-differentiated and minority rights. Although India's constitution cannot totally impede India's stride towards becoming a more illiberal and less tolerant democracy, it continues to offer checks and balances, and be employed by various dissenting forces, including those parts of judiciary, media, other state institutions and civil society who do not concur with the Hindu ideology of the BJP.

The case of India seems unparalleled given the BJP's audaciously conspicuous agenda of Hindu nationalism; yet, to an extent it reflects a global phenomenon of changing social attitudes towards minorities, immigrants and other culturally "unassimilable" communities. In many Western democracies, massive sociopolitical shifts in societies characterized by transnationalism, immigrant-driven demographic changes, reconfiguration of ideas of political sovereignty and deterritorialization of religion have created a situation of uneasiness and tension in response to increasing cultural diversities. Some societies have responded by receding away from multicultural commitments towards integration or assimilation if not majoritarianism such as in Europe. There is an increasing burden on cultural minorities to be "better citizens" and integrate into the hegemonic national frame. Demands for cultural recognition by the minorities are viewed apprehensively as reifying cultural differences at the cost of national unity and universal individual rights. There has been a backlash against multiculturalism and prompting of critical debates around the multiple meanings and interpretations of multiculturalism; what remains incontrovertible is the fact that we live in spatial realities that are marked by extreme diversities. Notwithstanding the critique of multiculturalism, it remains a difficult yet significant challenge to ensure that rights and cultural practices of minorities are not trampled over while also making possible a "third space." Homi Bhabha's idea of "third space" denoting a hybrid cultural identity is an important challenge for multiculturalism—it allows communities to move beyond cultural essentialism, merge different cultural elements and create new meaningful identities (Bhabha, 1990). Notwithstanding the complex debates and dilemmas entailed in multiculturalism, engaging constructively with it remains imperative to countering the threats of majoritarianism.

Notes

1 For an elaborate discussion on partition, refer to Zaminar (2007) and Butalia (2015)
2 BR Ambedkar himself belonged to a low caste and was known as the civil rights leader who called for annihilation of the caste system. He took a leading part in drafting the Indian Constitution and advocated inclusion of guarantees/protections for specific groups including the Scheduled Castes (lower-caste Hindus) and Scheduled Tribes.
3 Fundamental Rights as contained in part 3 of the Indian constitution, specifically Article 15 and 16, provide special protection for Scheduled Castes, Scheduled Tribes and Other Backward Castes for purposes of education and employment.
4 For instance, Article 15 of the Indian constitution forbids discrimination on grounds of religion, race caste or sex; Article 16 (4) provides for affirmative action for the advancement of any socially, and educationally backward classes of citizens or for the Scheduled Castes and the Scheduled Tribes; Article 17 abolished untouchability; Article 25 guarantees freedom to profess, practice and propagate religion; Article 29 confers rights on any section of the citizens residing in the territory of India or any part thereof having a distinct language, script or culture of its to conserve the same; Article 30 offers rights to all minorities based on religion or language to establish and administer educational institutions of their choice.
5 The Congress Party, for instance, quite conspicuously associated itself with secular ideology. However, it did not shy away from opportunistically appeasing one religious community or the other for electoral gain. It is argued that the party catered to minority demands to gain votes. But it also used the "Hindu card" when it needed to expand and win Hindu constituencies.
6 Jawaharlal Nehru, the first Prime Minister of India, had a major role in shaping the constitutional conception of Indian secularism. In his view, the nation state must be secular and not officially recognize religion. The state should have equal respect for all religions and must not discriminate on the basis of religion. However, the state is not hostile to religion and in fact, acknowledges the value of religion for the people of the country. These views are strongly reflected in the Indian constitution. Apart from Nehru, constitutional idea of secularism is also shaped by MK Gandhi—another prominent anti-colonial leader of India.
7 The 1980s witnessed the rise of caste and social justice politics resulting in lower-caste political mobilization and emergence of regional leaders who belonged to the lower and lower middle-caste groups.
8 Cultural and political organizations affiliated to the BJP include Rashtriya Swayam Sewak Sangh (RSS), Vishwa Hindu Parishad (VHP) and Bajrang Dal (BJD). These organizations operate at the grassroots level and have a widespread network or branches at all levels of society—cities, towns and villages. They play a key role in

mobilizing the Hindu community, engaging Hindus in various cultural or religious activities and disseminating the organization's anti-Muslim ideology.
9 Killings in the name of cow protection have started since 2015. The first such mob lynching took place on September 28, 2015, when a Hindu mob attacked and killed a 52-year-old Muslim, Mohammed Akhlaq, for allegedly slaughtering a cow. Many such attacks took place in the following years and violence against Muslims was normalized, mainly due to the complicity of the BJP.
10 So far, there are no such official documents in India by which citizenship can be proved. Many Indians, including internal migrants, slum dwellers and poor people, do not possess even common official documents (Aadhaar card, Voter card, Ration card) that are used as identity cards in various states of India.

References

Apoorvanand. 2021. "India's "Love Jihad" Laws: Another Attempt to Subjugate Muslims." Aljazeera. Retrieved October 2021 from, https://www.aljazeera.com/opinions/2021/1/15/indias-love-jihad-laws-another-attempt-to-subjugate-muslims.

Bajpai, R. 2015. "Multiculturalism in India: An Exception?" Institute of Culture, Religion and World Affairs. Retrieved 11 September 2021 from, https://www.bu.edu/cura/files/2015/06/bajpai-paper-formatted.pdf

Bajpai, R. 2017. "Why Did India Choose Pluralism? Lessons from a Postcolonial State." Global Centre For Pluralism. Retrieved 11 September 2021 from, https://www.pluralism.ca/wp-content/uploads/2017/12/India_EN.pdf

Banting, K. and W. Kymlicka. 2006. *Multiculturalism and the Welfare State: Recognition and Redistribution in Contemporary Democracies*. New York: Oxford University Press.

Bhabha, H. K. 1990. "The Third Space." In *Identity: Community, Culture, Difference*, J. Rutherford (ed.) London: Lawrence and Wishart, 207–221.

Bhargava, R. 1994. "Giving Secularism Its Due." *Economic and Political Weekly 29* (28): 1784–1791.

Bhargava, R. 2011. "States, Religious Diversity, and the Crisis of Secularism." Open Democracy. Retrieved 6 October 2021 from, https://www.opendemocracy.net/en/states-religious-diversity-and-crisis-of-secularism-0/

Bhatia, M. 2013. "Secularism and Secularization: A Bibliographical Essay." *Economic and Political Weekly*, 48(50): 103–110.

Bhatia, M. 2020. *Rethinking Conflict at the Margins: Dalits and Borderland Hindus in Jammu and Kashmir*. Cambridge, UK: Cambridge University Press.

Bhatia, M. 2021. "Citizenship as Politics and Performance of Religious Identity: Hindu Refugees from Sindh." *Sociological Bulletin* 71 (1), OnlineFirst.

Bhatia, K. and R. Gajjala. 2020. "Examining Anti-CAA Protests at Shaheen Bagh: Muslim Women and Politics of the Hindu India." *International Journal of Communication 14*: 6286–6303.

Butalia, U. 2015. *Partition: The Long Shadow*. New Delhi: Penguin.

Chandrachud, A. 2020. "Secularism and the Citizenship Amendment Act." *Indian Law Review 2*: 138–162.

Chatterji, J. 2012. "South Asian Histories of Citizenship, 1946–1970." *Historical Journal 55* (4): 1049–1071.

Chatterji, A., T. Hansen and C. Jaffrelot (eds.). 2019. *Majoritarian State: How Hindu Nationalism Is Changing India*. New York: Oxford University Press.

Dirks, N.B. 2011. *Castes of Mind: Colonialism and the Making of Modern India*. Princeton: Princeton University Press.

Ganguly, M. 2019. "Dissent Is "Anti-National" in Modi's India." *Human Rights Watch*. Retrieved 5 November 2021 from, https://www.hrw.org/news/2019/12/13/dissent-anti-national-modis-india#

Gottschalk, P. 2001. *Beyond Hindu and Muslim: Multiple Identity in Narratives from Village India*. Delhi: Oxford University Press.

Gudavarthy, A. 2018. *India After Modi: Populism and the Right*. New Delhi: Bloomsbury

Hewitt, V. 2007. *Political Mobilisation and Democracy in India: States of Emergency*. London: Routledge.

Jaffrelot, C. 1996. *The Hindu Nationalist Movement in India*. New York: Columbia University Press.

Jaffrelot, C. 1998. *Religion, Caste, and Politics in India*. Delhi: Primus.

Jodhka, S.S. 2021. "Farmers in India Have Been Protesting for 6 Months, Have They Made Any Progress?" *The Conversation*. Retrieved 12 November 2021 from, https://theconversation.com/farmers-in-india-have-been-protesting-for-6-months-have-they-made-any-progress-161101

Khan, D-S. 2004. *Crossing the Threshold: Understanding Religious Identities in South Asia*. London: I. B. Tauris.

Kymlicka, W. 1996. *Multicultural Citizenship: A Liberal Theory of Minority Rights*. New York: Oxford University Press.

Mahajan, G. 1998. *Identity and Rights: Aspects of Liberal Democracy in India*. Delhi: Oxford University Press.

Mahajan, G. 2005. "Indian Exceptionalism or Indian Model: Negotiating Cultural Diversity and Minority Rights in a Democratic Nation-State." In *Multiculturalism in Asia*, Will Kymlicka and Baogang He (eds.) Oxford: Oxford University Press, 288–313.

Mogul, R. and E. Mitra. 2021. "Man in India Arrested Over Alleged Rape Threats to Cricket Star Virat Kohli's Infant Daughter." *CNN*. Retrieved 3 November 2021 from, https://www.cnn.com/2021/11/12/sport/virat-kohli-abuse-arrest-intl-hnk/index.html

Narayan, B. 2021. *Republic of Hindutva*. Delhi: Penguin.

Palishkar, S. 2014. "India's 2014 Lok Sabha Elections Critical Shifts in the Long Term, Caution in the Short Term." *Economic and Political Weekly* 49 (39): 39–49.

Parekh, B. 2017. *Rethinking Multiculturalism: Cultural Diversity and Political Theory*. London: Macmillan Education.

Prabhu, N. 2020. *Middle Class, Media and Modi: The Making of a New Electoral Politics*. Los Angeles: Sage.

Ranade, S. 2021. "Modi Is on a Civilisational Mission." *The Wire*. Retrieved 3 November 2021 from, https://thewire.in/politics/modi-is-on-a-civilisational-mission-dont-mind-a-few-grand-lies

Rastogi, P. 2020. *Postcolonial Disaster: Narrating Catastrophe in the Twenty-First Century*. Evanston: Northwestern University Press.

Roy, R. and P. Wallace. 2007. *India's 2004 Elections: Grass-Roots and National Perspectives*. Delhi: Sage.

Sagar, A. and O. Sircar. 2021. "The Crisis of Citizenship in Our Time." *Jindal Global Law Reviewer* 12: 1–8.

Seshadri, E. 2020. "CAA and the Devaluation of Secular India." *The Hindu Centre for Politics and Public Policy*. Retrieved 5 September 2021 from, https://www.thehinducentre.com/the-arena/current-issues/article30789891.ece.
Stein, B. and D. Arnold. 2010. *A History of India*. Oxford: Wiley.
Teltumbde, A. 2016. *Dalits: Past, Present and Future*. Delhi: Routledge.
Tejani, S. 2007. *Indian Secularism: A Social and Intellectual History, 1890–1950*. Bloomington: Indiana University Press.
Uddin, S. 2011. "Beyond National Borders and Religious Boundaries: Muslim and Hindu Veneration of Bonbibi." In *Engaging South Asian Religions: Boundaries, Appropriations, and Resistances*, Mathew N. Schmalz and Peter Gottschalk (eds.) New York: State University of New York Press, 61–82.
Vanaik, A. 1997. *The Furies of Indian Communalism: Religion, Modernity, and Secularization*. New Delhi: Verso.
Withnall, A. 2019. "Triple Talaq: India Criminalises Muslim Instant Divorce." *Independent*. Retrieved 15 September 2021 from, https://www.independent.co.uk/news/world/asia/triple-talaq-bill-india-instant-divorce-islam-muslim-modi-bjp-a9029446.html
Zamindar, V.F.–Y. 2007. *The Long Partition and the Making of Modern South Asia: Refugees, Boundaries, Histories*. New York: Columbia University Press.

PART 4
Multiculturalism's Meaning and Value

11
OH CANADA, YOUR HOME'S ON NATIVE LAND

Narratives of the Missing in a Multicultural Home

Kiera L Ladner, Hope Ace, Marcus Closen and Dane Monkman

First Words

Canadian political scientist Peter H Russell often tells of his entrance into the realm of Indigenous politics in 1974 when he was called up to Yellowknife to speak with members of the Dene nation (whose territory is now occupied by Canada). He was asked how the British Crown gained sovereignty over the Dene and how it was that this claimed sovereignty was now transferred to the Canadian state. These daunting questions can be answered with reference to papal doctrine, international law and constitutional law; however, the best explanation may be "legal magic" (Russell, 2021; McNeil, 2018). In many ways, everything since this act of legal magic has been a cover-up—specifically, a narrative covering up genocide and the theft of Turtle Island (what many Indigenous peoples call North America). This narrative in Canada, much like those of other settler societies, is characterized by a settler amnesia whereby the country's history is constructed as beginning with settlers and pioneers (casting explorers as the part of the imperial narrative) and thus as a story of peaceful settlement wherein the land is not stolen (Behrendt, 2016: 190). It is a narrative quite removed from the many misdeeds of settler colonialism and imbued with discourses of peace, order, good governance, multiculturalism, rights and inclusion. This is the Canadian narrative. It is a story of mythologized exceptionalism in which Canada itself is presented as everything that is not American and as having a history so very different than the violence that defined the American colonial experience.

But there are other narratives that reject the very premise of the Canadian myth of Crown sovereignty being peacefully proclaimed (and accepted) over near empty lands. Narratives which do not ignore the rich political and legal landscape over which Canada was created. Narratives which address not only the pluralism that "pre-ceded" Canada (and its legal magic) but which also address the pluralism (and the denial) on which Canada is founded. But these are not the Canadian narrative. Instead, they are the stories told by "the other nations." They are the narratives told by those nations whose lands Canada occupies and those nations who have been denied a place within the Canadian statecraft despite Canada's commitment to legal, cultural and political pluralism (through policies such as multiculturalism, official bilingualism and its adherence to both civil and common law). Indeed, for Indigenous peoples, Canada is founded on pluralism and its denial.

While Canada is founded on pluralism and its denial, it is important to understand that Indigenous lands over which Canada claims sovereignty and occupies as a nation state have always been imbued with an understanding of legal, political and cultural pluralism. In fact, legal, political and cultural pluralism have long been central to the histories and narratives of Indigenous nations both prior to and since "discovery" and colonization. It is important to understand that Indigenous nations have always had a fundamentally different understanding of territory, power, philosophical, legal and political traditions that were grounded in (or expressions of) kinship and the relationality between human beings, non-human beings, and the land (Mills, 2017). Needless to say, this represents an entirely different political and legal tradition from that which developed out of the enlightenment and the expansion of the state (Scott, 1998). Thus, while Indigenous nations were not part of the Westphalian state tradition, they had their own international system whereby sovereign nations created political and legal orders that governed internal and external national relations—all within a philosophical context or paradigm which was fundamentally grounded in pluralism and relationality. As far back as oral histories can account, treaties have been used by Indigenous nations as tools to create and maintain multinational pluralism, amending and establishing territories, as well as the means by which multiple nations exist within shared territories. This is evidenced by how the Dish With One Spoon Treaty negotiated between the Haudenosaunee and the Anishinaabe secured and maintained the means by which multiple nations would live and prosper in shared territories such as the lands that became Tkaronto—or what is colonially called Toronto (Simpson, 2008; Jacobs and Lytwyn, 2020: 200).

Since treaties were already being used to establish how nations lived together, they became the means by which Indigenous peoples dealt with the invaders. As colonization ensued through trade and settlement, treaties were used by Indigenous nations to establish relations between nations (Indigenous and alien/invader/imperial) or how two nations would live together in Indigenous territories. Some of these treaties provided the newcomers with some semblance of (limited) "treaty rights" to settle and to engage in farming or fishing, whereas others did not. Likewise, other treaties limited newcomers to existing settlements or simply did not address any right to occupy or take up Indigenous lands. Some of these treaties dealt with the creation of peace and friendship between Indigenous peoples and the newcomers (possibly dealing with matters of territory and security through the establishment of an alliance). Meanwhile others dealt with matters of trade. While the treaties between Indigenous nations and newcomer nations (and the church) dealt with a multiplicity of matters, most address the ways multiple nations could live together (but separate) on Indigenous lands with all nations continuing to live in accordance with their own legal, political and cultural traditions. It is this acknowledgement, according to scholars such as Henderson and Ladner, that enables treaty federalism and allows for the development of a Canadian constitutional order on Indigenous lands alongside Indigenous constitutional orders (Henderson, 1994: 241; Ladner, 2005: 923).

In essence, treaties continue the longstanding tradition of legal, political and cultural pluralism that existed prior to colonization. But while it is important to understand that the treaties are part of a continuous narrative which embraces pluralism, this is not Canada's story. As noted above, Canada's story has been one of legal magic manifested in a simple invocation of Crown sovereignty. As a narrative, legal magic is perpetuated by the courts through its constant reification of Crown sovereignty and the assertion that Indigenous sovereignties were reconciled with Crown sovereignty at contact (Russell, 2021). Similarly, one could argue that the narrative has been continuously perpetuated by Canadian governments through policy initiatives such as PE Trudeau's White Paper on Indian Policy (1969) and his announcement of a federal policy of multiculturalism (1971).

While many view multiculturalism as embracing pluralism and envisioning a new national narrative distinct from its colonial roots through an organic generative process, for Indigenous peoples this is not the case. True, multiculturalism acts as a celebration of diversity and an attempt to recast Canada's identity as inclusive rather than an English and/or French melting pot. However, Canadian multiculturalism as both a policy and a vision, spoke of Canada as an immigrant nation, or as a settler society founded by two nations which had been transformed through post-war immigration. This policy spoke of Canada as a home, first with two nations and then to a "strange multiplicity" of peoples from around the world (Tully, 1995); and of a need to create and redecorate Canada as a home capable of embracing all peoples. But Canada's policy of multiculturalism can be read as a rebuff of the nations within and unfulfilled promises of pluralism. In particular, the individualized language of equity, diversity, equality and inclusivity imbues the discourse of multiculturalism, and attempts to reconcile diversity and inclusivity with a history of racism and exclusion. However, this does little to address the dispossession and subjugation of Indigenous nations and the continued denial of legal and constitutional pluralism.

This chapter explores multiculturalism through the lens of a settler narrative (particularly the narrative of home) demonstrating how—from the vantage of Indigenous nations—this longstanding narrative remains unchallenged and unchanged by multiculturalism. We argue that instead of providing a means of embracing pluralism and inclusion for Indigenous nations, multiculturalism sustains the colonial narrative and continues to obfuscate and deny Indigenous peoples the right to exist as sovereign and autonomous nations within their homelands as members of a multicultural and multinational treaty family. In affirming this argument, this chapter addresses settler narratives and pluralism historically and contemporaneously through discourses of a national home and multiculturalism in Canada as well as New Zealand and Australia.

Narratives of a Pretend Nation

According to Blackfoot legal scholar and quantum philosopher Leroy Little Bear,

> Having gone back and forth across the country, many times, I have come to the conclusion that what I know about Canada is that it is a "Pretend Nation." And let me tell you why. ... Well, a definition of a nation is that a nation is a group of people, or a society that has a common culture, history, customs, language, traditions, art, and religion. ...
>
> ... The only way Canada, as we've said, will become a true nation is to embody the Indigenous roots of the territory that it claims. Thousands of generations of Native Americans (for instance, Blackfoot people) have existed on the back of, what we call, Turtle Island. They have developed and embodied icons, images, symbols. And, those have become embodied in the customs, traditions, values, beliefs, and so on. They are embodied in our stories, in our songs, in our ceremonies. They have become part of that relationship with the land. That's what you can call and refer to as being Indigenous. Until that embodiment comes about for Canada, Canada will continue to have an identity problem. Until that embodiment comes about, Canada will continue to be a pretend nation. Canada will continue to be a nation that exists only on paper.
>
> Now, the Canadian Constitution and other conventions that make up the Canadian Constitution, are all administrative in nature. If you look through the documents from 1867 to 1982, all those thirty-some documents that today make up the Canadian Constitution are all administrative in nature. They say nothing about who are the Canadians, what is Canada all about? There is nothing in the documents about how they are connected to the land.
>
> *(Little Bear, 2017: 36–42)*

As scholars such as Judith Pryor (2008) have argued, the national myths and the national identity of settler states are often expressed through and become constitutional narratives. These nations begin with the arrival of colonial envoys who bring the laws and traditions of the imperial nations and their sovereignties onto seemingly empty lands; lands already inhabited yet claimed by colonial nations by means of European/international law. Settler nations—particularly Anglo-settler states—begin as a legal act or as a "legal" claim or assertion of sovereignty over another's homelands or territories. While Quebec's national narrative is somewhat different, it too begins with that "act of discovery" and thus, a legal assertion of France's claim over Indigenous homelands. The real difference is in the legal magical narrative which is constructed with France as ally to Indigenous nations and of its colonies somehow occupying lands which either are not Indigenous, or which are not dispossessed. It is this act of "legal" dispossession that serves as the foundation for the creation of the settler state while also functioning as the nation's origin story. For instance, in the case of Australia, it is Captain Cook's use of legal magic or his act of claiming the land which he "discovered" in its entirety for the British Crown that functions as Australia's origin story and which serves to connect the nation and its citizens to the earliest "known" story of this land.

Although the constitutional documents of settler nations like Canada and Australia are "administrative in nature" and do little to create an identity or a relationship to the land, law (both textual and performative) creates and sustains the narrative of these nations. More specifically, it is the import of settler state laws and traditions into Indigenous homelands—viewed as empty spaces by colonizing forces—that create and sustain the settler nation. But these lands were not empty; they were already home to other complex and established nations. For settler societies/nations (including Quebec), settler colonialism is a dispossession not a discovery, and it should be understood as a home invasion rather than an attempt to create a new homeland or a new nation in an empty/Indigenous space.

This colonial dispossession has created new narratives in the attempt to establish a new home on Indigenous lands, grounded by the dispossession and exclusion of Indigenous nations. Arguably, these settler nations have not just been established through law or legal narrative but rather through the construction of a national home (or homes) and narratives of home. Though the narrative and metaphor of home is exceedingly problematic for a multitude of reasons (including the gendering of public/private spheres), Margaret Davies has shown that the metaphor of home can be effectively used in reference to Australian colonialism, nation-building, and the "political-legal imaginary of the state" (Davies, 2014: 154). Building from the work of scholars such as Iris Marion Young and Sara Ahmed, Davies recognizes that the narrative of home within setter states such as Australia is an ambivalent, constitutive process which can be simultaneously inclusive and exclusive while providing the flux and belonging of both rootless mobility and rooted stability (Davies, 2014: 160).

As a political value, therefore, home may be a useful (though non-universalizable) concept because it promotes a sense of connection, common purpose and material wellbeing. At the same time, the process of contestation in constructing and maintaining a home must not disappear from view. Equally important, feminists can never forget that a "good" home is sometimes nothing more than a veneer for a place of violence and destructiveness (Davies, 2014: 160).

Settler nations are in large part constructed as "a repudiation of home" (Britain/Europe) and a "repudiation of Aboriginal homelands," and yet somehow still reflective of the "empire as a political and cultural home" to their nations—be that Anglo-Celtic or in Canada's case, the French and the English (Davies, 2014: 169). In recreating cultural and political homes, settler nations are rooted in curation and transplanting to extend the imperial homeland across the waters. This was done by importing religions, economies, cultures, architectures and invasive species (flora and fauna including British rabbits, blackbirds, sparrows and starlings). As these colonies grew into nation states and immigration expanded to include individuals from other European countries (as well as non-European labor), these new countries maintained their imperial roots such that there continued to be a privileging of imperial cultural, political, legal and social orders. While this struggle to both repudiate and recreate the homeland was very different for Quebec and other French (including Acadian) settlements due to different colonial strategies, imperial abandonment and the socio-political realities of forced coexistence and domination by the larger English colonial power, there is little doubt that both the French and the English settler societies were "founded on a fictitious blank slate" (Davies, 2014: 169). This fictive tabula rasa (re)created, privilege and sustained imperial cultural, political, institutional, legal and social orders.

While the histories and experiences are different, as settler societies emerged as entities unto themselves, they struggled to create nations or a new home (quite separate from the colonizing nation) or to find a "sense of home and belonging" for those who the state chose to include on the "fictitious blank slate" (Davies, 2014: 173). These new nations used restrictive settlement/ethnic sentiment to develop a home by (re)decorating the void of the Indigenous nations and their legacies of legal and political pluralism which somehow ceased to exist as anything but a mythical past. This is very much evident in Canada, Australia and New Zealand where Indigenous peoples (and non-Europeans) were mostly excluded from the state and the creation of home/the national narrative. Despite treaties in both Canada and New Zealand, Indigenous peoples in all three countries were largely removed from their lands and moved to reserves (Canada), missions (Australia) or in the case of Māori (New Zealand) who endured the raupatu (confiscation) which left most Iwi (tribes or nations) with one percent of their lands and most of their peoples landless. Indigenous peoples were not part of the nation—they were removed so that new settler nations could be built.

Beyond the exclusion of Indigenous peoples, apart from those Francophones already in Canada (in Quebec and beyond), these were largely imagined as Anglo or Anglo-Celtic nations despite the fact that these were settler nations (which required immigrants), and all sought to build "white nations" through racially selective immigration policies, and immigrants willing to start a new life in an Anglo nation. These settler societies constructed a "home" for their white, dominantly Anglo national narrative (in spite of Quebec's existence), on homelands which Indigenous peoples refused their extinction and non-white immigrant laborers treated as fodder refused to vacate following projects such as constructing the essential railroad. Settler nations were thus dependent upon ignoring treaties (New Zealand declaring treaty as a legal nullity) and pursuing more brutal genocidal policies of "civilization," "assimilation" and "elimination." This also encouraged the finding of new ways to "deal with" existing racial policies (such as Canada's Chinese Head Tax between 1885 and 1923) and effectively closing borders to all non-Europeans. Nonetheless, their narratives remained unchanged until well into the post-war period.

Settler state narratives become embodied in the consciousness of the body politic though a variety of textual and performative means including constitutional as well as war narratives, education, law, policy and the creation of cultural artifacts such as national anthems, art, music and literature. These in turn fuel the national romanticism that the settler states rely on to promote unity and uphold colonial power dynamics which continue to support the claims of sovereignty. This works to create and recreate an understanding of the settler nation as home—thereby replacing the narrative of coloniality with that of an independent nation and a national home (and a redecorating of Indigenous homelands). For example, within the Canadian national anthem in the English language version, the opening phrase "Oh Canada, our home and native land" suggests, this is Canada's native land such that it is the birthplace and home to its two nations. This is perhaps more explicit when considering the first and final lines of the French language version of the anthem, "O Canada! Land of our ancestors ... Will protect our homes and our rights." It is interesting to note that both official language versions are completely different and thus the anthems speak of two nations, and while each refers to their national homes, neither acknowledges the mere existence of Indigenous nations.

It comes as no surprise that until quite recently, Anglo and binational settler nations were mythologized as settler homelands without meaningful pasts (as in pre-colonial histories) or presents; futures would only be made meaningful through settlement and civilization (or so the story goes). Settler nations engaged settler-colonial logics resulting in dispossession and genocide (Wolfe, 2006). Though treaties were negotiated in much of Canada and New Zealand, and both countries mythologize their treaty histories as peaceful and honorable, dispossession was nevertheless achieved and sustained through state-sanctioned violence, oppression and genocidal policies. Although treaties in Canada and New Zealand were to have secured rights for Indigenous and non-Indigenous nations within the settler states, neither settler nations nor their claimed territories could be home to Indigenous peoples (as individuals or as nations). These were intentionally constructed as homes for British/French/European offspring; and what was once an Indigenous home was redecorated and reimagined to look more like the settler homelands and to ground that sense of belonging and being.

As generations of settlers developed roots and were joined by new waves of settlers, migrants, immigrants and refugees, Indigenous histories (pre-colonial and colonial) went largely ignored as territories were re-storied and new histories and cultures were created thus covering up the truth. As Thomas King said: "one of the most surprising things about Indians is that we're still here. After some 500 years of vigorous encouragement to disappear, we're still here" (King, 2003). But it is not simply that Indigenous peoples are still here that comes as a surprise. As Australian historian Henry Reynolds reminds us, the truth was never told. Settler society did not know because they were not told about Indigenous histories or the violent truths of colonialism and the establishment of the Australian settler nation because of the mythologized past of peaceful settlement, the supposed civilization of the "savage"/"savage land," and narratives of social Darwinism (Reynolds, 2000). What is more, not only were they not told, but in the case of Australia, Reynolds concludes that settler Australia might be unable to reconcile itself, or to "accommodate the indigenous interpretation of the past" or to create a shared history (Reynolds, 2000: 175). Instead, generations "have deferred dealing with these great problems and in so doing bequeathed them to their descendants" (Reynolds, 2000: 184). No doubt Indigenous peoples in Canada and New Zealand would say the same.

Multiculturalism—Expanding the Narrative

Indigenous peoples know of a much different narrative of Canada than that which is told with reference to Canadian multiculturalism. The story of multiculturalism is most often told as having "extended the rafters" and "remodeled" or "redecorated" the Canadian home to make it a more welcoming, more inclusive place to live as immigration in the post-war period increasingly included peoples from countries other than the United Kingdom or France and other parts of Europe. In many ways, it was simply a logical response to the changing socio-cultural fabric of Canada that had been brought about by decades of "other" European "settlement" of the Canadian west (as agriculturalists), of townships (as laborers), and the transformation of Canada's immigration policies in 1962 by Prime Minister Diefenbaker which was a decisive step towards ending racial exclusion as a primary consideration for immigration (if only on paper). This goal was more substantively realized in 1967 with Canada's implementation of the point system.

As an idea that developed outside of the political arena, multiculturalism in a bilingual English and French framework can be read as a means to absorb and celebrate the cultural mosaic without transforming the (national) narrative or the home that had been built by the two founding nations and the waves of European settlers who had joined them. At its core, multiculturalism can be viewed as creating a more accurate and reflective narrative of home (the new mosaic) that was both essential for the unity of the settler state whilst still promoting a national romanticism that disguises the violent history of the past, present and future of colonialism (the home invasion). As an organic generative response to a maturing nation, multiculturalism promoted a new sense of home predicated on the idea that the home could be redecorated as both a textual and performative space. The multicultural version of home could be continuously recreated as a singular non-assimilative nation comprised of two founding cultures/nations that could also preserve the cultural freedom of all individuals and provide recognition of the cultural contributions of diverse ethnic groups to Canadian society. In reality, multiculturalism was not a substantially transformative modification of the Canadian narrative for most Canadians.

While multiculturalism was a textual recognition of the shifting composition of Canada, it must also be read as an intricate piece of PE Trudeau's brand of liberalism. His vision fundamentally tried to alter the meaning of the settler nation and the home that was created for two nations by reimagining it as a single bilingual nation without an "official culture," comprised of multiple ethnicities, unified by an identity forged through a rights-bearing citizenry, and commitment to assist immigrants in "overcoming barriers," "acquiring at least one official language," and supporting "integration" to the "national life" (Canada, 1971: 8545). In other words, it was a policy of "preserving, enhancing and sharing the multicultural heritage of Canada by eliminating barriers in participation of all individuals and communities in public life" (Srikanth, 2012: 17).

Viewed in relation to the other major policy tools that were used to realize PE Trudeau's liberal vision (including the *Official Languages Act*, 1969; the White Paper of Indian Policy, 1969; and the *Canadian Charter of Rights and Freedoms*, 1982), multiculturalism should be read primarily as a gesture towards building a singular bilingual Canadian nation which included multiculturalism as a performative freedom related to food, dance and cultural costumes. It was not a meaningful shift towards or transformation of society into a "cultural mosaic" given the state maintained its sanction and preferential treatment of the two "founding nations" (and their linguistic, legal, political, cultural and societal institutions and traditions). To put this another way, multiculturalism promoted the idea of Canada as home to a great diversity of people and it attempted to create a sense of home and belonging. But it was nonetheless premised on the idea of one home and an attempt to destabilize the nations within—yet another attempt at subsuming Québécois by the larger, more powerful Anglo-Canadian identity.

Almost immediately, Canada proclaimed multiculturalism a success—comparing itself to other Western states and proclaiming its tolerance of diversity through the birth of a friendly peaceful nation that represents a multiplicity of identities. But this too is a story representative of Canada's mythologized exceptionalism that has been widely questioned and debated within Canadian society and the academy. As Burman explains,

> multiculturalism is so easily framed by politicians and media outlets as self-evidently good because it asks nothing of a White Canadian mainstream, other than tolerance; it mandates no change in the order of social hierarchies, it requires no sacrifice, no territorial concession. It interpolates on a mostly symbolic register, which makes it fundamentally incommensurable with Indigenous justice claims.
>
> *(Burman, 2016: 363)*

For Burman, Indigenous justice claims include land, sovereignty, language and treaty rights. For Indigenous peoples, Canada's multiculturalism policy represents the reification of the colonial narrative of two founding nations and a federal policy attempting to extend the rafters and create a home for all within these two nations on top of Indigenous nations and their territories/homelands. Indeed, as Vernon explains, "multicultural policy was not designed to address the political needs of ethnic or Indigenous peoples in Canada but to further exalt French and English Canada as the 'two founding races'," seen in perpetuity as "the legitimate heirs of the rights and entitlements proffered by the state" (Vernon, 2016: 94). It should be noted however, that Quebec has rejected multiculturalism because it fails to embrace the identity of Canada as two nations.

Multiculturalism failed to transform Canada's (national) narratives and romanticism or address the continuous violent genocide and dispossession of Indigenous peoples which continues to be fundamental to the establishment of the settler nation and the creation of a Canadian home. As MacDonald explains, multiculturalism "insufficiently recognize[s] the sui generis rights of Aboriginal peoples, while similarly failing to address the continuing economic, social, and political inequalities between Aboriginal and settler populations" (2014: 65). Thus, the façade of multiculturalism provided a means to dismiss this violent colonial past and offered a pathway of inclusion only if it did not question or threaten the settler state or its narrative of home (Kymlicka, 2011). Such notions of a shared nation were to have replaced the distinction of Indigenous sovereignty and rights to self-determination (Sabzalian, 2019: 314).

Arguably, multiculturalism represents a national romanticism that veils the violence of settler colonialism as the state conveys itself as embracing pluralism while deploying the same eliminatory policies (civilization, assimilation and dispossession) as always deployed by the state despite the treaties. Thus, the state continued to neglect its responsibilities as treaty partner and the nation-to-nation relationship with Indigenous peoples (and agreements of legal, cultural and political pluralism). Instead, the state maintained a paternalistic relationship designating Indigenous sovereignty to be outside the bounds of state recognition and denying any form of pluralism other than that which was developed to bring newcomers into the "Canadian family." For Indigenous nations, multiculturalism further exalts whiteness, such that in treating Indigenous nations as part of the cultural mosaic and not overturning the dominant colonial policy paradigm, multiculturalism "reproduced the colonial erasure of Aboriginal peoples as the original presence in the country;" this erasure we continue to see reproduced in multicultural state policies and programs in Anglo-settler nations (Vernon, 2016: 94).

Throughout Canada's history, colonial violence was legally mandated through eliminatory and assimilatory policies such as residential schools; after all, the mantra of Canadian residential schools was "kill the Indian, save the child." By means of a number of Canadian policies and policy tools including the *Indian Act*, Indigenous peoples were to have been legislated out of existence and forcibly assimilated. While many would argue that the era of forced assimilation continues through the colonial domination of the state and its politics of recognition (Coulthard, 2014: 46–49), there is no doubt that assimilation was the end goal of the Trudeau Government's 1969 White Paper on Indian Policy. The intent of this liberal policy was to enable the Indian people "to be free—free to develop Indian cultures in an environment of legal, social and economic equality with other Canadians" (Canada, 1969). This was to be achieved through the elimination of the *Indian Act,* the termination of treaties, the legal assimilation of all status Indians, the elimination of reserves (they were to be re-allocated as individually held private property), and the legal assimilation of all status Indians (thereby the removal of all legal distinctions and distinctions-based treatment). Trudeau's brand of liberal statecraft made it abundantly clear that Indigenous nations (and for that matter, individuals) were not part of the Canadian settler state and there was no place for Indigenous nations within the settler dominion or in their own Indigenous/national homelands; they did not belong, and government policies sought to exclude and/or eliminate.

As a policy, multiculturalism should not be viewed separately from the 1969 White Paper, the *Official Languages Act,* or later the 1982 Charter of Rights and Freedoms—all were tools through which Trudeau set out to create his vision of a just society. Multiculturalism became a tool to ignite and continue to unite all members of the body politic who have been accepted and embraced into the new home and it was also synonymously used to veil the violence of colonialism and the dispossession of Indigenous peoples which is fundamental to the new home. Multiculturalism allowed for a narrative of inclusion and acceptance while implicitly controlling and limiting distinctions-based rights such that the policy sustained the narrative of the 1969 White Paper. Trudeau's vision of Canada was predicated on the dismissal of the distinctness of Indigenous nations and with that, Indigenous rights and treaty responsibilities. This is most evident when viewed through the lens of law because "the law under liberal democracy continues to remain mono-cultural and common law cannot rise above the existing dominant culture" (Vernon, 2016: 19). Further, as MacDonald states, "Trudeau's 'White Paper liberalism' was entirely consistent with Western European political ideals, which privileged the individual as the central unit of a political system, while seeking to balance the freedom and equality of individuals operating in society" (2014: 74). PE Trudeau tried to destabilize Quebec nationalism with a singular nation or just society characterized by multiculturalism, bilingualism and a rights-bearing citizenry with no official culture. Despite his efforts, Canada continues to be depicted both past and present as two nations. Since the 1990s, however, the idea of Canada having three founding nations, or three pillars came to increasingly infiltrate Canadian politics. This has been without transformative affect, and the persistence of a two-pillar narrative continues dominate, making Indigenous sovereignty invisible in order to further support the binational relationship between Canada and Quebec which exists within dominant culture and state institutions, constituting a home invasion masked by multicultural acceptance. Multiculturalism continues to conceal the true nature of the Canadian home invasion within Indigenous nations' territories as they continue to deflect their treaty responsibilities towards Indigenous sovereign nations. The promotion of the two-pillar system entrenching French and English Canada as the two founding nations distorts the truth of the violent foundation and history of the state based on theft.

Multiculturalism Today: Official Languages and Indigenous Peoples

Canada still relies on narratives of its own identity to inform itself. Sometimes these narratives run against one another, especially when the story of multiculturalism is considered alongside the narrative of the two founding nations and the resulting policy of official bilingualism in Canada. Canadian bilingualism continues to be a subject of great debate, frequently alongside (or as it intersects with) multiculturalism. Canada as a country is bilingual as defined by the 1969 *Official Languages Act*. Public servants, members of the government and various officials are required to speak (and often read) both English and French. It comes as no surprise that there has been no movement to provide formal recognition to other settler languages despite multiculturalism and multilingual educational programming across several jurisdictions. Despite the prominence of the discourse of three founding nations (Indigenous, French and English) and the recognition of Aboriginal and treaty rights within the *Constitution Act*, 1982, it was the recognition of Indigenous language rights in self-government agreements and land claims that allowed governments such as Nunavut to declare their languages to be "official languages." It was only in 2019, in celebration of the International Year of Indigenous Languages, that the Canadian government passed its *Indigenous Languages Act*. Though this legislation does provide some nominal recognition of rights and affirms that "Indigenous languages are at the core of reconciliation with Indigenous peoples and are fundamental to shaping the country" (Canada, 2019), it does not abrogate or derogate from Canada's official languages (and the rights provided them) thereby reinforcing the narrative of two founding nations. The home has been redecorated, and little place is left for the recognition and/or inclusion of Indigenous nations and their cultures, languages, laws and political traditions (much of which was to be protected by treaty).

The debate over bilingualism as a mainstay of Canadian society and culture came up again in 2021 in the nomination and appointment of Mary Simon as Governor General. In what should have been seen as a win for Canada, Prime Minister Justin Trudeau nominated an Indigenous person to the role for the first time and did so with recognition that this was "a historic moment in the nation's history;" one where Mary Simon would provide leadership as Canada engages in reconciliation (Trudeau, 2021). However, Mary Simon did not, at the time, speak French fluently and a flurry of complaints began to arrive to the official languages commissioner (*Montreal Gazette*, 2021). Bilingualism, to Canadians, means not any two languages, but the "correct" two languages. Mary Simon's bilingualism was seen by some as not sufficiently bilingual, despite her fluency in English *and* Inuktitut. Thus, Indigenous peoples, in their own land, are not recognized as sufficiently proficient in language if they are not proficient in *both* English and French. It should be noted that French language education was not provided at federally run schools (well into the 1990s), including the one which Mary Simon was forced to attend.

While the Canadian government "recognized" Indigenous languages in 2019 and has accorded them some legislative protection and affirmed that the constitutional recognition of Aboriginal and treaty rights contains language rights, the state does not regard them as Canadian languages, or worthy of being part of bilingualism. The *Official Languages Act* in Canada recognizes two "official" languages. The *Constitution Act*, 1982 provides through Section 27 a recognition of Canada as a multicultural society; in Section 25 it recognizes that Aboriginal rights are not abrogated by any other section of the Constitution. Yet, Indigenous peoples are not provided the same language or cultural recognition provided to either English or French Canada as the two dominant categories of Canadian life. While multiculturalism is seen as the foundation of Canadian constitutionalism post-patriation, the recognition for Indigenous peoples and their distinct languages and cultures remains underdeveloped.

Bilingualism in Canada, as can be seen in the examples above, does not mean any two languages, it means English and French. Proficiency in any other language is disregarded, regardless of how long those languages may have been spoken. So much for the suggestion that reconciliation has been "baked into" Canadian politics or the claim that the three nations/three pillars understanding of Canada (past, present and future) has become the dominant narrative in Canadian politics. Canada in 2021—after 50 years of multiculturalism and nearly 40 years of constitutionally recognized Aboriginal and treaty rights—is still a nation comprised of two nations. Despite a narrative that embraces multiculturalism, Indigenous rights, tolerance and reconciliation, both Indigenous peoples and "other" Canadians are to be somehow reconciled with and absorbed into a singular bilingual nation. Put more bluntly, Indigenous peoples are to be reconciled with Canada's two nations—one of which is officially multicultural, while the other practices interculturalism (which recognizes cultural difference but promotes assimilation into Québécois culture in an attempt to strengthen Quebec in this uneven relationship)—and their claims of sovereignty over the entirety of Indigenous lands, Indigenous peoples, Indigenous laws and Indigenous cultures.

This is a critical issue, not simply a matter of language law or the regulation of language in Canada's institutions. In terms of justice, bilingualism's exclusion of Indigenous languages also serves to exclude Indigenous legal traditions and those who can speak to them without the need to interpret them in a completely different language or from the vantage of another's cultural and legal tradition (be that common or civil law; see for example Borrows, 2010). Justices of the federal courts are one such group where linguistic proficiency in both English and French is seen as a requirement of the job. Nominees to the Supreme Court of Canada are criticized if not somewhat proficient in both English and French, providing a significant barrier to Indigenous lawyers who might be nominated to the highest court (Stefanovich, 2021). Despite multiculturalism and Canada's empty words of recognition and reconciliation, Indigenous peoples and their languages and legal traditions continue to be dispossessed and treated as though they do not exist, or at very least do not matter. This is easily done when their home is entirely redecorated with new trappings of English and French.

While the Justin Trudeau government is in the process of implementing its legislation recognizing Indigenous languages, the Department of Justice has launched an action plan to enhance English and French bilingual capacity of the federal judiciary but has no plan to recognize any other language or any obligation to provide other means of interpretation. The Canadian state still does not recognize the rights of some people to be able to speak their own languages in proceedings in court but has plans to require all Justices to be able to carry out their work in two of the languages. Questions remain about how committed Canada can or wants to be in enabling the use of any language other than the two official languages, and if the support for or use of these languages will ever be made as accessible as French is to be in English Canada. The situation is dire considering the state of most Indigenous languages following years of government-sanctioned violence aimed at genocide, and the fact that these languages represent intellectual and cultural archives of Indigenous nations. Indigenous languages are the means through which to understand Indigenous legal, political and cultural traditions—traditions that were to have been protected by the treaties. Given the role of the Canadian Court in giving meaning to treaties and Aboriginal rights (and thus, Indigenous legal, cultural and political orders), and the absence of expertise in Indigenous legal traditions (alongside common and civil legal traditions), Justin Trudeau's move to shore up the Court's language requirements speaks volumes about the persistence of the two founding nations narrative and the limitations of both multiculturalism and Indigenous rights.

A 2016 survey points to the attitudes of Canadians toward cultural minorities and what "limits" Canadians would tolerate in terms of the cultural mosaic, versus cultural assimilation (Environics Institute, 2015). Canadians want a multicultural society within limits but are unwilling to tolerate significant differences. Cultural minorities (those that are not white anglophones or Francophones) seem to be asked "to go along to get along," and anyone who falls outside the scope of the two is seen to be outside those limits of toleration. Indigenous languages therefore fall outside the scope of what bilingualism means to Canada. Indigenous peoples, their cultures, their legal traditions and their languages remain largely unacknowledged in Canada. While some languages are recognized by the state, the practice of multiculturalism has not yielded recognition for historical or ongoing cultural, legal, political and/or linguistic dispossession (a destruction tantamount to genocide) of Indigenous peoples.

Yet, other countries have provided important examples of how this can be "managed" in a way that does not yield the same problems. The situation does not have to be the way that Canada seems to insist that it must be. If Canada is a nation of pillars, then the addition of another pillar should not be a challenge to recognize Indigenous peoples. Indeed, this has been carried out elsewhere; notable places like Hawai'i and New Zealand have made a great deal of progress in terms of not only recognizing Indigenous cultural, linguistic, legal and political traditions, but also honoring, implementing or enabling Indigenous rights. In the case of New Zealand, the 1970s brought about a reimagining of the nation (and its underlying narratives) premised on a recognition that the Treaty of Waitangi served as the "birthplace of the nation" and "its founding document." Through the *Treaty of Waitangi Act* of 1975, New Zealand finally pushed ahead with the treaty's implementation, establishing the

Waitangi Tribunal to deal with claims, instilling four treaty principles to guide Parliament (such that the principles are to be reflected in law and policy), and providing for a new relationship between treaty partners (the foundation for the country and its future). By 1987 when Parliament recognized Māori as an official language (with the same standing as English), New Zealand had institutionalized biculturalism legislatively as it proceeded to implement the treaty in an increasingly multicultural nation. Despite the "absence of a comprehensive multiculturalism policy in New Zealand … governments have responded by acknowledging multicultural realities, while maintaining the unique status of Māori under the Treaty of Waitangi" (Smits, 2019: 119).

Final Thoughts

Despite colonial legacies, New Zealand's language laws demonstrate the possibility that assimilation is not the only way for settler societies to respond to Indigenous nations. The *Official Languages Act* in Canada advances an assimilationist end, pushing everything and everyone into one of two language boxes, but other former colonies and dominions provide evidence that this does not need to be. Biculturalism—or in Canada's case, triculturalism—can exist alongside Canadian multiculturalism (and Quebec's interculturalism), as a relationship between Indigenous nations and their English and French counterparts. Treaties can be brought back from declarations of "legal nullity" to become "foundational documents." While the situation in New Zealand is far from perfect, the understanding of treaty as the foundation of the nation state and the continued resurgence of Māori and their political, legal and cultural traditions offers at least a glimmer of hope and possibility.

For Indigenous peoples, multicultural policy in Canada is a framework of assimilation into two singular nations, which systematically ignores Indigenous peoples as nations within their own legal, political and cultural traditions. These traditions have been recognized, affirmed and protected through treaties, the oft-proclaimed narrative of three nations/pillars and, in turn, Canadian constitutional law. While the "multi-" in multiculturalism means many, it effectively recognizes only the two (English and French) cultures of Canada and requires that cultures fit into one of the two already institutionalized. It creates a home with a different window dressing and with different meals on the table, but it has not transformed Canada's dominant settler narrative or sense of home—Canada is still home to two nations and all others, including Indigenous peoples, must take up residency within. While Canada recognizes bilingualism in only the "correct" two languages and relegated all other languages to secondary status, its attitude toward Indigenous languages is particularly problematic and part of a larger program of linguistic and cultural exclusion and assimilation. Perhaps, as the story advances it will come to include the narratives that it has traditionally excluded. Other cases provide evidence that this does not need to be the end, and that multiculturalism in Canada could be reshaped in order to recognize Indigenous nations and advance reconciliation meaningfully.

References

Behrendt, Larissa. 2016. *Finding Eliza: Power and Colonial Storytelling / Larissa Behrendt.* St Lucia, QLD: University of Queensland Press.
Borrows, John. 2010. *Canada's Indigenous Constitution.* Toronto, ON: University of Toronto Press.
Burman, Jenny. 2016. "Multicultural Feeling, Feminist Rage, Indigenous Refusal." *Cultural Studies, Critical Methodologies 16* (4): 361–372.
Canada. Department of Indian Affairs and Northern Development. 1969. *Statement of the Government of Canada on Indian Policy, 1969.* [Ottawa].
Canada. House of Commons Debates, 8 October 1971 (Right Hon. P. E. Trudeau, LPC). https://parl.canadiana.ca/view/oop.debates_HOC2803_08/811?r=0&s=1
Davies, Margaret. 2014. "Home and State: Reflections on Metaphor and Practice." *Griffith Law Review 23* (2): 153–175.
Environics Institute. 2015. *Canadian Public Opinion About Immigration and Multiculturalism.* Toronto: Environics Institute for Survey Research.
Henderson, James Youngblood. 1994. "Empowering Treaty Federalism." *Saskatchewan Law Review 58* (2): 241–330.
Indigenous Languages Act S.C. 2019, c. 23. https://laws-lois.justice.gc.ca/eng/acts/i-7.85/page-1.html
Jacobs, Dean M. and Victor P. Lytwyn. 2020. "Naagan Ge Bezhig Emkwaan: A Dish with One Spoon Reconsidered." *Ontario History 112* (2): 191–210.
King, Thomas. 2003. *The Truth about Stories: A Native Narrative.* Toronto, ON: House of Anansi Press.
Kymlicka, Will. 2011. "Multicultural Citizenship within Multination States." *Ethnicities 11* (3): 281–302.
Ladner, Kiera L. 2005. "Up the Creek: Fishing for a New Constitutional Order." *Canadian Journal of Political Science / Revue Canadienne de Science Politique 38* (4): 923–953.
Little Bear, Leroy. 2017. "Canada is a Pretend Nation: REDx Talks — What I Know Now about Canada." In *Surviving Canada: Indigenous Peoples Celebrate 150 Years of Betrayal*, Kiera L. Ladner and Myra J. Tait (eds.) Winnipeg, MB: ARP Books, 36–42.
MacDonald, David B. 2014. "Aboriginal Peoples and Multicultural Reform in Canada: Prospects for a New Binational Society." *Canadian Journal of Sociology 39* (1): 65.
Mcneil, Kent. 2018. "Indigenous and Crown Sovereignty in Canada." In *Resurgence and Reconciliation*, Michael Asch, John Borrows and James Tully (eds.) Toronto, ON: University of Toronto Press, 293–314.
Mills, Aaron. 2017. "Driving the Gift Home." *The Windsor Yearbook of Access to Justice 33* (1): 167.
Montreal Gazette. 2021. "Probe Launched after 400 Complaints Over New GG's Lack of French." *Montreal Gazette*, July 19, 2021. https://montrealgazette.com/news/local-news/probe-launched-after-400-complaints-over-new-ggs-lack-of-french.
"Prime Minister Announces The Queen's Approval of Canada's next Governor General." *Prime Minister of Canada.* Canada, July 6, 2021. Prime Minister's Office. https://

pm.gc.ca/en/news/news-releases/2021/07/06/prime-minister-announces-queens-approval-canadas-next-governor.

Pryor, Judith. 2008. *Constitutions Writing Nations, Reading Difference*. New York: Birbeck Law Press.

Reynolds, Henry. 2000. *Why Werent We Told?: A Personal Search for the Truth about Our History*. Ringwood, VIC: Penguin Books.

Russell, Peter H. 2021. *Sovereignty: The Biography of a Claim*. Toronto, ON: University of Toronto Press.

Sabzalian, Leilani. 2019. "The Tensions between Indigenous Sovereignty and Multicultural Citizenship Education: Toward an Anticolonial Approach to Civic Education." *Theory and Research in Social Education* 47 (3): 311–346.

Scott, James C. 1998. *Seeing Like a State: How Certain Schemes to Improve the Human Condition Have Failed*. New Haven, CT: Yale University Press.

Simpson, Leanne. 2008. "Looking after Gdoo-Naaganinaa: Precolonial Nishnaabeg Diplomatic and Treaty Relationships." *Wicazo sa Review* 23 (2): 29–42.

Smits, Katherine. 2019. "Multiculturalism, Biculturalism, and National Identity in Aotearoa/New Zealand." In *Multiculturalism in the British Commonwealth: Comparative Perspectives on Theory and Practice*, 1st ed., Richard T. Ashcroft and Mark Bevir (eds.) University of California Press, 104–124. http://www.jstor.org/stable/j.ctvr7fcvv.9.

Srikanth, H. 2012. "Multiculturalism and the Aboriginal Peoples in Canada." *Economic and Political Weekly* 47 (23): 17–21.

Stefanovich, Olivia. 2021. "Bilingualism Requirement for SCC Justices Creates "Needless Barrier" for Indigenous Candidates, Critics Say." *CBC*, March 31, 2021. https://www.cbc.ca/news/politics/supreme-court-proposed-official-languages-reform-1.5969707.

Tully, James. 1995. *Strange Multiplicity: Constitutionalism in an Age of Diversity*. Cambridge: Cambridge University Press.

Vernon, Karina. 2016. "To the End of the Hyphen-Nation: Decolonizing Multiculturalism." *English Studies in Canada* 42 (3): 81–98.

Wolfe, Patrick. 2006. "Settler Colonialism and the Elimination of the Native." *Journal of Genocide Research* 8 (4): 387–409. https://parl.canadiana.ca/view/oop.debates_HOC2803_08/811?r=0&s=1

12
BLACK LIVES MATTER, SOCIAL JUSTICE, AND THE LIMITS OF MULTICULTURALISM

Debra Thompson

Introduction

In the summer of 2020 protests against police violence broke out in cities across the United States and around the world. Ignited by Minneapolis police officer Derek Chauvin's on-duty murder of George Floyd and united by the assertion that Black lives matter, these protests were the largest, most diverse and longest lasting protests in American history, with estimates suggesting that about 15 to 26 million people in the United States alone participated in demonstrations in June 2020 (Buchanan et al., 2020). In cities across Canada, as well as places as diverse as Brussels, London, Seoul, Sydney, Rio de Janeiro and Madrid, "Black Lives Matter" has become a global rallying cry against nationally distinct, but globally analogous manifestations of anti-Black racism and police brutality (Kirby, 2020). In France, for example, Black Lives Matter protestors organized under the banner "Justice for Adama," a young Black man who died in French police custody in 2016, while in Great Britain protestors in Bristol threw a statue of Edward Colston, an enslaver, into the harbor and sparked a public debate over the how the country remembers its role in the transatlantic slave trade. In Canada and the United States, protestors similarly graffitied or toppled monuments to colonialism and the Confederacy and echoed the demand for municipal governments to defund the police—a call for a shift in thinking around the provision of public safety in cities across North America.

The emergence of Black Lives Matter (BLM), its global appeal and grassroots resilience over the past several years, and the incredible shift in public support for the movement in 2020 were neither easy nor inevitable. There have been sustained moments of vicious backlash against the movement's organizers, aims and strategies. The refrain "All Lives Matter," as well as the pro-police assertion that "Blue Lives Matter," were immediately adopted as direct, antagonistic responses to what was perceived as a divisive and unnecessary focus on Black communities. Once Donald Trump won the American presidency in 2016, his administration openly attacked BLM, frequently using its existence as a rallying point for the white nationalist right. Beyond the United States, activists were frequently accused of importing American-derived racism to foreign contexts, where these circumstances, critics argued, simply did not apply.

Putting the empirical question of the global appeal, diffusion, presence and relevance of BLM beyond the United States aside for the moment, the existence of BLM and the durability of the backlash towards the movement reveals an interesting tension endemic of advanced democracies. On one hand, BLM should not be controversial in multicultural societies. Multiculturalism as a policy and approach to diversity management is based on the basic liberal precepts of individualism, equality and universalism. BLM has long asserted, since its earliest days, that the discourse is not "*only* Black Lives Matter," but rather, "Black Lives Matter, *too.*" According to co-founder Alicia Garza (2014), BLM is:

> an ideological and political intervention in a world where Black lives are systematically and intentionally targeted for demise. It is an affirmation of Black folks' contributions to this society, our humanity, and our resilience in the face of deadly oppression.

The struggle to guarantee and protect the civil and political rights of Black citizens is not unlike multiculturalism, which provides different forms and levels of public recognition to minority communities. Both are, arguably, premised on fulfilling the central precepts of democratic rule, including representation, participation, competition, civil and political liberties and respect for minority rights. On the other hand, it is telling that BLM has often been critiqued and rejected by the political establishment for being "too radical." More to the point, the fact that BLM arose in many of the same countries that openly, emphatically promote and value multiculturalism as a social ideal should give us pause: if multiculturalism has been so effective at incorporating racial minorities into predominately white societies, then why did BLM come into being at all?

There is a reason why multiculturalism has not become the rallying cry for a new generation of activists. In this chapter, I argue that multiculturalism has, at least in the Canadian and American contexts, proven wholly insufficient to challenge persistent racial economic inequality, rampant political suppression, and the frequent, violent encounters with the state experienced by Black populations. As one of the most important social movements of the 21st century, BLM has exposed the conceptual limits of the multicultural model. Though leftist and Indigenous critiques have been leveled against liberal multiculturalism since its inception, BLM's intervention is something quite different. The discourse of BLM and the demands of the Movement for Black Lives go beyond the scope of multiculturalism and, drawing from Black feminism and the Black radical tradition, instead use the precepts of abolition democracy to emphasize the political, economic, and moral imperatives of social justice.

Multiculturalism and Racial Justice

The meaning and scope of multiculturalism in democratic societies has, of course, been extensively discussed by others, including several chapters in this volume. Christian Joppke defines multiculturalism as a pervasive political movement in Western democracies that pursues equal rights and public recognition for ethnic, racial, religious or sexually defined groups, especially in countries that were once more homogenous on those same terms (Joppke, 1996). Coming into being in the last few decades of the 20th century, it represents a concerted and purposeful shift away from older models of diversity management of the early and mid-20th century that prioritized the assimilation of immigrants into dominant national cultures. Multiculturalism emphasizes the importance of the public recognition of identities but was also developed to address the persistence of racial and ethnic hierarchies in liberal democracies, especially in terms of economic inequalities, underrepresentation in political institutions, social stigmatization or cultural invisibility (Kymlicka, 2012: 6). Kymlicka and Banting's Multicultural Policy Index identifies eight policies as the most common forms of multiculturalism, including political affirmation of multiculturalism, multicultural school curricula, public media representation, dress code exemptions, dual citizenship, funding of cultural activities, bilingual education and affirmation action programs.[1] The multicultural ideal also gained traction in international organizations, as states ratified the United Nation's International Convention on the Elimination of All Forms of Racial Discrimination and the European Union issued the Racial Equality Directive and the Employment Equality Directive in 2000.

The sweeping adoption of multicultural norms and policies was not without its critics. While much has been said about the conservative critique that multiculturalism is conceptually divisive and pragmatically unnecessary, a more damning set of critiques emerges from those on the ideological left. First, in its equivocation of race and culture, multiculturalism enables both the preservation of white domination in settler societies and the reconstitution of national identities as a culturally tolerant, cosmopolitan whiteness (Bannerji, 2000; Thobani, 2007; Haque, 2012). Secondly, multiculturalism is inextricably connected to racial capitalism and neoliberal imperatives. As such, multiculturalism as a discourse is far less about equality than it is a mechanism to sustain the embedded inequities of global capitalism, create cosmopolitan, self-sufficient market actors and commodify diversity and cultural affinities (Abu-Laban and

Gabriel, 2002; Melamed, 2011). Thirdly, multiculturalism is conceptualized as cultural and not racial, and institutional rather than structural, and so multicultural ideologies purposefully make claims about the diversification of society without directly challenging any of the social, cultural, political or economic arrangements that maintain white supremacy (Walcott, 2019). Finally, multiculturalism is a national strategy that works to undermine Indigenous claims to sovereignty, giving primacy to whitewashed processes of recognition reconciliation rather than Indigenous-led resurgence of traditional ways of knowing and being (Coulthard, 2014; Simpson, 2017).

On the whole, in the struggle for racial justice neither the ideology nor the instrumentality of multiculturalism is up to the task. Indeed, in Canada, where multiculturalism is cemented into the national imaginary, it is frequently and faithfully used to deny the existence of racial inequality. As Keith Banting and I have recently argued, Canadian multiculturalism has been largely ineffective at combatting racial economic inequality, in part because it was never intended to serve that purpose. Though there have been a few short-lived moments when the policy focused on combatting racial discrimination, it has, more often than not, left critical racial issues unresolved (Banting and Thompson, 2021).

For example, Black unemployment rates are higher than the national average, average employment incomes are lower, and wage gaps between Black and white populations are significant and persist into second and third generations (Block, Galabuzi and Tranjan, 2019). Nearly 24% of the Black population lives below the low-income measure (after tax)—a common proxy for poverty—compared to 12.2% of the white population and nearly one-third of Black children have a low-income status (Block, Galabuzi and Tranjan, 2019; Houle, 2020). According to a recent national survey of Black Canadians, 70% report having experienced racism, nearly one in five say that they have been unfairly stopped by the police, and upwards of 90% confirm there is racism in both the healthcare sector and in employment (Foster et al., 2021). Canada's first and only Black Deputy Minister was appointed in February 2020, and in March 2021 more than 600 Black public servants joined a class action lawsuit against the federal government, alleging systemic discrimination in federal workplaces (Laucius, 2021). In the arena of criminal justice, a major focus of BLM organizing, Black Canadians are 3.5% of the national population but 8.6% of the federally incarcerated population. When incarcerated, Black inmates are overrepresented in admissions to "segregation," disproportionately involved in use-of-force incidents, and are more likely to be classified as maximum security (Canada, 2017). A recent study on federal inmates' risk assessments found that these highly consequential reports, which determine where offenders serve their sentences, access to rehabilitative programs, visitation privileges and odds of getting parole, are "fundamentally, powerfully biased against Indigenous and Black inmates, placing them in higher security classifications and assigning them worse odds of successfully re-entering society" (Cardoso, 2020). In essence, multiculturalism fails to account for the ways that specifically Canadian racial orders have policed Black lives from slavery to the present day (Maynard, 2017).

It is not necessarily the case that BLM and multiculturalism are incompatible, but rather that there are conceptual limitations that compromise multiculturalism's usefulness as a weapon to combat the endemic white supremacy of settler societies. It is deeply liberal and far more focused on the recognition of diverse identities and cultures than the dismantling of racial and colonial orders. Its universalistic undertones are incapable of addressing the specificities and nuances of anti-Black racism, or in advocating for either targeted positive action, such as race-specific affirmative action programs or reparations for slavery. Multiculturalism as a policy and a paradigm is also silent about the ongoing violence of internal colonialism and complicit in the continuing exploitative practices of racial capitalism. In many ways, the very presence of grassroots movements such as Black Lives Matter and Idle No More, an Indigenous protest movement in Canada that emerged in 2012 and brought national attention to ongoing struggles for Indigenous sovereignty, points to the inadequacy of multicultural discourses. Moreover, racialized and Indigenous peoples do not necessarily desire integration or incorporation into polities that are founded on white supremacy; they seek to fundamentally transform them.

Black Lives Matter and Abolition Democracy

The origins of BLM are, by this point, fairly well known. The hashtag #BlackLivesMatter is widely credited to three Black women, Opal Tometi, Alicia Garza and Patrisse Cullors, created in the wake of George Zimmerman's acquittal in the murder of Trayvon Martin in 2014. The movement ignited after the police officer Darren Wilson killed Black teenager Michael Brown in Ferguson, Missouri, caught fire when officers of the Baltimore Police Department were charged (but not convicted) in the police-involved death of Freddie Gray, and then spread to cities across America and around the world. Though there are "official" BLM chapters in the United States, Canada and the United Kingdom that operate under the organizational structure of the Black Lives Matter Global Network, the broader movement is comprised of dozens of local and national formations, adjacent and autonomous organizations and "political quilters" that supply the connective tissue of the movement through leadership training, political education and strategic support (Ransby, 2018).

On its face, BLM as a social movement most explicitly challenges the disturbingly pervasive nature of police violence towards Black populations. The most egregious form of this violence is deadly force, which is used so disproportionately against Black populations that in the United States one in every thousand Black men can expect to be killed by the police (Edwards et al., 2019). Some of the names of the dead are familiar, by now. Eric Garner was killed in Staten Island, New York when put in an illegal chokehold by officer Daniel Pantaleo; Garner's words, "I can't breathe," have become a haunting refrain of the movement since his death in 2014. A few months later, Cleveland police officer Timothy Loehmann shot 12-year-old Tamir Rice within two seconds of arriving in the public park where Rice was playing with a toy gun. Philando Castile was shot and killed during a traffic stop near Minneapolis in 2016 after telling police officer Jeronimo Yanez he had a licensed firearm in his vehicle; Castile's girlfriend and her four-year-old daughter were in the car at the time. Stephon Clark was shot in his grandmother's backyard in Sacramento, California, in 2018, holding only a cell phone. Other names, especially those of Black women and Black trans women, are too frequently forgotten. The #SayHerName campaign, spearheaded by legal scholar Kimberlé Crenshaw and the African-American Policy Forum, sought to bring more awareness to the unique gendered and racial violence that Black women face at the hands of law enforcement, as well as those women killed at the hands of the police, including Rekia Boyd, Sandra Bland and Breonna Taylor.

BLM also contributed to a heightened awareness of what Michelle Alexander (2010) calls the "New Jim Crow"—the conceptualization of the system of mass incarceration as "a stunningly comprehensive and well-disguised system of racialized social control that functions in a manner strikingly similar to Jim Crow" (4). In fact, a notable success of the discourse of BLM is the illumination of the rampant systemic racism in every facet of the criminal justice system, including the War on Drugs, broken windows policing, three strikes laws and mandatory minimum sentencing, as well as the detrimental social and political consequences that follow when citizens are labeled as felons, including voting disenfranchisement. The movement has challenged the proliferation of the carceral state, the prison-industrial complex and its relationship to racial capitalism, the militarization of the police, the increasingly punitive and criminalizing tone of immigration and poverty management policies, the uneven and unequal distribution of public goods, the precarious legitimacy of democratic institutions and the fraudulence of simplistic claims about the inevitability of racial progress (Taylor, 2016; Thompson and Thurston, 2018).

The Canadian chapters of BLM are similarly invested in confronting the disproportionately targeted and violent policing of Black communities. The original Toronto Coalition of BLM emerged in November 2014 after a Missouri grand jury declined to indict Darren Wilson for killing Michael Brown. It was not simply an emulation of the organizing in the United States; rather, BLM-Toronto sought to

> create not just a space for solidarity, but one that centred the experience of Black communities in Canada ... We were seeking to rupture the

violent way that Canada attempts to absent us; it was a radical, geographic shift in our understandings of Blackness in the Americas.

(Hudson and Diverlus 2020: 7)

Satellite sites of Black Canadian organizing, including BLM chapters in Toronto, Vancouver, Montreal and Edmonton, seek to challenge the systemic racialized violence of the Canadian police toward Black people and center Black voices in the struggle, especially those who are queer, trans, women, differently abled, poor, undocumented, immigrant and otherwise marginalized. Though the "new Jim Crow" is frequently conceptualized as a uniquely American phenomenon, the broad concerns of Canadian BLM chapters are similar to those articulated by activists in the United States, especially in regard to disproportionate and deadly police violence toward Black populations. The additional challenge for these activists, however, is the formidable obstacle of a national discourse and social consensus that rarely acknowledges the realities and specifically Canadian manifestations of racism (Thompson, 2020).

It was not until Minneapolis police officer Derek Chauvin murdered George Floyd in May 2020 that the movement experienced an unprecedented resurgence and massive, though somewhat temporary, shift in white public opinion (Samuels, 2021). The drivers of this moment were a confluence of unique factors. Most obviously, the COVID-19 pandemic set the stage for the protests in several ways: the disproportionate burden of the disease on racialized communities, the experiences of vulnerability and precarity that enabled white people to empathize with Black pain, and the questions of how societies understand and operationalize the idea of the common good (Ajadi and Thompson, 2021). The video of George Floyd's murder—incontrovertible, horrific, viral and emergent at precisely the same moment when large parts of the population were in lockdown and more attuned to their social media feeds—came on the heels of two other high-profile murders of Black citizens: Breonna Taylor's police-involved killing in St. Louis, Missouri, and the racially-motivated murder of Ahmaud Arbery in Glynn County, Georgia. In the more than five years prior to Floyd's murder, BLM had built a movement infrastructure and an established messaging that was ready to mobilize and could now resonate with a broader audience. The location of the initial uprisings mattered as well: Minneapolis has a long history of radical and grassroots organizing that helped bring people into the streets. The responses to the protests also inadvertently fueled the fire. President Trump threatened to deploy troops to quash the protests (one tweet used the ominous phrasing, "when the looting starts, the shooting starts") and urged state governors and law enforcement officials to take a more forceful approach, claiming that protestors were agitators from "the radical left." This line in the sand made it more likely that Democrats and others who had opposed Trump since he won the 2016 election would choose to align themselves in opposition. The police response also escalated the situation in many cities across North America, as they used tear gas and rubber bullets against unarmed, largely peaceful protestors and intensified the public's awareness of endemic state violence.

The protests soon became about much more than BLM. As Tobi Haslett (2021) writes,

> Something deeper and more disruptive had breached the surface of social life, conjuring exactly the dreaded image the conspiracy theorists refused to face. This was open black revolt: simultaneous but uncoordinated, a vivid fixture of American history sprung to life with startling speed ... But what emerged under the banner of blackness was soon blended with other elements, flinging multi-racial crowds against soldiers and police.

The singular, pointed cruelty inflicted upon George Floyd was propelled to an American, and even worldwide, democratic crisis.

In ideological terms, BLM is markedly distinct from and more radical than the entrenched liberalism of multiculturalism. Emerging from the Black Marxist understanding that chattel slavery was as much an economic system of control as it was political and social, the Black radical tradition is defined by Cedric Robinson as "the continuing development of a collective consciousness informed by the historical struggles for liberation and motivated by the shared sense of obligation to preserve the collective being, the ontological totality" (1983: 171). The Black radical imagination, Chicago activist Charlene Carruthers writes, is rooted in anti-slavery and anti-colonial movements of the 19th and early 20th centuries, builds on the legacies of the Haitian Revolution, the Student Nonviolent Coordinating Committee and the Combahee River Collective, and dreams of "a world without prisons, without gender-based violence, where definitions of valuable work are transformed, and where the land we live on is liberated alongside its peoples" (2018: 19–20).

Black feminist politics have also been an ideological core of the movement. BLM clearly takes inspiration from the intersectional, feminist approach articulated by the Combahee River Collective in its 1977 statement, which criticized white feminist movements steeped in racism and Black liberation movements that ignored sexism (Taylor, 2017). Black feminist politics, language, sensibilities and traditions are premised on the idea that "the personal is political, and the political is profoundly personal" (Ransby, 2018: 106). The movement is inherently intersectional, meaning that it emphasizes and understands the interaction among various categories of difference, such as race, gender, class and sexual orientation, to produce interlocking systems of domination and subjective identity positions (Crenshaw, 1991; Hancock, 2007; Nash, 2008; Cho, Crenshaw and McCall, 2013). This intersectional, feminist, radical praxis has meant that movement organizers have struggled to challenge the ways that the media and public tend to focus on the male victims of police violence, while the police violence, sexualized violence and intimate partner violence faced by Black girls and women and especially Black trans women goes unaddressed. The call to "Say Her Name" is an attempt to illuminate the adultification of Black girls and the erasure of violence against Black women (AAPF, 2015).

The ideological orientation of BLM stands in contrast to the central tenets of liberalism, such as the individualistic orientation of political rights and the taut connection between individual and property rights. While multiculturalism is preoccupied with the recognition of individual and group identities within a liberal democratic framework, the Movement for Black Lives is premised on the transformation of our society as we know it. Even as the events that initially gave rise to BLM are widely understood as exemplary of a uniquely American "race problem," BLM is a global movement. It can be read as a continuation of the long tradition of Black internationalism, which is characterized by a conscious interconnection across the disparate settlements of the African diaspora and the interlocution of Black struggles beyond boundaries, including those created by oceans, empires, states and nations (West et al., 2009). A more diasporic orientation about the struggles that connect Black people across national borders and the resonance of BLM's calls to bring awareness to issues of police brutality, mass incarceration, racial inequality and anti-Black racism across the globe demonstrate that the state has invariably been a source of racial domination. There is, therefore, good reason to be skeptical of the emancipatory potential of state action in the name of multiculturalism.

In essence, BLM seeks to move democratic societies toward what WEB Du Bois (1935/1998) called "abolition democracy." In his landmark work on the Reconstruction era, *Black Reconstruction in America, 1860–1880*, Du Bois wrote of the enormous, unrealized democratic potential of Reconstruction. The era was about more than the extension of the formal rights of citizenship to the formerly enslaved; it could have been a total transformation of the exploitative capitalist system that entraps Black and white workers alike. Because the failure—but really, the sabotage—of Reconstruction sutured enduring and morphing forms of racial domination to democratic citizenship in the United States, liberal democracy will continue to serve the interests and protect the political status of the white citizen (Olson, 2004). Scholar-activist Angela Davis (2005), drawing on Du Bois's original formulation, argues that the comprehensive abolition of slavery would have required entirely new institutions to incorporate the formerly enslaved into the policy. This, obviously, did not happen; instead, Davis argues that surviving institutions such as the death penalty and prisons must be abolished if we are to achieve a democracy in its fullest, most substantial form. "Racism," Davis writes, "is something that is far deeper than that which can be resolved through processes of diversification and multiculturalism" (2005: 94).

These abolitionist aims have animated BLM's resurgence in 2020, with clear, repeated messaging about the necessity of defunding, and eventually, abolishing the police. "Enough," powerhouse organizer Mariame Kaba (2020) wrote in the *New York Times* at the height of the protests. "We can't reform the police. The only way to diminish police violence is to reduce contact between the public and the police." Across the United States, state legislatures moved to create new or strengthened police accountability systems that collect, analyze and publish data on police use of force, officer-involved deaths, officer-involved sexual conduct cases and other forms of police misconduct. At the city level, reforms require officers to break the "blue wall of silence" and report unreasonable or excessive force, the redirection of police budgets toward community alternatives, the removal of police officers from public schools, and, in the case of New York City, limits on police officers' qualified immunity from civil action for unreasonable search and seizure or the use of excessive force.

Scholars have proposed that we might think of the uprisings of 2020 as a "Third Reconstruction." In American history, Reconstruction was the period that followed the end of the Civil War, characterized by the incorporation of formerly enslaved people of African descent into American democracy. The rapid advancement of civil rights in the decades following the end of the Second World War are often referred to as the "Second Reconstruction." In this sense, 2020 was a similar moment of national reckoning with the many ways that democratic social, economic and political systems continue to exploit, dominate, control, expunge, ruin and incarcerate Black populations (Codrington, 2020). It is a moment, the prolific Black Studies scholar Robin DG Kelley argues, characterized by the most visionary conception of abolition in American history. This Third

> Reconstruction [is] not simply, better jails, better police, better training. It's: no police, it's no jails, no prisons. It's creating a new means of justice that's not based on criminalization but based on affirmation and reparation ... here is an opportunity to actually transform not just the nation, but the entire world.
>
> *(Kelley 2020)*

But, like the era of Redemption, lynch mobs and legalized segregation that followed the failure of the First Reconstruction, and the War on Drugs that punished the communities that marched for civil rights in the Second Reconstruction, this Third Reconstruction will, inevitably, be followed by a disproportionate backlash and a retrenchment of new, perhaps more malleable forms of racial inequality. The recent "culture war brawl" over critical race theory is a point in case: Republicans at local, state and national levels are trying to block curriculums that emphasize America's history of racism or the continued existence of systemic racism (Gabriel and Goldstein, 2021). This is likely just the beginning.

Conclusion

Fifty years of multiculturalism has not resolved entrenched racial inequality in democratic societies. In Canada and the United States, the introduction of multicultural policies and discourses coincided with the shift from the explicit, legalized forms of racial discrimination of the early 20th century to more subtle, covert, but nevertheless systemic forms of racism. Fifty years later, racism remains embedded throughout society, including in those institutions thought to be at the forefront of redistributive, egalitarian social moorings, including the tax system, public education, higher education, healthcare, environmental protection, migration policy and more. In addition, citizen involvement with the state is too frequently conceptualized as operationalizing the democratic ideal of civic engagement, when the reality for many Black and Indigenous people is quite the opposite. Joe Soss and Vesla Weaver (2017) argue that race-class subjugated communities most often interact with the "second face of the state, "the activities of governing institutions and officials that exercise social control and encompass various modes of coercion, containment, repression, surveillance, regulation, predation, discipline, and violence" (567). Questions of liberal-democratic inclusion through multicultural framings are fundamentally inadequate to capture the ways that various modes of democratic governance that are frequently entwined with policing (as is the case with immigration policy, welfare policy and child protective services, for example) work to stigmatize, supervise and repress communities of color.

In a fairly short amount of time, BLM has emerged as a more radical critique of persistent racial inequality in democratic societies than older and institutionally entrenched multicultural frameworks. This is not to say that the movement is perfect, perfectly progressive, or even coherent. Since its emergence in 2014 there have been serious fractures within the movement about whether to promote revolution or reform, challenges to its legitimacy, questions about its transparency and accountability, and near-constant accusations of corporate and political cooptation. Writing on the five-year anniversary of BLM in 2019, Keeanga-Yamahtta Taylor (2019) noted that "measured by the number of formal organizations it sprouted, the movement was barely ever alive, but it thrived in the hearts and minds of young black people who ached to be heard and seen."

Nevertheless, BLM is arguably the most important, and by some measures the most successful, social movement of the 21st century. In this chapter, I have suggested that the very existence of BLM in Canada and the United States, two countries that pride themselves on the idea that they are racially and ethnically diverse democracies, demonstrates the limits of the multicultural model in the struggle for racial justice. BLM arose to challenge circumstances of deadly police violence and has expanded over the years to incorporate an agenda aimed at dismantling various forms and instruments of racial domination in the system of mass incarceration, the carceral state and other vectors of state power. In contrast to multiculturalism's explicit commitment to liberal ideals, BLM's more radical ideological grounds raise the question of whether the striking racial inequality that characterizes both Canada and the United States is the outcome of liberal democracy operating exactly as it was intended. The appropriate response, then, can only be abolition, which to paraphrase Ruth Wilson Gilmore, requires that we change just one thing—everything.

Note

1 https://www.queensu.ca/mcp/home

References

Abu-Laban, Yasmeen and Christina Gabriel. 2002. *Selling Diversity: Immigration, Multiculturalism, Employment Equity, and Globalization*. Toronto: University of Toronto Press.

African American Policy Forum. 2015. *Say Her Name: Resisting Police Brutality against Black Women*. New York: Center for Intersectionality and Policy Studies, Columbia University.

Ajadi, Tari and Debra Thompson. 2021. "The Two Pandemics of Anti-Black Racism and COVID-19 are Tied Together." *Globe and Mail*, May 22. https://www.theglobeandmail.com/opinion/article-the-two-pandemics-of-anti-black-racism-and-covid-19-are-tied-together/

Alexander, Michelle. 2010. *The New Jim Crow: Mass Incarceration in the Age of Colorblindness*. New York: The New Press.

Bannerji, Himani. 2000. *The Dark Side of the Nation: Essays on Multiculturalism, Nationalism, and Gender*. Toronto: Women's Press.

Banting, Keith and Debra Thompson. 2021. "The Puzzling Persistence of Racial Inequality in Canada." *Canadian Journal of Political Science* 54 (4): 870–891.

Block, Sheila, Grace-Edward Galabuzi, and Ricardo Tranjan. 2019. *Canada's Colour Coded Income Inequality*. Ottawa: Canadian Centre for Policy Alternatives.

Buchanan, Larry, Quoctrung Bui, and Jugal K. Patel. 2020. "Black Lives Matter May Be the Largest Movement in U.S. History." *New York Times*, July 3, 2020. https://www.nytimes.com/interactive/2020/07/03/us/george-floyd-protests-crowd-size.html

Canada. 2017. *Annual Report: Office of the Correctional Investigator, 2016–2017*. https://www.oci-bec.gc.ca/cnt/rpt/pdf/annrpt/annrpt20162017-eng.pdf

Cardoso, Tom. 2020. "Bias Behind Bars: A Globe Investigation Finds a Prison System Stacked against Black and Indigenous Inmates." *Globe and Mail*, October 24. https://www.theglobeandmail.com/canada/article-investigation-racial-bias-in-canadian-prison-risk-assessments/

Carruthers, Charlene A. 2018. *Unapologetic: A Black, Queer, and Feminist Mandate for Radical Movements*. Boston: Beacon Press.

Cho, Sumi, Kimberlé Williams Crenshaw, and Leslie McCall. 2013. "Toward a Field of Intersectionality Studies: Theory, Applications, and Praxis." *Signs* 38 (4): 785–810.

Codrington III, William. 2020. "The United States Needs a Third Reconstruction." *The Atlantic*, July 20. https://www.theatlantic.com/ideas/archive/2020/07/united-states-needs-third-reconstruction/614293/

Coulthard, Glen. 2014. *Red Skin, White Masks: Rejecting the Colonial Project of Recognition*. Minneapolis: University of Minnesota Press.

Crenshaw, Kimberlé. 1991. "Mapping the Margins: Intersectionality, Identity Politics, and Violence against Women of Color." *Stanford Law Review* 43 (6): 1241–99.

Davis, Angela. 2005. *Abolition Democracy: Beyond Empire, Prisons, and Torture*. New York: Seven Stories Press.

Du Bois, W.E.B. 1935/1998. *Black Reconstruction in America, 1860–1880*. New York: the Free Press.

Edwards, Frank, Hedwig Lee, and Michael Esposito. 2019. "Risk of Being Killed by Police Use of Force in the United States by Age, Race-Ethnicity, and Sex." *Proceedings of the National Academy of Sciences of the United States of America* 116 (34): 16793–98.

Foster, Lorne, Stella Park, Hugh McCague, Marcelle-Anne Fletcher, and Jackie Sikdar. 2021. *Black Canadian National Survey Interim Report, 2021*. Toronto: Institute for Social Research, York University. https://blacknessincanada.ca/wp-content/uploads/2021/05/0_Black-Canadian-National-Survey-Interim-Report-2021.2.pdf

Gabriel, Trip and Dana Goldstein. 2021. "Disputing Racism's Reach, Republicans Rattle American Schools." *New York Times*, June 1. https://www.nytimes.com/2021/06/01/us/politics/critical-race-theory.html

Garza, Alicia. 2014. "A Herstory of the #BlackLivesMatter Movement." *The Feminist Wire*, October 7. http://www.thefeministwire.com/2014/10/blacklivesmatter-2/

Haque, Eve. 2012. *Multiculturalism within a Bilingual Framework: Language, Race, and Belonging in Canada*. Toronto: University of Toronto Press.

Hancock, Ange-Marie. 2007. "When Multiplication Doesn't Equal Quick Addition: Examining Intersectionality as a Research Paradigm." *Perspectives on Politics* 5 (1): 63–79.

Haslett, Tobi. 2021. "Magic Actions: Looking Back on the George Floyd Rebellion." *n+1 Magazine*, May 7. https://nplusonemag.com/online-only/online-only/magic-actions/

Houle, René. 2020. *Changes in the Socioeconomic Situation of Canada's Black Population, 2001 to 2016*. Ottawa: Statistics Canada. https://www150.statcan.gc.ca/n1/en/pub/89-657-x/89-657-x2020001-eng.pdf?st=yqmomlgI

Hudson, Sandy and Rodney Diverlus. 2020. "The Origin Story of Black Lives Matter Canada." In *Until We Are Free: Reflections on Black Lives Matter in Canada*, Rodney Diverlus, Sandy Hudson and Syrus Marcus Ware (eds.) Regina: University of Regina Press, 3–16.

Joppke, Christian. 1996. "Multiculturalism and Immigration: A Comparison of the United States, Germany, and Great Britain." *Theory and Society* 25 (4): 449–500.

Kaba, Mariame. 2020. "Yes, We Mean Literally Abolish the Police." *New York Times*, June 12. https://www.nytimes.com/2020/06/12/opinion/sunday/floyd-abolish-defund-police.html

Kelley, Robin D.G. 2020. "Scholar Robin D.G. Kelley on How Today's Abolitionist Movement Can Fundamentally Change the Country." *The Intercept*, June 27. https://theintercept.com/2020/06/27/robin-dg-kelley-intercepted/

Kirby, Jen. 2020. ""Black Lives Matter" has Become a Global Rallying Cry against Racism and Police Brutality." *Vox*, June 12, 2020. https://www.vox.com/2020/6/12/21285244/black-lives-matter-global-protests-george-floyd-uk-belgium

Kymlicka, Will. 2012. *Multiculturalism: Success, Failure, and the Future*. Washington, DC: Migration Policy Institute.

Laucius, Joanne. 2021. "More than 600 Come Forward in Class-Action Lawsuit Alleging Systemic Discrimination against Black Public Servants." *Ottawa Citizen*, March 29. https://ottawacitizen.com/news/local-news/more-than-600-come-forward-in-class-action-lawsuit-alleging-systemic-discrimination-against-black-public-servants

Maynard, Robyn. 2017. *Policing Black Lives: State Violence in Canada from Slavery to the Present*. Halifax: Fernwood Publishing.

Melamed, Jodi. 2011. *Represent and Destroy: Rationalizing Violence in the New Racial Capitalism*. Minneapolis: University of Minnesota Press.

Nash, Jennifer C. 2008. "Re-thinking Intersectionality." *Feminist Review 89*: 1–15.

Olson, Joel. 2004. *The Abolition of White Democracy*. Minneapolis: University of Minnesota Press.

Ransby, Barbara. 2018. *Making All Black Lives Matter: Reimagining Freedom in the Twenty-First Century*. Oakland: University of California Press.

Robinson, Cedric J. 1983. *Black Marxism: The Making of the Black Radical Tradition*. London: Zed Press.

Samuels, Alex. 2021. "How Views on Black Lives Matter Have Changed – And Why that Makes Police Reform So Hard." *FiveThirtyEight*, April 13. https://fivethirtyeight.com/features/how-views-on-black-lives-matter-have-changed-and-why-that-makes-police-reform-so-hard/

Simpson, Leanne Betasamosake. 2017. *As We Have Always Done: Indigenous Freedom Through Radical Resistance*. Minneapolis: University of Minnesota Press.

Soss, Joe and Vesla Weaver. 2017. "Police Are Our Government: Politics, Political Science, and the Policing of Race-Class Subjugated Communities." *Annual Review of Political Science 20*: 565–91.

Taylor, Keeanga-Yamahtta. 2016. *From #BlackLivesMatter to Black Liberation*. Chicago: Haymarket Books.

Taylor, Keeanga-Yamahtta (ed.). 2017. *How We Get Free: Black Feminism and the Combahee River Collective*. Chicago: Haymarket Books.

Taylor, Keeanga-Yamahtta. 2019. "Five Years Later, Do Black Lives Matter?" *Jacobin*, September 30. https://jacobinmag.com/2019/09/black-lives-matter-laquan-mcdonald-mike-brown-eric-garner

Thobani, Sunera. 2007. *Exalted Subjects: Studies in the Making of Race and Nation in Canada*. Toronto: University of Toronto Press.

Thompson, Debra. 2020. "The Intersectional Politics of Black Lives Matter." In *Turbulent Times, Transformational Possibilities? Gender and Politics Today and Tomorrow*, Fiona MacDonald and Alexandra Dobrowolsky (eds.) Toronto: University of Toronto Press, 240–257.

Thompson, Debra and Chloe Thurston. 2018. "American Political Development in the Era of Black Lives Matter." *Politics, Groups and Identities 6* (1): 116–119.

Walcott, Rinaldo. 2019. "The End of Diversity." *Public Culture 31* (2): 393–408.

West, Michael O., William G. Martin, and Fanon Che Wilkins (eds.). 2009. *From Toussaint to Tupac: The Black International Since the Age of Revolution*. Chapel Hill: University of North Carolina Press.

13
HUNGARY AND THE PARADOXES OF ILLIBERAL ANTI-MULTICULTURALISM

Zsolt Körtvélyesi

Introduction

Ask anyone and it is very likely that they wouldn't associate multiculturalism with developments dominating the news cycle on, and political developments in, Hungary in recent years. This chapter takes up this lack of connection and shows how, amid developments that undermine the rule of law, constitutionalism and democracy, multiculturalist insight can and should play a critical role in understanding and mapping out Hungary's societal, political and institutional present and future.

There are various possible ways to explore multiculturalism's relevance in Hungary, including highlighting the plight of the Roma, the largest domestic minority in Hungary as well as the struggles of other minorities living in Hungary, and other co-ethnic communities or "kin minorities" (i.e., Hungarians living in neighboring states). Multiculturalist insight could also be vital in providing a critical lens for Hungarian immigration and integration programs and domestic and external responses to illiberal deviation. What further complicates an application of multiculturalist insight to Hungary is that some policy areas (e.g., asylum, visa or basic rule of law requirements) are both regulated by the European Union (which Hungary joined in 2004 with other countries in the region) and are related to the freedom of movement that is central to the pursuit of European integration. It is therefore impossible to provide here a satisfactory overview of all of these areas and to evaluate all of them in line with the multitude of existing multiculturalist approaches. Consequently, this chapter's objectives are modest; it provides an overview of a few key policies and I limit my discussion to liberal multiculturalism.

DOI: 10.4324/9781003197485-19

To be clear, liberal multiculturalism is a normative approach embedded in liberalism[1] that rules out some policy decisions and mandates others, promotes group-specific policies and is based on the rejection of a homogenous, unitary nation state (Kymlicka, 2007a: 61). Will Kymlicka lists, among other liberal multicultural policies, the recognition of self-government rights, territorial autonomy, official language status, affirmative action and guarantees of representation, allowing dual citizenship, support for cultural activities and the adoption of multiculturalism in school curricula (Kymlicka, 2010: 36–37). In contrast to this, what I term "illiberal anti-multiculturalism" refers to a reactionary trend, in Hungary and beyond, that not only harkens to a perverse fantasy of ethnic homogeneity (i.e., a state of zero immigration and a view of the Roma as a burden on the nation), but that also undermines liberal tenets like judicial independence or equal rights and, ultimately, democracy.

The chapter focuses on post-1990 policy developments, and the context in which they were implemented, as they relate to multiculturalism. 1990 marks the first democratic elections after the state socialist era and a turn towards the West, with influences including liberal democracy and multiculturalism. The chapter argues that this influence had mixed results and a limited impact on policies that could be empathically read as liberal multiculturalist but that remained compatible with nationalist goals. This is manifest in policies targeting domestic minorities as well as measures aimed at Hungarian minorities living in neighboring countries. It is therefore not so surprising that these policies could be made compatible with the illiberal anti-multiculturalist bent of the post-2010 regime. Since 2010, Prime Minister Viktor Orbán has won three consecutive elections and he has been building a regime that has explicitly broken with Western ideals of multiculturalism and liberalism. In brief, any semblance of liberal multiculturalism there may have been in Hungary has withered away. This chapter documents key policy changes to address the question of how this could happen so easily.

The chapter starts by looking at domestic policies related to national minorities living in Hungary. It then moves on to an examination of an external ethnic citizenship policy targeting Hungarians in neighboring countries that also has internal consequences (such as impacting the right to vote in Hungarian elections) and that, as we shall see, is particularly pertinent to a discussion on multiculturalism. "Dual citizenship," that is to say the policy to allow non-residential naturalization with an ethnic preference, is discussed in a separate section as it has become both a key element in shaping the official concept of the nation as well as a means to recruit new votes for the regime. The chapter then provides an overview of the post-2010 regime in light of its incoherent relationship to multiculturalist claims. The chapter's conclusion remarks on how the challenges posed by the post-2010 regime to the broadly liberal European framework can be understood in light of multiculturalist discussions on liberal responses to illiberal minorities. My hope is that this overview will allow the reader not only to understand, through the Hungarian example, the troubled reception of liberal multiculturalist ideas in the post-communist post-accession era in Central Europe, but also to see that liberal multiculturalism may perhaps yet play a vital role in addressing current challenges in Hungary and Central Europe.

Democratic Transition and Multiculturalism

Multiculturalism became a central point of discussion in Hungary within the context of the democratic transition of 1989/1990 although multicultural concerns have long been important in Hungary due to the country's multiethnic reality. The "nationalities question" (Wank, 1997: 131–146) has been widely credited for the breakup of the Habsburg monarchy (the Austro-Hungarian Empire). This resulted in the loss of more than two-thirds of the territories of the Kingdom of Hungary, close to two-thirds of the population, including one-third of ethnic Hungarians, per the Treaty of Trianon (Romsics, 2020). Combined with the nationalizing policies of neighboring countries, this made Hungary a strong advocate of minority protection in the interwar period, albeit with limited success (Romsics, 2000: 17–24). The question of Hungarians living in neighboring countries, a sensitive issue quickly condemned as an expression of irredentism, was largely shelved during the larger part of the communist era, in the name of internationalism.[2] It was the run-up to the change of regime in the 1980s that brought renewed interest in the field. This was manifested by the Hungarian state's interest in the living conditions of Hungarian communities living in neighboring states—there were three million Hungarians living in neighboring states.[3] This topic also became one of the drivers of opposition politics before the regime change.

In Hungary, the Constitution as revised in 1989 recognized national (ethnic) minorities as "a constituent part of the state" (The Constitution of Hungary 1949: Art. 68-1 of Act No. XX, after the 1989 amendments, as in application up to 2012) and used a mix of a political and a cultural concept of the nation, with "responsibility" also for the fate of Hungarians living "beyond the borders" (The Constitution of Hungary 1949: Art. 6-3 of Act No. XX, after the 1989 amendments, as in application up to 2012). A Minorities Act was adopted in 1993 that granted far-reaching rights, including collective self-governments, for minorities living in Hungary (Hungarian Minority Act 1993: No. LXXVII). While the historical precedents from the 19th century were invoked, at the end of the 20th century, this was a very different country. By this time Hungary could be described as a state with minorities that are:

> relatively small in number and territorially dispersed in terms of settlement ... [who] feel firmly attached to the state and its dominant culture

... [who] are at an advanced stage of linguistic-cultural assimilation ... [and who] have not been politically mobilized along ethnic lines.

(Sansum and Dobos 2020: 251–252)

If we compare this ethnic landscape to legislation on minorities, a puzzle is revealed: the largely homogenous ethnic composition of the country[4] hardly justifies the robust legal framework elaborated to address the needs of nationalities living in Hungary. It is even more perplexing to look at the specifics of the regulations; one realizes that it is a misfit for the needs of the actual minorities whose concerns it is meant to address, and that the adopted legal framework does not mirror the needs of the groups that have been largely assimilated. For instance, multilingualism is supported, whereas most of the minorities are assimilated to the extent that languages ceased to be a source of contention or discrimination. The Roma in fact constitute three communities, the Romungro, with Hungarian as their mother tongue, the Vlach and the Boyash communities, but are recognized as one minority. Roma communities are anyway more in need of proper integration policies and traditional equality measures, as opposed to separation, including social policies, housing, school desegregation and addressing other forms of exclusion. More than half of the households experience forms of exclusion, including residence and housing, education and employment[5] (Váradi and Virág, 2014: 61). The Jewish minority is divided on whether its members should seek recognition as a nationality, and despite some attempts, remains without recognition due to internal resistance. As a result, the representation of Jewry in Hungary relies on religious organizations—hardly a satisfactory solution for non-religious people.

An overtly permissive legal regulation was created on the basis of self-identification, leading to instances of "ethnobusiness," which is to say identifying as a minority for personal gain.[6] Minority self-governments also became a vehicle for majority interests to co-opt minority representation; in some cases, this took place quite directly due to the long-time issue of non-minority citizens being able to participate in electing minority representatives (Majtényi, 2005: 401–402). The extensive framework can be compared to the building of the Hungarian Parliament: the system of minority self-governments is similarly outsized for current realities, a misfit that can only be explained by looking beyond the current borders of the country. Similarly, in a region where states rarely venture to "overperform" in the area of minority rights, Hungary wanted to create a model for the region, with the explicit recognition of collective rights.[7] Not only was this model *not* based on multiculturalist convictions, it also failed to respond to the needs and specificities of the relevant domestic minorities thus failing to live up to multiculturalism's key normative principles.

The puzzle of the misfit, or "overperformance," is easily resolved if one sees the legal regulation for what it was meant to be in the first case: a showcase for the world that was not primarily intended for domestic consumption (Sansum and Dobos 2020). In fact, Hungary sought to set a regional standard that would benefit Hungarians living in the neighboring countries, which was more of a concern for the Hungarian legislature than was the fate of minorities within the country. This was a low-cost move intended to position Hungary internationally as a state sensitive to the fate of minorities as well as human rights, a kinstate with credibility, and a high achiever in "Europeanisation," that is to say the adoption of European norms. The developments in the post-Yugoslav region, with territorial autonomy in Serbia or the Croatian case which seems to have built on the Hungarian model (Petričušić, 2015: 55; Sansum and Dobos, 2020: 252), might even suggest that the model worked. Paradoxically, the Hungarian model has proven to be less effective for most Hungarian communities, particularly those in Romania, in Slovakia and in Ukraine.

On the regional level, whatever initial enthusiasm there was for the Hungarian model soon wore out, and disappointment followed regarding how far liberal conditionality could actually reach. This was partly due to a domestic resistance to liberal norms that had appeared early and strong (as discussed, e.g., in Kymlicka and Opalski, 2002) and that were initially followed not because of any real domestic political support for their substance but due to a desire "catch up with the West." The meager results have also been confirmed by multiculturalist literature critically assessing the standards created by the European regime on national minorities (Kymlicka, 2007a: 245–246). This not only led to disappointment but also to a push to look for alternatives. If Europeanisation and minority rights would not bring improvement, perhaps political mobilization could work. Yet ethnic Hungarian parties in Slovakia, Romania and Serbia spent years in coalition governments but with limited results.[8] In what follows, I look at one aspect of where minorities looked for help: how Hungarian *citizenship* became the epicenter of minority claims where both sides (the Hungarian governments and Hungarian minority politicians in neighboring countries) could demonstrate success.

The Strange Politics of National Borders

Just as with minority self-governments, legislation on Hungarian citizenship seems to align itself with multiculturalism. Allowing persons belonging to minorities living in a home state but also feeling attachment to a kin state to have the citizenship of both countries is a way of recognizing the dual belonging.[9] The idea of deterritorializing citizenship and virtualizing borders can be seen as moves in line with Western and European liberal ideas. Contributing to a borderless Europe—how more liberal can one get?[10]

The national political consensus coalesced initially around not granting citizenship to Hungarians living in neighboring countries. An important argument in the debate on whether naturalization should be available to Hungarians living in neighboring states centered on the problem that this shift would lead to the (quicker) flight of Hungarians and thus to the weakening of these minority communities. However, the logic of nationalist bidding forced Fidesz—a right-wing populist and nationalist political party in Hungary led by Victor Orbán—to embrace the expansion of citizenship, turning against its previous position. It was a right-wing nationalist association—the World Alliance of Hungarians—that initiated a referendum on the issue; arguing against citizenship expansion seemed to be a difficult position to take for a party that sought to be seen as the standard-bearer of national unification. The issue was articulated in Hungarian public discussions as a discussion on "dual citizenship," which seems like somewhat of a misfit for an ethnic preferential rule on non-resident naturalization. In the end, the referendum itself was invalid due to a low turnout but it nonetheless locked Fidesz in a pro-expansion position.

Already in 1993, with the adoption of the new Act on Hungarian Nationality, strong preference was given to ethnic Hungarians, allowing them to naturalize after one year of residence, as opposed to the general eight-year rule (*Cf.* Act No. LV on Hungarian Nationality 1993: Art. 4-1-a and 4-3). This was brought down to zero years by the left-liberal coalition after the citizenship referendum, meaning that naturalization of ethnic Hungarians could start at taking up residency in the country. The first policy move of the incoming Fidesz government in 2010 was to allow naturalization from abroad, resulting in the addition of over one million new Hungarian citizens to a country with a population of just under ten million people. In response to these developments, Slovakia promptly moved to adopt a "counter-law" establishing a ban on dual citizenship[11] and Ukraine has effectively criminalized the issue (BBC News, 2018; Wesolowsky, 2020).

Parallel to these developments, the non-resident or external ethnic citizenship category (i.e., "dual citizenship/nationality" in the Hungarian debate) came to be seen as a panacea to all the potential difficulties associated with minority life, despite the fact that it could do little to actually alleviate the hardships of minority status locally (Bárdi, 2017: 147, 149–150). This notion became increasingly popular given the fact that Hungary, as the kin state, could do little to counter inequality and to live up to the commitment to keep these communities alive; not that this reality was publicly acknowledged in any way, shape or form. To the contrary, the 2010 amendment was celebrated as the single most important move after the shock of 1920—the breaking up of the Kingdom of Hungary by the Treaty of Trianon which left many Hungarians finding themselves minorities in states that they did not see as their own and where they were often treated with hostility. In fact, the offer to naturalize members of these minorities has been presented as an undoing of Trianon and the rhetoric of unification reached such a point that the Parliament was described, by its president, a prominent Fidesz politician, as representing the entire nation (Kövér, 2014)—effectively excluding all non-resident Hungarians who, still a majority, did not apply for citizenship.

In light of these developments, it becomes increasingly clear that what might appear as a multiculturalist policy of "dual citizenship" and deterritorialization is far better understood as a key part of a nationalist policy with irredentist overtones. To put it bluntly: any appearance of the inclusive character of extending citizenship is quickly cast aside by evidence of the state's clear ethnic preference.[12] Furthermore, it is also clear that the domestic political calculations have been the main driver for this decision. Public opinion related to the extension of the franchise is, by contrast to wide public support for external ethnic citizenship, a domestically divisive issue: a national poll showed that two-thirds of Hungarians support citizenship for non-resident ethnic Hungarians while there is a clear majority opposing their right to vote in Hungarian elections (Publicus, 2017). While Fidesz denied that extending the franchise was in any way a consideration, that was exactly what took place and gratitude for nationality (as an official recognition of Hungarian-ness) was expressed in votes with 95–96% of new non-resident citizen votes going to Fidesz,[13] which helped to maintain the regime in place.

Extending the franchise also meant that new non-resident citizens could also vote in referenda. As we will see in the next section, the regime, by this time, had made sure, through the now less-than-independent institutions like the National Electoral Commission and the Constitutional Court, that all opposition referenda initiatives have effectively been blocked and that referenda are only used to support government positions. In 2016, one such government initiative was let through, despite being unconstitutional on three separate grounds. The referendum, where voters overwhelmingly supported the government position but where the result was deemed invalid due to a low turnout, asked whether voters wanted to allow the European Union to order "the compulsory settlement of non-Hungarian citizens to Hungary." The referendum was held as part of a campaign with xenophobic messages and racial overtones that started in 2015 (and that is still ongoing) advocating a policy of zero immigration, the defense of Hungary as a homogeneous Hungarian country (and Europe as a Christian continent), and the building of a fence on the southern border. Trying to convince new external citizens to participate and to boost turnout, government messages have appeared in Serbia, among other countries, calling for a support, from the other side of the fence, for the strengthening of border protection from "illegal immigrants" (i.e., asylum seekers coming from conflict zones). That message seems designed to invoke, in the Hungarian community in Serbia, the still vivid memories of Hungarians crossing that same border to seek the protection of Hungary from the Yugoslav war or the more distant memory of Hungarians fleeing in the other direction, from the communist dictatorship and the purge after the 1956 revolution.[14] Whatever the case may be, it shows that there is a seemingly multiculturalist policy, such as dual citizenship which cannot be extricated from domestic level political calculations, and that may have little if anything at all to do with the recognition and accommodation of diversity.

De-Democratization and Multiculturalism

In this section, I bring together the two preceding sections and broaden this chapter's perspective to explore how policies relevant for multiculturalism (e.g., minority rights, citizenship and immigration) can be linked to deviations from liberal-democratic standards. The post-2010 Hungarian regime under the premiership of Viktor Orbán has been described in various ways: as an illiberal democracy (Buzogány, 2017: 1307–1325; Pap, 2017), as a hybrid regime (Krekó and Enyedi, 2018: 39–51) and as either an electoral or competitive authoritarianism (Shedler, 2013; Levitsky and Way, 2010). Populism is also a recurring label for the regime, but it has proven hard to situate the regime ideologically given that it combines neoliberal, statist, nationalist, conservative elements (Bartha, Boda and Szikra, 2020: 71–81). Despite the difficulty in coming up with a clear understanding of post-2010 Hungary, it is nonetheless quite clear that some aspects of the regime's decision-making can be readily described as "illiberal," a term that, ironically, the regime sometimes uses to describe itself (Orbán, 2014).

An "illiberal" regime stands in stark contradistinction to the liberal and constitutionalist element of post-1945 (and post-1990) standards of democracies. In an illiberal regime, the lack of a commitment to constitutionalism (and in some cases, an outright anti-constitutionalism) means both that the pursuit of power is unconstrained by rule of law considerations and that, once it has been obtained, maintaining power is the overriding motivation behind all government actions. The rise of illiberalism in Hungary has been facilitated by a weak and divided opposition and by weak institutional protection, that is to say a disproportionate electoral system with the sole requirement of a two-thirds majority in Parliament to overhaul the constitutional structure. All of this has resulted in the adoption of the Fundamental Law of Hungary[15] along with the adoption of a series of laws that have attacked the independence of key players in Hungarian politics and society, including the judiciary (Kovács and Scheppele, 2018: 189–200; Szente, 2021: 1316–1326), civil society (Gerő et al., 2020: 119–139), academia (Bárd, 2020: 87–96; Körtvélyesi, 2020) and media (Polyák, 2019: 279–303). This has also contributed to the continuation of the regime.

The functioning of the regime—variously described as illiberal, anti-constitutionalist, de-democratizing or autocratizing—has been amply covered in the literature (Krekó and Enyed, 2018; Pap, 2017; Bozóki and Hegedűs, 2018: 1173–1189). Consequently, this chapter focuses on how the regime's functioning relates to multiculturalism. For the sake of simplicity and as an exercise in applied normative reasoning, the following explores post-2010 measures and contrasts them to the expectations of normative multiculturalist theory as well as to the standards, evidenced in claims made by the regime, regarding the desired regulations applying to Hungarians living in neighboring states.[16]

As we saw in the preceding discussion on dual citizenship and the deterritorialization of citizenship, some of the entrenched policies that continued after 2010 could be viewed, at least on the surface, as multiculturalist and embedded within a legal framework providing for strong minority rights including collective rights and self-government. In making no attempt to shatter this illusion, the regime, in line with these and other pre-2010 policies, has positioned itself as a supporter of minority rights on the international level.[17] For example, the regime's goals regarding ethnic Hungarian communities in neighboring countries can be easily described as trying to make the respective home states multiculturalist with regard to language use, education, territorial autonomy and self-government with dedicated minority institutions, strong forms of non-discrimination and equality, including equity in public offices, affirmative measures (e.g., in participation in public life), the toleration of dual (external ethnic) citizenship, and maintaining ties across borders along ethnic lines.

However, a closer look at existing policies and political rhetoric shows that they serve very different purposes than the recognition and accommodation of diversity. We have seen how the ethnicized system of preferences presents itself as a genuinely nationalist policy in the case of external citizenship. Focusing here on how these various elements connect to the regime, it is apparent that even this policy is designed to bring votes that help to sustain the regime. There is a double self-selection of voting non-resident citizens: only those who took Hungarian citizenship can vote and not all of them register for voting. The institutional structure set up to support would-be citizens with naturalization is intimately linked to Fidesz-loyal political entities (Kovács, Körtvélyesi and Nagy, 2015: 106–110). The financial support for Hungarian communities that in itself could be good policy is in fact used to secure a loyal base outside Hungary's borders (Bárdi, 2017: 151–154). The expansion of the citizenry and the franchise, combined with a closely held and increased transborder funding (Kovács, 2020: 1146–1165) results in the export of autocratization, weakening independent Hungarian minority organizations and media in the neighboring countries (Sipos, 2018). The electoral system is built on open discrimination that only allows voting by mail to citizens without a registered address in Hungary and not to emigrant voters who left Hungary in great numbers.[18] The extension of the citizenry has thus served as a means to extend the operation of the regime. New citizens are also used to boost the cohort of voters through an unlawful scheme to mass-register addresses for non-resident voters in localities close to the border.[19]

Minority self-governments show a similar pattern domestically.[20] The most important change to the new Minority ("Nationalities") Act adopted in 2011 was the introduction of representation for national minorities in Parliament (Act No. CLXXIX on the Rights of Nationalities 2011), in the form of a speaker or, in the case of election through a preferential quota, an MP with full rights (Dobos, 2014). The latter possibility was promptly used by the governing party to secure a seat for a German representative who is a former Fidesz member and who declared his automatic support for government initiatives in all cases going beyond minority-relevant topics (Majtényi, Nagy and Kállai, 2018). This means that even the preferential parliamentary representation for internal minorities serves as a tool to maintain power in a regime that, in actuality, tolerates no real autonomies. The status of minorities was also weakened in an important if largely symbolic sense. The Venice Commission, scrutinizing the Fundamental Law, found that domestic minorities are presented as "not part of the people behind the enactment of the Constitution," adding that a proper constitution "should be seen as the result of the democratic will-formation of the country's citizens as a whole, and not only of the dominant ethnic group" (European Commission for Democracy Through Law, 2011).

In line with this interpretation the Fundamental Law, the Prime Minister stated his wish to maintain the homogeneity of Hungary (Euractiv, 2017) and adopted explicitly anti-multiculturalist rhetoric, in line with European political declarations on the death of multiculturalism (echoing similar statements from political leaders such as Angela Merkel, David Cameron and Nicolas Sarkozy). In the regime's rhetoric, one can often hear a related criticism of the "failing West," a place with so-called "no-go zones" and a region from where residents rightly seek refuge in countries, such as Hungary.[21] Quite ironically though, politicians have proclaimed the end of multiculturalism in countries such as France, Germany and Britain, where there had been no considerable attempt to implement multiculturalism in the first place; in fact, many of multiculturalism ostensible failures stem, if anything, from multiculturalism's *absence* rather than as a result of its implementation (Kymlicka, 2007b). Similarly, the backlash against multiculturalism has emerged in Hungary without any meaningful discussion or engagement, not to speak of adoption, of multiculturalism as a driver of state policies. By contrast, the regime continues to make bold multiculturalist declarations regarding neighboring countries that, it claims, should support and maintain the "Hungarian world," and "parallel societies"[22] with robust linguistic, educational and other cultural rights, territorial autonomies and a toleration for dual citizenship.[23]

At the domestic level, the regime's positioning is quite different. The illiberal anti-multiculturalist positioning of the regime includes hate speech by officials, repeated government narratives that foster xenophobia,[24] billboard and media campaigns in a controlled media landscape (Polyák, 2019), letters from the Prime Minister and questionnaires with leading questions sent out to all citizens (Bognár, Sik and Surányi, 2018). The government's positioning also includes a racist video message with explicit reference to skin colors produced by János Lázár, the second most important government official at the time, wherein he sought to depict the results of disastrous Western policies in the streets of Vienna (Gergely and Groendahl, 2018). This position was also evidenced by corresponding policy measures that included the strategic use of violence[25] and hunger (denial of food)[26] in relation to asylum seekers.

What is often willfully overlooked by mouthpieces of this illiberal anti-multiculturalism positioning is that behind the slogan of defending Hungary from invaders lies a very different reality: Hungary is hardly a destination for asylum seekers.[27] It is a country where the longstanding concern has not been immigration but instead emigration[28] and where immigration of non-ethnic Hungarians has historically been driven by government-sponsored programs (with tens of thousands of immigrants from non-EU countries obtaining the right to settle in Hungary (Molnár, 2021) and a now-defunct visa for money program).[29]

The exploitation of the refugee crisis by illiberal anti-multiculturalists has allowed the regime to consolidate a voter base that seemed on the verge of dissipating, and it has provided an opportunity for the regime to maintain a type of "moral panic" (Gerő and Sik, 2020: 39–58) and to create the appearance of a need for constant securitization (Majtényi, Kopper and Susánszky, 2019: 173–189). Many voters, including those in distant Roma villages, now fear imaginary dangers like the possibility that their neighborhoods are going to be overrun by terrorists and, according to a more recent government campaign, that their children may now be at risk of forced sex reassignment surgery. Unfortunately, due to effective government propaganda, voters are also downplaying the real existing threat of COVID-19 and, at one point, Hungary found itself in the top tier for COVID-19-related deaths per capita.[30]

Migration-related campaigns have also ensured that Hungarians have yet to face the fact that, in a country with a shrinking population that is immigrant-sending rather than immigrant-receiving, strategic thinking on migration would be timely.[31] Paradoxically, Hungary is in full denial: talk focuses on zero immigration, combined with a policy to bring in foreign workers, often from outside the EU, for jobs with low qualification requirements.[32] This is a combination that did not work particularly well for Germany, and it will be of little help if resulting failures can be blamed on multiculturalism. Multiculturalism should be exactly the approach that must be discussed—particularly focusing on its insights on what can make integration and engagement with diversity successful.

Tragically, remedying this lacuna faces other challenges. The campaigns built on hatred of different groups ("illegal immigrants," LGBTQI people or simply "liberals," "Soros mercenaries," etc.) labelled as a threat to the "homogenous" nation clearly resonate with anti-minority as well as anti-Hungarian narratives and policies in neighboring countries.[33] More broadly, the systemic trend to undermine the rule of law and constitutionalism, giving rise to added scrutiny by the European Union,[34] is also contrary to the interests of minority Hungarians. The move to undo constitutionalism and to eliminate autonomies clearly runs counter to multiculturalist goals; centralization and undermining the rule of law are clear dangers for minorities, including Hungarians in the neighboring states. To use but one example, the Equal Treatment Authority, the equality body established in 2003 as part of EU conditionality, was abolished in 2020.[35] A similar move in Romania, abolishing the National Council for Combating Discrimination, an important protector of equality and headed by an ethnic Hungarian, would be a considerable blow to the rights of Hungarians living there. Furthermore, the attack on the independence of key institutions, the logic of centralization and "ennemification" results in an anti-pluralism that not only makes the regime incompatible with multiculturalism, but also with sustaining a functioning democracy (which shows the mistake of the approaches that describe the regime as a "democracy with an adjective"). And, when the state of democracy and the rule of law in Hungary is questioned, the regime quickly shifts to arguments based on sovereignty, national identity and existential threats to the nation, combined with Russia-like policies targeting "foreign agents" domestically (Gerő et al., 2020). This is contrary not only to how the regime, as we have seen, happily campaigns and exerts influence in neighboring countries, but also to the interest of Hungarian minorities that legitimately fear similar behavior from their home states.

Responding to Illiberal Politics: Is There a Future for Multiculturalism?

What lessons do the past three decades of Hungarian politics contribute to our thinking on multiculturalism? The ethnocentric exclusivist approach is proving to be an enduring phenomenon in Central Europe (Vachudova, 2020: 318–340). In the case of Hungary, we have seen that some measures can be mistaken for multiculturalist policies but turn out to be really veiled nationalism (as in the case of non-residential citizenship) and, even in cases where multiculturalism seems to apply, policies can be redeployed to achieve opposing results (as in the case of co-opting domestic minority representation). Does this mean that legal-institutional guarantees are meaningless, that they can be misused and even contribute to support authoritarian strategies? The Hungarian story underlines the importance of constitutional assumptions behind implementing multiculturalism. As soon as liberalism is neglected, or worse, abandoned, whatever real or hoped-for multiculturalism also falls.

However, there are still grounds for hope. First, the illiberal position is unsustainable over the long-term given that illiberals themselves are bound to recognize, or (re)discover, the value of liberal and multiculturalist principles when they find themselves are in a minority situation. Second, if one is looking for optimism at all costs, one could also claim that the illiberal and anti-multiculturalist regime is helping to build and activate liberal multiculturalists that could provide genuine support for multiculturalist policies after the fall of the current regime. Third, despite its failings, the international context still seems to be set against the type of illiberalism present in Hungary.

Before I turn to this third aspect, let me briefly mention an example that speaks to the first two reasons for optimism. For one, while Fidesz is seen in opposition to the ideals of liberal multiculturalism, this was even more true for extreme right-wing Jobbik, a party that became a national political force by thematizing "gypsy criminality," a racist rhetoric alleging an inherent link between Roma ethnicity and criminality (Karácsony and Róna, 2011: 61–92). The party first achieved electoral success and was seated in Parliament in 2010 and saw, as an opposition party, the adoption of many of its policies by Fidesz. Jobbik soon realized how this was detrimental to its own interests. For example, the regime could use the State Audit Office to go after Jobbik but not after Fidesz for similar campaign funding schemes (Keller-Alánt, 2020); government media could launch smear campaigns that included surveillance tactics against Jobbik leaders;[36] and a Jobbik billboard campaign could be brought to an unceremonious end by the adoption of legal amendments (Transparency International Hungary, 2017). Gábor Vona, the former Jobbik premier and now public commentator, publicly acknowledged how these developments triggered a rethinking of his (and his party's) positions (Partizán, 2019). The party has since retreated on some of its extremist positions, publicly apologizing for earlier anti-Roma, anti-Semitic and anti-LGBTQI statements, and it now finds itself as an established force of the united opposition. Many still question the genuineness of Jobbik's shift (which can also be explained on strategic grounds), but it has certainly been considerable for a party with such extreme positions[37] and whose voting base is now being lectured by party leaders on the importance of the basic tenets of inclusion and constitutionalism.

Can the international context also play an important role in inducing a genuine multicultural shift in Hungary? The international context is not immediately reassuring with what has been described as the populist Zeitgeist, with occasional concessions even from institutions meant to protect human rights against such deviations.[38] Yet, the Hungarian regime is not embedded in the context that the country experienced in the interwar period. It is part of a set of international organizations explicitly committed to the liberal goals of human rights, democracy and the rule of law, even if we see spectacular failures like in the case of treating asylum seekers.[39] The weakness of related conditionality is apparent; liberal approaches tend to hesitate when it comes to bringing about changes based on personal convictions.[40] Shallow or fake compliance, without real commitment, has long been the name of the game (Batory, 2016: 685–699; Noutcheva, 2009: 1065–1084). Given that European integration rests on key assumptions regarding not only shared values like democracy, the rule of law and human rights, but also good faith cooperation, deviations that undermine these commitments risk undermining the European Union project. Making the underlying assumptions of European integration explicit and making good on these promises has become imperative, and the illiberal challenge has been instrumental in providing the political momentum for this to happen.

In thinking about the right type of responses, commitments to pluralism—also in the form of a Treaty clause protection "national identity" (Treaty on European Union 2012: Article 4-2)—and to democracy and the rule of law will need to be balanced carefully. I have argued elsewhere that multiculturalist debates concerning the limits of toleration and illiberal minorities are helpful for devising a consistent and effective response to illiberal deviations within the EU (Körtvélyesi, 2020: 567–600; See also Körtvélyesi and Majtényi, 2021: 500–523). It is clear that not all elements that deviate from common European values (like human rights, the rule of law, democracy and pluralism) can and should be sanctioned. However, where governments go too far (e.g., by undermining judicial independence, itself a key tenet of European integration) the lack of effective responses can undermine the very functioning of the system. Deciding what "going too far" means requires a transparent framework that enforces liberal principles consistently. Faced with a comparable dilemma, Will Kymlicka argued that in deciding when (not) to tolerate illiberal elements, we should consider factors like the gravity and nature of violations, combined with a regard for aspects like internal support and historical agreements (Kymlicka, 1996: 152–172). A similar normative framework is required for managing diversity in the European polity committed to liberal pluralism.

Multiculturalist approaches can also help devise institutional settings that encourage compliance, i.e., behavior that remains within the zone of toleration. Ayelet Shachar describes "transformative accommodation" as a promising approach to shared governance that can protect the most vulnerable (Shachar, 2001: 117–145). She devises a scheme under which individuals dissatisfied with the regulation under one framework can opt to the other framework, which creates a bidding process where the two structures compete for authority (Shachar, 2001: 117–145). EU law is full of such options under the wide application of mutual recognition, from education and family law to asylum decisions. This dynamic could be exploited to act against norms curtailing rights in areas of shared (national and supranational) powers. For example, the common problem of a captured public prosecutor's office could be counterbalanced by accession to the European Public Prosecutor's Office that can act where national authorities failed to act. Furthermore, the diversion of immense European funds to oligarchs and otherwise to sustain an illiberal regime could be alleviated by a distribution mechanism that combines supranational, domestic and local decision-making. In this context what makes the multiculturalist framework particularly useful is that it can address the problem of illiberalism in a coherent and sustainable way that emphasizes the positive aspect of accommodating diversity: that is to say, the need to create a community of solidarity[41] that allows for the mutual sacrifices and redistribution—two ideas on which the Union rests.

In brief, the post-1990 Hungarian story can be read as a lesson in the limitations of democratic transitions and on the importance of looking for genuine commitments beyond simply formal, institutional changes. This applies particularly to multiculturalism: as we have seen, seemingly multiculturalist policies can be redeployed to support an illiberal anti-multiculturalist agenda. Applying authentic multiculturalist insights can help in upholding liberal democratic commitments and in the design coherent and effective democratic guarantees. What might lead this to happen in Hungary? Even for a regime that is committed to undermining pluralism on various levels, the question of managing diversity is undoubtedly set to resurface on the European level, under the slogan of a right to national difference and national identity. No matter how hard people try to get rid of multiculturalism, the central dilemmas, debates, arguments and proposals unavoidably reappear, and question attempts to go back to a monochromatic vision of societies.

Notes

1 This should not be understood in the party-political sense, but as a broader commitment to some key foundational principles among which are democracy, the rule of law and human rights. Regarding the troubled relationship between liberalisms and diversity, see Levy (2015).
2 Although note Rogers Brubaker's argument that the view that nationalism somehow returned after it had been oppressed, under a Freudian reading (the thesis on "the return of the repressed"), downplays existing continuities (Brubaker, 1998: 285–288).
3 Both numbers trend downwards. On the data for Hungary, see the table from the Central Statistics Office of Hungary: https://www.ksh.hu/stadat_files/nep/hu/nep0001.html. On data for ethnic Hungarians in the neighboring states, see Gyurgyík, Horváth and Tamás (2010: 72).
4 The larger groups of national minorities (Croats, Germans, Romanians, Serbs, Slovaks, Slovenes) all fall under 0.5%, most of them not more than 0.1%, with absolute numbers in the thousands and low ten thousands. The only exception is the Roma, often discussed separately, as not "national" but "ethnic" minority. Estimates of the number of Roma in Hungary range in the hundred thousands (Kapitány, 2015: 69–101; Morauszki and Papp, 2015: 142).
5 Kymlicka also notes the difficulty of placing the Roma in a typology of minorities (Kymlicka, 2002: 74–76; 2007b: 391; see also Rövid, 2011: 1–22).
6 The initial law resulted in many non-minority votes cast for lists meant for minorities, undermining the idea of minority self-representation (Pap, 2013: 126–128). For later modifications meant to address this, see Dobos, 2014.
7 The logic actually goes back to the socialist era (Sansum and Dobos, 2020: 255).
8 For a regional overview on Hungarian ethnic parties, see Csilla, László and Balázs (2018).
9 At least in the case of immigrant groups (Kymlicka, 2010: 37). For a discussion specifically on kin-minorities and external citizenship, see Bauböck (2007: 2393–2447).
10 For an account supporting such trends, see, e.g., Spiro (2006: 207–233).
11 With exceptions, this means that those who are found to have naturalized lose their Slovakian citizenship. For a debate on the moves in the two countries: Bauböck (2010).

12 With a strange twist, it was the 2010 amendment that formally "de-ethnicized" the preferential rule. This does not mean, however, that the resulting practice was not overwhelmingly ethnic (Körtvélyesi, 2020: 783–784).
13 In 2014, 122,638 of the 128,429 votes went to Fidesz; in 2018, 216,561 out of 225,025 votes. Voting by mail is only available to citizens without registered address in Hungary, which practically corresponds to new citizens in the neighbouring countries. Results from the site of the National Election Office: https://static.valasztas.hu/dyn/pv14/szavossz/en/levjkv_e.html; https://www.valasztas.hu/levelszavazas-jegyzokonyv.
14 For an account from the border, see Feischmidt (2020: 441–456).
15 For an early commentary, see Tóth (2013).
16 This can also be read as a reversal of the regime's favourite argument on "double standards." For the narrative, see, e.g., Harper (2017).
17 It supported, e.g., the "Minority SafePack" European citizens' initiative for strengthening EU action for minorities (Fidesz, 2020).
18 Official statistics register 490,000 Hungarian citizens living in European Economic Area countries (EU Member States plus Switzerland, Liechtenstein, Iceland and Norway), mostly in Germany, Austria and the UK. See Gödri and Horváth (2021: 227–250).
19 A recent proposal is meant to address this and legalize the practice, raising fears of voting fraud (Hungarian Civil Liberties Union, 2021).
20 For a parallel and short overview of electoral tinkering with minorities both within and beyond the borders, see Majtényi, Nagy and Kállai, 2018.
21 "Of course we can give shelter to the real refugees: Germans, Dutch, French, Italians; scared politicians and journalists; Christians who had to flee their own country; those people who want to find here the Europe that they lost at their home" (Euronews, 2017).
22 For an assessment of "ethnic parallelism" in the case of Hungarians in Romania, see Kiss and Kiss (2018: 227–247).
23 In the reading of Rainer Bauböck, to the extent that some elements are contradicting each other, for the coexistence of external (dual) citizenship and territorial autonomy cannot be reconciled as normative claims (Bauböck, 2007).
24 Which is precipitously rising (Messing and Ságvári, 2018). People who would admit asylum seekers into the country virtually disappeared from the polls (Simonovits, 2020: 162).
25 Illegal pushbacks (Hungarian Helsinki Committee, 2020: 23–27).
26 Denial of food (United Nations, 2019).
27 The destination is usually "the West," i.e., countries like Germany, Austria and the United Kingdom (UN Migration Agency, 2017).
28 With close to half a million, or 5% of the total population, having left the country, according to official statistics (Gödri and Horváth, 2021).
29 In European comparison: Surak (2020: 1–19).
30 Coronavirus pandemic is the deadliest in Hungary in the entire world (Portfolio, 2021).
31 In fact, a migration strategy was adopted in 2013, but it is no more than a box-ticking exercise for the EU that so fundamentally contradicts migration policy ever since to render it meaningless (Government of Hungary, n.d.).
32 The numbers have increased for the past few years (Kálmán, 2020).
33 In large part as a result of surviving reflexes of "minoritized majorities" (Kymlicka, 2007: 185–186).
34 See the report of the European Parliament that initiated the procedure under Article 7 of the Treaty on European Union, often described as the "nuclear option." European Parliament resolution of September 12, 2018, on a proposal calling on the Council to determine, pursuant to Article 7(1) of the Treaty on European Union,

the existence of a clear risk of a serious breach by Hungary of the values on which the Union is founded (2017/2131(INL)).
35 The powers were transferred to the ombudsperson's office, headed by a government loyalist. A related but earlier move concerning minorities came ten years earlier, when the stand-alone ombudsperson for minority issues was demoted and became a largely powerless—even in the standards of an ombudsperson—deputy to the now sole ombudsperson.
36 Accusations included being a Muslim convert, a homosexual and a terrorist and having an affair. See, e.g., Juhász et al. (2017: 13) and Rádi (2018).
37 For an overview in English: (The Economist, 2017).
38 See the argument that the European Court of Human Rights seems more and more willing to give in to arguments on "requirements of living together" or "social integration," to the detriment of human rights: Henrard and Vermeersch (2020: 809–825).
39 See, e.g., Lavenex (2018: 1195–1212).
40 It is hard not to see a parallel with liberal integration policies. For a debate, see Bauböck and Joppke (2010).
41 In a message delivered in Budapest, the Pope lectured on some of basics of Christian teachings and multiculturalist toleration, in a country led by a government that poses as the protector of Christian Europe: "Your country is a place where men and women from other peoples have long lived together. Various ethnic groups, minorities, religious confessions and migrants have made yours a multicultural country. This is something new and, at least initially, can be troubling. Diversity always proves a bit frightening, for it challenges our securities and the status quo. Yet it also provides a precious opportunity to open our hearts to the Gospel message: 'Love one another as I have loved you' (Jn 15:12). In the face of cultural, ethnic, political and religious diversity, we can either retreat into a rigid defense of our supposed identity, or become open to encountering others and cultivating together the dream of a fraternal society. I recall with pleasure that in 2017, here in this European capital, you assembled with representatives of the other Episcopal Conferences of Central and Eastern Europe to affirm once again that attachment to one's own identity must never become a motive of hostility and contempt for others, but rather an aid to dialogue with different cultures. Dialogue without negotiating away one's own attachment." (Pope Francis, 2021).

References

Act No. CLXXIX of 2011 on the Rights of Nationalities.
Act No. LV of 1993 on Hungarian Nationality.
Arunyan, A. 2018. "How Hungary and Ukraine Fell Out over a Passport Scandal." *Open Democracy*, available [online]: <https://www.opendemocracy.net/en/odr/how-kyiv-and-budapest-fell-out-over-zakarpattya/>.
Bárd, P. 2020. "The Rule of Law and Academic Freedom or the Lack of It in Hungary." *European Political Science* 19 (1): 87–96. <https://doi.org/10.1057/s41304-018-0171-x>.
Bárdi, N. 2017. "Álságos állítások a magyar etnopolitikában. A külhoni magyarok és a budapesti kormányzatok magyarságpolitikája [Hypocritical Claims in Hungarian Ethnopolitics. Hungarians Abroad and the Hungarian Nationality Politics of Budapest Governments]." In *Hegymenet. Társadalmi és politikai kihívások Magyarországon [Uphill. Social and political challenges in Hungary]*, A. Jakab, L. Urbán (eds) Budapest: Osiris, 130–155.

Bartha, A., Z. Boda and D. Szikra. 2020. "When Populist Leaders Govern: Conceptualising Populism in Policy Making." *Politics and Governance* 8 (3): 71–81. <https://doi.org/10.17645/pag.v8i3.2922>.
Batory, A. 2016. "Defying the Commission: Creative Compliance and Respect for the Rule of Law in the EU." *Public Administration* 94 (3): 685–699. <https://doi.org/10.1111/padm.12254>.
Bauböck, R. 2007. "Stakeholder Citizenship and Transnational Political Participation: A Normative Evaluation of External Voting." *Fordham Law Review* 75 (5): 2393–2447.
Bauböck, R. 2010. "Dual Citizenship for Transborder Minorities? How to Respond to the Hungarian-Slovak Tit-for-Tat." *Working Paper* (Robert Schuman Centre for Advanced Studies, European University Institute, available [online]: <https://cadmus.eui.eu//handle/1814/14625>.
Bauböck R. and C. Joppke. 2010. "How Liberal Are Citizenship Tests?" *Working Paper*, Robert Schuman Centre for Advanced Studies, European University Institute, available [online]: <https://cadmus.eui.eu/handle/1814/13956>.
BBC News. 2018. "Diplomats Thrown out in Ukraine-Hungary Passport Row." *BBC News*, sec. Europe, available [online]: <https://www.bbc.com/news/world-europe-45753886>.
Bognár, E., E. Sik and R. Surányi. 2018. "The Case of Hungary – de Wilde Goes Wild." *CEASEVAL Research on the Common European Asylum System*. Chemnitz: CEASEVAL, available [online]: <http://ceaseval.eu/publications/08_BognarSik_Suranyi_The_case_of_Hungary.pdf>.
Bozóki, A. and D. Hegedűs. 2018. "An Externally Constrained Hybrid Regime: Hungary in the European Union." *Democratization* 25 (7): 1173–1189.
Brubaker R. 1998. "Myths and Misconceptions in the Study of Nationalism." In *The State of the Nation. Ernest Gellner and the Theory of Nationalism*, J. Hall (ed.) Cambridge: Cambridge University Press.
Buzogány, A. 2017. "Illiberal Democracy in Hungary: Authoritarian Diffusion or Domestic Causation?" *Democratization* 24 (7): 1307–1325.
Central Statistics Office of Hungary. 2021. Available [online]: <https://www.ksh.hu/stadat_files/nep/hu/nep0001.html>.
Csilla, F., S. László and V. Balázs (eds.). 2018. *Etnikai pártok Kelet-Közép-Európában, 1989–2014*. Budapest: MTA TK Kisebbségkutató Intézet.
Dobos, B. 2014. "Between Importing and Exporting Minority Rights: The Minority Self-Governments in Hungary." In *Autonomy Arrangements around the World: A Collection of Well and Lesser Known Cases*, L. Salat, S. Constantin, A. Osipov and I. Gergő Székely (eds.) Cluj-Napoca: Romanian Institute for Research on National Minorities, 275–298.
EurActiv. 2017. "Orbán Calls "Ethnic Homogeneity" a Key to Success." *EurActiv*, available [online]: <https://www.euractiv.com/section/justice-home-affairs/news/orban-calls-ethnic-homogeneity-a-key-to-success/>.
European Commission for Democracy Through Law (Venice Commission). 2011. "Opinion no. 621/2011 on the New Constitution of Hungary, CDL-AD(2011)016, 20 June 2011, para. 40." available [online]: <https://www.venice.coe.int/webforms/documents/default.aspx?pdffile=CDL-AD(2011)016-e>.
European Parliament Resolution. 2018. *The Situation in Hungary*, available [online]: <https://www.europarl.europa.eu/doceo/document/TA-8-2018-0340_EN.pdf>

Euronews. 2017. "Hungarian PM: We Welcome Refugees Fleeing Germany, France and Italy." *Euronews*, available [online]: https://www.euronews.com/2017/02/11/hungarian-pm-we-welcome-refugees-fleeing-germany-france-and-italy.

Feischmidt, M. 2020. "Deployed Fears and Suspended Solidarity along the Migratory Route in Europe." *Citizenship Studies* 24 (4): 441–456. <https://doi.org/10.1080/13621025.2020.1755157>.

Fidesz. 2020. "The Success of Minority SafePack is the Success of All Hungarians." available [online]: <https://fidesz-eu.hu/en/the-success-of-minority-safepack-is-the-success-of-all-hungarians/>.

Gergely, A. and B. Groendahl. 2018. "Facebook Restores Hungarian Minister's Anti-Migrant Video." *Bloomberg*, available [online]: <https://www.bloomberg.com/news/articles/2018-03-07/facebook-blocks-hungarian-minister-s-whites-vs-migrants-video>.

Gerő, M. and E. Sik. 2020. "The Moral Panic Button. Construction and Consequences." In *Europe and the Refugee Response: A Crisis of Values?*, E. M. Goździak, I. Main and B. Suter (eds.) New York: Routledge, 39–58. <https://doi.org/10.4324/9780429279317>.

Gerő, M., P. Susánszky, A. Kopper and G. Tóth. 2020. "Strategies for Survival: Human Rights Organizations' Responses to the Closing of Political Opportunity Structures in Hungary." *Politologický Časopis* 27 (2): 119–139, <https://doi.org/10.5817/PC2020-2-119>.

Gödri, I. and V. Horváth. 2021. "Nemzetközi vándorlás [International Migration]." In *Demográfiai portré*, J. Monostori, P. Őri and Z. Spéder (eds.) Budapest: KSH Népességtudományi Kutatóintézet, 227–250. <https://demografia.hu/kiadvanyokonline/index.php/demografiaiportre/article/view/2835/2725>.

Government of Hungary. 2013. "The Migration Strategy and the Seven-Year Strategic Document Related to Asylum and Migration Fund Established by the European Union for the Years 2014–20." available [online]: <http://belugyialapok.hu/alapok/sites/default/files/Migration%20Strategy%20Hungary.pdf>.

Gyurgyík, L., I. Horváth and K. Tamás. 2010. "Demográfiai folyamatok, etno-kulturális és társadalmi reprodukció." In *Határon túli magyarság a 21. században: konferenciasorozat a Sándor-palotában, 2006–2008*, B. Botond (ed.) Budapest: Köztársasági Elnöki Hivatal, 69–123.

Harper, J. 2017. "Hungarian MEP decries "EU's Double Standards"." *DW*, available [online]: <https://www.dw.com/en/hungarian-mep-decries-eus-double-standards/a-38760955>.

Henrard, K. and P. Vermeersch. 2020. "Nationalism with a Human Face? European Human Rights Judgments and the Reinvention of Nationalist Politics." *Nationalities Papers* 48 (5): 809–825. <https://doi.org/10.1017/nps.2019.103>.

Hungarian Civil Liberties Union. 2021. "Legalizálja a fiktív lakcím létesítését egy frissen elfogadott salátatörvény." available [online]: <https://tasz.hu/cikkek/legalizalja-a-fiktiv-lakcim-letesiteset-egy-frissen-elfogadott-salatatorveny>.

Hungarian Helsinki Committee. 2020. "Country Report: Hungary. 2020 Update. Asylum Information Database." *European Council on Refugees and Exiles*, available [online]: <https://asylumineurope.org/wp-content/uploads/2021/04/AIDA-HU_2020update.pdf>.

Hungarian Minority Act. 1993. No. LXXVII, in *European Yearbook of Minority Issues* (2005–2006) 5: 420–469.

Juhász, A., B. Hunyadi, E. Galgóczi, D. Róna, P. Szicherle and E. Zgut. 2017. *The Year of Rearrangement – The Populist Right and the Far-Right in Contemporary Hungary*. Budapest: Political Capital – Social Development Institute.

Kálmán, A. 2020. "Ötszörösére nőtt a Magyarországon dolgozó külföldiek száma négy év alatt, közelítünk a vendégmunka-alapú társadalomhoz [The Number of Foreigners Working in Hungary Grew Five-Fold in the Past Five Years, We are Approaching a Guestworker-Based Society]." *24.hu*, available [online]: <https://24.hu/fn/gazdasag/2020/04/28/vendegmunka-kulfoldi-munkavallalo-gazdasag-migracio/>.

Kapitány, B. 2015. "A Magyarországi Történelmi Kisebbségi Közösségek Demográfiai Viszonyai És Perspektívái 1990–2011 Között." *Demográfia* 58 (3): 69–101.

Karácsony, G. and D. Róna. 2011. "The Secret of Jobbik. Reasons behind the Rise of the Hungarian Radical Right." *Journal of East European & Asian Studies* 2 (1): 61–92.

Keller-Alánt, Á. 2020. "Mi felett őrködik valójában az Állami Számvevőszék? – II. rész [What does the State Audit Office really watches over? Part II]." *Szabad Európa [Radio Free Europe]*, available [online]: <https://www.szabadeuropa.hu/a/allami-szamvevoszek-domokos-laszlo-partok/30851607.html>.

Kiss, T. and D. Kiss. 2018. "Ethnic Parallelism: Political Program and Social Reality: An Introduction." In *Unequal Accommodation of Minority Rights: Hungarians in Transylvania*, Palgrave Politics of Identity and Citizenship Series, T. Kiss, I. Gergő, T. Toró, N. Bárdi and I. Horváth (eds.) Cham: Springer International Publishing, 227–247. <https://doi.org/10.1007/978-3-319-78893-7_5>.

Körtvélyesi, Z. 2020a. "Fear and (Self-)Censorship in Academia." *Verfassungsblog* (blog), available [online]: <https://verfassungsblog.de/fear-and-self-censorship-in-academia/>.

Körtvélyesi, Z. 2020b. "Nation, Nationality, and National Identity: Uses, Misuses, and the Hungarian Case of External Ethnic Citizenship." *International Journal for the Semiotics of Law - Revue Internationale de Sémiotique Juridique* 33 (3): 771–798. <https://doi.org/10.1007/s11196-020-09731-8>.

Körtvélyesi, Z. 2020c. "The Illiberal Challenge in the EU: Exploring the Parallel with Illiberal Minorities and the Example of Hungary." *European Constitutional Law Review* 16 (4): 567–600, <https://doi.org/10.1017/S1574019620000322>.

Körtvélyesi, Z. and B. Majtényi. 2021. "Justifying Supranational Responses to the Anti-Constitutionalist Challenge: Applying Liberal Multiculturalism as a Background Theory." *Global Constitutionalism* 10 (3): 500–523. <https://doi.org/10.1017/S2045381720000258>.

Kovács, K., Z. Körtvélyesi and A. Nagy. 2015. "Margins of Nationality. External Ethnic Citizenship and Non-Discrimination." *Perspectives on Federalism* 7 (1): 85–116. <https://doi.org/10.1515/pof-2015-0005>.

Kovács, K. and K. L. Scheppele. 2018. "The Fragility of an Independent Judiciary: Lessons from Hungary and Poland—and the European Union." *Communist and Post-Communist Studies* 51 (3): 189–200, <https://doi.org/10.1016/j.postcomstud.2018.07.005>.

Kovács, E. 2020. "Direct and Indirect Political Remittances of the Transnational Engagement of Hungarian Kin-Minorities and Diaspora Communities." *Journal of Ethnic and Migration Studies* 46 (6): 1146–1165.

Kövér, L. 2014. "Kövér László köszöntő beszéde [Inaugural Speech of László Kövér]." *Parliament of Hungary*, available [online]: <https://www.parlament.hu/hu/web/guest/elnoki-koszonto>.

Krekó P. and Z. Enyedi. 2018. "Orbán's Laboratory of Illiberalism." *Journal of Democracy* 29 (3): 39–51. <https://doi.org/10.1353/jod.2018.0043>.

Kymlicka, W. 1996. *Multicultural Citizenship: A Liberal Theory of Minority Rights.* Oxford: Oxford University Press.

Kymlicka, W. 2002. "Western Political Theory and Ethnic Relations in Eastern Europe." In *Can Liberal Pluralism Be Exported?: Western Political Theory and Ethnic Relations in Eastern Europe,* W. Kymlicka and M. Opalski (eds) Oxford: Oxford University Press, 13–105.

Kymlicka, W. and M. Opalski. 2002. *Can Liberal Pluralism Be Exported?: Western Political Theory and Ethnic Relations in Eastern Europe.* Oxford: Oxford University Press.

Kymlicka, W. 2007a. *Multicultural Odysseys: Navigating the New International Politics of Diversity.* Oxford: Oxford University Press.

Kymlicka, W. 2007b. "National Cultural Autonomy and International Minority Rights Norms." *Ethnopolitics* 6 (3): 379–393. <https://doi.org/10.1080/17449050701487389>.

Kymlicka, W. 2010. "The Rise and Fall of Multiculturalism?: New Debates on Inclusion and Accommodation in Diverse Societies." In *The Multiculturalism Backlash. European Discourses, Policies and Practices,* S. Vertovec and S. Wessendorf (eds.) London: Routledge, 32–49.

Lavenex, S. 2018. ""Failing Forward" Towards Which Europe? Organized Hypocrisy in the Common European Asylum System." *Journal of Common Market Studies* 56 (5): 1195–1212.

Levitsky, S. and L.A. Way. 2010. *Competitive Authoritarianism: Hybrid Regimes after the Cold War,* Cambridge: Cambridge University Press.

Levy, J.T. 2015. *Rationalism, Pluralism, and Freedom.* Oxford: Oxford University Press.

Majtényi, B., Á. Kopper and P. Susánszky. 2019. "Constitutional Othering, Ambiguity and Subjective Risks of Mobilization in Hungary: Examples from the Migration Crisis." *Democratization* 26 (2): 173–189. <https://doi.org/10.1080/13510347.2018.1493051>.

Majtényi, B. 2005. "What Has Happened to Our Model Child? The Creation and Evolution of the Hungarian Minority Act." *European Yearbook of Minority Issues* 5 (1): 397–469. <https://doi.org/10.1163/22116117-90000055>.

Majtényi, B., B. Nagy and P. Kállai. 2018. ""Only Fidesz" – Minority Electoral Law in Hungary." *Verfassungsblog* (blog), available [online]: <https://verfassungsblog.de/only-fidesz-electoral-law-in-hungary/>.

Messing V. and B. Ságvári. 2018. "Looking behind the Culture of Fear. Cross-National Analysis of Attitudes towards Migration." *Friedrich Ebert Stiftung - European Social Survey,* available [online]: <https://cps.ceu.edu/sites/cps.ceu.edu/files/attachment/article/3014/messing-sagvari-fes-study-march-2018.pdf>.

Molnár, D. 2021. "Húszezer ukrán, hatezer kínai, háromezer vietnami és kétezer dél-koreai állampolgár is kapott tartózkodási engedélyt tavaly." *24.hu,* available [online]: <https://24.hu/belfold/2021/11/08/tartozkodasi-engedely-ukran-kinai-vietnami-magyarorszag-statisztika/>.

Morauszki, A. and A. Papp Z. 2015. "Ethnic Revival? The Methodology of the 2011 Census and the Nationalities of Hungary." *Minority Studies* 18: 141–160.

Nándor, B. 2017. "Álságos állítások a magyar etnopolitikában. A külhoni magyarok és a budapesti kormányzatok magyarságpolitikája." In *Hegymenet. Társadalmi és politikai kihívások Magyarországon,* J. András and U. László (eds.) Budapest: Osiris, 130–155.

Noutcheva, G. 2009. "Fake, Partial and Imposed Compliance: The Limits of the EU's Normative Power in the Western Balkans." *Journal of European Public Policy* 16 (7): 1065–1084. <https://doi.org/10.1080/13501760903226872>.

Orbán, V. 2014. Prime Minister Viktor Orbán's Speech at the 25th Bálványos Summer Free University and Student Camp, available [online]: <https://2015-2019.kormany.hu/en/the-prime-minister/the-prime-minister-s-speeches/prime-minister-viktor-orban-s-speech-at-the-25th-balvanyos-summer-free-university-and-student-camp>.

Pap, A.L. 2013. "Overruling Murphy's Law on the Free Choice of Identity and the Racial-Ethnic-National Terminology-Triad: Notes on How the Legal and Political Conceptualization of Minority Communities and Membership Boundaries is Induced by the Groups' Claims." In *The Interrelation between the Right to Identity of Minorities and Their Socio-Economic Participation*, K. Henrard (ed.) Leiden; Boston: Brill | Nijhoff, 115–155. <https://doi.org/10.1163/9789004244740_006>.

Pap, A.L. 2017. *Democratic Decline in Hungary: Law and Society in an Illiberal Democracy*. London: Routledge.

Partizán. 2019. "Interjú Vona Gáborral." [Interview with Gábor Vona], *Partizán*, available [online]: <https://www.youtube.com/watch?v=8nR7goY6Us0>.

Petričušić, A. 2015. "Non-Territorial Autonomy in Croatia." In *Managing Diversity through Non-Territorial Autonomy*, T. H. Malloy, A. Osipov and B. Vizi (eds.) Oxford: Oxford University Press, 53–68. <https://doi.org/10.1093/acprof:oso/9780198738459.003.0004>.

Polyák, G. 2019. "Media in Hungary: Three Pillars of an Illiberal Democracy." In *Public Service Broadcasting and Media Systems in Troubled European Democracies*, E. Polońska and A. Bozóki (eds), Cham: Springer, 279–303. <https://doi.org/10.1007/978-3-030-02710-0_13>.

Pope Francis. 2021. "Apostolic Journey of His Holiness Francis to Budapest, on the Occasion of the Concluding Holy Mass of 52nd International Eucharistic Congress, and to Slovakia – Meeting with the Bishops – Address of His Holiness." available [online]: <https://www.vatican.va/content/francesco/en/speeches/2021/september/documents/20210912-budapest-vescovi.html>.

Portfolio. 2021. "Coronavirus Pandemic is the Deadliest in Hungary in the Entire World." *Portfolio*, available [online]: <https://www.portfolio.hu/en/economy/20210422/coronavirus-pandemic-is-the-deadliest-in-hungary-in-the-entire-world-479550>.

Publicus. 2017. *Határon túli magyarok egyes jogairól [On Certain Rights of Hungarians Living Beyond the Borders]*, available [online]: <https://publicus.hu/blog/hataron_tuli_magyarok_egyes_jogairol/>.

Rádi, A. 2018. "Opposition Politicians Suing Dozens of Government-Aligned Propaganda Outlets for Character Assassination." *Átlátszó*, available [online]: <https://english.atlatszo.hu/2018/06/13/opposition-politicians-suing-dozens-of-government-aligned-propaganda-outlets-for-character-assassination/>.

Romsics, I. 2000. "A Magyar Külpolitika Útja Trianontól a Háborúig." *Rubicon* 9: 17–24.

Romsics, I. 2020. "Le passé qui ne passe pas. The Treaty of Trianon and Its Repercussions." *Erdélyi Krónika*, available [online]: <http://erdelyikronika.net/2020/06/03/the-treaty-of-trianon-and-its-repercussions/>.

Rövid, M. 2011. "One-Size-Fits-All Roma? On the Normative Dilemmas of the Emerging European Roma Policy." *Romani Studies* 21 (1): 1–22.

Sansum, J.M. and B. Dobos. 2020. "Cultural Autonomy in Hungary: Inward or Outward Looking?" *Nationalities Papers 48* (2): 251–266. <https://doi.org/10.1017/nps.2019.80>.

Schedler, A. 2013. *The Politics of Uncertainty. Sustaining and Subverting Electoral Authoritarianism.* Oxford: Oxford University Press.

Shachar, A. 2001. "Transformative Accommodation: Utilizing External Protections to Reduce Internal Restrictions." In *Multicultural Jurisdictions: Cultural Differences and Women's Rights*, 1st ed., A. Shachar (ed.) Cambridge University Press, 117–145, <https://doi.org/10.1017/CBO9780511490330>.

Simonovits, B. 2020. "The Public Perception of the Migration Crisis from the Hungarian Point of View: Evidence from the Field." In *Geographies of Asylum in Europe and the Role of European Localities*, IMISCOE Research Series, B. Glorius and J. Doomernik (eds.) Cham: Springer, 155–176. <https://doi.org/10.1007/978-3-030-25666-1>.

Sipos, Z. 2018. "NERdély 1.: Így hódította meg az erdélyi magyarságot a Fidesz, [This Is How Fidesz Conquered Transylvanian Hungarians]." *Átlátszó Erdély*, available [online]: <https://atlatszo.ro/napi-politika/nerdely-1-igy-hoditotta-meg-az-erdelyi-magyarsagot-a-fidesz/>.

Spiro, P.J. 2006. "Perfecting Political Diaspora." *New York University Law Review 81* (1): 207–233.

Surak, K. 2020. "Who Wants to Buy a Visa? Comparing the Uptake of Residence by Investment Programs in the European Union." *Journal of Contemporary European Studies* 1–19. <https://doi.org/10.1080/14782804.2020.1839742>.

Szente, Z. 2021. "Stepping into the Same River Twice? Judicial Independence in Old and New Authoritarianism." *German Law Journal 22* (7): 1316–1326. <https://doi.org/10.1017/glj.2021.69>.

The Constitution of Hungary. 1949. Art. 68–1 of Act No. XX, after the 1989 amendments, as in application up to 2012.

The Constitution of Hungary. 1949. Art. 6–3 of Act No. XX, after the 1989 amendments, as in application up to 2012.

The Economist. 2017. "Hungary's Jobbik Party Tries to Sound Less Extreme." *The Economist*, available [online]: <https://www.economist.com/europe/2017/11/15/hungarys-jobbik-party-tries-to-sound-less-extreme>.

Tóth, G.A. 2013. *Constitution for a Disunited Nation: On Hungary's 2011 Fundamental Law.* Central European University Press.

Transparency International Hungary. 2017. "Plakáttörvény-módosítás: alkalmatlan és Alaptörvény-ellenes [Amendment of the Act on Billboards: Inadequate and Anticonstitutional]." *Transparency International Hungary*, available [online]: <https://transparency.hu/hirek/plakattorveny-modositas-alkalmatlan-es-alaptorveny-ellenes/>.

Treaty on European Union 2012.

United Nations. 2019. "United Nations, Migrants, Asylum Seekers Detained in Hungary "Deliberately Deprived of Food": UN Human Rights Office." available [online]: <https://news.un.org/en/story/2019/05/1037811>.

UN Migration Agency (IOM). 2017. "Migration Flow to Hungary. First Half of 2017 Overview." available [online]: <https://hungary.iom.int/sites/g/files/tmzbdl176/files/documents/HU%20Handout%202017I.pdf>.

Vachudova, M.A. 2020. "Ethnopopulism and Democratic Backsliding in Central Europe." *East European Politics 36* (3): 318–340. <https://doi.org/10.1080/21599165.2020.1787163>.

Váradi M. and T. Virág. 2014. "Faces and Causes of Roma Marginalization: Experiences from Hungary." In *Faces and Causes of Roma Marginalization in Local Contexts: Hungary, Romania, Serbia*, J. Szalai and V. Zentai (eds.) Budapest: Center for Policy Studies, Central European University, 34–65.

Wank, S. 1997. "Some Reflections on the Habsburg Empire and Its Legacy in the Nationalities Question." *Austrian History Yearbook 28*: 131–146. <https://doi.org/10.1017/S0067237800016350>.

Wesolowsky, T. 2020. "Singing Off-Key? Kyiv, Budapest Clash Over Rights of Ethnic Hungarians In Ukraine." *Radio Free Europe/Radio Liberty*, sec. Ukraine, available [online]: <https://www.rferl.org/a/kyiv-budapest-clash-over-rights-of-ethnic-hungarians-in-ukraine/30984297.html>.

PART 5
Multiculturalism, Pandemic, Populism and the Political Right

14
RETHINKING MEMBERSHIP UNDER A PANDEMIC CRISIS

Anna Triandafyllidou

Introduction

A brief review of political decisions and policy developments that took place in the months following the pandemic outbreak in February 2020—most of which continue to this day (April 2021)—signals that these have been unique and rather unprecedented. They cut across and "bypassed" formerly rigid distinctions between legal and irregular migrants or asylum seekers, citizens and aliens, permanent and temporary workers. The pandemic emergency has led to selective border closures (and openings) and has prompted important political and symbolic questions about what community, solidarity, belonging and civic responsibility mean. In this chapter, I review some of these emergency measures with a view of arguing that the pandemic may have prompted us to rethink the basis of membership in a political community, beyond our current debates about (multicultural) citizenship.[1]

Border closures that took place in the emergency in February and March 2020 initially made rigid distinctions between citizens and others: in the EU the closures excluded EU citizens, in Canada the border restrictions initially excluded both citizens and permanent residents but left out temporary residents. However, after a few days the government also excluded from border closures those who are on temporary status but effectively residing in the country. During spring 2020, it soon became apparent that there was a need of ensuring that everyone in the territory of a country is covered by the public health system and enjoys some basic protections. Thus, many European countries (including, for instance, Spain, Portugal, Poland and Germany) implemented blanket extensions of stay permits for all foreigners during the spring of 2020 to avoid people losing their legal status under the lockdown (EMN,

DOI: 10.4324/9781003197485-21

2020). Similar measures were taken in Canada, Chile, Israel and New Zealand, while Italy implemented a regularization program between May and August 2020 with a view of providing status to illegally staying aliens working in the agriculture and care sectors. Some countries implemented different facilitation procedures like allowing for online renewals of permits, as in the Netherlands, or automatically renewing the status of people who had lost it during the pandemic, as happened in Canada, until the end of 2020, to give them more time to gather necessary documents or find a new job or both (EMN, 2020). One may argue that such measures had an ethnocentric objective: COVID-19 is a contagious disease; ensuring access to health services for all regardless of status, did not only protect the health and life of those concerned but overall public health. While this may be true, one cannot forego the fact that extensions of legal status and efforts to keep everyone in safety were expansive and inclusive rather than exclusionary.

The pandemic has also brought forward important reflections on essential work casting light on the fact that many of the services deemed "essential" are provided by migrant or refugee workers with precarious status, who are normally seen as non-members of the polity, and may not even have a pathway to long term residency or citizenship. This has kick-started a reflection on the boundaries of membership to a community, on solidarity towards fellow members of the community who may be citizens, permanent residents or temporary workers, and on the responsibility that comes with citizenship. Even in a country like Canada that prides itself on being the first "post-national state" (as the then newly elected Canadian Prime Minister Justin Trudeau put it in a December 2015 interview with a *New York Times* journalist) and where public opinion towards immigration has been consistently positive in the past 15 years and growing even more positive in the latest Environics survey of fall 2020 (Environics, 2018, 2020), the pandemic has raised important challenges as regards border management, protection provided to refugee claimants and who qualifies to be a member of the Canadian society and polity.

Beyond concerns about cultural and religious diversity within the polity and considerations of multicultural citizenship as these have been analyzed by multiculturalism theorists like Tariq Modood (2013) or Will Kymlicka (2015) or also sociologists of multiculturalism like myself (Triandafyllidou et al., 2011; Modood et al., 2006), the pandemic has brought forward a new dimension of membership that cuts across notions of national membership. The value of human life and the importance of health, and the recognition that services to the community that protect life and health (both directly as care and indirectly as, for instance, ensuring food security or essential good provision) are invaluable—have come to the forefront as important dimensions or qualities of membership over and beyond considerations of legal status or cultural and ethnic diversity issues. In this chapter I develop further some initial critical reflections (Triandafyllidou, 2022) on whether the pandemic emergency can lead to both policy and analytical innovation in matters of membership and citizenship.

It is my contention that this crisis exposes several alternatives of community and membership that we need to consider that may not necessarily be tied to the legal relationship between the individual and the state expressed in the classical notion of national citizenship (Baubock, 2018). The exceptional character of the COVID-19 emergency has both reinforced the importance of citizenship as a priority marker of who belongs and who is to be allowed access to the country or access to emergency benefits during the pandemic crisis. At the same time, the emergency has pushed the boundaries of what I will call "*effective membership*" further to include everyone present in the territory. We may even argue that the pandemic emergency has given rise to an alternative mode of membership that could be termed *jus domicilii* (Stavilă, 2013) and is based on effective presence in the territory of the state.

Citizenship, Effective Residence and Border Closures

The COVID-19 virus has proven to be truly transnational, moving fast across not only national borders but also across ethnic communities, social classes, cities and small towns, ignoring territorial borders and sovereign governments. Despite this transnational character, the virus has pointed to how much countries, governments and even health authorities are interdependent under the emergency, yet states reacted initially by prioritizing their own citizens. Weighing their obligations towards solidarity and protection of citizens has led to border closures—the most notorious of which was US President Donald Trump's sudden closure of the US border to all EU citizens in March 2020. Under pandemic circumstances, citizens have been allowed to return to their own country but "others"—notably temporary residents, their family members, international students and visitors or distant family members of citizens—have been banned from entry. The rationale of these decisions has relied on a balancing act between a health risk, on one hand, and belonging and solidarity, on the other. Those who do not belong fully to the nation state need to stay out, at least temporarily.

The border closure has also affected those seeking international protection. Their right to apply for asylum was temporarily *de facto* suspended in many countries such as Canada (for people coming from the US) or Greece (mostly for those crossing via Turkey). One might argue that there was a trade-off between the reasons that favor admission (solidarity toward citizens, obligations toward refugees, immigration objectives) and the possible health risks that come from admitting people (citizens or others) arriving from abroad. There seemed to be, in other words, a cost-benefit analysis where the moral obligation of protecting refugees was simply discounted.

The rationale of solidarity and interdependence and the trade-off between protecting citizens vs assisting aliens under the pandemic emergency merits some further discussion though. There are two different facets of this argument; one concerns the extent to which citizens have a priority over "others," even if those others are temporary residents of the country and hence partly members of the political community. While in theory the answer to this argument may be straightforward, in practice this is less the case as one wonders how one should classify temporary residents (under different legal statuses) who effectively have strong ties with their "host" country in the sense that they live, work, pay taxes, contribute to the community, send their kids to school and participate in public life even if they do not have political rights. The second facet concerns the level of civic responsibility that we are entitled to expect from citizens who should behave in a way that protects their fellow citizens. But then how do we account for temporary residents who make a special civic contribution to the community under the emergency situation, notably through working in essential and risky sectors?

Layers of Membership

The pandemic and related international border restrictions have emphasized the existence of different layers of membership within each country. Such membership layers which distinguish citizens from residents and those from total aliens are not new and immigration and enforcement policies have played an important role in (re-)constructing imagined communities of "aliens" (Aleinikoff, 1995; Romero, 1998). The pandemic has pushed the boundaries of these different layers, blurring and redrawing their contours. The emergency has raised important clarification questions: where does the boundary between insiders and outsiders effectively lie and who should be in or out? For instance, should people with temporary status be given exemptions from border restrictions or should they be excluded? What matters most: their effective residence or their immigration status? Similarly, should asylum seekers be included—with respect to the international right of asylum—or should this right be suspended during the pandemic?

We can imagine the effective population of a country as a set of concentric circles (see also Triandafyllidou and Veikou, 2002): the inner group includes the citizens, those who belong and who have a clear and stable legal relationship with the state. The citizens are expected to take priority in terms of protection of their right to life and health, both as regards their protection through reduced international mobility but also through access to the public health or welfare system. At the same time, they are expected to show loyalty and solidarity to fellow citizens, which in the case of the pandemic emergency may include adhering to the guidelines of the authorities or, for instance, restraining from international but also domestic travel with a view to avoid spreading the virus.

Even though public measures regarding public health and border closures sought to reinforce a sense of community and civic responsibility using war-related metaphors ("fight" the virus; we are all "soldiers" in this fight; "we are all in this together;" Isaacs and Priesz 2021; Musu 2020), they failed to acknowledge and address a creeping racism that took anti-Asian overtones—as the COVID-19 virus was identified by some (like former US President Donald Trump) as the "Chinese" virus—seriously affecting the feeling of safety and well-being of citizens belonging to specific ethno-cultural backgrounds (Heidinger and Cotter, 2020; Zhang et al., 2020). People looking East Asian took the brunt of this racism much as it happened also during the SARS epidemic in 2003 and the H5N1 bird flu in 2005 affecting very negatively not only their rights as citizens but also their feelings of belonging (Lee and Waters 2020). Thus, this inner circle of citizens was layered, and some were seen as "lesser" citizens than others. Prioritizing citizens in general in the "fight" against the pandemic did not address these issues and rather inadvertently by their xenophobic overtones might have unleashed such public expressions of racism.

Turning, however, to the question of residence and our concentric circles, in immigration countries like Canada or Australia or the US, people accepted as permanent immigrants (e.g., green card holders in the US, so-called PRs in Canada) are treated like citizens for what concerns their socio-economic rights, including, for instance, access to public health or family reunification rights. In other countries with significant immigrant populations, like Britain or Germany, this status is called "the right of abode" and is given to people who were initially temporary migrants but have acquired long-term resident status. Transnational entities like the European Union create an additional layer of belonging as European citizenship gives EU citizens who live in another member state equal rights with those of the citizens of that country (Baubock, 2019). Such people who are not citizens but who have an enhanced residence status have been treated under the pandemic like citizens and the pandemic actually has somehow reinforced their belonging to the in-group.

A gray zone of belonging and exclusion has cast its shadow over people with temporary status who have been admitted to a country for a specific period, whether for study or work, and who are likely to be relatively recent arrivals. These have faced significant hardship (Raghuram and Sondhi, 2020) as the permits of some expired during the lockdowns while others lost their jobs and hence risked losing their status as a result of the pandemic (Wright, 2020). The pandemic, though, has forced countries to consider what Canada has termed the "effective residence" of temporary aliens. Hence, beyond the issue of citizenship, the pandemic has brought to the fore the notion of "effective membership." It forced governments to ask where people live habitually, where they send their kids to school, where they pay taxes or have health coverage. The pandemic pushed this outer circle of transient members of the community into the inner circle of those who effectively live in the country for what concerned border restrictions (from which they were exempted). At the same time these transient members were internally excluded in some countries as they did not have access to emergency unemployment or family benefits (as happened for instance for temporary migrants in Germany and for Syrian refugees in Turkey). While effective membership may thus still seem tentative, the pandemic has raised the question of whether this notion of effective residence can be codified into law. For instance, it could include consular protection if found temporarily abroad under a sudden border closure, or the right to reunite with second-degree family members such as elderly parents or adult children who may find themselves cut off from extended family during the pandemic restrictions.

Refugees as Outcasts

While for temporary migrants maybe the dilemmas of border restrictions and service provisions were easier to solve through an inclusive approach, the dilemmas raised by asylum seekers entering a country to seek protection or temporary migrants whose status has expired raised more difficult decisions (Jubilut and Silva, 2020; Godoy and Bauder, 2020). In the face of increasing contagions and scarce health resources, the balance would clearly tip over prioritizing citizens and legal residents. At the same time legal instruments ensuring a general human rights approach like the Canadian Charter of Rights and Freedoms (1982) or the EU Charter of Fundamental Rights (2012) would call for the inclusion of people with precarious status under the protection net of the welfare state and health system. Effectively a review of relevant approaches in the EU and OECD countries has revealed that states have opted for universal coverage particularly regarding access to health services during the pandemic for all people present in their territory regardless of status (EMN, 2020). The approach there was two-pronged: on one hand, special measures were taken to extend legal status or also regularize those without status and, on the other, health coverage was provided for all with concerted efforts for sharing information in different languages in most EU and OECD countries (EMN, 2020: 8).

In other countries, though, like the UAE or Singapore (Molho, 2020) such protections were not afforded to temporary migrant workers who were often locked up in their dormitories to prevent contagion when cases were discovered in their community. Several lost their job and no protection was afforded them; they had to live off their savings while waiting for repatriation flights (Irudaya and Arrokiaraj, 2022; Sahin Mencutek, 2022). In addition, those temporary workers or asylum seekers who work in the informal labor market—as is the case for many Syrians in Turkey, Lebanon or Jordan—the closure of the catering and tourism industries left them without their basic means of subsistence and facing important administrative and linguistic barriers in accessing information about health and sanitation measures.

Asylum seekers posed important dilemmas to countries with long traditions of asylum like EU countries or Canada (George, 2020; Abji et al., 2020; Ellis, 2020). For those inside the country, the approach has been inclusive in affording them protections based on both a human rights perspective and with a view to overall limiting the spread of the virus in the community. However, there were often inhumane practices too (Flynn and Welsford, 2020): for example, in Greece asylum seekers in the metropolitan area of Athens or the Aegean islands were confined in reception centers when positive cases were discovered. The crowded living conditions in these centers did not prevent the virus from spreading within those communities—while access to healthcare was also limited or non-existent (Molnar and Braam, 2020)—but priority was given to keeping the virus in the camps and avoiding its spread among the wider community of citizens outside the camp. The border in those cases was recreated within the state, separating those who do not belong from those who belong (Rosinska and Pellerito, 2022). Similar approaches were documented in the US too where detention centers became COVID-19 hotspots (Boris, 2022).

Refugee claimants seeking protection by crossing international borders were however the most vulnerable and most exposed category where the pandemic showed how citizenship is prioritized over an international right to asylum or an international respect of human rights. Asylum seekers were pushed back from the Canadian border to the US (Ellis, 2020) and prevented from entering Greece from Turkey. While in both cases there are international safe third country agreements in place that could legally justify the move, in both cases those pushed back were in vulnerable conditions and the countries to which they were pushed back are not particularly safe. The Federal Court of Canada in fact ruled on July 23, 2020 that the Canada–US Safe Third Country Agreement (STCA) violates the Canadian Charter of Rights and Freedoms by allowing Canada to send refugee claimants back to the US.[2] Despite these challenges, it was clear that the inner political community of members could not "afford" to help aliens under the pandemic emergency by allowing them to enter the country. Similar challenges were documented in South Africa (Rugunanan, 2020) and in Singapore and Malaysia (Petcharamesree, 2020).

Expanding Membership

The pandemic has exposed the fissures and dilemmas in our understanding of the limits and hierarchies of membership and solidarity. As it happened in Canada, the US, Germany, Italy, Spain or Poland many of the frontline workers in senior care homes, farms or food processing plants were people with precarious status, notably seasonal migrants, asylum seekers waiting for their application to be processed or mere sojourners without the right to work. They performed their "citizenship duty" even if they had no secure legal status and did not belong to the community. Indeed, this argument sparked a controversy in Quebec, Canada, in June 2020 when asylum seekers employed in senior care homes—which were hard hit by the pandemic—mobilized, asking to obtain permanent residency status as a recognition of their contribution to the safety and care of community members (Levitz and Kestler d'Amours, 2020). The Quebec Premier refused but after further negotiations with the federal government, a special path to permanent residency was announced by the federal minister, Marco Mendicino, on August 14, 2020—this program has come to be known as the "Guardian Angels" Program. Minister Mendicino explained the decision by reflecting on the fact that these asylum seekers put themselves at risk day after day in the pandemic and "they demonstrated a uniquely Canadian quality" (argued Mendicino) "in that they were looking out for others and so that is why today is so special" (Seidle, 2020).

The Canadian government took further bolder and unprecedented measures in February and April 2021. It first lowered significantly (on February 13, 2021) the points necessary to apply for permanent residency inviting all temporary residents who had sent a preliminary application and were physically present in the country. And most recently, on April 14, 2021, it announced an innovative pathway to permanent residence for over 90,000 essential workers and international graduates thus giving an accelerated path to permanent residency for people who are employed in the healthcare system as well as the agri-food sector (even though the latter was not mentioned anywhere in the announcement). The justification for these exceptional decisions, while perhaps ethno-centric in that it privileges the well-being of the country, it also signals what I call "effective membership." Those invited to apply are people who contribute to the community, in crucial sectors, even though they do not have a long-term status, read the Immigration Refugees Citizenship Canada (IRCC) announcement. "The focus of this new pathway will be on temporary workers employed in our hospitals and long-term care homes and on the frontlines of other essential sectors, as well as international graduates who are driving the economy of tomorrow" (IRCC 2021, April 14). Unfortunately, by June 17, 2021, of the 20,000 slots available for people employed in care, less than 2,000 applications had been received (Alboim and Cohl, 2021) which actually might raise questions about the discrepancy between the official rhetoric and the actual implementation of the related program.

The question thus arises whether the pandemic had a *polarizing effect* on our understanding and practice of membership: while it pushed people with temporary status towards the inner circle through the notion of effective membership and service to the community, it pushed outside those who may have needed protection the most, the refugee claimants making their way through the border or confined in refugee camps. The pandemic has recreated borders within the territory of the nation state by unleashing anew, anti-minority discrimination and prejudice, while also creating closed refugee camps or migrant dormitories and assigning different mobility rights to citizens/permanent residents and temporary residents. The latter face some discretion at the border if an immigration officer questions the necessity of their presence in the country or they have to prove through additional pieces of evidence that they regularly and effectively reside in the host country.

While many states used their emergency and quarantine laws, and in this sense acted lawfully in exercising delegated legislative authority to declare an exception, they ended up stripping asylum seekers from their right to seek asylum. While a restrictive perspective seeking to evade international obligations in relation to asylum may have been a longer trend, it was exacerbated during the pandemic, leading to the situation that Agamben (2005, see Humphreys, 2006) specified: they exercised their power in deciding on the exception and suspended the juridical order because of the serious crisis threatening the state and its "legitimate" population. Thus, protecting the most basic rights of asylum claimants to seek refuge is annulled. Border closures, such as between Canada and the US preventing any asylum claimant from entering Canada or those on the Greek islands, reinforce a sense of national solidarity among citizens and permanent residents and a transnational solidarity among sovereign states, but leave in limbo, in a "space of exception" (Agamben, 2005, as explained in Humphreys, 2006), those who are among the most vulnerable populations: notably asylum seekers and irregular migrants seeking entry. They fall into this zone of active abandonment that is neither inside nor outside the polity, it is just there at the border (Pinelli, 2018).

Eventually the pandemic had a mixed effect on membership and issues of protection, covering some and leaving others terribly exposed, it has certainly pushed the boundaries of membership in different directions, disregarding concerns about cultural or religious diversity and centering considerations on "service to the community." While this may be particularly visible in the case of the Canadian discourse and policy, it has been a relevant topic in many countries including, for instance, Italy, where essential (but irregular) migrant workers were given the option to legalize their status. From an epistemological perspective, the pandemic pushes us to consider how the sociology of multiculturalism can make innovative contributions to multiculturalism as a political theoretical model forcing us to rethink the moral obligations towards different layers of our community and how we weigh moral obligations towards citizens, members and aliens in relational and not just absolute terms. How can employment that serves the community become an inroad to membership? It remains for now an open question whether these developments will lead to a different type of multicultural citizenship that over and above considerations of cultural and religious values, will foreground the notion of civic membership or whether soon after the pandemic emergency is over, we will go back to our usual "multiculturalism backlash" debates.

Notes

1 This chapter is a revised version of Triandafyllidou's "Spaces of Solidarity and Spaces of Exception: Migration and Membership During Pandemic Times," (2022: 3–21) in A. Triandafyllidou (ed.) *Migration and Pandemics: Spaces of Solidarity and Spaces of Exception*, Cham: Springer Open (IMISCOE Research Series) https://link.springer.com/book/10.1007/978-3-030-81210-2
2 The Federal Court of Appeal upheld the appeal of the government against the original decision of August 2020 and ruled (on April 15, 2021) that the agreement between Canada and the United States to treat each other as "safe countries" for refugees does not violate the Charter of Rights and Freedoms.

References

Abji, S., M. Pintin-Perez and R. Bhuyan. 2020. "In Canada, Non-Status Women are Being Left Behind." *Open Democracy*. https://www.opendemocracy.net/en/pandemic-border/anada-non-status-women-are-being-left-behind/. Accessed 28 February 2021.
Agamben, G. 2005. *State of Exception*. Chicago: University of Chicago Press.
Alboim, N. and K. Cohl. 2021. "Equitable Access: Implementing the Temporary Resident to Permanent Resident Pathway." CERC Policy Brief no. 3/2021. https://www.ryerson.ca/content/dam/cerc-migration/Policy/CERCMigration_PolicyPaper03_June2021.pdf.
Aleinikoff, A.T. 1995. "The Tightening Circle of Membership." *Hastings Constitutional Law Quarterly* 22 (915). https://repository.uchastings.edu/hastings_constitutional_law_quaterly/vol22/iss4/1.
Baubock, R. (ed.). 2018. *Debating Transformations of National Citizenship*. Cham, Switzerland: Springer. https://www.springer.com/gp/book/9783319927183. Open Access.
Baubock, R. (ed.). 2019. *Debating European Citizenship*. Cham, Switzerland: Springer, https://www.springer.com/gp/book/9783319899046.
Boris, E. 2022. "Vulnerability and Resilience in the Covid-19 Crisis: Race, Gender, and Belonging." In *Migration and Pandemics*, A. Triandafyllidou (ed.) Cham: Springer Open, 65–84.
Canadian Charter of Rights and Freedoms. 1982. https://laws-lois.justice.gc.ca/eng/const/page-15.html.
Ellis Claire. 2020. "COVID-19: Canada Locks Its Gates to Asylum Seekers." https://www.opendemocracy.net/en/pandemic-border/covid-19-canada-locks-its-gates-asylum-seekers/.
Environics. 2018. "Focus Canada – Winter 2018 Canadian Public Opinion About Immigration and Minority Groups." https://www.environicsinstitute.org/docs/default-source/project-documents/focus-canada-winter-2018---immigration-and-minority-groups/focus-canada-winter-2018-survey-on-immigration-and-minority-groups---final-report.pdf?sfvrsn=ede94c5f_2.
Environics. 2020. "Focus Canada – Fall 2020 Canadian Public Opinion About Immigration and Refugees." https://www.environicsinstitute.org/docs/default-source/project-documents/fc-fall-2020---immigration/focus-canada-fall-2020---public-opinion-on-immigration-refugees---final-report.pdf?sfvrsn=bd51588f_2.
EU Charter of Fundamental Rights. 2012. https://ec.europa.eu/info/aid-development-cooperation-fundamental-rights/your-rights-eu/eu-charter-fundamental-rights_en.

European Migration Network, EMN. 2020. "Inform Number1 Eu and OECD Member States Responses to Managing Residence Permits and Migrant Unemployment During the Covid-19 Pandemic." https://ec.europa.eu/migrant-integration/library-document/inform-1-eu-and-oecd-member-states-responses-managing-residence-permits-and_en.

Flynn, M. and K. Welsford. 2020. "COVID-19 Reveals the Inherent Vindictiveness of Migration Detention." *Open Democracy*. https://www.opendemocracy.net/en/pandemic-border/covid-19-reveals-inherent-vindictiveness-migration-detention/. Accessed 28 February 2021.

George, U. 2020. "Will Canada Give Its Foreign Essential Workers Their Rights?" *Open Democracy*. https://www.opendemocracy.net/en/pandemic-border/will-canada-give-its-foreign-essential-workers-their-rights/. Accessed 28 February 2021.

Godoy, M. and H. Bauder. 2020. "What Can We Learn from Latin America's Solidarity Cities?" *Open Democracy*. https://www.opendemocracy.net/en/pandemic-border/what-can-we-learn-from-latin-americas-solidarity-cities/. Accessed 28 February 2021.

Heidinger, L. and A. Cotter. 2020. *Perceptions of Personal Safety Among Population Groups Designated as Visible Minorities in Canada During the COVID-19 Pandemic*. Ottawa, StatsCanada. https://www150.statcan.gc.ca/n1/en/pub/45-28-0001/2020001/article/00046-eng.pdf?st=SV8zedqq.

Humphreys, S. 2006. "Legalizing Lawlessness: On Giorgio Agamben's State of Exception." *The European Journal of International Law* 17 (3): 677–687. https://doi.org/10.1093/ejil/chl020.

IRCC. 2021. "14 April, New Pathway to Permanent Residency for over 90,000 Essential Temporary Workers and International Graduates." https://www.canada.ca/en/immigration-refugees-citizenship/news/2021/04/new-pathway-to-permanent-residency-for-over-90000-essential-temporary-workers-and-international-graduates.html.

Irudaya, R.S. and H. Arokkiaraj. 2022. "Return Migration from the Gulf Region to India Amidst COVID-19." In *Migration and Pandemics*, A. Triandafyllidou (ed.) Cham: Springer Open, 207–226

Isaacs, D. and A. Priesz. 2021. "Isaacs, Covid 19 and the Metaphor of War." Editorial, *Journal of Paediatrics and Child Health* 57: 6–8.

Jubilut, L. and J.C. Silva. 2020. "COVID-19 at the Brazil-Venezuela Borders: The Good, the Bad and the Ugly." *Open Democracy*. https://www.opendemocracy.net/en/pandemic-border/covid-19-brazil-venezuela-borders-good-bad-and-ugly/. Accessed 28 February 2021.

Kymlicka, W. 2015. "Solidarity in Diverse Societies: Beyond Neoliberal Multiculturalism and Welfare Chauvinism." *Comparative Migration Studies* 3: Article number: 17. https://comparativemigrationstudies.springeropen.com/articles/10.1186/s40878-015-0017-4.

Lee, Suyeon and Sara F. Waters. 2020. "Asians and Asian Americans' Experiences of Racial Discrimination During the COVID-19 Pandemic: Impacts on Health Outcomes and the Buffering Role of Social Support." *Stigma and Health,* Vol. 2, No. 999, 000 ISSN: 2376-6972. http://dx.doi.org/10.1037/sah0000275.

Levitz, S. and J. Kestler d'Amours. 2020. "Asylum seekers on front lines of COVID_19 to have chance at permanent residency." *The Canadian Press*, August 14, https://www.cp24.com/news/asylum-seekers-on-front-lines-of-covid-19-to-have-chance-at-permanent-residency-1.5064978.

Modood, T. 2013. *Multiculturalism,* 2nd edition. London: Polity Press.
Modood, T., A. Triandafyllidou and R. Zapata-Barrero (eds.). 2006. *Multiculturalism, Muslims and Citizenship: A European Approach.* London: Routledge.
Molho, J. 2020. "Will the 'Singapore Model' Survive the Pandemic?" *Open Democracy.* https://www.opendemocracy.net/en/pandemic-border/will-the-singapore-model-survive-the-pandemic/. Accessed 28 February 2021.
Molnar, P. and D. Braam. 2020. "Refugees at Increased Risk of Coronavirus due to Barriers to Healthcare." *The Conversation.* https://theconversation.com/refugees-at-increased-risk-of-coronavirus-due-to-barriers-to-healthcare-137217. Accessed 28 February 2021.
Musu, C. 2020. "War Metaphors Used for COVID-19 are Compelling but also Dangerous." 8 April 2020. https://theconversation.com/war-metaphors-used-for-covid-19-are-compelling-but-also-dangerous-135406
Petcharamasree, S. 2020. "COVID-19 in Southeast Asia: Non-Citizens Have a Right to Protection Too." *Open Democracy.* https://www.opendemocracy.net/en/pandemic-border/covid-19-southeast-asia-non-citizens-have-right-protection-too/. Accessed 28 February 2021.
Pinelli, B. 2018. "Control and Abandonment: The Power of Surveillance on Refugees in Italy, During and After the Mare Nostrum Operation." *Antipode 50* (3): 725–747. https://doi.org/10.1111/anti.12374.
Raghuram, P. and G. Sondhi. 2020. "Stuck in the Middle of a Pandemic: Are International Students Migrants?" *Open Democracy.* https://www.opendemocracy.net/en/pandemic-border/stuck-middle-pandemic-are-international-students-migrants/. Accessed 28 February 2021.
Rajan, S. Irudaya and H. Arrokiaraj. 2021. "Return Migration from the Gulf Region to India Amidst COVID-19." In *Migration and Pandemics,* A. Triandafyllidou (ed.) Cham, Switzerland: Springer, 207–226.
Romero, V.C. 1998. "Expanding the Circle of Membership by Reconstructing the "Alien": Lessons from Social Psychology and the "Promise Enforcement" Cases." *University of Michigan Journal of Law Reform 1.* https://repository.law.umich.edu/mjlr/vol32/iss1/2
Rosińska, A. and E. Pellerito. 2022. "Essential or Expendable? Immigrants and Workers' Rights in the Domestic Workers' Activism in the US Under the Pandemic." In *Migration and Pandemics,* A. Triandafyllidou (ed.) Cham: Springer Open.
Rugunanan, P. 2020. "'South Africa Belongs to All Who Live In It', COVID-19 Showed It Does Not." *Open Democracy.* https://www.opendemocracy.net/en/pandemic-border/south-africa-belongs-to-all-who-live-in-it-covid-19-showed-it-does-not/. Accessed 28 February 2021.
Sahin Mencutek, Z. 2022. "Voluntary and Forced Return Migration under a Pandemic Crisis." In *Migration and Pandemics,* A. Triandafyllidou (ed.) Cham: Springer Open. 185–206.
Seidle, Leslie. 2020. "Issue 41: Should Canada Regularize the Immigration Status of Asylum Seekers Helping Fight COVID-19?" 26 May. https://maxpolicy.substack.com/p/issue-41-should-canada-regularize. Accessed 12 January 2021.
Statistics Canada. 2020. "COVID-19 Disruptions and Agriculture: Temporary Foreign Workers." Release date: April 17.
Stavilă, Andrei. 2013. *Citizens-Minus and Citizens-Plus: A Normative Attempt to Defend Citizenship Acquisition as an Entitlement Based on Residence.* Florence, Italy: European University Institute.

Triandafyllidou, A. 2022. "Spaces of Solidarity and Spaces of Exception: Migration and Membership During Pandemic Times." In *Migration and Pandemics: Spaces of Solidarity and Spaces of Exception*, A. Triandafyllidou (ed.) Cham: Springer Open, forthcoming in the IMISCOE Springer series, 1–20.

Triandafyllidou, A. and M. Veikou. 2002. "The Hierarchy of Greekness. Ethnic and National Identity Considerations in Greek Immigration Policy." *Ethnicities* 2 (2): 189–208.

Triandafyllidou, A., T. Modood, and N. Meer (eds.). 2011. *European Multiculturalisms. Cultural, Religious and Ethnic Challenges*. Edinburgh: Edinburgh University Press.

Wright, R. 2020. "Vulnerable and Unprotected in the US: It Only Takes Political Will." *Open Democracy*. https://www.opendemocracy.net/en/pandemic-border/vulnerable-and-unprotected-us-it-only-takes-political-will/. Accessed 28 February 2021.

Zhang, W., L. Chai, J. Fan, P. Wang, X. Wei and L. Yang. 2020. "COVID-19, Racial Discrimination, and Psychological Distress." *Annals of Epidemiology*. https://doi.org/10.1016/j.annepidem.2020.08.032

15

IMPERILED MULTICULTURALISM? COVID-19, RACISM AND NATION-BUILDING IN AUSTRALIA

Tim Soutphommasane

The history of Australian multiculturalism has closely tracked that of its Canadian cousin. Following Canada's landmark adoption of official multiculturalism in 1971, and to some extent in emulation, Australia was the second country to endorse multiculturalism as policy in 1973. Since then, multiculturalism has formed a core feature of Australian nationhood, in particular, its formal articulation by political leaders and government. It has been integral to a certain reinvention of Australian national identity. Once, the Australian national self-image was emphatically defined by racial and cultural homogeneity, as expressed through the infamous White Australia policy that restricted non-European immigration. But in recent decades Australia has celebrated the cultural diversity of its population. Even amid populist ructions during the 1990s, and more recent political turbulence, Australia's official multiculturalism has endured. There is consistently high public support expressed for cultural diversity; no prime minister has yet walked away from a policy of multiculturalism. Such stability contrasts with more fleeting and abandoned multicultural experiences elsewhere, most notably in parts of Europe.

Yet how stable and enduring is Australia's multicultural policy settlement? While frequently lauded as a success—political leaders from all mainstream persuasions routinely boast that Australia "is the most successful multicultural country in the world"—Australia's multiculturalism shows signs of fragility. Debates about free speech, race and identity have arguably fed social division and created forms of ideological "culture war" polarization. There has been a recent resurgence of populist nationalism, and alarming growth in right-wing extremism. The COVID-19 pandemic has exacerbated these trends, stirring up anti-Asian racism, and lending momentum to disinformation campaigns and conspiracy theories aligned with fringe political movements. Combined with

DOI: 10.4324/9781003197485-22

the near total closure of Australia's borders during the pandemic, not only to the rest of the world but also between its states and territories, these developments signal a shift in Australian political culture. Australia risks retreating from being an open, globalized and triumphantly multicultural country to its old "Fortress Australia" ways, one ever anxious and fearful of external threats.

This chapter explores the historical development of multiculturalism in Australia and examines the effects of COVID-19 and populist nationalism. I argue that recent events illustrate structural vulnerabilities within Australia's multiculturalism, as well as a lapse in the country's nation-building imagination. For Australia's multiculturalism to emerge from the pandemic intact, rather than imperiled, there will need to be an emphatic renewal of multicultural nation-building and of systemic anti-racism efforts.

Australia's Multiculturalism

Australian society has always contained diversity and pluralism. Among the original Indigenous occupants of the continent, there were some 700 First Nations speaking more than 250 languages, all long before the British First Fleet arrived in 1788. Among the arrivals on the First Fleet were soldiers, sailors and convicts with ancestral origins in Europe, Africa and the Middle East. The goldfields of New South Wales and Victoria in the 19th century were populated by prospectors and others from a multitude of nationalities. Yet today's multicultural society is, in many respects, the distinctive creation of the second half of the 20th century. It is the product of the successive waves of mass immigration following the Second World War. During that time, a cumulative eight million people have immigrated to this country, and with them a new mix of ethnicities and cultures (Phillips et al., 2010; Australian Bureau of Statistics, 2021).

Australia adopted a policy of multiculturalism in the 1970s amid this postwar experience. As with Canada in 1971, Australia's endorsement of multiculturalism reflected the political pressures of the time and a desire for new policy settlements. The Canadian experience was shaped by rising Québécois nationalism: "multiculturalism within a bilingual framework" reflected the Trudeau government's embrace of multiculturalism to accommodate both the claims made by immigrant "ethnic" groups and by French-speaking minorities. The Australian one, meanwhile, reflected a desire from political elites to draw a line under the opprobrious history of the White Australia policy (in place from 1901 until its final abolition in the 1970s), which restricted immigration from non-European countries and increasingly attracted international criticism (Tavan, 2005). Although the most infamous manifestation of the policy, the dictation test (in which prospective immigrants were required to pass a dictation test in a European language), was abolished in 1958, remnants of it remained right until 1973.

Even though by the 1960s fewer immigrants were coming from Britain, Ireland and northern Europe—with an increasing number coming from southern Europe—there was still an expectation that immigrants would assimilate to Anglo-Celtic Australian norms. Assisted passage was offered to immigrants from Britain and Europe, but not to those from outside Europe. Immigration officials retained a discretionary right to determine whether an arrival was sufficiently European to be allowed in.

At the outset, then, multiculturalism was expressed as a repudiation of White Australia and an affirmation of democratic citizenship. In a speech in 1973 that invoked multiculturalism for the first time, the Minister for Immigration, Al Grassby, acknowledged that mass immigration had rendered any aspiration of fully assimilating newcomers to the "Australian way of life" untenable (Grassby, 1973: 3). Instead, it was time to enlarge the national identity, and ensure Australia's new arrivals would be free "to make their own distinctive contribution to the family of the nation" (Grassby, 1973: 9). According to Grassby, the goal should be to ensure that all Australians would be proud to declare, in their different accents, "I am Australian"—just as Roman citizens in antiquity could boast, "Civis Romanus sum" (Grassby, 1973: 9). The embrace of multiculturalism was supported by legislative developments at the federal level, namely, the enactment of the *Racial Discrimination Act 1975*, which prohibited any discrimination, exclusion, restriction or preference based on race, ethnicity or national origin. The new legislation, in the words of then Prime Minister Gough Whitlam, "writes it firmly into our laws that Australia is in reality a multicultural nation, in which the linguistic and cultural heritage of the Aboriginal people and of peoples from all parts of the world can find an honored place" (Whitlam, 1985: 506).

Multiculturalism's advent was undoubtedly a response to the social reality of cultural diversity. But in the Australian case, the practice of multiculturalism has not always neatly mapped on to the multiculturalism often expounded by theorists concerned with the politics of identity. It has diverged from the multiculturalism described by theorists in terms of special or group-differentiated rights for minorities (Joppke, 2001: 446). As practiced in Australia, multicultural policy has not been an offer just for minorities, nor can it be reduced to the offer of group-differentiated rights and measures. Rather, it has been consistently couched in the language of integration and concerned with ensuring the inclusion of citizens of all backgrounds into the political community and culture (Jayasuriya, 1997: 23; Soutphommasane, 2005: 405; and see Chapter 1 by Will Kymlicka on multiculturalism as citizenization in this volume).

The evolution of Australia's multiculturalism has reflected the ideological bearings of successive governments. Following the Whitlam Labor government's (1972–1975) initial formulation, the Fraser Liberal-Country coalition government (1975–1983) lent multiculturalism a "cultural pluralist" focus, viewing immigrants as consisting of relatively distinct ethnic groups and the role of policy as concerned with supporting the maintenance of cultural identities. The Hawke and Keating Labor governments (1983–1996) provided a more explicit emphasis on multiculturalism as citizenship: the policy conferred all Australians with a right to express their individual cultural identity, but this was accompanied by "an overriding and unifying commitment" to accept the liberal democratic structure and principles of Australian society. Although the years of the Howard Liberal-National coalition government (1996–2007) saw a prime ministerial aversion to even referring to the word "multiculturalism," Howard stopped short of abandoning the policy, instead shifting emphasis towards social cohesion and cultural harmony. During the second half of the Rudd and Gillard Labor governments (2007–2013), there was a renewed commitment to multiculturalism, based on an acceptance of democratic values and of the need for improved access and equity in the provision of government services to Australians from all backgrounds.

In more recent times, the state of Australian multicultural policy has been markedly ambivalent. There was no policy statement of multiculturalism, for example, during the life of the Abbott Liberal-National coalition government (2013–2015). The stance of Abbott as prime minister invited questions about his commitment to the policy, given his public statements about multiculturalism suggesting "migrants assimilate in their own way and at their own pace" to the "Australian way of life" (Narushima, 2010). Moreover, during the periods of the Abbott and Turnbull (2015–2017) governments, the government embarked upon two campaigns to repeal racial hatred provisions in the *Racial Discrimination Act*, the de facto legislative expression of multiculturalism (which I will discuss below). When the Turnbull Liberal-National coalition government (2015–2017) released its multicultural policy statement in 2017, it seemed to retreat from previous emphases on cultural liberty, social justice and the need for government responsiveness to cultural diversity. Some observers suggest that Australia's multicultural policy had now assumed a "post-multiculturalist posture," in which government has mainstreamed its approach to cultural diversity, with only limited attention to the structural inequalities experienced by immigrants and minorities (Levey, 2019: 466).[1]

Any dilution of government policy, though, does not necessarily reflect a cooling of public sentiment towards multiculturalism. If anything, there has been consistent and overwhelming public support of multiculturalism. According to the most recent Scanlon Foundation "Mapping Social Cohesion" survey, the longest-running annual national survey of its type, 84% of Australian respondents agreed that "multiculturalism has been good for Australia," with 71% agreeing that "accepting immigrants from many different countries makes Australia stronger" (Markus, 2021: 67–68, 102). Moreover, such levels of agreement have been consistently found over the past 14 years since the Scanlon survey was first administered: for more than a decade, more than 8 in

10 Australians consistently say that it has been good for Australia. On this basic question, there is no doubt that multiculturalism is something of a triumph.

On other measures, too, there is a strong case to be made about the success of Australia's multiculturalism. There is strong civic integration of immigrants, as reflected in the high rates of naturalization among those who settle in Australia. An estimated 80% of immigrants with more than ten years' residence in the country become Australian citizens, though the path from immigrant arrival to citizenship has been complicated by temporary migration. In areas such as education and employment, Australian society does not exhibit patterns seen in many other liberal-democratic societies, where significant numbers of immigrants and their descendants experience entrenched, generational socio-economic disadvantage. The children of immigrants, on average, outperform the children of Australian-born parents with respect to educational performance. The children of immigrants constitute a higher proportion of people in highly skilled occupations than the children of Australian-born parents. Perhaps reflecting how Australia's immigrant intake has skewed towards skilled migration since the 1970s, multiculturalism has been characterized by relatively strong social mobility (see Soutphommasane, 2012: 66–70; Hartwich, 2011: 2–3).

And yet, there is a paradox within Australia's multiculturalism. For all its apparent strengths, it exhibits a certain fragility. While there is resounding majority support for multicultural diversity, there is also significant anxiety and suspicion about aspects of multiculturalism. Nearly half of Australian respondents to the Scanlon Foundation's social cohesion study held negative views towards Chinese people, as well as Iraqis and Sudanese (Markus, 2021: 80). More than 40% held negative attitudes towards Lebanese people, with 37% of respondents holding a negative attitude towards Muslims (Markus, 2021: 80). For a supposedly successful multicultural nation, these are high levels of negative sentiment towards multiple ethnic and cultural groups from non-European backgrounds. What does it say that Australians from Chinese, Iraqi, Sudanese, Lebanese and Muslim backgrounds, according to these recent findings, are regarded by so many of their fellow Australians with distrust, hostility, even hatred?

The COVID-19 Pandemic, Race and the Politics of Sovereignty

One part of the answer lies in the COVID-19 pandemic. Australia avoided the worst effects of the COVID-19 pandemic, with the Australian government response proving effective in suppressing the numbers of infection since the coronavirus was first detected in March 2020. Even so, the country has not been immune from one of the pandemic's effects: its unleashing of xenophobia, hatred and racist scapegoating. Just as in North America and Europe, there has been a surge in anti-Asian racism, initially linked to the coronavirus's origins in Wuhan, China. Community advocates have recorded hundreds of instances of Asian-Australians experiencing verbal abuse, threats and even physical attacks in the months following the pandemic's outbreak (Zhou, 2020). According to a 2021 study of attitudes within the Chinese-Australian community conducted by the Lowy Institute, 37% of Chinese-Australians said they have been racially discriminated against in the past 12 months, with 18% of Chinese-Australians saying they have been physically threatened or attacked in that time because of their Chinese heritage (Kassam and Hsu, 2021: 17). Such experiences have coincided with an alarming increase in right-wing extremist activity, though coronavirus racism has by no means been confined to fringe elements. The virus threat has, if anything, provided cover for the expression of racism among a wider constituency.

The COVID-19 pandemic reinforced some pre-existing trends, particularly relating to anti-Chinese and anti-Asian racism. There has for some time been growing unease about Chinese and Asian buyers outbidding "local" Australians at house auctions or acquiring agricultural land. Moreover, since 2017 there has been a marked deterioration of bilateral relations between Australia and China (Kassam and Hsu, 2021: 3). Fears about the Chinese Community Party's influence in, if not interference with, public institutions have spilled over into a more general antagonism against Chinese-Australians. There has been growing suspicion towards Australians with Chinese heritage, with even one federal parliamentary inquiry questioning several Chinese-Australians about their allegiance to Australia (Hurst 2020). Such distrust has accelerated during the pandemic. Within Australia, alongside the casting of Chinese people as spreaders of the coronavirus, and conspiracy theories about the Chinese government creating COVID-19, there were widely circulating but unfounded rumors about Chinese and Asian people on "tourist buses" raiding supermarkets in regional towns for supplies during the early days of Australia's lockdown. Some Chinese-Australians were criticized for organizing for medical supplies to be shipped to China during the early stages of the pandemic. If there has been such marked hostility against Chinese people during COVID-19, it has not emerged from nowhere, but rather from existing anxieties and prejudices (Soutphommasane, 2020: 214).

More broadly, there has in recent years been a challenge to Australia's multiculturalism from the global ascendency of populist nationalism. The tone and language of politics has arguably shifted to favor those on the side of nativism and protectionism. Even though there has been no formal abandonment of multiculturalism, Australian politics has involved a new normalization of racism within public discourse. There has been an intensification, in particular, of culture war criticisms of multiculturalism and "political correctness" from the right of politics. Most notably, with the vocal support of sections of media, the Liberal-National coalition government has twice sought during the past decade to weaken federal racial hatred laws against acts that "offend, insult, humiliate or intimidate" others on the grounds of race. Supported by then Attorney-General George Brandis's statement that Australians had "a right to be bigots," those agitating for change gave license to people to believe that venting racism could be justified as the exercise of free speech.[2]

There have also been outright attempts by some political leaders to stir racial fears and criticize multiculturalism. In 2018, for example, there was panic about an "African gangs" crisis in Melbourne, triggered by comments by then Home Affairs Minister, Peter Dutton, that Victorians were so cowed by African gang violence that they refrained from going out to restaurants at night. In a separate intervention, Dutton also proposed that white South African farmers be given "special attention" for fast-tracked humanitarian visas because of their alleged persecution on the grounds of race (no such policy was ever enacted). During the same year, then Minister for Citizenship and Multicultural Affairs, Alan Tudge, warned that Australia was veering towards a "European separatist multicultural model." Not to be outdone, in October 2018 Pauline Hanson proposed a motion in the Senate to acknowledge "the deplorable rise of anti-white racism and attacks on Western Civilization" and "that it is okay to be white" (repeating a well-known white supremacist slogan). The motion was only narrowly defeated, with 23 government senators voting in support of the motion, though the government recanted its support following public outcry, claiming that its senators' votes were the result of an administrative error (Soutphommasane, 2019: 44–46).

Political posturing on race did not abate during the COVID-19 pandemic, not even with the global anti-racism moment generated by Black Lives Matter protests. If anything, they fed a certain enthusiasm for the culture wars. For example, while the death of George Floyd at the hands of police in Minneapolis in May 2020 focused attention in many countries on institutional racism, anti-racism protests in Australia were quickly dismissed by some as leftist excesses. Prime Minister Scott Morrison criticized protests against Aboriginal deaths in custody for "importing" the issue of institutional racism into domestic political debate, suggesting that anti-racism protests have been "taken over" by "politically driven leftwing agendas." He also stated that racism in the country could not be compared with that in the United States because "there was no slavery in Australia," a statement for which he later apologized, following public criticism that he was indifferent to historical experiences of racial injustice (Murphy, 2020).

There has also been a deepening ambivalence in Australia's official stance towards right-wing extremism during the pandemic. Australia's security agencies have, in recent years, issued consistent warnings about the growing threat of far-right nationalism and white supremacist movements operating within Australia—one revealed all too starkly when an Australian white supremacist killed 51 people in two mosques in Christchurch, New Zealand, in 2019. The Australian Security Intelligence Organization has also warned that COVID-19 had created opportunities for right-wing extremists to recruit new followers, amid resentment against government lockdowns to counter the pandemic's spread (Christodoulou, 2020). However, following strong objections from some government senators against the terminology of "right-wing" extremism, in March 2021, ASIO announced it would no longer refer to "right-wing extremism," instead adopting the language of "ideologically motivated violent extremism" to describe threats associated with white supremacist and white nationalist groups (Galloway, 2021).

Accompanying the rise in racism and intensification of race politics, COVID-19 has created—or, in some cases, revealed—a troubling exclusion and marginalization of immigrants. It was immigrants, after all, who worked disproportionately in parts of the economy most directly hit by lockdowns and by economic contraction, such as hospitality and retail services. Emergency measures such as the multi-billion-dollar JobKeeper wage subsidy program excluded a number of key categories of immigrant visa-holders, including international students. At the height of the pandemic's impact in 2020, there were long queues of international students waiting for free meals in Sydney and Melbourne, illustrating the precarious economic position of many of them. In addition, some of the more punitive aspects of Australia's pandemic response have been implemented in communities containing significant immigration populations. This includes the tough lockdowns imposed on inner-city public housing towers in Melbourne in 2020, and the deployment of Australian Defence Force personnel to assist in the enforcement of stay-at-home public health orders in southwest Sydney in 2021. Arguably, the pandemic has exposed some glaring deficits in Australian multiculturalism—namely, the inability of federal and state governments to craft policy responses that account for diversity, and that avoid stigmatizing or punishing immigrant communities.

Then there has been another development. Perhaps the most significant effect of the pandemic has been to return a "Fortress Australia" mentality to its political culture (Soutphommasane and Stears, 2020). The closure of Australia's borders in March 2020 guaranteed that politics in Australia would again be defined in terms of borders and national security. There were echoes of Australia's hardline response to asylum seekers arriving by boat during the 2000s and 2010s. It was no accident that, when the federal parliament sat for the first time after the pandemic hit, Prime Minister Morrison spoke of the government's response as being about "defending and protecting Australia's national sovereignty," as though COVID-19 were an enemy combatant in war (Morrison, 2020). For nearly two years up until February 2022, Australia's borders were effectively closed to nearly everyone not a citizen or permanent resident, with a stringent cap on arrivals. Net overseas migration went negative, an unprecedented state of affairs since the end of the Second World War. Moreover, the Fortress Australia stance was not merely directed at foreign outsiders; it was turned on Australians themselves. More than 35,000 Australian citizens were still unable to return home more than 18 months into the pandemic, with many left questioning the worth of their passports. After all, what value does citizenship have if a citizen can't exercise a right to return home during a time of need?

Even within the nation itself, borders were closed between several states for extended periods, with many fearful of fellow Australians importing COVID-19 from interstate. Following a resurgence of the virus in Victoria in July 2020, various media reports in New South Wales and Queensland referred to incursions from "Mexicans" from the south, and even to the "Melbourne virus." One year on, in July 2021, during the outbreak of the Delta variant, the Western Australian Labor premier Mark McGowan openly entertained the idea of maintaining an indefinite "hard border" with New South Wales. At the level of state politics, politicians have discovered that closing their borders to compatriots has been wildly popular among voters. In November 2020, Queensland Labor premier Anastacia Palaszczuk was resoundingly re-elected, with her government's closure of Queensland borders used to demonstrate her strong stance on the pandemic. Similarly, Mark McGowan won a landslide victory in March 2021, with voters in Western Australia rewarding his government's handling of the pandemic.

The election of a new Labor government in May 2022 possibly signals a political reset. The new government has stated a desire to kick start the nation's immigration program (Galloway, 2022). That said, it remains unlikely the country will see a return in the near future to pre-pandemic levels of international travel, tourism and immigration. There has perhaps been a shift away from an open, globalized Australia to a more closed, parochial Australia. Immigration has historically been a vital ingredient of the modern Australian economy and society. Yet the experience of COVID-19 has cast immigration as an unambiguous threat to Australia's national sovereignty, with attendant implications on Australia's multiculturalism.

Multicultural Fragility and Nation-Building

The fragility of Australia's multiculturalism has, in many ways, been revealed through its legislative absence and the conduct of national politics. Unlike Canada, with its *Canadian Multiculturalism Act 1988* and the recognition of multiculturalism in its Charter of Rights and Freedoms, Australia does not yet have a legislative charter or constitutional statement enshrining its commitment to multiculturalism. Official adherence to multicultural policy relies upon periodic renewal by governments, whose ideological proclivities lead to disruptions and discontinuities (though that is by no means something confined to multiculturalism). Even then, the current formal expression of multiculturalism has raised questions about the substance of federal policy. The closest Australia comes to providing legislative expression to multiculturalism is through the *Racial Discrimination Act*, which prohibits racial discrimination and racial hatred, enables complaints about unlawful conduct to be made to the Australian Human Rights Commission and establishes the office of Race Discrimination Commissioner to advocate for racial equality and tolerance. But, as noted above, even the de facto legislative expression of multiculturalism has endured significant challenges, with the prolonged contests over the appropriate limits on free speech and the legal definition of racial hatred.

Evidence of multicultural fragility grows upon closer examination of the substance of multicultural commitments. To be fair, an assessment of Australia's multiculturalism should not be confined to the federal level: the presence of multiculturalism legislation at the state and territory levels in Australia, with accompanying statutory agencies responsible for conducting multicultural policy, means there is a robust local infrastructure that supports any multiculturalism projected nationally (Jupp, 2011: 51). Even so, the policy cupboard has been rather bare. At the federal level, aside from the delivery of grants for community groups and support for English language programs, multiculturalism is more symbolic than substantive as policy. For example, only with a new federal Labor government has there been renewed funding of dedicated anti-racism initiatives—the first time since that has happened since 2015 (Dreyfus and Giles, 2022). While the new funding committed (US$4.8 million) is significantly higher than that committed the last time Australia had a national anti-racism strategy from 2012 to 2015 (a mere US$1.25 million over four years), the quantum remains modest. Compare this with Canada, where the Trudeau government is spending total of US$76 million over three years on an anti-racism campaign aimed at countering the rise in racism linked to right-wing extremism (Jones, 2021).

Any renewal of multiculturalism will require a strengthened anti-racism commitment. After all, there are few graver threats to a multicultural society than racist prejudice and discrimination. If there is to be an anti-racist commitment, it must begin with the conduct of politics. As noted, there has been a politicization of race in recent years. While race politics is by no means new, there has been a coarsening of political sentiments. It has become increasingly common to find, for example, the charge that anti-racism has become the real racism in society today; that the most dangerous racism is that which is now supposedly directed at white Australians, the source of which is an ideological multiculturalism aligned with "cultural Marxism." It is tempting to understand this as a symptom of a global political shift towards nationalist populism. Brexit in the United Kingdom and the Trump presidency in the United States have emboldened some on the conservative right in Australia to be more aggressive in asserting claims about "reverse racism," and in expressing grievances on behalf of a white majority (Soutphommasane, 2018: 44).

The institutional character of Australian society, though, reflects something far from multicultural ascendancy. For all of Australia's success in multicultural social mobility, there appears to be a ceiling on this achievement. Using statistical modeling based on the 2016 census results on ancestry, the Australian Human Rights Commission (AHRC) estimated in 2018 that 58% of the Australian population have an Anglo-Celtic background, 18% have a European background, 21% have a non-European background and 3% have an Aboriginal or Torres Strait Islander background (Australian Human Rights Commission, 2018: 7). Based on its analysis of close to 2,500 senior leaders in business, politics, government and higher education, the AHRC found that almost 95% of leaders at the senior executive levels (chief executives and group executives, and their equivalents) have an Anglo-Celtic or European background (Australian Human Rights Commission, 2018: 8). Of the 372 chief executives and equivalents it identified, 97% have an Anglo-Celtic or European background (Australian Human Rights Commission, 2018: 9). Just over 94% of federal parliamentarians have an Anglo-Celtic or European background (with 4% having a non-European background and 1.5% having an Indigenous background) (Australian Human Rights Commission, 2018: 12). Although the recent federal election of May 2022 has resulted in the most culturally diverse Parliament ever represented (Soutphommasane, 2022), it is still some way from being broadly reflective of Australian society.

This has been one obvious limit to Australia's multicultural achievement: so little of its diversity is represented in the leadership of its institutions. The country pales in comparison with other similar liberal democracies that have multicultural and multiracial populations. At the time of writing, Canada's 30-odd strong cabinet features seven members who are "visible minorities." The majority of Joe Biden's 25-strong cabinet is non-white. In Britain, politicians from black and minority ethnic backgrounds fill three of the four "great offices of state." In New Zealand, the 20-strong cabinet features five ministers who are Māori.

There are multiple reasons why Australia's cultural diversity has not yet made its mark on the country's institutional character, some four decades since non-European immigrants began arriving in Australia in significant numbers. Structural barriers, including discrimination, are undoubtedly present, though they may not alone explain the status quo. Another explanation may be that it reflects the history of Australia's multicultural evolution. When multiculturalism was introduced in the 1970s, the change did not so much emerge from a groundswell of popular sentiment as reflect a top-down initiative, the presence of immigrant ethnic politics notwithstanding. Multiculturalism came almost as a gift from government, rather than something that had been decisively fought over—and won.

It is ironic, then, that political elite support for multiculturalism—for a long time, bipartisan and assured—is now proving more fickle. Historically, multiculturalism was driven by political leaders. But there has now emerged a gap between the strong headline support for multiculturalism and the deep ambivalence, if not hostility, towards multiculturalism from some elements of the conservative right in Australian politics. With some exceptions, nearly every politician is happy to declare that Australia is the most successful multicultural country in the world; yet that may also imply that they believe the work of multiculturalism has largely been done.

This itself may reflect Australia's historical experience in integrating immigrants. In its original expression, multiculturalism was in large part aimed to ensure that the immigrants and refugees who arrived in the immediate postwar years had their opportunity to become part of the family of the nation. With the increasing emphasis on skilled immigration from the 1970s onwards, much of the work of multicultural integration shifted from the state to the labor market and civil society. The nation-building ambition behind Australia's immigration program, and multicultural policy stance, has in the process lost some of its driving power. For decades following the Second World War, the nation-building rationale of immigration was axiomatic. Political leaders understood the need to build an immigration program that accepted as serving the national interest, and as enlarging the nation. People understood that those who came to Australia did so with ambitions to set up a new life and would in time become citizens and Australians.

This path to citizenship is no longer as clear as it may once have been. During the past two decades, migration has become market-driven with the advent of temporary migration. The old statist model, in which Australia's migration intake was set centrally by the federal government, is no longer. Right up until the pandemic, temporary migration was the engine of Australia's immigration program, which in recent years has been dominated by arrivals of skilled workers, international students and holidaymakers. Although many who arrive in Australia as temporary migrants end up as permanent residents and eventually citizens, their path is not viewed the way as the permanent settler-citizens of the past (Mares, 2016). The temporary migrant's place in society is a more vulnerable and contingent one, and their contribution to society understood primarily in economic terms rather than civic. The vice of the "guest worker" model, one that Australia had historically avoided by adopting a "multicultural citizenship" model to immigration, has inadvertently crept into its political culture. Only now, it seems, are policymakers beginning to change their minds—as evidenced by the new Labor government's move in September 2022 to rebalance Australia's migration program in favor of permanent immigration (O'Neil and Giles, 2022).

The hitherto preference for temporary immigration does go some way, though, to explaining the treatment of immigrants during COVID-19. There was little political difficulty for the Australian government to exclude many immigrants from emergency COVID-19 economic measures. Where a country views immigration primarily as a market exercise, concerned with extracting immediate economic benefit from immigrants, immigrants can become viewed as guests who can be returned home. It was all too revealing that, as the pandemic hit Australia, Prime Minister Scott Morrison told international students to return to their home countries, saying that "Australia must focus on its citizens and its residents" (McCauley and Chung, 2020).

Conclusion

Multiculturalism has been a nation-building success in Australia, with the national identity now incorporating a strong affirmation of cultural diversity. There is strong and stable public support for multiculturalism, backed by relatively high levels of social cohesion and mobility in Australia. International indexes of multiculturalism place Australia at the top of the league table, based on the apparent comprehensiveness of its multicultural policies (Tolley, 2011). The success of multiculturalism has been both normative—the vast majority of Australians are accepting of differences and are comfortable with a country that consists of many ethnicities and cultures—and semiotic—the vast majority of Australians accept and celebrate a story about Australian society that has welcomed all comers and extended equal citizenship to all within society.

However, Australia's multiculturalism is both robust and fragile. At the federal level, multiculturalism has only a de facto legislative instrument in the form of the *Racial Discrimination Act*, which has itself come under sustained political and ideological challenge. Official adherence to multiculturalism has in recent times been more rhetorical than substantive. Moreover, multiculturalism has yet to transform the institutional character of Australian life, which remains stubbornly Anglo-Celtic and far removed from the kind of multicultural diversity evident within the population and the official depiction of the national identity. If multiculturalism were meant to ensure structural change to society's institutions and ensure that the diversity of a population could be reflected in the places where power resides, then this has not yet happened. Australia's multiculturalism has been a more modest one, with the cultural norms and complexion of the country's Anglo-Celtic majority still very much imprinted within its major institutions.

The COVID-19 pandemic created additional challenges. It unleashed racialized fear and anger, particularly directed at Asian-Australians—in the process, reinforcing forms of anti-Asian racism that have been building as a result of rising geopolitical tensions between Australia and China, and mounting concerns about Chinese Communist Party influence within Australia. If anything, the pandemic has also seen an intensification of culture wars politicking around race, one linked to a resurgence of nationalist populism and right-wing extremism.

But there has been an arguably deeper, structural blow that COVID-19 has struck against multiculturalism. As part of the government response to the pandemic, Australia's borders from March 2020 to February 2022 were more or less closed to the world, with borders also closed at points between several states within the country itself. It is unlikely that a return to pre-pandemic levels of immigration will occur for at least a few years, if it does at all. Given the close historical association between multiculturalism and immigration, this may create or reinforce a certain public complacency towards the work of multiculturalism. There is a prospect that multiculturalism is considered a case of "mission accomplished," with no urgent need for multicultural policy if fewer immigrants are coming to Australia, rather than an ongoing project of civic integration. The risk is that Australia beats a retreat to the false security of "Fortress Australia," with borders closed off from the world and its people fearful of outside threats. If multiculturalism is to emerge from the pandemic intact, there will be a need for Australia's political debate to rediscover its nation-building imagination.

Notes

1 For accounts of the historical development of multiculturalism in Australia, see, e.g., Jupp, 2011; Soutphommasane, 2012; Levey, 2019.
2 For discussion of the debates about free speech, racism and the *Racial Discrimination Act*, see Soutphommasane, 2015; Soutphommasane, 2019.

References

Australian Bureau of Statistics. 2021. "Migration, Australia: Statistics on Australia's International Migration, Internal Migration (Interstate and Intrastate), and the Population by Country of Birth." 23 April 2021. https://www.abs.gov.au/statistics/people/population/migration-australia/2019-20

Australian Human Rights Commission. 2018. *Leading for Change: A Blueprint for Cultural Diversity and Inclusive Leadership Revisited*. Sydney: Australian Human Rights Commission. https://humanrights.gov.au/sites/default/files/document/publication/Leading%20for%20Change_Blueprint2018_FINAL_Web.pdf

Christodoulou, Mario. 2020. "ASIO Briefing Warns that the Far-Right is Exploiting Coronavirus to Recruit New Members." *Australian Broadcasting Corporation News*, June 12, 2020. https://www.abc.net.au/news/2020-06-12/asio-briefing-warns-far-right-is-exploiting-coronavirus/12344472#:~:text=Right-wing%20extremists%20now%20make%20up%20around%20a%20third,individuals%20is%20now%20second%20only%20to%20Sunni%20extremists.

Dreyfus, Mark and Giles, Andrew. "Labor Commits to New Anti-Racism Strategy." Media Statement, 13 May 2022. https://www.andrewgiles.com.au/media-centre/media-releases/labor-commits-to-new-anti-racism-strategy/

Galloway, Anthony. 2021. ""Words Matter": ASIO to Stop Referring to "Right-Wing" and "Islamic" Extremism." *The Age*, March 17, 2021. https://www.theage.com.au/politics/federal/words-matter-asio-to-stop-referring-to-right-wing-and-islamic-extremism-20210317-p57bme.html.

Galloway, Anthony. 2022. "Skilled migration: Australia could fall behind warns Immigration Minister Andrew Giles." *Sydney Morning Herald*, 21 August 2022.

https://www.smh.com.au/politics/federal/immigration-minister-warns-australia-could-fall-behind-on-skilled-migrants-20220818-p5baxm.html.

Grassby, Al. 1973. *A Multi-Cultural Society for the Future*. Canberra: Australian Government Publishing Service. http://www.multiculturalaustralia.edu.au/doc/grassby_1.pdf.

Hartwich, Oliver Marc. 2011. *Selection, Migration and Integration: Why Multiculturalism Works in Australia (And Fails in Europe)*. Sydney: Centre for Independent Studies. https://www.cis.org.au/publications/policy-monographs/selection-migration-and-integration-why-multiculturalism-works-in-australia-and-fails-in-europe/.

Hurst, Daniel. 2020. "Eric Abetz Refuses to Apologize for Demanding Chinese-Australians Denounce Communist Party." *Guardian Australia*, October 16, 2020. https://www.theguardian.com/australia-news/2020/oct/16/eric-abetz-refuses-to-apologize-for-demanding-chinese-australians-denounce-communist-party.

Jayasuriya, Laksiri. 1997. *Immigration and Multiculturalism in Australia*. Nedlands: School of Social Work and Social Administration, University of Western Australia.

Jones, Ryan Patrick. 2021. "Asian Canadians See Flaws in Federal Anti-Racism Strategy." *Canadian Broadcasting Corporation News*, April 8, 2021. https://www.cbc.ca/news/politics/anti-racism-strategy-asian-canadians-1.5977980.

Joppke, Christian. 2001. "Multicultural Citizenship: A Critique." *European Journal of Sociology 42* (2): 431–447.

Jupp, James. 2011. "Politics, Public Policy and Multiculturalism." In *Multiculturalism and Integration: A Harmonious Relationship*, Michael Clyne and James Jupp (eds.) Canberra: Academy of the Social Sciences in Australia, 41–52. https://press-files.anu.edu.au/downloads/press/p113381/pdf/book.pdf.

Kassam, Natasha and Jennifer Hsu. 2021. *Being Chinese in Australia: Public opinion in Chinese communities*. Sydney: Lowy Institute. https://interactives.lowyinstitute.org/features/chinese-communities.

Levey, Geoffrey Brahm. 2019. "The Turnbull Government's "Post-Multiculturalism" Multicultural Policy." *Australian Journal of Political Science 54* (4): 456–473. http://dx.doi.org/10.1080/10361146.2019.1634575.

Mares, Peter. 2016. *Not Quite Australian: How Temporary Migration Is Changing the Nation*. Melbourne: Text Publishing.

Markus, Andrew. 2021. *Mapping Social Cohesion: The Scanlon Foundation Surveys*. Melbourne: Scanlon Foundation Research Institute. https://scanloninstitute.org.au/sites/default/files/2021-02/SC2020%20Report%20Final.pdf.

McCauley, Dana and Laura Chung. 2020. "Coronavirus Australia: Scott Morrison Tells International Visitors to Go Home." *Sydney Morning Herald*, April 3, 2020. https://www.smh.com.au/politics/federal/go-home-scott-morrison-tells-international-visitors-20200403-p54gu2.html.

Morrison, Scott. 2020. "Ministerial Statement, Australian Parliament House." April 8, 2020. https://www.pm.gov.au/media/ministerial-statement-australian-parliament-house-act-080420.

Murphy, Katharine. 2020. "Scott Morrison: Black Lives Matter Protesters Should Be Charged if They Defy Advice and March." June 11, 2020. https://www.theguardian.com/australia-news/2020/jun/11/scott-morrison-if-black-lives-matter-protesters-defy-advice-and-march-they-should-be-charged.

Narushima, Yuko. 2010. "Obey the Law at Least, Abbott Tells Migrants." *Sydney Morning Herald*, January 22, 2010. https://www.smh.com.au/national/obey-the-law-at-least-abbott-tells-migrants-20100122-mqox.html.

O'Neill, Clare and Andrew Giles. 2022. "Australia's Migration Future". Joint Media Statement, 2 September 2022. https://minister.homeaffairs.gov.au/ClareONeil/Pages/australias-migration-future.aspx.

Phillips, Janet, Michael Klapdor and Joanne Simon-Davies. 2010. "Migration to Australia since Federation: A Guide to the Statistics." Background Note, Parliamentary Library of Australia. www.aph.gov.au/binaries/library/pubs/bn/sp/migrationpopulation.pdf.

Soutphommasane, Tim. 2005. "Grounding Multicultural Citizenship: From Minority Rights to Civic Pluralism." *Journal of Intercultural Studies* 26 (4): 401–416.

Soutphommasane, Tim. 2012. *Don't Go Back to Where You Came From: Why Multiculturalism Works*. Sydney: NewSouth Books.

Soutphommasane, Tim. 2015. *I'm Not Racist But … 40 Years of the Racial Discrimination Act*. Sydney: NewSouth Publishing.

Soutphommasane, Tim. 2018. "Race and Representation: Challenging the Myth of the Mainstream." *Griffith Review* 61: 43–50.

Soutphommasane, Tim. 2019. *On Hate*. Melbourne: Melbourne University Press.

Soutphommasane, Tim. 2020. "Multiculturalism is a Strength." In *Upturn*, Tanya Plibersek (ed.) Sydney: NewSouth Publishing, 210–219.

Soutphommasane, Tim. 2022. "We're about to have Australia's most diverse parliament—but there's still a long way to go". *The Conversation*, 24 May 2022. https://theconversation.com/were-about-to-have-australias-most-diverse-parliament-yet-but-theres-still-a-long-way-to-go-183620.

Soutphommasane, Tim and Marc Stears. 2020. "Two Australias." Thesis Eleven (online). https://thesiseleven.com/2020/08/28/two-australias/.

Tavan, Gwenda. 2005. *The Long, Slow Death of White Australia*. Melbourne: Scribe Publications.

Tolley, Erin. 2011. *Multiculturalism Policy Index: Immigrant Minority Policies*. Kingston: Multiculturalism Index Policy Project, School of Policy Studies, Queen's University. https://www.queensu.ca/mcp/sites/webpublish.queensu.ca.mcpwww/files/files/immigrantminorities/evidence/ImmigrantMinoritiesApr12.pdf.

Whitlam, Gough. 1985. *The Whitlam Government 1972–1975*. Melbourne: Penguin Books.

Zhou, Naaman. 2020. "Asian Australians Threatened and Spat on in Racist Incidents Amid Coronavirus." *Guardian Australia*, July 24, 2020. https://www.theguardian.com/australia-news/2020/jul/24/asian-australians-threatened-and-spat-on-in-racist-incidents-amid-coronavirus.

16

IMMIGRATION, MULTICULTURALISM AND TOLERANCE

Canada's Two Images

Paul May

Introduction

Canada is highly regarded internationally when it comes to immigration and to the integration of ethnocultural minorities; in fact, one might say that Canada's international "image" is unmistakably positive. To be sure, there is a lot to support this image. Canada has the highest rate of immigrants in the world as a proportion of its population (Pew Research Center, 2019a), and Canadians on the whole are generally more open to ethnocultural diversity compared to the population of other countries (The Environics Institute for Survey Research, 2019). The comparative literature on immigration tends to confirm this image: several key studies carried out on more than 50 countries (i.e., Migrant Integration Policy Index, 2020; European Union Democracy Observatory, 2017; Multicultural Policy Index, 2020) each rank Canada as the leading country in terms of immigrants' right to education and health or in terms of commitments to anti-discrimination policies.[1]

The evidence presented in this chapter brings into question the veracity of this image; in brief, materials discussed in this chapter show that Canada is in fact not as open to immigration as one might believe if one were to only rely on the country's international image. The chapter develops this argument through a comparison of the immigrant selection process in Canada, in the United States and, more generally, in the countries of the European Union. While the comparative literature on migrants' rights measures the rights of migrants according to a diverse set of criteria (such as access to education, to the labor market and to political participation), I choose here to focus exclusively on the immigrant selection process. This criterion greatly determines the other factors usually used to measure the rights of migrants. Indeed, a policy that provides

DOI: 10.4324/9781003197485-23

relatively easy access to healthcare and education, but which excludes the most precarious and vulnerable categories of the population from access to its territory, cannot be seen as genuinely open to immigration. Perhaps more importantly, particularly given this book's main theme, the immigration selection process can be seen as a critical precursor to multiculturalism; consequently, a restrictive process may very well suggest a determination in the types of diversity that are acceptable in the receiving society.

This chapter analyzes the selection process in operation in Canada, in the United States and in the countries of the European Union as it concerns the three categories of immigrants recognized by the administration of these three political entities: "economic," "family" and "humanitarian." I have chosen these three political entities because they are the top three destinations for immigrants (Migration Observatory, 2021). This comparison will highlight the greater selectivity of Canadian immigration policies, and put into perspective the positive image enjoyed by Canada in terms of the rights of immigrants. It will show that immigrants to Canada, even if they can benefit from an ensemble of cultural rights once they have obtained permanent residence, must go through a selection process that is harsher than the selection process in most other countries.

Following an overview of the relevant literature, the chapter develops its main argument in three parts. Part 1 describes a "Canadian paradox:" on the one hand, Canada receives one of the highest number of immigrants in proportion to the country's population while, on the other hand, Canada places great emphasis on the needs of its national economy, which has the effect of neglecting populations who are not considered of immediate use and importance to the economy. Part 2 examines refugee policy (refugees, in Canada, are accepted under the "humanitarian" category) using the example of Syrian refugees accepted into Canada in 2015–2016. I will show that, for geographical reasons, Canada does not face the same logistical challenges as European countries in receiving refugees, yet Canada still selects certain categories of refugees to the detriment of others, sometimes even overlooking people in the most precarious of situations. Part 3 of the chapter shows that, contrary to what one might believe given the country's international image, Canada's immigration system has actually been highly praised by parties of the political right in Europe. These parties see in the Canadian immigration system's selectiveness a source of inspiration for reforming national policies in their respective countries. In the eyes of these political parties, Canada is not the welcoming country open to ethnocultural diversity, as its international image would suggest. Canada's real "image," to these parties, is that of a calculating and utilitarian manager of immigration.

In sum, this chapter highlights an oft-overlooked Canadian duality. On the one hand, Canada receives a large number of immigrants and Canadian governments have implemented some of the most elaborate multicultural policies in the world (Multicultural Policy Index, 2020), including measures such as affirmative action, language rights and reasonable accommodation (Kymlicka, 1998). On the other hand, Canada also has an exclusionary side: Canadian governments have also developed one of the most selective immigration systems in the world, including in the area of the reception of refugees. Paradoxically, while Canada provides the basis for much of the theorizing on multiculturalism and is one of the first countries to adopt multiculturalism policies (and is often a source of inspiration for progressive forces around the world), Canada also provides a blueprint for right-wing political parties seeking to regulate and to reduce immigration. This chapter's main conclusion is that Canadian multiculturalism must be viewed alongside Canadian immigration policies.

Review of the Literature

The academic literature on migration ranks Canada among the countries that are the most open to immigration and the most respectful of migrant rights. The literature has three main facets.

The first facet measures, quantitatively, the rights of migrants and different ethnocultural minorities in various countries. It includes studies such as: the Migrant Integration Policy Index (2020), the European Union Democracy Observatory (2017) and the Multicultural Policy Index (2020). These studies use a series of indicators to measure the rights of migrants (such as access to permanent residence, access to work, access to housing, etc.) and the rights of ethnocultural minorities (such as bilingual curriculum, exemptions for dress codes in public administrations, etc.). For each indicator, countries are rated according to the more or less progressive nature of their legislation. In the case of the Multicultural Policy Index, for example, countries are rated with a score ranging from 0 (meaning complete lack of policy), 0.5 (partial policy adoption) or 1 (clearly stated policy). In each of these indices, Canada ranks among the highest scoring countries, both in terms of the rights of migrants and the rights of ethnocultural minorities. The Multicultural Policy Index gave Canada a score of 7 out of 8 for 2020, which was exceeded only by Australia's perfect score of 8 out of 8; the Migrant Integration Policy Index for 2019 ranks Canada in third position;[2] while the European Union Democracy Observatory does not provide a ranking of countries, it nonetheless identifies Canada as the most advanced country in terms of immigrant access to citizenship and to political participation.

A second facet of the literature features surveys carried out at regular intervals and the analysis of survey data. The comparative analysis of public opinion, for example, reveals a globally positive vision of immigration in Canada which contrasts with a more restrained or conservative attitude that prevails in other countries, to such an extent that some authors speak of a kind of "Canadian exceptionalism" (Bloemraad, 2012). To cite only the most recent studies, a survey published in 2019 by the Pew Research Center shows that Canada stands out from other Western democracies by the high proportion of its population who believe that immigration "makes the country stronger" (Pew Research Center, 2019b). Another major poll conducted in 2019 by the Environics Institute shows that the topic of immigration and refugees is low on the list of concerns of Canadians, far behind concern over the economy, the environment or international tensions (The Environics Institute for Survey Research, 2019). These attitudes contrast starkly with those in other countries, most notably the United States (Gallup World Poll, 2019). Additionally, a 2020 comparative study measuring the degree of acceptance of migrants in 145 countries around the world places Canada at the top of the list (Gallup World Poll, 2020).

A third facet of the literature examines the use of immigration and diversity to advance Canada's economic interests on the international stage. Supported by Canada's provincial governments and by private communications firms, the Canadian federal government projects an image of a dynamic, friendly country that is open to all forms of ethnic, religious and sexual diversity. This is what is commonly understood as "nation branding."[3] In recent years, this strategy has been used extensively by capitalist countries in the worldwide competition to increase their soft power and attractiveness on the international scene. In this context, Canada's diverse, educated, multicultural workforce is often portrayed as an asset in global competition: documents targeting investors celebrate the "diverse workforce" and "diverse, confident, creative, entrepreneurial people" (Investcanada, 2020). Openness to ethnocultural diversity is often among the indicators assessed by such agencies when they measure nation-branding potential (Brandfinance, 2017). Canada's nation branding is regularly ranked high by various research firms that advise governments and companies on investments (see Future Brand Country Index, 2019; Anholt-Ipsos Nation Brands Index, 2020; Forbes, 2018). Despite the apparent appeal of Canada's nation branding, some scholars have been critical of what they view as the instrumentalization of multiculturalism, which has reduced diversity to a mere competitive advantage in post-Fordist capitalist economies and a distraction from a politics of redistribution (Barry, 2001; Abu-Laban and Gabriel, 2002; Gitlin, 1995; Michaels, 2007; Miller, 2006).

Although each facet of the literature provides a different perspective, they nevertheless converge to emphasize the relatively open character of the Canadian immigration system and the country's greater acceptance of immigrants; in brief they paint an image of Canada as being "tolerant." The following sections in this chapter point, by contrast, to the restrictive nature of Canadian immigration policy thus highlighting an oft-overlooked feature in the current literature and, in turn, qualifying this point of convergence.

Methodological Sources and Theoretical Framework

This chapter draws from two methodological sources in order to develop its main argument. The first are government websites that collect immigration data: the Canadian Department of Immigration, US Homeland Security and the European Parliament and Eurostat. These three sources provide detailed information and the most up-to-date figures on three key categories of immigration: economic, family, humanitarian. I also rely on the United Nations High Commissioner for Refugees (UNHCR) website, which focuses particularly on the issue of refugees, to allow for comparisons between refugee policies in different countries. The second source is gathered from organizations carrying out studies on immigration from a comparative perspective: the OECD, the World Economic Forum and the Pew Research Center. These are the main independent international organizations that provide data on migration across the world by using different indicators (such as skill level, or the ratio of men to women in different categories of migrants in different countries). In the case of migration—my focus in this chapter—these sources allow us to compare the various measures implemented by states to select immigrants deemed eligible to enter the immigration process.

Part 1: Canada: A Selective Immigration System, Which Largely Excludes Precarious and Unskilled Applicants

This section shows that the process of selecting immigrants to Canada is carried out to the detriment of more precarious categories of migrants. I first explain how the Canadian immigration system works, and I then illustrate how this results in a composition of the immigrant population that is different from that of other Western countries. In fact, immigrants to Canada are on average significantly more skilled and many speak one of the country's two official languages (English and French); this means that they have far easier access to the receiving country's labor market than do immigrants in other immigrant-receiving countries (Kymlicka and Walker, 2012), particularly European countries (see Chapter 2 in Alba and Foner, 2015).

Canada is the country that receives the most immigrants in proportion to its population. The percentage of citizens who were born abroad is also particularly high (20.6%, compared to 12.6% in the United States and 13% in Germany). In 2019, 341,000 people—which is to say more than 1% of Canada's total population—acquired permanent residency. Overall, the total of those acquiring permanent residency has followed an upward curve, going from 271,835 in 2015 to 286,510 in 2017, 321,055 in 2018 and 341,180 in 2019 (Government of Canada, 2020). The plan for future years was announced by Marco Mendicino, Canada's Minister of Immigration, Refugees and Citizenship. The aim is to welcome over 400,000 permanent residents per year until 2023. This objective may prove difficult to reach because of the COVID-19 pandemic, which is limiting population movements; however, this announcement indicates a desire to continue the upward trajectory established in previous years. These data are often cited by experts and academics to emphasize Canada's openness with respect to immigration. However, they paint a partial picture of the situation and hide a contradictory development: while Canada[4] is indeed welcoming an increasing number of immigrants, it also has an extremely selective immigration system, especially in comparison with other Organisation for Economic Co-operation and Development (OECD) countries. To fully understand this selectiveness, it is necessary to look at the administrative procedure that immigrant applicants have to go through.

The heart of the immigration system is based on awarding points to applicants; this point system has the explicit purpose of ensuring that newcomers will be able to integrate into the job market rapidly thanks to their language skills as well as to their diplomas, acquired either in their country of origin or in Canada. The point system was first introduced in 1967 (Green and Green, 2004), at a time when officials sought to break with a system that had overwhelmingly favored immigrants from European countries. The pool of potential migrants has been expanded to all countries by evaluating applicants on the basis of their individual credentials, rather than on their ethnic or country origin. The point system was considered more meritocratic by the Liberal government of Prime Minister Lester B Pearson and was designed especially for that purpose. The result is that over the last 30 years, the selective aspect of immigration has clearly been accentuated. For example, in 1985, there were slightly more "family class" immigrants (in other words, people selected because of their family ties with Canadian citizens) than "economic class" immigrants (in other words, people selected on the basis of their professional skills), but by 2008 the proportions had been inversed, with 149,000 "economic class" immigrants compared with only 65,000 "family class" immigrants (Statistics Canada, 2012). In 2020, the figures were 196,658 and 91,311, respectively.

The Canadian immigration system has been modified many times since its creation. The last major overhaul of the system took place in 2015, when the "Express Entry" approach was put in place. The "Express Entry" approach takes the form of an online application platform providing rapid access to permanent residency for the most highly qualified applicants, in particular for professionals in high demand, such as engineers, computer scientists and healthcare professionals. In practice, permanent residency candidates are given points according to an ensemble of factors: some of the criteria that award more points are being young, having a sought-after diploma and fluency in at least one of Canada's two official languages (Government of Canada, 2020). Candidates with the highest scores are invited to submit applications for permanent residency. Each application takes about six months to process, which is fast compared to other liberal democracies (Bloemraad, 2012). Applicants who do not obtain a high score are not invited to apply for permanent residence. Thus, people over the age of 40, without university qualifications, with health problems or who do not specialize in a sought-after professional field, tend to be greatly penalized by the grading system.

The selective character of the Canadian immigration system stands out clearly when compared to that of the United States, as shown by an analysis of the US Department of Homeland Security. In 2016 in Canada, 63% of immigrants were accepted in the "economic" category, 24% in the "family" category and 13% in the "humanitarian" category (Immigration Refugees and Citizenship Canada, 2017). In the same year in the United States, the distribution was almost the opposite: 63% of immigrants were accepted in the "family" category, 21% in the "humanitarian" category and only 13% in the "economic" category (US Department of Homeland Security, 2017).[5] One of the repercussions of Canada's selection system is that immigrants' level of education is higher on average in Canada than in the United States. According to the Migration Policy Institute, in 2016, approximately half of the immigrants to Canada had a university diploma, compared with only 21% of the native-born population. In the United States, 30% of the 38.2 million immigrants aged 25 and over had a level of university education at least equal to a bachelor's degree, compared with 32% of the native-born population.

A comparison with other Western democracies, especially EU countries, leads to the same observation. An analysis of OECD data at global level shows that the proportion of immigrants who have attained tertiary level (a term used by the World Bank and the United Nations to define university level degrees) is on average 20% in Western European countries. In some countries, for example in New Zealand, Luxembourg and Israel, immigrants are proportionally over-represented in universities. It should be noted that in countries that have adopted a point system there is higher than average proportion of immigrants with university degrees: this is certainly the case of both Canada and Australia, where 60% and 47% respectively of adult immigrants hold a university level degree. Conversely, in Germany, France, Italy and Spain, the proportion of immigrants among post-secondary graduates is smaller than immigrants' overall proportion of the total population. This percentage drops to 11% in Slovenia, 12% in Italy and 19% in Greece. This is largely due to the fact that these countries have immigration policies that select migrants less on the basis of educational qualifications and language skills. Here again, Canada belongs to the category of countries, along with Luxembourg, Qatar and Israel, that receives a high proportion of immigrants, while at the same time, selecting immigrants scrupulously on the basis of their qualifications and excluding those which are not deemed immediately useful to the country's economy.

Additionally, Canada has one of the most restrictive visa issuance policies in the world. In this regard, the World Economic Forum ranks Canada 120th in the world out of a total of 136 surveyed countries, ranking Canada behind countries such as Albania, Estonia and Kazakhstan. This selectivity in the issuance of visas is specifically intended to avoid the presence of undocumented migrants, as migrants often become undocumented by staying in the country without having renewed their visa (World Economic Forum, 2017: 121).

In brief, Canada adopts a utilitarian approach in its immigration policies. The rigor of the immigrant selection process results in the composition of the immigrant population being different, in terms of gender, national origins and level of qualification compared to that of Europe. While this utilitarian approach has also been implemented in Europe—as evidenced by the introduction in 2009 of the "blue card" aimed at attracting the most qualified immigrants into the "global competition for talent" (OECD, 2016)—it is clear that applicants for immigration, particularly those with few qualifications based on selection criteria, still have more access to the immigration system in European countries than they would to Canada's immigration system (Beauregard et al., 2021; Gill, 2021). Canada's image is therefore open, but in reality, the immigration process is more selective than in other Western democracies, which comes to light when analyzing both the immigration process and the composition of the immigrant population.

Part 2: Humanitarian Crisis and Harsh Selection Criteria: The Syrian Refugee Experience in Canada

This part focuses on policies towards refugees. I will show that, in this area, in certain regards, Canada practices a much harsher selection than other Western countries, which contrasts with Canada's international reputation for openness. I illustrate my point by narrowing the temporal focus to 2014–2016, a period in time during which there was an influx of asylum seekers from Syria as a result of the Syrian Civil War.

When Canada welcomed 46,700 refugees, including 33,266 Syrians, beginning in late 2015 (UNHCR, 2017), this was widely celebrated in the media. Prime Minister Justin Trudeau, himself, went to the Toronto Pearson International Airport to welcome refugees personally and, in front of eager news cameras, handed out winter coats and chatted about the Canadian winter. This gesture was praised by Ban Ki-Moon, the then Secretary-General of the United Nations, who stated that Canada was "generous" in its refugee policy (United Nations, 2016). Yet, here again, the analysis of empirical sources reveals that, if we put the figures relating to the reception of refugees from Canada in comparative perspective with those of other countries, it becomes imminently clear that Canadian policy is no more progressive and no more open than policies implemented in other liberal democracies.

Administratively, Canada distinguishes between two categories of refugees (Waldman, 2021). The first category is that of resettled refugees, which includes Syrians settled in 2015–2016. These are individuals who were in refugee camps, such as those in Lebanon or Jordan, that were administered by the

UNHCR and who were then selected by the Canadian federal government to come to Canada. This process meant that resettled refugees were checked for criminal records, that they received a medical examination, that they were registered through the use of biometric measurements including an iris scanner (Government of Canada, 2020). Furthermore, Canada only accepted families, single women and children. Single men were excluded, except for those few who were in a position to establish evidence of persecution because of their membership of the LGBTQ community (International Migration Outlook, 2020). This measure sparked condemnation from Amnesty International on the grounds that the exclusion of single men, seen as a "potential threat," contributed to fueling the negative stereotypes that already exist about Arabs and/or Muslims (Amnesty International, 2015).

Refugees admitted to Canada can be sponsored by the government or by the private sector (such as businesses, community groups and religious organizations). Sponsors identify specific individuals, families or communities in UNHCR camps. They facilitate the resettlement process by providing financial support, by helping to find accommodation, and by facilitating the schooling of children. Although these measures aim to facilitate integration in the best possible conditions, they can also be seen as a means of filtering applicants for resettlement. In fact, by sponsoring certain people to the detriment of others according to (what amounts to) subjective criteria left up to private or community organizations to determine, it could be argued that refugee sponsorship actually reinforces an already selective refugee selection process.

A second category of refugees is those who flee their country of origin and who come to Canada to seek asylum directly by presenting themselves at the border, whether by land, sea or air. Syrian refugees welcomed to Canada in 2015–2016 do not fall within this category. Refugees in this category go through the relevant administrative procedures only when they arrive at the Canadian border. After their documents are checked, they sometimes have to wait several months for a response from Canadian immigration services to find out whether or not they will be granted refugee status. Here, a crucial element should be noted: in Canada, the proportion of refugees who fall into this category is very small compared to the proportion of resettled refugees (Government of Canada, 2020). This is mainly because access to Canadian territory is more difficult for geographic reasons. Canada is bordered by two oceans, and unlike the United States and certain European countries, Canada does not border a country or region where economic hardship and conflict has compelled people to leave their home and seek to emigrate elsewhere. As a result, Canada has relatively few asylum applications to process in any given year. And, when comparing the number of asylum applications to the population of the country for 2015–2016, Sweden (1.83%), Austria (1.47%) and Germany (1.44%) rank at the top of the list, whereas Canada comes in at 22nd (0.11%) (see International Migration Outlook, 2020). In brief, while the Trudeau government was applauded for welcoming Syrian refugees in 2015 and 2016, it must be kept in mind both that these resettled refugees underwent a very strict selection process, and, more generally, that Canada actually processes a far lower number of asylum claims each year than any other Western democracy.

Part 3: Canada's Immigration System: A Model for Right-Wing Political Parties?

European right-wing political parties (e.g., the German *Christlich Demokratische Union*, the British Conservatives or the French party *Les Républicains* for example) which want to look tough on immigration to cater to their electoral base have lauded the highly selective nature of the Canadian immigration system. More specifically, they sometimes praise the Canadian immigration system for its supposed effectiveness and as a model to follow, particularly when it comes to regulation and tying immigration to the needs of the economy. In addition, immigration policy under conservative governments and those contending with rising right-wing challengers shows an increasing Canadian influence. These phenomena are evident in the United Kingdom, France and Germany.

Since officially leaving the European Union on January 31, 2020, the United Kingdom has implemented a new immigration system. Following what had been promised by the *Leave* camp during the Brexit referendum, the Boris Johnson-led Conservative government adopted measures that limit the arrival of low-skilled immigrants (UK Government, 2020). The new immigration system is organized according to a point system, which has many similarities to the one that exists in Canada. Applicants for immigration to the United Kingdom are evaluated according to a scale defined by the Minister of State for Immigration; applicants obtain a score depending on their diplomas, their professional sector of activity and their mastery of the English language (UK Government, 2021). For example, a job offer from an approved employer gives the applicants 20 points, an English level B1 (i.e., evidence of an intermediate grasp of or semi-fluency in English) gives 10 points and a doctorate in a scientific discipline 20 points. To obtain a "skilled worker visa," 70 points are required, Priti Patel, the British Home Secretary, argued that the new system will "bring overall migration numbers down" while attracting "the brightest and the best from around the globe" (UK Government, 2020). When discussing the system's design, Boris Johnson explicitly stated that it was inspired by a "Canadian and Australian-style points-based system" (Migration Observatory, 2021) centered on the economic usefulness of migrants.

French right-wing political parties and political leaders have also applauded the Canadian immigration system, sometimes by name but also implicitly by invoking its key features. Former President Nicolas Sarkozy (2007–2012), a member of *Union pour un Mouvement Populaire* (UMP), which became *Les Républicains* in 2015, often used managerial and utilitarian rhetoric when discussing immigration. He frequently employed the term "chosen immigration" ("immigration choisie")—this term was also widely used by other UMP speakers and in the party's political program—in referring to the idea that France was penalized by waves of immigration that were mostly underqualified and unsuited to the job market. An analysis of parliamentary debates between the years 2010 and 2020 shows that UMP deputies present the Canadian immigration system as an example to follow due to its supposed "pragmatic" and "selective" character (May, 2016); the Canadian system is further contrasted to a French system perceived as too permissive and as largely consisting, much to the UMP's discontent, of family reunification immigration rather than of economic immigration. In 2013, Jean-François Copé, the then president of the UMP, traveled to several Canadian cities to discuss questions of immigration with Canadian civil servants. Once back in France, he proposed to "return to a system of economically chosen immigration, like Canada, in order to avoid being the most attractive country for illegal immigrants" (Viprey, 2013).

There is also evidence in France of a contagion from the right. President Emmanuel Macron, founder of the centrist *La République En Marche!*, also took up an instrumental approach to immigration in preparation for the 2022 French presidential elections. Macron chose to take measures aimed at reducing immigration it would seem both in response to public opinion demanding reinforced border controls (IFOP, 2019) and in light of the electoral challenges presented by three right-wing parties (i.e., *les Républicains, le Rassemblement National* and *Reconquête!*) all of whose leaders have been calling for the implementation of more restrictive immigration policies. The inspiration for a new French immigration system under Macron would likely be inspired by the Canadian system. In a 2019 press release, Macron approved of "the Canadian model" which allows the establishment of immigration quotas, with a set number of immigrants allowed to receive a visa for each category, as well as a reduction of family reunification immigrants (Présidence de la République, 2019).

During Angela Merkel's successive terms as Chancellor of Germany (2005–2021) one can see a gradual change towards an immigration system based on the selection of individuals considered most suitable for the labor market, coupled with a growing willingness to pay less attention to humanitarian concerns, and this despite Germany welcoming nearly one million Syrian refugees in 2015–2016. As early as 2005, a bill on immigration was introduced in the Reichstag that included a point system similar to the one in Canada[6] (Tometten, 2018). According to the bill, successful applicants would receive a permanent residence card only if they were specialized in specific high value-added technological sectors. While the bill did not pass at that time, the idea of drawing lessons from a Canadian-style immigration system continues to gain ground, albeit tacitly.

Since 2013, under the influence of Minister of the Interior Thomas de Maiziere, Germany has moved towards the establishment of a binary immigration system, favoring the arrival of skilled workers and seeking to limit low-skilled family immigration, as the latter is perceived as less useful to the country. It is still too early to know whether the government of Olaf Scholz, elected in September 2021, will depart from this utilitarian logic. Whatever may happen, the path that has been thus far laid out by successive conservative governments is one that mobilizes narratives related to entrepreneurial management. For example, a good immigration policy has to "attract" "skills," and "talents;" "value-added" immigration with increased "efficiency" are required to compete in a "global economy"; and, the aim of immigration is to attract "young," "dynamic" workers, with "skills" (especially students) best suited for the contemporary economy (Federal Government of Germany, 2022). In sum, this language evokes the Canadian immigration system not for its openness and welcoming nature, but rather for its supposed economic rationality and its alignment with capitalist logic.[7]

Conclusion

Canada's international image has long been tied to ethnocultural diversity and, more specifically, to multiculturalism in the form of guaranteed cultural and specific linguistic minority rights. Furthermore, large chunks of the academic literature on migrant rights highlight the fact that immigrants' access to education, social services and the labor market is generally better in Canada than it is in other Western democracies (a development that has been partly attributed to the success of Canada's multicultural policies). And, for Canadians, being welcoming to immigration and to ethnocultural diversity is a key feature of national belonging and pan-Canadian national identity. This identity also continues to define Canada's international image, one that also been articulated as a way of differentiating Canadians from their American neighbors.

However, the evidence presented in this chapter brings the veracity of this image into question. As this chapter has shown, a vital duality is overlooked if one buys the image of Canada as a paragon of virtue when it comes to immigration and ethnocultural diversity. The chapter's discussion of the selection process of immigrants from "economic" and "humanitarian" categories reveals, respectively, a tendency to attract a specific type of highly qualified immigrants, those who can be readily integrated into the labor market, and the exclusion of vulnerable migrant populations. Contrary to what one might have expected, the comparison between Canadian, American and European immigration systems demonstrates that the immigrant selection process in Europe and the United States is less harsh. All of this suggests that there is a duality when it comes Canadian multiculturalism. On the one hand, Canada is uncontestably a global leader in the design and implementation of multiculturalism policies. On the other hand, Canadian multiculturalism, understood as welcoming of demographic diversification and an openness to all, is an image (or self-image) that does not hold up under scrutiny.

Notes

1. This text deals specifically with immigrants, not migrants in general. An immigrant is a person who crosses an international border, and who becomes a permanent resident in another country. Migration can occur within the borders of the same country, as well as across international borders (Boucher and Guest, 2018).
2. The Migrant Integration Policy Index (MIPEX) measures integration policies (such as education, health, family reunification, etc.) towards migrants in 56 countries across the globe. For the year 2019, Canada is behind only Sweden and Finland.
3. Nation branding is a marketing strategy that uses the tools and techniques of commercial marketing to make a country more attractive to tourists, investors and skilled workers.
4. In Canada, immigration is managed jointly by the provinces and the federal government. However, in this chapter, I do not take account of this distinction, and I use the term "Canada" because it refers to the Canadian state as a whole. I follow the term used by the literature on the subject (see for instance, Irene Bloemraad, *Becoming a Citizen*, 2016).
5. In both Canada and the United States, the family-based category designates permanent residents who may sponsor foreign relatives to come to the country.
6. Bill BT-Drs. 15/420.
7. The Canadian immigration system has also been praised by the European right for altogether different, and disturbing, reasons. In 2010, Markus Ferber, a member of the Christian Social Union in Bavaria (the Bavarian sister party of the Christian Democratic Union) and member of the European parliament, made some extremely controversial comments in praise of the Canadian model, falsely suggesting that it drew from eugenics: "Canada is much further ahead with this and requires immigrant children to have a higher IQ than native-born children. Humanitarian motives such as reuniting families cannot be the only immigration criteria in the long term." Although these highly offensive remarks reveal a clear lack of knowledge of the Canadian immigration system, they show that, at least in the imagination of some right-wing political actors, Canada is understood as country that clearly favors a utilitarian instead of a humanitarian approach to immigration.

References

Abou-Chadi, Tarik and Werner Krause. 2020. "The Causal Effect of Radical Right Success on Mainstream Parties' Policy Positions - A Regression Discontinuity Approach." *British Journal of Political Science 50* (3): 829–847.

Abu-Laban, Yasmeen and Christina Gabriel. 2002. *Selling Diversity Immigration Multiculturalism, Employment Equity, and Globalization*. Peterborough: Broadview Press.

Alba, Richard D. and Nancy Foner. 2017. *Strangers No More: Immigration and the Challenges of Integration in North America and Western Europe*, Princeton University Press.

Albahari, Maurizio. 2016. *Crimes of Peace: Mediterranean Migrations at the World's Deadliest Border*. Philadelphia: University of Pennsylvania Press.

Amnesty International. 2015. https://www.amnesty.ca/syria/refugee-resettlement-serves-to-protect-the-most-vulnerable-among-the-refugees/.

Anderson, Christopher G. 2013. *Canadian Liberalism and the Politics of Border Control, 1867–1967.* Vancouver: University of British Columbia Press.

Barry, Barry. 2001. *Culture and Equality: An Egalitarian Critique of Multiculturalism.* Cambridge, MA: Harvard University Press.

Beauregard, Pierre-Loup, Alain-G. Gagnon, and Jean-Denis Garon. 2021. "Managing Immigration in the Canadian Federation: The Case of Quebec." In *International Affairs and Canadian Migration Policy, Canada and International Affairs*, Y. Samy and H. Duncan (eds.)Cham: Springer International Publishing, 227–245.

Bloemraad, Irene. 2012. *Understanding "Canadian Exceptionalism" in Immigration and Pluralism Policy.* Washington, DC: Migration Policy Institute.

Boucher, Anna and Justin Gest. 2018. *Crossroads Comparative Immigration Regimes in a World of Demographic Change.* Cambridge and New York: Cambridge University Press.

Brandfinance. 2017. https://brandfinance.com/wp-content/uploads/1/bf_nation_brands_2017.pdf.

de la République, Présidence. Élysée 2019. https://www.elysee.fr/emmanuel-macron/2019/01/13/lettre-aux-francais.

Environics Institute for Survey Research. 2019. https://www.environicsinstitute.org/docs/default-source/project-documents/focus-canada-fall-2019---immigration-refugees/focus-canada-fall-2019-survey-on-immigration-and-refugees---final-report.pdf?sfvrsn=56c2af3c_2.

European Parliament. 2017. https://www.europarl.europa.eu/news/en/headlines/society/20170629STO78630/asylum-and-migration-in-the-eu-facts-and-figures

Eurostat. 2020. https://ec.europa.eu/eurostat/statistics-explained/index.php/Asylum_statistics#Age_and_gender_of_first-time_applicants.

Federal Government of Germany. 2022. https://www.make-it-in-germany.com/en/visa-residence/skilled-immigration-act.

Fenge, Terry and Jim Aldridge (eds.). 2015. *Keeping Promises: The Royal Proclamation of 1763, Aboriginal Rights, and Treaties in Canada.* Montreal and Kingston: McGill-Queen's University Press.

Forbes. 2018. https://www.forbes.com/best-countries-for-business/list/.

Future Brand Country Index. 2019. https://www.futurebrand.com/uploads/FCI/FutureBrand-Country-Index-2019.pdf.

Gallup World Poll. 2019. https://news.gallup.com/poll/249092/americans-say-government-immigration-lead-woes.aspx?utm_source=alert&utm_medium=email&utm_content=morelink&utm_campaign=syndication.

Gallup World Poll. 2020. https://news.gallup.com/poll/320669/canada-migrants-sixth-place.aspx.

Gill, Jasmine. 2021. Canada's Position in the Global Competition for Talent. In *International Affairs and Canadian Migration Policy, Canada and International Affairs*, Y. Samy and H. Duncan (eds.) Cham: Springer International Publishing, 111–129.

Gitlin, Todd. 1995. *The Twilight of Common Dreams: Why America is Wracked by Culture Wars.* New York: Metropolitan Books.

Government of Canada. 2014–2019. https://www.international.gc.ca/education/report-rapport/strategy-strategie-2014/index.aspx?lang=eng.

Government of Canada. 2020. https://www.canada.ca/en/immigration-refugees-citizenship/corporate/publications-manuals/annual-report-parliament-immigration-2020.html.

Green, Alan G. and Green, David. 2004. "The Goals of Canada's Immigration Policy: A Historical Perspective." *Canadian Journal of Urban Research 13* (1): 102–139.

Immigration Refugees and Citizenship Canada. 2017. https://www.canada.ca/en/immigration-refugees-citizenship.html.

Immigroup. 2019. https://www.immigroup.com/news/illegal-immigration-canada

Institut français d'opinion publique. https://www.ifop.com/publication/les-francais-et-limmigration-6/.

ICEF Monitor. 2014. https://monitor.icef.com/2014/01/canadas-new-international-education-strategy-aims-for-450000-students-by-2022/.

International Migration Outlook. 2020. https://www.compareyourcountry.org/migration?cr=oecd&lg=en&page=2&visited=1.

Investcanada. 2020. https://www.investcanada.ca/why-invest/workforce?creative=490955700622&keyword=%2Bcanada%27s%20%2Bdiversity&matchtype=b&network=g&device=c&gclid=EAIaIQobChMIiszTndWR7wIVzdrVCh1-BgM4EAAYASAAEgJj_fD_BwE.

Just, Aida. 2017. "The Far-Right, Immigrants, and the Prospects of Democracy Satisfaction in Europe." *Party Politics 23* (5): 507–525.

Kelley, Ninette and M.J. Trebilcock. 1998. *The Making of the Mosaic: A History of Canadian Immigration Policy*. Toronto and Buffalo: University of Toronto Press.

Kymlicka, Will. 1998. *Finding Our Way: Rethinking Ethnocultural Relations in Canada*. Toronto and New York: Oxford University Press.

Kymlicka, Will and Kathryn Walker. 2012. *Rooted Cosmopolitanism Canada and the World*. Vancouver: University of British Columbia Press.

Kymlicka, Will. 2018. "The Rise and Fall of Multiculturalism? New Debates on Inclusion and Accommodation in Diverse Societies." *International Social Science Journal 68* (227–228): 133–148.

May, Paul. 2016. "Ideological Justifications for Restrictive Immigration Policies: An Analysis of Parliamentary Discourses on Immigration in France and Canada (2006–2013)." *French Politics 14* (3): 287–310.

Michaels, Walter Benn. 2007. *The Trouble with Diversity: How We Learned to Love Identity and Ignore Inequality*. 1. Holt paperback (ed.) [Nachdr.]. New York: Metropolitan Books.

Migration Observatory. 2021. https://migrationobservatory.ox.ac.uk/resources/primers/policy-primer-the-uks-2021-points-based-immigration-system/.

Miller, David. 2006. "Multiculturalism and the Welfare State: Theoretical Reflections." In *Multiculturalism and the Welfare State*, K. Banting and W. Kymlicka (eds.) Oxford: Oxford University Press, 322–338.

New York Times, December 8, 2015. https://www.nytimes.com/2015/12/13/magazine/trudeaus-canada-again.html.

Norris, Pippa. 2020. "Measuring Populism Worldwide." *Party Politics 26* (6): 697–717. https://doi.org/10.1177/1354068820927686.

Opendemocracy. 2020. https://www.opendemocracy.net/en/pandemic-border/are-canadians-changing-their-attitude-migration-due-covid-19/.

Organisation for Economic Co-operation and Development. 2016. https://www.oecd.org/migration/europe-is-underachieving-in-the-global-competition-for-talent.htm.

Pew Research Center. 2016. https://www.pewresearch.org/global/2016/08/02/number-of-refugees-to-europe-surges-to-record-1-3-million-in-2015/.

Pew Research Center. 2019b. https://www.pewresearch.org/global/2019/03/14/around-the-world-more-say-immigrants-are-a-strength-than-a-burden/.

Ryan, Phil. 2010. *Multicultiphobia*. Toronto and Buffalo: University of Toronto Press.
Statistics Canada. 2012. https://www150.statcan.gc.ca/n1/pub/91-209-x/2011001/article/11526/tbl/tbl-eng.htm#a1.
Stein, Sharon. 2018. "National Exceptionalism in the "EduCanada" Brand: Unpacking the Ethics of Internationalization Marketing in Canada." *Discourse: Studies in the Cultural Politics of Education 39* (3): 461–477.
Tometten, Christoph. 2018. "En Allemagne, quelle loi pour une terre d'immigration?" *Revue des droits de l'homme*. Actualités Droits-Libertés.
UK Government. 2020. https://www.gov.uk/government/news/home-secretary-announces-new-uk-points-based-immigration-system.
UK Government. 2021. https://www.gov.uk/government/publications/uk-points-based-immigration-system-employer-information/the-uks-points-based-immigration-system-an-introduction-for-employers.
UNHCR. 2017. https://www.unhcr.org/en-us/news/press/2017/4/58fe15464/canadas-2016-record-high-level-resettlement-praised-unhcr.html.
United Nations. 2016. https://news.un.org/en/story/2016/02/522042-canada-ban-applauds-countrys-commitment-resettle-25000-syrian-refugees.
US Department of Homeland Security. 2017. https://www.dhs.gov/sites/default/files/publications/2016%20Yearbook%20of%20Immigration%20Statistics.pdf.
Viprey, Mouna. 2013. "Immigration choisie, immigration subie : du discours à la réalité." *La Revue de l'Ires 64* (1): 149–169.
Waldman, Lorne. 2021. *Canadian Immigration and Refugee Law Practice*. Markham: Lexisnexis Canada.

CONCLUSION

Towards a New Diversity Politics for the 21st Century? Building on Multiculturalism through Solidarity

Yasmeen Abu-Laban, Alain-G Gagnon and Arjun Tremblay

Using the annual Multiculturalism Day in June of 2021 as an occasion to signal the upcoming 50th anniversary of official multiculturalism in Canada (October 8, 2021), Canadian Prime Minister Justin Trudeau, who has staunchly supported the policy that his father Pierre Trudeau introduced in 1971, offered a sober assessment on its impact and on the current state of majority–minority relations in Canada. In Justin Trudeau's words:

> This year, we mark an important anniversary. Fifty years ago this fall, Canada became the first country in the world to adopt a policy of multiculturalism, which was later enshrined in law through the Canadian Multiculturalism Act. While we have made important progress toward a more inclusive and equitable society since then, much work remains to be done. Every day, far too many racialized Canadians, Indigenous peoples, and religious minorities continue to face systemic racism, discrimination, and a lack of resources and opportunity.
>
> Sadly, over the last year and a half, the COVID-19 pandemic has revealed and deepened social, health, and economic disparities, and seen a rise in threats and violence against many of these communities. The tragic events of the past several weeks are painful reminders that Canada has not always lived up to its ideals, and that many Canadians continue to feel fear and insecurity simply because of the colour of their skin, their background, or their faith.
>
> *(Trudeau, 2021)*

The tragic events of the preceding weeks that Trudeau references included the locating of, through ground-penetrating radar (Austen, 2021), the first of

DOI: 10.4324/9781003197485-24

thousands of bodies of missing Indigenous children who lost their lives at state- and church-run Indian residential schools in operation from the 1880s to the 1990s. Trudeau's comments also came just after a man, suspected of consuming white supremacist materials, used a vehicle to murder a Muslim family, killing four on June 6, 2021, in London, Ontario (Yun, 2022).

Given that a Canadian political leader who backs multiculturalism cannot square it with ongoing inequities and death, it is perhaps not surprising that several of the volume's contributors are wary of multiculturalism's promise. In what follows, we review the findings of the preceding chapters to showcase points of overlap and disagreement when it comes to defining multiculturalism, to weighing its utility and effectiveness, and to assessing its value as a 21st century politics of diversity. Our overview indicates the necessity of being attuned both to how multiculturalism is understood, as well as to its temporal and historical context. Therefore, rather than positioning multiculturalism as an unalloyed good (or bad) phenomenon, we argue that its promise stems from being a possible entry point into a larger politics of solidarity. Put differently, as a politics of diversity, we suggest that multiculturalism *may* potentiate solidarity at national and international levels, but this requires ongoing engagement as well as reflection by policy-makers and publics alike.

Situating and Comparing the Findings: This Volume

This volume set out to interrogate the future of "multiculturalism" in the 21st century as a form of diversity politics. Multiculturalism, as we have seen, has extended from its Canadian roots as a 1971 national policy response, to become a term that has been taken up by policymakers, publics and scholars in many different contexts globally. Despite multiculturalism's rapid ascent and global reach, it is clear that in Canada and beyond, there are debates about multiculturalism in terms of its value, efficacy and the likelihood of its survival. This necessarily tempers any enthusiastic or categorical embrace of the concept, particularly by those concerned by the gross inequities stemming from settler colonization, colonialism and slavery. Indeed, any categorical assertions of multiculturalism's future rest uneasily with ongoing forms of socio-economic and racialized inequality, the post 9/11 proliferation of anti-Muslim racism, xenophobic right-wing populist attacks on dislocation and migration and the exacerbation of anti-Asian discrimination during the COVID-19 pandemic.

In this concluding chapter, we provide an overview of the diverse findings of authors in this volume to offer a reflection on both the Canadian and international comparative dimensions of multiculturalism as a form of diversity politics. It is clear that contributors to this volume do not speak with one voice. The chapters differ, sometimes in significant fashion, when it comes to their understanding of what multiculturalism is, how it should be understood, how it works, who it benefits, as well as whether multiculturalism should be reformed, abandoned or transformed. Below we reflect on each of these dimensions.

Multiculturalism's Terminological Complexity

As indicated in the volume's introduction, while the term "multiculturalism" was coined in Canada, even here it was subject to different understandings. This terminological complexity is only amplified when we turn to the global context. Not surprisingly then, this volume's contributors highlight multiculturalism's many usages and, in so doing, take up its terminological complexity. Although some may argue that this terminological complexity is counterproductive to the comparative study of multiculturalism, we aim to show in the following pages that multiculturalism's conceptual elusiveness is in fact a boon for several reasons. Most notably, multiculturalism's terminological complexity helps to provide a more comprehensive and accurate picture of the ebb and flow of the politics of diversity.

Some chapters in this volume (i.e., Bloemraad, Gouws) engage multiculturalism's terminological complexity directly. For example, Irene Bloemraad's chapter acknowledges that multiculturalism is often used as a descriptor of "demographic pluralism"—a usage of multiculturalism that refers to immigrant-generated diversity. Bloemraad notes how this usage sometimes, but not always, includes Indigenous peoples and national minorities under its descriptive ambit. Additionally, Bloemraad takes up a recurring definition in comparative studies of multiculturalism and points to multiculturalism as a term that refers to both a "range of policies that aim to recognize and accommodate ethnoracial and religious diversity and … [to] a public discourse that affirms and valorizes diversity in origins, culture and religions" (Bloemraad, Ch. 2: 39). Similarly, Amanda Gouws's chapter addressing South Africa discusses multiculturalism as a "concept" and employs the term multicultural as a descriptor of societies consisting of multiple cultures and of specific kinds of diversity-oriented "policy frameworks … [that provide] every individual with a cultural reference point and sense of belonging to a particular ethnic community" (Gouws, Ch. 5: 97).

Other chapters in this volume (i.e., Kymlicka, Triandafyllidou, Modood, Teo, Thompson, Körtvélyesi) center on one particular understanding of multiculturalism rather than engaging it on multiple fronts. For instance, multiculturalism is sometimes understood as distinct and characteristic of the age of migration and as inextricably linked to state citizenship and to membership in political communities. This understanding of multiculturalism is deployed in chapters by Will Kymlicka, Anna Triandafyllidou, Tariq Modood and Terri-Anne Teo. Taken together, these chapters explore multiculturalism as a means to enhance the scope and facilitate the acquisition of citizenship rights (i.e., "multiculturalism-as-citizenization," see Kymlicka's chapter), as a set of rights traditionally associated with a narrow sense of "national membership" rather than a more broadly defined and encompassing "effective membership" (see Triandafyllidou chapter) and (in chapters by Modood and Teo) as a framework that captures the extent of minority involvement in the construction of state citizenship, here understood not as rights-based citizenship but as citizenship in the form of a "sense of belonging" (Bloemraad et al., 2008: 154).

Chapters by Debra Thompson and by Zsolt Körtvélyesi examine multiculturalism as types of public policies; more specifically, types of public policies that recognize and accommodate the cultures, languages, religions and customs of polyethnic minorities (which is to say minorities borne out of individual and familial immigration). This understanding of multiculturalism is most commonly associated with Will Kymlicka and Keith Banting's collaborative scholarship (addressed in this volume's introduction) which has resulted in the creation of the Queen's University Multiculturalism Policy Index (MPI).

Eschewing the top-down approach to defining multiculturalism advanced by the MPI, some chapters in the volume (i.e., Freeman-Maloy and Tatalovich, Soutphommasane, Bhatia) take a more explicitly bottom-up approach to developing highly contextualized definitions of multiculturalism. For example, Maloy Freeman and Tatalovich argue that American multiculturalism is mainly evidenced by policies that accommodate Americans of limited English proficiency. In her chapter, Bhatia contends that Indian multiculturalism predates its Western counterparts and that, as opposed to other forms of multiculturalism, it has emerged alongside state secularism in the form of the constitutional recognition of cultural pluralism and the enshrinement of "institutional and political measures for accommodation of various groups" (Bhatia, Ch. 10: 184). And Soutphommasane shows that Australian multiculturalism, in contrast to most other forms of state and official multiculturalism, was originally wedded to the development of an anti-racist policy agenda.

Several chapters in this volume (i.e., Eisenberg, Ladner et. al., May, Mathieu) discuss Canadian multiculturalism and highlight its origins in national level public policy in the early 1970s. These chapters also weave a rich historical and contextual tapestry that brings to light features of Canadian multiculturalism that may sometimes go overlooked in broader comparative discussions. For one, chapters by Avigail Eisenberg and by Kiera Ladner, Hope Ace, Marcus Closen and Dane Monkman situate the development of Canadian multiculturalism within the context of settler colonialism and show that, in contrast to certain theoretical understandings, multiculturalism as a political project in Canada effectively excluded and maybe even demobilized Indigenous peoples. Offering a different take on Canadian multiculturalism, beyond the context of settler colonialism, Paul May draws a distinction in his chapter between an outwardly projected inclusionary vision of Canadian multiculturalism as it relates to immigrants and immigration and a restrictive immigration regime that shapes Canada's multicultural demographic reality. And, examining Canada as a multinational state, Félix Mathieu's chapter distinguishes between, on the one hand, multiculturalism as Canada's federal model of pluralism and, on the other, interculturalism as a sub-state model for accommodating polyethnic diversity, particular to the context of a minority nation.

While most chapters in this volume explore multiculturalism at the domestic level, Dolores Morondo Taramundi's chapter is unique in that it ties into a discussion on the design and proliferation of international multicultural norms and laws (see Kymlicka, 2013; de Sousa Santos, 2017; Delgado-Moreira, 2017). Morondo Taramundi's chapter contributes to this discussion by showing how European supranational organizations have, at different times, defined cultural diversity as an "interstate," "trans-state" or "intrastate" "issue" and that, more recently, cultural diversity has come to be "associated with immigration flows and the processes of globalization" (Morondo Taramundi, Ch. 7: 132). In turn, addressing these "issues" is primarily interlinked with the aims of protecting vulnerable groups and ensuring political stability within and across European democracies.

In brief, the chapters in this volume show that the term "multiculturalism" is multifaceted and that its meanings differ both in relation to context and sometimes to observer. While some might clamor for a unified definition of multiculturalism, we see three main advantages to the multiplicity of understandings and meanings of multiculturalism advanced in this volume.

Firstly, this multiplicity provides a more comprehensive account of multiculturalism's complex cross-national emergence and increases the comparative ambit of discussions on multiculturalism to include Australia, North America, Western Europe, Asia, South Asia, South-East Asia and Eastern Europe. Consequently, this volume may help to address a criticism that has been leveled against the MPI. As previously noted, the MPI traces annual policy commitments (from 1960 onwards) to an "accommodating approach to diversity" across 21 countries. To be sure, the MPI plays a critical role in demonstrating the existence of a variety of multiculturalism policies (MCPs) in political contexts where the term multiculturalism is largely absent and even derided in public discourse. Yet the MPI has been criticized on the grounds that its typology of MCPs has a distinctly "Canadian flavour" (Entzinger, 2006: 187) and that it may not accurately reflect multiculturalism's origins and development in other countries. The chapters in this volume, in particular those that take a bottom-up approach to defining and describing multiculturalism, flesh out multiculturalism's objectives and its institutional, social and political manifestations all the while acknowledging Canadian centrality in multiculturalism's origins and development.

Secondly, contradictory multicultural trends are better captured by scholarship that does not rely on a single indicator of multiculturalism's meaning and effect. By discussing multiculturalism as a demographic phenomenon relating to increased population diversity, as a form of citizenship and belonging, as a type of policy, and against the backdrop of different cultural diversity "issues," this volume paints a more accurate picture of multiculturalism's global trajectory and highlights its contradictions. Consequently, we cannot categorically confirm either suspicions that we are now bearing witness to the "retreat from multiculturalism" (Joppke, 2004) or be overly comfortable about the overall health of diversity politics as evidenced, in part, by the persistence and even global expansion of multiculturalism policies, even when taking into account contextual as well as definitional diversity (Banting and Kymlicka, 2013).

Thirdly, and the point to which we turn in the following section, this multiplicity is significant when considering the unique challenges of the 21st century. Specifically, it provides a distinct combination of cross-national and sometimes distinct (*sui generis*) measures that may pave the way not merely for describing empirical variation, but for a normative reimagining of multiculturalism's effectiveness given the complexities of the 21st century.

Multiculturalism's Mixed Record of Effectiveness

The chapters in this volume also add to an ongoing discussion on multiculturalism's effectiveness. As a package, evidence presented in this volume suggests that multiculturalism's record at its semicentennial is neither one of unmitigated successes nor of complete failures: it is mixed.

A discussion on multiculturalism's effectiveness took center stage in scholarship on multiculturalism during the first decade of the 21st century following a shift in the Netherlands in public discourse on immigration as well as in immigrant integration policies. Indeed, scholarly texts have described the debate with titles such as "The Demise of Dutch Multiculturalism" (Carle, 2006), "The Rise and Fall of Multiculturalism: The Case of the Netherlands" (Entzinger, 2014) and "From Toleration to Repression: The Dutch Backlash against Multiculturalism" (Prins and Saharso, 2010). The changes captured in scholarship on Dutch multiculturalism inevitably raised the question as to why a country with an ostensibly strong commitment to cultural and religious recognition would pare down its multiculturalism policy framework. The most direct answer to this question was provided by Christian Joppke in "The Retreat from Multiculturalism in the Liberal State: Theory and Policy" (2004). Joppke argues that a "retreat" of multiculturalism evident in the Netherlands (and elsewhere) is attributable to three factors: a "re-assertiveness of the liberal state" (a concept that remains ill-defined); a lack of public support for multiculturalism policies; and, perhaps most importantly, to the failure of multiculturalism policies "with respect to the socio-economic marginalization and self-segregation of migrants and their children" (Joppke, 2004: 244).

An ensuing scholarship on multiculturalism's effectiveness has taken this assessment to task and yielded a variety of different perspectives and assessments.

One of the key contributors to this endeavor has been Will Kymlicka who has, on his own and in collaboration with Keith Banting, provided evidence of multiculturalism's positive effects on democratic values (Kymlicka, 2010), interpersonal trust (Banting and Kymlicka, 2004) and national solidarity (Kymlicka and Banting, 2006). Within the Canadian context, Banting and Kymlicka (2010) have demonstrated that multiculturalism has a positive impact on immigrant integration and on societal attitudes of the majority toward new arrivals, but that Canada is still grappling with persistent anti-Indigenous and other forms of racism.

According to some chapters (i.e., Ladner et. al., Eisenberg, Mathieu) in this volume, not only is multiculturalism *not* working, it may also be counterproductive to the development of a more inclusive politics of diversity. For one, despite multiculturalism's apparent success in Canada, it may also be hindering the development of a pluri-national politics that centers Indigenous peoples and Indigenous legal traditions and that recognizes minority nations. This assessment of Canadian multiculturalism advances that Canada's official policy of multiculturalism is embedded within a settler-colonial narrative that embraces a language of individual empowerment and that its enshrinement is effectively "a rebuff of the nations within" (Ladner et al., Ch. 11: 203). Canada's multiculturalism policy is also critiqued for doing nothing to recognize and empower Indigenous legal and political authority (Eisenberg's chapter). Moreover, in regard to the Francophone minority nation of Quebec, it has been critiqued for failing to recognize imbalances in power between groups and for reaffirming, although implicitly, a monist nation-state framework (Mathieu's chapter).

Multiculturalism's effectiveness is also brought into question by its failure to provide remedies to racialized exclusions. Debra Thompson's chapter clearly brings to light this indicator of multiculturalism's *in*effectiveness by showing that even in countries with robust multiculturalism policy frameworks (Canada and the United States) one can witness "persistent racial economic inequality, rampant political suppression, and the frequent violent encounters with the state experienced by Black populations" (Thompson, Ch. 12: 221). There is even evidence that policy responses associated with multiculturalism can be redeployed to serve illiberal anti-multicultural objectives. As we saw in Zsolt Körtvélyesi's chapter, Hungary's Fidesz government promoted dual citizenship not as a policy intended to facilitate the immigrant integration process but as "nationalist policy with irredentist overtones" (Körtvélyesi, Ch. 13: 235).

Additionally, multiculturalism, understood in particular ways, may prevent the development of a politics of diversity that recognizes the importance of religious identities. Tariq Modood argues that this is the main conceptual and theoretical limitation of the politics of diversity proposed by what might be termed the "Canadian School of Multiculturalism" (Tremblay, 2021). More specifically, he argues that:

> For a multiculturalist it is disappointing that whilst recognizing the significance of the individual spiritual dimension so central and important for many religious adherents, there is no equivalent appreciation of the religious communities in which most individuals come to acquire and live out the significance of religion
>
> *(Modood, Ch. 9: 168)*

To be clear, some contributors to this volume disagree that multiculturalism is ineffective and exclusionary. Rather, they suggest that multiculturalism is still effective and also inclusionary, albeit in different ways and to varying degrees. To be sure, Tim Soutphommasane does argue that Australian multiculturalism has been unable to respond effectively to the anti-Asian racism exacerbated by the COVID-19 pandemic. But he also states that "an assessment of Australia's multiculturalism should not be confined to the federal level" (Ch. 15: 274) and that multicultural frameworks at the state-level are far more "robust" (ibid.). Irene Bloemraad, for her part, addresses both the limitations and utility of immigrant-centered multiculturalism policies. On the one hand, she argues that while there is no indication that multiculturalism policies negatively impact immigrant socio-economic integration, there is also scant comparative evidence of their positive effects in this matter. On the other hand, Bloemraad shows that "there is a stronger evidentiary case for the arguments that multicultural policies and discourse facilitate political and civic incorporation" (12) and that there is preliminary evidence that countries with strong institutional and policy commitments to multiculturalism have thus far been able to stave off right-wing anti-immigrant populism.

Similarly, Will Kymlicka's chapter provides evidence for multiculturalism's "real but incomplete citizening effects" (Ch. 1: 19). More specifically, Kymlicka argues that multiculturalism (at least within the Canadian context) has been effective in challenging "hierarchies of worthiness" (9) and that "multiculturalism is associated with higher levels of public support for the right of minorities to access welfare benefits, to have cultural accommodations, and to share political power" (9). However, Kymlicka does concede that multiculturalism's effects remain "incomplete" given the persistence of anti-Black and anti-Muslim prejudices.

Multiculturalism's Near- and Longer-Term Future

Contributors to this volume also have different outlooks when it comes to multiculturalism's future. Several contributors believe that there must be a change to the status quo and, accordingly, they present a range of possible frameworks to either reform or to perhaps even replace multiculturalism. Debra Thompson presents an alternative to multiculturalism in the form of the Movement for Black Lives and abolition democracy. Specifically, Thompson argues that "[while] multiculturalism is preoccupied with the recognition of individual and group identities within a liberal democratic framework, the Movement for Black Lives is premised on the transformation of our society as we know it" (13). Following from this, abolition democracy seeks to upend exploitative capitalism and advocates "the necessity of defunding, and eventually, abolishing the police" (15).

Another framework is articulated in chapters by Eisenberg and by Ladner et. al. Taken together, these chapters advance two major reforms to Canada's existing multicultural policies and institutions with the aim of undoing the "legal magic" of Canada's settler colonial narrative, ensuring responsiveness to Indigenous nations, and recognizing Indigenous legal and political authority. For Eisenberg, this means complementing Canadian official multiculturalism with a three-pronged approach that: 1. affirms the domestic application of the United Nations Declaration of the Rights of Indigenous People (UNDRIP); 2. develops legal pluralism by "displacing the state as the final source of law and authority" (Ch. 4: 81); and 3. embraces a radical ethical pluralism that challenges the hegemony of Euromodern perspectives. For Ladner et. al., Canada can draw inspiration from the *Treaty of Waitangi Act* of 1975 which "[provided] a new relationship between treaty partners" (24) and, concomitantly, enshrine "triculturalism" alongside federal-level official multiculturalism and interculturalism in Quebec.

Some alternative frameworks focus on how liberal democracies are addressing religious diversity. Sticking with the context of Quebec, Mathieu's chapter articulates an alternative to the liberal multicultural litmus test for minority claims-making, which allows for minority group-rights if they are responses to "external pressures" but not if they seek "internal restrictions." Mathieu instead advocates for the adoption of the so-called "Oakes test" to evaluate the legitimacy and liberalness of the cultural majority's exercise of the *ad hoc* preference principle and, in turn, he argues that the current ban on religious symbols for all public workers in positions of authority in Quebec is an excessive rights infringement on religious minorities. In his chapter, Tariq Modood advocates an alternative to the multicultural theories developed by the Canadian school of multiculturalism seeing as how they have a tendency to omit what he sees as the centrality of religion as a key identity marker. The approach that he advocates—one that is aligned with the Bristol School of Multiculturalism (see Brahm Levey, 2019)—would entail the "multiculturalizing accommodation of public inclusion of religious minorities" (15) and provide a space of minority faiths in public education and public institutions.

Clearly, not every chapter advocates moving on from the multicultural status quo. Most notably, Will Kymlicka develops a compelling argument for maintaining "citizenist multiculturalism" warts and all, rather than shifting to "some form of 'post-national' multiculturalism, in which state citizenship is decentered" (18). In brief, he argues that the "idea of society as a common possession" is integral to the development of social democracy and progressive politics; therefore, an understanding of multiculturalism bound to citizenship is worth maintaining.

Keeping the foregoing discussion in mind, in the final section we turn to considering multiculturalism's promises and potential. We discuss multiculturalism's future at three levels: in relation to the ideas propelling its founding in many countries, the costs and benefits of its removal, as well as its potential normative value considering the issues that confront us in the 21st century.

Beyond This Volume: The Costs and Benefits of Multiculturalism's Removal and Reimagining a Politics of Solidarity

In light of the issues and uncertainties identified by authors addressing varied contexts in this volume, we find it useful to bluntly consider the question: what are the costs and benefits of multiculturalism? Here it is worth considering what has typically been the main intention behind the establishment of a politics of multiculturalism. In most countries, the stated intention was to give a voice to communities disenfranchised from the political process or excluded from the social ladder and who oftentimes had a sense of being second-class citizens in their country of adoption (as immigrants) or in their country of citizenship (as minorities). Put differently, and certainly with respect to the Canadian case, multiculturalism was the outcome of struggles by minorities encountering inequities and discrimination (Abu-Laban, 2014).

Over time, and with institutionalization as a state response, multiculturalism as a "politics of diversity" appears to have lost some of its appeal in many countries. To be sure, as an initial state response to demands for equity and fairness, multiculturalism reflected a way in which countries that were experiencing social and political tensions could develop options as well as promote "social cohesion" or what we prefer to call solidarity. Hence settler societies such as Australia and Canada expressed a desire to create new opportunities for minority immigrants and their offspring. In these countries, there was a feeling among policymakers that much more ought to and could be done to give everyone her/his/their chance in the workplace as well as in political institutions. In brief, the feeling was that a successful politics of multiculturalism could contribute to creating the conditions of success for all citizens.

While the intention justifying the implementation of multiculturalism may generally have been positive and even inclusionary, the end result has not always been the one expected. In some cases, the call for the institutionalization of a politics of diversity led to backlash among members of the majority culture(s). This backlash embodied the sentiment that, instead of contributing to a *rapprochement* among all citizens, such a politics alienated citizens from one another or formalized a distance between communities. Perhaps this could explain in part why, during the 2000s, some political leaders in countries such as France, Germany and the United Kingdom started to heavily criticize not only the politics of diversity but also the term multiculturalism itself, for its supposed implications of disunity.

Recent years have seen the rise of arguments favoring white supremacist logics, such as that of *le grand replacement* (the great replacement) advanced by France-based author Renaud Camus in 2012. This conspiracy theory suggests that hordes of immigrants from North Africa and Sub-Saharan Africa are threatening to topple white Christian Europe, and it has been influential for far-right extremists responsible for mass shootings in places of worship like the Tree of Life synagogue in Pittsburgh in 2018 and the mosque attacks in Christchurch, New Zealand in 2019 (McAuley, 2019). In other words, we may now be witnessing a shift from a critique of multiculturalism as one of several models of immigrant integration to an anti-multiculturalism more clearly steeped in racist paranoia.

We are also now witnessing the mobilization of different understandings of multiculturalism and citizenship. In most country settings, from the 1990s onwards, the focus came to move away from a position where diversity was encouraged, to a perception that multiculturalism could not serve the basic functions of democratic participation and shared citizenship. In the United Kingdom, for example, the opportunity to enshrine official multiculturalism was at the turn of the millennium displaced by attempts to entrench "community cohesion" and, more recently, "muscular liberalism." Paradoxically, the drive for shared citizenship at the national level in Canada was accompanied by a paring down of fiscal commitments to official multiculturalism (Tremblay, 2019). In Quebec, democratic participation and shared citizenship are now being discussed against the backdrop of state secularism rather than interculturalism (see Gagnon and Tremblay, forthcoming) and in the context of an institutional reaffirmation of the majority language. Additionally, in the post-9/11 period Canada, the UK and other Western countries have also made formal citizenship for immigrants more difficult to obtain through testing on cultural/civic integration, as well as through immigration policies favoring temporary as opposed to permanent residents (Abu-Laban, Tungohan and Gabriel, forthcoming 2023).

Yet, citizenship and citizen participation in democratic societies remains critically important to the politics of diversity. Returning to the case of Canada, it is notable that Prime Minister Justin Trudeau, in dealing with the contradictions attending the 50th anniversary of multiculturalism, held that "the Government of Canada must and will continue to take meaningful action to right past wrongs, fight racism and discrimination, and foster a fairer, more equitable society" (Trudeau, 2021).

But the case of Canada also shows that multiculturalism in the first instance was a response to *civil society mobilization*, and we suggest that it is such civil society organizing that holds promise to the extent that it is solidaristic. Solidarity is an outcome not only of state actions and emphases—whether on citizenship, or international norms and policies—but also what happens in civil society. In other words, civil society is critical to potentiating solidarity, and therefore a more solidaristic multiculturalism.

The conditions which gave rise to multiculturalism in the 1960s and 1970s were part of broader social demands that also gave rise to movements for national self-determination, anti-racism, gender equality, LGBTQ+ rights, Indigenous sovereignty and decolonization. This civil society basis and context of multiculturalism is sometimes forgotten in the focus only on state policies, or their absence, or what politicians and policymakers say about multiculturalism. However, keeping the social basis in mind can be helpful for thinking in a more fulsome way about the possibilities of multiculturalism in the 21st century.

Formally, multiculturalism is concerned with issues like race, ethnicity, language, cultural traditions and religion. However, feminist theorists have drawn attention to intersectionality and the complex identities and positionalities people hold owing not only to race, ethnicity, language, cultural traditions and religion, but *also* class, gender identity, geographic location, citizenship status and other markers of identity and difference. From such complexity has come a greater understanding of the organizing needed to challenge inequities on the ground as well as the demand for greater reflexivity, that is, attention to the oppression not only of one's own but also the oppression of others (Keskinen, 2021). This has also been identified by Nira Yuval-Davis (1999; 2018) as transversal politics. Transversal politics forms an alternative to zero-sum games spinning around identity politics (Yuval-Davis, 2018: 163). It is this transversal idea of solidarity that we, as editors of this volume, find powerful.

There is no reason that an emboldened multiculturalism could not be a more solidaristic and transversal form of diversity politics. For this to happen and for multiculturalism to be a truly efficacious politics of diversity for the 21st century, policymakers and scholars must continue to grapple with the impact of colonialism, institutionalized racism, anti-Indigenous historical legacies and the strengthening of xenophobic and white supremacist movements. They must also face the challenges of the 21st century head on and in so doing, recognize the increasing importance of religious identities in liberal democracies, the plight of minorities within minorities and the demands of minority nations, the dearth of rights and poor treatment of non-citizens, the growing economic inequalities underscored by COVID-19 the pandemic and the fallout of a now-mainstream mono-cultural right-wing populism. Indeed, we would argue that this is the only way multiculturalism could be a meaningful form of diversity politics in the years ahead. Anything less would give reason to those who call multiculturalism a failure.

References

Abu-Laban, Yasmeen. 2014. "Reform by Stealth: The Harper Conservatives and Canadian Multiculturalism." In *The Multiculturalism Question: Debating Identity in 21st Century Canada*, Jack Jedwab (ed.) Montreal and Kingston: School of Policy Studies, Queen's University and McGill-Queen's University Press, 149–172.

Abu-Laban, Yasmeen, Ethel Tungohan and Christina Gabriel. Forthcoming 2023. *Containing Diversity: Canada and the Politics of Immigration in the 21st Century*. Toronto: University of Toronto Press.

Austen, Ian. 2021. "How Thousands of Indigenous Children Vanished in Canada." *The New York Times* (7 June). https://www.nytimes.com/2021/06/07/world/canada/mass-graves-residential-schools.html [Accessed 10 May 2023].

Banting, Keith and Will Kymlicka. 2004. *Do Multiculturalism Policies Erode the Welfare State?* Kingston: School of Policy Studies, Queen's University.

Banting, Keith and Will Kymlicka. 2010. "Canadian Multiculturalism: Global Anxieties and Local Debates." *British Journal of Canadian Studies 23* (1): 43–72.

Banting, Keith and Will Kymlicka. 2013. "Is There Really a Retreat from Multiculturalism Policies? New Evidence from the Multiculturalism Policy Index." *Comparative European Politics 11* (5): 577–598.

Bloemraad, Irene, Anna Korteweg and Gökçe Yurdakul. 2008. "Citizenship and Immigration: Multiculturalism, Assimilation, and Challenges to the Nation-State." *Annual Review of Sociology 34* (1): 153–179.

Brahm Levey, Goeffrey. 2019. "The Bristol school of multiculturalism." *Ethnicities 19*: 200–226

Carle, Robert. 2006. "Demise of Dutch Multiculturalism." *Society 43* (3): 68–74.

Delgado-Moreira, Juan M. 2017. *Multicultural Citizenship of the European Union*. London: Routledge.

Entzinger, Han. 2006. "The Parallel Decline of Multiculturalism and the Welfare State in the Netherlands." In *Multiculturalism and the Welfare State,* Keith Banting and Will Kymlicka (eds.) Oxford: Oxford University Press, 177–201.

Entzinger, Han. 2014. "The Rise and Fall of Multiculturalism: The Case of the Netherlands." In *Toward Assimilation and Citizenship: Immigrants in Liberal Nation-States,* Christian Joppke and Ewa Morawska (eds.) London: Palgrave Macmillan, 59–86.

Gagnon, Alain-G. and Arjun Tremblay. Forthcoming. "Interculturalism and the Plea for an Informal Constitution: Responding to the Challenge of Polyethnicity in Québec." In *A Written Constitution for Québec?,* Richard Albert, Léonid Sirota and Patrick F. Baud (eds.) Montreal and Kingston: McGill-Queen's University Press.

Joppke, Christian. 2004. "The Retreat of Multiculturalism in the Liberal State: Theory and Policy." *The British Journal of Sociology 55*: 237–257.

Keskinen, Suvi. 2021. "Antiracist Feminism and the Politics of Solidarity in Neoliberal Times." In *Feminisms in the Nordic Region: Neoliberalism, Nationalism and Decolonial Critique*, Gender and Politics, Suvi Keskinen, Pauline Stoltz and Diana Mulinari (eds.) London: Palgrave Macmillan, 201–221.

Kymlicka, W. 2010. "Testing the Liberal Multiculturalist Hypothesis: Normative Theories and Social Science Evidence." *Canadian Journal of Political Science 43*: 257–271.

Kymlicka, W. 2013. *Multicultural Odysseys: Navigating the New International Politics of Diversity*. Oxford: Oxford University Press.

Kymlicka, W. and Banting, K. 2006. "Immigration, Multiculturalism, and the Welfare State." *Ethics & International Affairs 20*: 281–304.

McAuley, James. 2019. "How Gay Icon Renaud Camus Became the Ideologue of White Supremacy." *The Nation* (17 June). https://www.thenation.com/article/archive/renaud-camus-great-replacement-brenton-tarrant/ [Accessed 10 May, 2022].

Prins, B. and S. Saharso 2010. "From Toleration to Repression: The Dutch Backlash Against Multiculturalism." In *The Multiculturalism Backlash: European Discourses, Policies and Practices*, Steven Vertovec and Susanne Wessendorf (eds.) London: Routledge, 72–99.

Santos, Boaventura de Sousa. 2017. "Toward a Multicultural Conception of Human Rights." In *Human Rights,* Robert McCorquodale (ed.) London: Routledge, 341–355.

Tremblay, Arjun. 2019. *Diversity in Decline? The Rise of the Political Right and the Fate of Multiculturalism.* London: Palgrave Macmillan.

Tremblay, Arjun. 2021. "Multiculturalism: Public Philosophy and Public Policy." In *Political Ideologies and Worldviews: An Introduction*, Valérie Vézina (ed.) Minneapolis: Open Textbook Library British Columbia Kwantlen Polytechnic University, 123–141.

Trudeau, Justin. 2021. "Statement by the Prime Minister on Multiculturalism Day." (27 June). https://pm.gc.ca/en/news/statements/2021/06/27/statement-prime-minister-canadian-multiculturalism-day [Accessed 10 May 2022].

Yun, Tom. 2022. "Suspect in Killing of Muslim Family in London, Ont. May Have Accessed Neo-Nazi Site on Dark Web: Documents." *CTV News* (March 15). https://toronto.ctvnews.ca/suspect-in-killing-of-muslim-family-in-london-ont-may-have-accessed-neo-nazi-site-on-dark-web-documents-1.5819479 [Accessed 10 May 2002].

Yuval-Davis, Nira. 1999 "What is 'Transversal Politics." *Soundings 12*: 94–98.

Yuval-Davis, Nira. 2018. "Recognition, Intersectionality, and Transversal Politics". In *Recognition as Key w/or Reconciliation: Israel, Palestine, and Beyond,* Vol. *118*, Yoram Meital and Paula M. Rayman (ed.) Brill, Boston: Social, Economic and Political Studies of the Middle East and Asia, 156–167.

INDEX

Page numbers in **bold reference tables.
**Page numbers in *italics* reference figures.

1619 Project 130
1776 Report 130
1990 Policy Statement on Immigration and Integration 157

abolition democracy 231–232
Aboriginal Peoples, survey questions *29*
Act on Hungarian Nationality (1993) 242
Act Respecting the Laicity of the State (Bill 21), Quebec 162
ad hoc preference principle 161–165
African National Congress (ANC) 100
African-American Policy Forum 228
AfriForum 115n7
Agamben, Giorgio 102, 110
age of migration 32–33
age of mobility 32–33
Alexander, Michelle 228
American English 121–124
Anglo-Saxon 121–122
Anishinaabe 206
anti-Asian racism: Australia 281; Covid-19 pandemic 267
anti-culturalism (Hungary) 244–251
anti-discrimination 175
anti-Muslim policies (India) 194
anti-Muslim racism (Islamophobia) 11
anti-Muslim sentiments 186
anti-national label 195
anti-racism (Australia) 285
Arbery, Ahmaud 229
Arnold, David 191
asylum seekers: during Covid-19 pandemic 269–271; Hungary 247
Australia 8, 12, 276–277; anti-Asian racism 281; blackface 70–71; citizenship 280; Covid-19 pandemic 280–284; Fortress Australia 283; guest workers 287; legal magic 209; multicultural fragility 284–288; multiculturalism 277–280; nation-building 284–288; populist nationalism 281–282; *Racial Discrimination Act* (1975) 278–279, 285, 288; racism 282; right-wing extremism 282–283
Australian Institute of Multicultural Affairs 8
authority: *vs.* identity 84–89; political authority 89–90

backlash against multiculturalism 52–55
Baines, Donna 21
Bajpai, Rochana 187–189
Banting, Keith 8, 27, 55, 189, 226, 311
bare habitance 104, 114
bare life 101, 102

324 Index

Barrett, Amy Coney 55
Beck, James M. 121
Belgium 142
belonging 62
Bernier, Maxime 53
Bharatiya Janata Party (BJP) 186, 190–191; creating a virulent Hindu India 193–196; protests 196–197
bicultural individuals 47
biculturalism 6
Bilingual Education act of 1968 (BEA) 129
bilingualism 217–218
Bill 21 (*An Act Respecting the Laicity of the State*) 162, 165
Bill 101 (*Quebec Charter of the French Language*) 161–162
Black feminist politics 230
Black First Land First 115n12
Black Lives Matter (BLM) 223–225, 233–234; abolition democracy 231–232; origins of 227–231; protests 223, 229–230
#BlackLivesMatter 110
Black trans women 231
Black women: police violence 228; violence against 231
blackface 69–71
Blackness 68, 70
BLM *see* Black Lives Matter
blue cards 299
border closures 4; Covid-19 pandemic 263–266
Borevi, Karin 8
Bosniak, Linda 21
Bouchard, Gérard 160, 163
Bourassa, Robert 156–157
Bristol School of Multiculturalism 171
British nationality 121
brownface 70–73
Bryce, James 127
BS v. Spain [2012] 47159/08 145
Buchan, John 125–126
Burman, Jenny 214
Bush, George W. 129

CAA (Citizenship Amendment Act), India 193–196
Canada 3–4, 292–294; 1990 Policy Statement on Immigration and Integration 157; *ad hoc* preference measures 161–165; asylum seekers during Covid-19 270; backlash against multiculturalism 53; bilingualism 216–218; Black Lives Matter 223, 228–229; Canadian Multiculturalism Policy (CMP) 153; citizenship 23–31; *Constitution Act* 217; cultural domination 84–86; Dish With One Spoon Treaty 206; diversity 28; financial assistance 51–52; immigration 294–295; Immigration Refugees Citizenship Canada (IRCC) 270; immigration selection process 296–303; inclusive citizenship 48–49; *Indian Act* 215; *Indigenous Languages Act* 217; interculturalism 156–157; language 125; minorities within minorities 141–142; narratives of a Pretend Nation 208–212; nation branding 295; national identity 54; *Official Languages Act* 216; origins of multiculturalism 5–7; permanent residency for Covid-19 frontline workers 270; Quebec Charter of the French Language (Bill 101) 161–162; Quebec Ministry of Immigration 156; racial inequality 226; rise of multiculturalism 43; Syrian refugee experience 299–301; temporary foreign workers (TFWs) 32
Canada-US Safe Third Country Agreement (STCA) 269
Canadian Charter of Rights and Freedoms 7, 165
Canadian exceptionalism 295
The Canadian Multiculturalism Act 7
Canadian Multiculturalism Policy (CMP) 153
Canadian narrative 205–206, 212–216
"Canadian-ness" 54
case law: *BS v. Spain* [2012] 47159/08 145; *DH and Others v. The Czech Republic* [2007] 57325/00 145; *Fernandez Martinez v. Spain* [2014] 56030/07 143; *IR v. JQ*, [2018] C-68/17 143; *R v. Oakes* (1 SCR 103) 164–165; *R v Sparrow* ([1990] 1SCR 1075) 95n2; *Santa Clara Pueblo v. Martinez*, [1978] 436 US 49 147n13
Castile, Philando 228
Catholic Church 143, 177
Caucasian 127
Chandrachud, Abhinav 195
Chinese-Australians 281
chosen immigration 302

Church of England 178–180
citizenist multiculturalism 34, 316
citizenization 21, 23–31
citizenship 21–22; Australia 280; Canada 23–31; Covid-19 pandemic 265–266; dual citizenship 238; end of 31–36; Hungary 241–243; inclusive citizenship 48–49
Citizenship Amendment Act (India) 193–196
citizenship rights 35
citizenship struggles 35
civic incorporation 48–52
civic integration 11
Civil Rights Act (1964) 129
civil society mobilization 318–319
Clark, Stephon 228
Cleveland, Grover 127
Clinton, Bill 129
CLRA (Communal Land Rights Act) 112
CMP (Canadian Multiculturalism Policy) 153
CoE (Council of Europe) 139
coercive assimilation 85
collective identification 45–48
colonial dispossession 209
colonial indirect rule 105
"The Colonial Legacy" 10
colonial occupation 103
colonial settlement 103
colonial violence 215
colonialism 88; settler colonialism 104–105; South Africa 100–101
common culture, United States 124–128
Communal Land Rights Act (CLRA) 112
community 35
Connick Jr., Harry 70
Constitution Act (Canada) 217
"Cook and share a pot of curry" day (Singapore) 67
Copé, Jean-François 302
Copenhagen criteria (1993) 139
Council of Europe (CoE) 139
Covid-19 pandemic 5, 264–265; Australia 280–284; border closures 263–266; citizenship 265–266; effective residence 267; expanding membership to non-citizens 269–271; layers of membership 266–268; refugees as outcasts 268–269; right-wing extremism 283

critical race theory 232
criticism of multiculturalism 11–12, 46–47
Crown sovereignty 207
cultural accommodation 87
cultural difference 84, 88, 137
cultural diversity 99, 134–136; Europe 137–141; immigration 140
cultural domination 84–85
cultural identity 84, 171
cultural pluralism 50
cultural protection 88
cultural purposes 85–86
culture, societal culture 155

Declaration of Official Languages Act (US) 119
decolonization 84, 87, 104; restructuring political authority 89–90; *see also* governance
de-democratization (Hungary) 244–248
dehumanization 34
democratic transition (Hungary) 239–241
demographic pluralism 310
Dene nation 205
Denmark 177
derogatory terms, genocide 111
DH and Others v. The Czech Republic, [2007] 57325/00 145
dictation tests (Australia) 277
discursive opportunity structure 50
Dish With One Spoon Treaty 206
distinct society 158
diversity 286; Canada 28; emphasizing 46; leadership 286; linguistic diversity 142; multinational democracies 154–156; *see also* cultural diversity
Du Bois, W.E.B. 231
dual citizenship 238, 242–243
dual identity 47
duality paradigm 160
Dutton, Peter 282

E pluribus unum 126
Economic Freedom Fighters (EFF) 100, 109
economic class immigrants 297
ECRML (European Charter for Regional or Minority Languages) 138–140
ECtHR (European Court of Human Rights) 142, 144

education: religion 180; Singapore 64
EFF *see* Economic Freedom Fighters
effective membership 265, 270, 311
effective residence 267
effectiveness of multiculturalism 313–315
The Elementary and Secondary Education Act (1965) 129
embodiment 101
end of citizenship 31–36
England 177
"English Plus" legislation 124
Equal Treatment Authority 248
Equal Treatment Directive 143
ethnic discrimination 127–128
ethnic ghettos 46
ethnic identity 47
ethnobusiness 240
ethno-cultural diversity 134, 137
ethnocultural minorities 155–156
ethnoreligious identities 179
Europe: cultural diversity 137–141; minorities within minorities 135, 141–145; minority protection 139; multicultural debate 137–141
European Charter for Regional or Minority Language (ECRML) 138–140
European Commission (EC) 137
European Court of Human Rights (ECtHR) 142, 144
European integration 249–250
European Union (EU) 237, 250–251; language 146n4; layers of membership 267; linguistic policy 138; religion 143–144
European Union Democracy Observatory 294
European values 144
exclusion of Indigenous peoples 210–211
expansion of multiculturalism 7–10
Express Entry approach (Canada) 297
external citizenship 245
external protection 163, 165

faith communities 172
family class immigrants 297
farm attacks (South Africa) 109
farm murders (South Africa) 109–112
farmers' protest (India) 197
FCPNM (Framework Convention for the Protection of National Minorities) 138–140
feminism, Black feminist politics 230

Fernandez Martinez v. Spain [2014] 56030/07 143
Fidesz 242–243, 249
financial assistance 50
First Reconstruction 232
Floyd, George 110, 229, 230, 282
Fortier, Anee-Marie 66
Fortress Australia 283
Framework Convention for the Protection of National Minorities (FCPNM) 138–140
France 8; immigration systems 301–302; Indigenous homelands 209; Justice for Adama 223; moderate secularism 177; Muslim immigrants 47
Fraser, Nancy 21
French-Speaking Quebecois 29
Fundamental Law of Hungary 244, 246
future of multiculturalism 315–317

Gagnon, Alain-G 160
Garner, Eric 227–228
Garza, Alicia 224
gender 112
genocidal logic of colonial pacification 105
genocide: derogatory terms 111; South Africa 101–102
Germany 24, 172; governance of religion 177; immigration systems 302–303; returnist multiculturalism 24
global migratory movements 4
Gordon, Linda 21
governance 89; internationalism 90–91; legal and political pluralism 91–93; radical pluralism and pluriverse 93–94; of religion, Western Europe 177–179
Grant, Madison 123
Grassby, Al. 278
Great Britain, Black Lives Matter protests 223
Greece, Covid-19 pandemic 269
group rights 144
"Guardian Angels" Program 270
guest workers (Australia) 287
gypsy criminality 249

Hanson, Pauline 282
Haslett, Tobi 230
Haudenosaunee 206
Hey Hey It's Saturday 70
Hindtuva 195
Hindu nationalism 190–193

Hindu-Muslim polarization, India 191
Hindu-Muslim violence 188
Hindus, India 193–196
"Hindutva" 191
home, narratives of 209–211
homini sacri 102
homo sacer 101–102
human dignity 34
human personhood 34
human rights 104
humanitarian crisis, Syrian refugee experience (Canada) 299–301
humanity 25
Hungary 237–238, 248–251; citizenship 241–243; de-democratization 244–248; democratic transition 239–241; dual citizenship 238; future of anti-multiculturalism 248–251; immigration 243; minorities 239–241; Minorities Act (1993) 239; minority self-governments 240, 245–246; national borders 241–243; racism 246; Roma 240
Hutchings, Kimberly 93–94
hyphenated identities 47

Iacovino, Raffaele 160
identity 174–175; *vs.* authority 84–89; land or place 100–101
Idle No More 227
illegal immigrants 243
illiberal anti-multiculturalism 238
illiberalism 244, 246–251
Illinois (US), language 124
immigrant incorporation 42
immigrant populations 43
immigrants: Covid-19 pandemic 283; membership commitment source **30**; post-secondary graduates 298; survey questions *28*
immigration: Canada 294–295; cultural diversity 140; Hungary 243, 247
Immigration Refugees Citizenship Canada (IRCC) 270
immigration selection process (Canada) 293, 296–299; Syrian refugee experience 299–301
immigration systems: Canada 293, 296–299, 301–303; France 301–302; Germany 302–303
inclusive citizenship 48–49
India 172, 186; Citizenship Amendment Act 193–196; constitution 187–189;
Hindu nationalism 190–193; National Register of Citizens (NRC) 194–195; protests 196–197; secularism 189–192; shift in socio-political dynamics 190–193; violence 196
Indian Act (Canada) 215
Indians, media representation of 71
Indigenous justice 214
Indigenous Languages Act (Canada) 217
Indigenous nations (Canada) 205–206
Indigenous peoples: authority 85, 88–89; Canadian narrative 212–216; exclusion of 210–211
Indigenous rights 87
institutional racism 282
integration 47, 159; European integration 249–250; of religious migrants 171–172
intercultural dialogue 141
interculturalism 6–8, 147n11, 153–154; Canada 156–157; characteristics of 161; as model of pluralism 157–161
internal constraints 163–165
International Covenant on Civil and Political Rights 90
International Labor Convention 90
internationalism 90–91
intersectionality 230–231, 319
interstate cultural diversity 137
intrastate cultural diversity 138, 140
IR v. JQ, [2018] C-68/17 143
IRCC (Immigration Refugees Citizenship Canada) 270
Islam 179

Jamal, Mahmud 55
Jews 175, 240
Jobbik 249
Jodhka, S. S. 197
Johnson, Boris 122, 301
Johnson, Samuel 122
Justice for Adama 223

Kavanaugh, Brent 55
Kelley, Robin DG 232
Kenney, Jason 54
Khan, Raeesah 72
"Kill the Boer, Kill the Farmer" 111
King, Thomas 212
Kochenov, Dimitry 21
Kohli, Virat 196
Kymlicka, Will 9–10, 87, 155, 163–164, 170–172, 180, 314, 316

laïcité 162
land, identity 100–101
Land Act (1913) (South Africa) 106
land expropriation (South Africa) 109, 114
land redistribution (South Africa) 107–108
land reform (South Africa) 106–113
Land Reform Process (South Africa) 107
land tenure reform (South Africa) 107
language: European Union 146n4; United States 119–124, 128–129
layers of membership, during Covid-19 pandemic 266–268
le grand replacement (the great replacement) 318
leadership, diversity 286
League of Nations 139, 146n5
Lee, Kuan Yew 64
legal and political pluralism 91–93
legal exemptions for Indigenous communities 86
legal magic 205, 209
Lesage, Jean 5
liberal multiculturalism 238
liberal pluralist secularism *see* open secularism
liberalism 216; muscular liberalism 318
libtards 187
linguistic diversity 142
linguistic policy, European Union 138
literacy tests 127
Little Bear, Leroy 208
Little India (Singapore) 68
"love Jihad" law (India) 194
Lutheran Church in Denmark 178

MacDonald, David B. 214, 216
Macklem, Patrick 90
Macron, Emmanuel 302
"Maîtres Chez Nous" ("masters in our own home") 5
majority nations 154
Malhi, Gurbax Singh 41
Māori 210
Marshall, T. H. 35
Martin, Trayvon 228
Martínez, Fernández 143
Martinez, Julia 147n13
Mbembe, Achille 103
McCormick, J. 124
McGowan, Mark 284
media representation of Indians (Singapore) 71

membership: during Covid-19 pandemic 266–271; effective membership 270
membership commitment questions **27**
membership penalties 34, 36
membership rights 35–36
membership stakes 35
Merkel, Angela 302
metaphor of home 209–211
migrant communities 146–147n10
Migrant Integration Policy Index 294
migrants, religious migrants 171–172
migration: age of migration 32; India 188; temporary migration 32; *see also* immigration
"The Millet Legacy" 10
minorities 139; ethnocultural minorities 155–156; Hungary 239–241; less worthy and less deserving 25; Singapore 68–71; worthiness 26
Minorities Act (1993), Hungary 239
minorities within minorities 134–135; Europe 137, 141–145
minority nations 154
minority protection 139–140
minority rights 134–135
minority self-governments (Hungary) 240, 245–246
minstrel performances 70; brownface 71–73
misrecognition 175
Mngxitama, Andile 111
moderate secularism 176–181
Modi, Narendra 186, 192–196
Modood, Tariq 315
moral contracts 159
moral panic 247
Morrison, Scott 282–283
MPI *see* Multiculturalism Policy Index
multicultural accommodation, religion and 174–176
multicultural citizenship 24, 33–34, 60; Singapore 62–66
multicultural fragility (Australia) 284–288
multicultural horizons 66
Multiculturalism Policy Index (MPI) 8, 45, 226, 294, 312
multiculturalizing moderate secularism 179–181
multilingualism 240
multinational democracies 153; diversity 154–156
multinationalism 170

multiracialism, Singapore 61–65
muscular liberalism 318
Muslim immigrants (France) 47
Muslims 191

narratives: of home 209–211; of a Pretend Nation, Canada 208–212
nation branding 295
national borders (Hungary) 241–243
national communities 154–155
National Education (NE), Singapore 64
national homes 209–211
national identification 47
national identity 54, 62, 180, 209, 250
national minorities 139
National Register of Citizens (NRC) 194–195
nationalities question, Hungary 239
nation-building (Australia) 284–288
naturalization (Hungary) 242
NE (National Education), Singapore 64
Nebraska (US), language 123
negative equality 175
Nehru, Jawaharlal 198n6
Nehruvian secularism 190
nested identities 47
Netherlands 8, 11; *Zwarte Piet* 70
"New Jim Crow" 228–229
New Zealand 210–212, 219–220
Ngidi, Lungi 110
No Child Left Behind Act (US) 129
non-citizens (Singapore) 66–68
non-procedural liberalism 172–173
non-racialism 100
Norway 177
NRC (National Register of Citizens) 194–195

Official Languages Act (Canada) 216
open secularism 172–174, 181
Orbán, Viktor 238, 242
"Other," Singapore 66
"othered" multiracial subjects (Singapore) 66–68

Pearson, Lester B. 5
People's Action Party (PAP), Singapore 63
permanent immigrants 34
permanent residency for Covid-19 frontline workers 270
permissive space 113
place, identity 100–101

pluralism 156; demographic pluralism 310; interculturalism 157–161; legal and political pluralism 91–93; radical pluralism and pluriverse 93–94
pluriverse 93–94
point system for immigration: Canada 297; United Kingdom 301
polarization 52
police violence 227–228, 231–232
policies on multiculturalism **9**
policy of integration 157
political authority, restructuring 89–90
political diversity 41
political incorporation 49–52
political secularism 176
populism: Hungary 244; language 122
populist nationalism (Australia) 281–282
post-citizenship view 31–36
"Postcolonial Nation-Building" 10
post-colonial settler state (South Africa) 105–106
post-secondary graduates 298
prevalence of the world "multiculturalism" *44*
Prohibition of Unlawful Religious Conversion Ordinance (2020), India 194
Protestantizing 174
protests: Black Lives Matter 223, 229–230; India 196–197
pseudo-secularism 192
public good, religion 178

quasi-multi-establishment states 172
Quebec Charter of the French Language (Bill 101) 161–162
Quebec Ministry of Immigration 156
questioning of multiculturalism effectiveness 11–12

R v. Oakes (1 SCR 103) 164–165
R v Sparrow ([1990] 1SCR 1075) 95n2
race riots (1964), Singapore 63–64
race-class subjugated communities 233
Racial Discrimination Act (1975), Australia 278–279, 285, 288
racial harmony (Singapore) 66
Racial Harmony Day (Singapore) 64, 72
racial inequality 226
racial justice 225–227
racial logic of power 102
racialization 101, 175

racism 231, 233; Australia 282; Covid-19 pandemic 267; Hungary 246; institutional racism 282; United States 128, 131; white racism 282
radical pluralism 93–94
"Rainbow Nation" 99
rape of Black women (South Africa) 112
"Rath Yatra" 191
Reconstruction (US) 127, 231–232
Rees-Mogg, Jacob 122
Reform Party (Canada) 53–54
refugee crisis, Hungary 247
refugees: Covid-19 pandemic 268–269; Syrian refugee experience (Canada) 299–301
religion 4, 171; education 180; European Union 143–144; multicultural accommodation and 174–176; state-religion connections 176; Western European governance of 177–179
religious migrants, integration of 171–172
restructuring, political authority 89–90
returnist multiculturalism 24, 34
reverse racism 285
Reynolds, Henry 212
Rice, Tamir 228
right of abode 267
right-wing extremism (Australia) 282–283
rise of multiculturalism 43–45
Robinson, Cedric 230
Roma 145, 237–238, 240, 249
rural safety (South Africa) 109–110

Santa Clara Pueblo v. Martinez, [1978] 436 US 49 147n13
Sarkozy, Nicholas 301
#SayHerName 228
Schlesinger, Arthur 119–120
school segregation, Roma children 145
Second Reconstruction 232
secularism 4, 172–173; India 189–192; moderate secularism 176–179; Nehruvian secularism 190; open secularism 181; political secularism 176; pseudo-secularism 192
selective immigration system (Canada) 296–299
self-determination 88
self-help groups (Singapore) 65
Seshadri, Elizabeth 194
settler colonialism (South Africa) 102–105, 209

settler narrative 208–212
settler nations 209–211
settler states, national identity 209
sexual violence 112
sexuality 112
Shanmugam, K. 72
shared membership 34–35
Sharma, Nandita 21
sickularism 187
sickulars 196
Simon, Mary 217
Simon Roche of Die Suidlanders 110
Singapore 61; brownface 70–73; media representation of Indians 71; minorities 68–71; multicultural citizenship 62–66; multiracialism 61–65; non-citizens 66–68; "Other" 66
Singh, Jasmeet 41
social movement 4
societal community 154
societal culture 155, 170
socio-economic integration 45–48
solidarity 317
Somers, Daryl 70
South Africa 99–101; farm murders 109–112; genocide 101–102; land reform 106–113; post-colonial settler state 105–106; sexual violence 112; sovereignty after settler-colonialism 102–104
sovereignty 101–104, 114; Crown sovereignty 207
state-religion connections 176; open secularism 174
Stein, Burton 191
stereotypes (Singapore) 69
"Stop the Steal" 121
Strom, Harry 6
Suidlanders 111–112
Sweden 8
Swift, Rodney B. 124
Syrian refugee experience (Canada) 299–301

Taylor, Breonna 228–229
Taylor, Charles 172–173
temporary foreign workers (TFWs) 32
temporary migrants (Australia) 287
temporary migration 32
temporary status 267
terminological complexity of multiculturalism 310–313
territorial self-autonomy 139

territory 103
TFWs (temporary foreign workers) 32
"Third Reconstruction" 232
third space 198
traitors 196
transformative accommodation 250
transstate cultural diversity 138–139
transversal politics 319
treaties 206–207; Canada-US Safe Third Country Agreement (STCA) 269; Dish With One Spoon Treaty 206; Treaty of Trianon 242; Treaty of Waitangi 219–220
treaty federalism 207
Treaty of Trianon 242
Treaty of Waitangi 219–220
"Triple Talaq bill" (India) 194
Trudeau, Justin 53, 61, 218–219, 299, 308, 318
Trudeau, Pierre 3, 6, 45–46, 207, 215–216
Trump, Donald 52, 122, 130, 224, 229, 265
Tudge, Alan 282

UMP (*Union pour un Mouvement Populaire*) 301–302
UNDRIP (United Nations Declaration of the Rights and Indigenous Peoples) 90–91
UNHCR (United Nations High Commissioner for Refugees) 296
Union pour un Mouvement Populaire (UMP) 301–302
United Kingdom 8; immigration systems 301
United Nations: Declaration of the Rights and Indigenous Peoples (UNDRIP) 90–91; High Commissioner for Refugees (UNHCR) 296
United States 8, 119–120; Black Lives Matter protests 223; common culture 124–128; Declaration of Official Languages Act 119; ethnic discrimination 127–128; immigrants 298; immigration integration 47; integration of religious migrants 171–172; language 119–124, 128–129; minorities within minorities 141–142; racism 128, 131; Reconstruction 127; Voting Rights Act 127, 129
United States Citizenship and Immigration Service (USCIS) 51–52
Universal Declaration of Human Rights 134
universal human rights 35
USCIS (United States Citizenship and Immigration Services) 51–52

Vernon, Karina 214
violence: colonial violence 215; India 196; police violence 227–228, 231; rape of Black women (South Africa) 112
visible minority populations 43
Voting Rights Act (US) 127, 129
vulnerable groups 145

Webster, Noah 122
welfare state 35
Western European governance of religion 177–179
White Australia policy 277
white genocide 110–111
white racism 282
white supremacist logics 318
white supremacist movement 282–283
whiteness 215
Whitlam, Gough 278
"willing buyer, willing seller" 108
women: Black women 228, 231; minorities within minorities 135; sexual violence (South Africa) 112
Wong, Lawrence 64
World Alliance of Hungarians 242
worthiness 26

Zwarte Piet 70

Printed in the United States
by Baker & Taylor Publisher Services